Cross and Flag
in Africa

2/2061192

Cross and Flag in Africa

The "White Fathers" during the Colonial Scramble
(1892–1914)

Aylward Shorter

ORBIS BOOKS
Maryknoll, New York 10545

Founded in 1970, Orbis Books endeavors to publish works that enlighten the mind, nourish the spirit, and challenge the conscience. The publishing arm of the Maryknoll Fathers and Brothers, Orbis seeks to explore the global dimensions of the Christian faith and mission, to invite dialogue with diverse cultures and religious traditions, and to serve the cause of reconciliation and peace. The books published reflect the views of their authors and do not represent the official position of the Maryknoll Society. To learn more about Maryknoll and Orbis Books, please visit our website at www.maryknoll.org.

Library of Congress Cataloging-in-Publication Data

Shorter, Aylward.
    The cross and flag in Africa: the white fathers during the colonial sramble (1892–1914) / Aylward Shorter.
        p. cm.
    Includes bibliographical references and index.
    ISBN-13: 978-1-57075-655-9 (pbk)
    1. White Fathers—Missions—Africa.   2. Catholic Church—Missions— Africa—History.   3. Africa—Church history.   4. Lavigerie, Charles Martial Allemand, 1825–1892.   I. Title.
    BV2300.W6S56 2006
    266'.2609034—dc22

                                                                                    2005029033

In memory of Richard Gray
1929–2005

Publication of this study was made possible through the generous assistance of Fr. Hermann Schalück OFM, National Director of the Pontifical Mission Societies in Germany (Missio Aachen) and Chairman of the Board of Missionswissenschäftliches Institut Missio, and that of Fr. Gérard Chabanon M.Afr., Superior General of the Missionaires of Africa.

CONTENTS

LIST OF ILLUSTRATIONS

Maps
(on pages xiv to xx)

Photographs
(on pages 96 to 105)

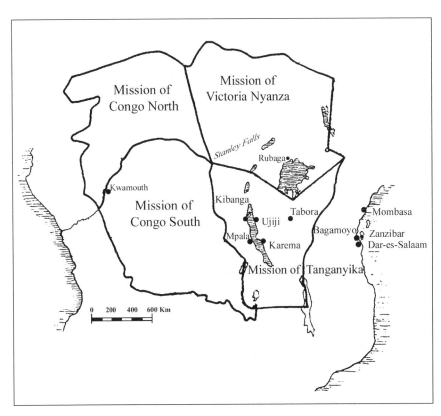

Map 1 – Missions of Equatorial Africa entrusted to
Cardinal Lavigerie 1878-1880

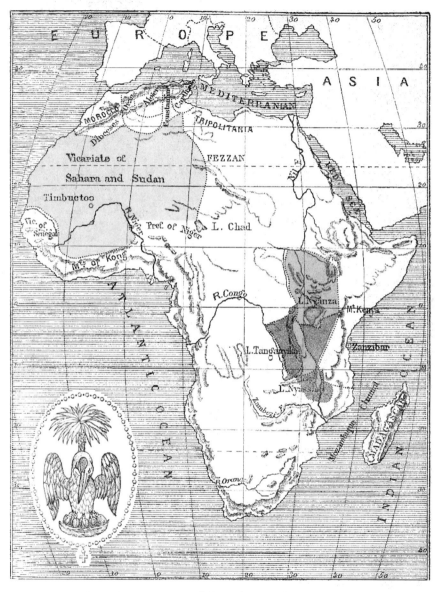

Map 2 – Missions of the White Fathers in 1891
(from a 19th century publication)

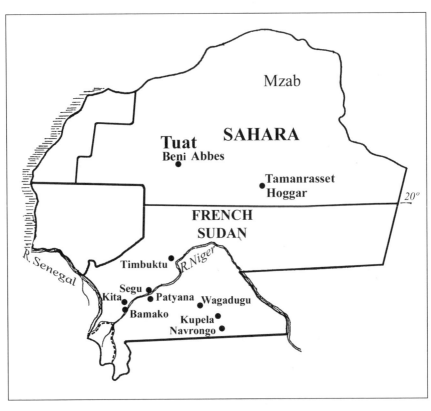

Map 3 – Sahara and Sudan 1901-1915

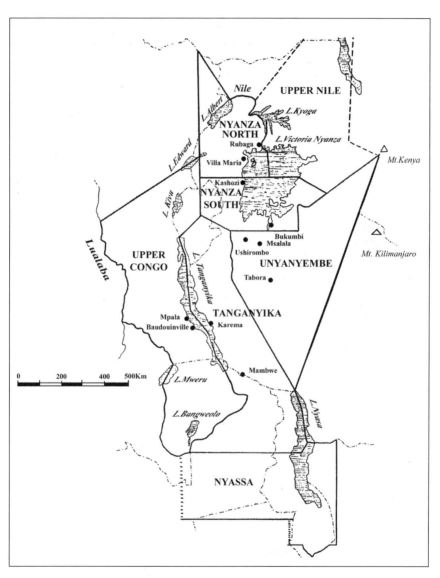

Map 4 – Missions of Equatorial Africa in 1894

Map 5 – Missions in German East Africa 1895-1912

Map 6 – Missions in German East Africa
after the creation of Kivu Vicariate

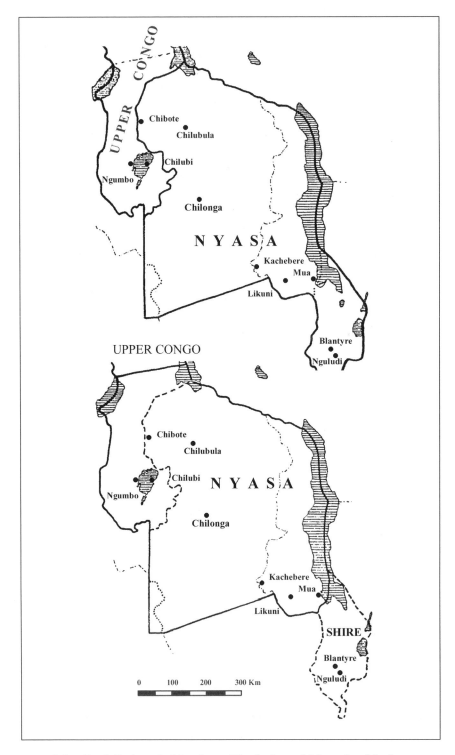

Map 7 – Missions in Northern Rhodesia and Nyasaland before
and after the 1911 border adjustment with Congo

PREFACE

The period 1892–1914 saw the high tide of the "scramble for Africa," the continent's dismemberment by rival European powers. During the same period the Society of Missionaries of Africa laid the foundations of the Catholic Church in what were to become fifteen African countries. This missionary society, popularly called the "White Fathers" because of the white Arab costume adopted by its members, was founded at Algiers in 1868 by Cardinal Charles Lavigerie. In November 1892 Lavigerie died, leaving his small society to face a major crisis. Its most hopeful mission, Uganda, was in danger of being lost. A handful of White Fathers were clinging tenuously to a few posts in the area of the Great Lakes, and the advance across the Sahara was blocked by fierce Tuareg tribesmen. For the next fifteen years, Africa was riven by successive waves of violence provoked by the slave trade, colonial aggression and anti-colonial resistance, accompanied by ecological and medical catastrophes. In spite of widespread violence and virulent epidemics, the White Fathers consolidated their position in equatorial Africa and penetrated the French Sudan.

When conditions became more settled, the Catholic missionaries found themselves confronting British, German and Belgian colonial administrations which were suspicious of their (mainly) French nationality and, in the case of the British and Germans, showed themselves more favourable to missionaries of Protestant denominations. In the French Sudan they faced an active anti-clericalism, which impeded educational and social development. In spite of these handicaps, the White Fathers not only converted thousands of individuals, but began the transformation of African society, and the formation of an indigenous Catholic leadership. They also began to adopt a style of churchmanship that was influenced consciously or unconsciously by African socio-cultural realities. This pioneering era ended with the First World War, as a result of which relations between missionaries and the colonial powers were profoundly changed.

A great deal of the credit for the realization of Lavigerie's dream and for the achievements of the White Fathers during this period goes to Léon Livinhac, first Catholic bishop in equatorial Africa and first superior general of the Society of Missionaries of Africa. These twenty-two years were the most active of his thirty-year superiorate. Livinhac took crucial decisions in Uganda and West Africa and he battled with anti-clericalism in France and the French colonies. More importantly, he held his missionary

society together through wise and consistent leadership and, in spite of many
obstacles, through regular communication with those in the field. Livinhac
managed Lavigerie's legacy, abandoning policies that were no longer relevant, accentuating others and confronting the problems posed by the colonial scramble.

This book examines the period 1892–1914. The first chapter deals with
the crises that followed Lavigerie's death and introduces the personality of
Livinhac, the man who resolved them. Chapter Two examines the White
Fathers' attitudes towards colonialism and those of colonial administrations
towards the Catholic missionaries. The success of the White Fathers was
mainly due to the personal qualities of their leaders. The story of the Society's
deployment is therefore told in this chapter through the biographies of the
principal actors. The book then goes on to treat the history of the period the-
matically. Thematic history always carries with it the danger of repetition,
since the same facts are successively considered under different angles. Every
effort, however, has been made to eliminate unnecessary repetition of the narrative in this account, though the same personalities and place names necessarily recur.

The third chapter studies the slave trade and its lingering effects, especially the slave wars around Lake Tanganyika. Orphanages and freed slave
villages were consequences of the aftermath of slavery. The White Fathers
needed armed auxiliaries to defend their mission "fortresses," and they frequently exercised civil power in the absence of effective colonial administration. Chapter Four examines the processes, content and agents of
evangelization. This includes the establishment of mission stations and their
operation, the revival of the early Christian catechumenate, and also especially the work of the catechists. Among the latter were the well-known doctor-catechists, some of whose biographies are given. The chapter concludes
with the evolution of the White Fathers' pastoral strategy towards Muslims,
influenced by the life and witness of the hermit Charles De Foucauld and
his White Father correspondents Charles Guérin and Henri Marchal.

Chapter Five is a pivotal chapter, since it deals with the White Fathers'
understanding of African languages and culture, and how this affected their
relationship with colonial officials and with the "pseudo-sciences" of colonialism. An attempt is also made to assess the early beginning of Africa's
impact on the church. The final chapter deals with the monopoly on education exercised by the missionaries in this period, and its importance for
evangelization. Education was the major area of conflict with missionaries
of other denominations, and the mutual antagonism of Protestants and
Catholics is discussed, as well as early glimmers of ecumenism. Also treated
in this chapter is the development of seminary education during the period
and its importance for producing a highly trained African clergy and as well
as a Catholic lay elite.

This book is one of the fruits of a history project launched by the General
Council of the Missionaries of Africa in 2001. According to François

Richard (Superior General, 1998–2004), this project has two basic purposes: to supply a deficiency in the historical study of the Society since the death of the founder, and to make better use of the General Archives of the Society (AGMAfr.).[1] Relatively little research has been carried out on the history of the Catholic Church in Africa in the years following the death of Cardinal Lavigerie. This book begins the task of filling the gap. The archives of the Society constitute an incalculable heritage for missionary history, church history and the history of Africa. Considerable investment is being made in the conservation of these assets, through the microfilming and initial digitalizing of a large part of the collection.[2] This book makes extensive use of these archives.

Probably the most important source is that of the *Chronique Trimestrielle* (*CT*). This is a series of printed extracts from mission diaries, running from 1878 to 1909, and intended to promote co-operation and communication within the Society. "These thousands of pages represent for the historian an inexhaustible mine of information on how the communities carried out their apostolate, their relationships with the people, their community life, their common prayer and the development of church structures."[3] They provide a bird's eye view, as it were, of the whole society. There were many practical difficulties in obtaining contributions for the *Chronique* and there are many mistakes in the spelling of names of persons and places as a result of the copying process. To correct these, as well as to learn about sensitive matters not covered by the extracts, it is necessary to go to the original Mission diaries themselves. Relevant diaries were studied in their entirety for the period covered by this book. The *Chronique* was replaced in 1912 by the internal bulletin of the Society, *Petit Echo*, which continues up to this day.

It was necessary to trawl through the minutes of General Council meetings for the period, but the correspondence of Léon Livinhac, which fills twelve shelves, is indexed, and it was possible to consult it selectively on a range of issues and events. It was also necessary to study the minutes of the 1894, 1900, 1906 and 1912 General Chapters. The dossiers of relevant individuals and institutions were also used. Printed internal sources, such as the instructions of Lavigerie, Livinhac and the Vicars Apostolic, as well as the Annual Reports of the Vicariates and the Necrological Notices were very useful. Texts of Constitutions, Directories, handbooks and catechisms were also relevant.

The archives of the Society contain a wealth of monographs, dissertations and other manuscripts by confreres, some of them published. A large

---

[1] Richard, François, *Superior General's Report 1998–2004*, Rome, Missiionaries of Africa, 2004, § 1.8.7.

[2] *Ibid.*; Ceillier, Jean-Claude and Page, Ivan, *Les sources écrites internes à la Société, Société des Missionaires d'Afrique*, Rome, Missionaries of Africa History Series, no. 4., p. 54.

[3] *Ibid.*, p. 25.

number of these were consulted, and it was felt that, for a general history of the present kind, it was not necessary to repeat the detailed archival research on which most of these are based. In addition many published books and articles by White Fathers and others were helpful to the research.

Behind the immediate research of the past two years lie thirty years of teaching, researching and writing in the countries of Eastern Africa in the fields of ethno-history and missiology. This has brought the author into contact with the local archives of missionary provinces and dioceses. However, until 2004 he had had no comparable experience of Francophone West Africa. This deficiency was supplied by a journey in February-March to Senegal, Mali and Burkina Faso, where he studied local archives, interviewed informants and visited historic sites.

Acknowledgements are due to many individuals and communities for help received in the course of preparing this book. In the first place to my *confrères* Jean-Claude Ceillier, Head of the Society's History Project, and Ivan Page, the Society's Archivist; then to Dr. Jonathan Bonk, Director of the Overseas Ministries Study Center in New Haven, Connecticut, where the author was Senior Mission Scholar and Research Associate of the Yale Divinity School for the second semester of 2002–2003; to Dr. Paul Stuehrenberg and the staff of the Day Missions Library at Yale; to historians of Africa who have given advice and encouragement, especially Professor Richard Gray, Emeritus of London University; Professor John Iliffe of Cambridge University; Professor Lamin Sanneh of Yale University; to historians in the Society: Joseph-Roger de Benoist, Hugo Hinfelaar, Francis Nolan, Dominique Arnauld and Armand Duval; to Marinus Rooijackers, who put at my disposal a series of working papers on the history of the White Fathers in Uganda; to *confrères* in Mali, José Morales and Patient Nshombo, who prepared the itinerary of my visit, and to Michel Robin who acted as guide; to *confrères* in Burkina Faso, Eugenio Bacaicoa, Georges Jacques and François de Gaulle for planning my visit and offering expert guidance. Then to Rev. Hans Boerakker MHM, Archivist of the Mill Hill Missionaries; Mrs. Sara Rodger, Assistant Librarian of Arundel Castle; the staffs of many libraries: the British Library; Cambridge University Library; the Library of the Missionary Institute London; St. Edward's College Library, Totteridge; the Library of Maison Lavigerie in Wagadugu and Downside Abbey Library.

Acknowledgements are also due to Sister Hildegunde Schmidt, Archivist of the Missionary Sisters of Our Lady of Africa (MSOLA) or "White Sisters," in Rome. The MSOLA are the sister society of the White Fathers, founded a year later in 1869 by Cardinal Lavigerie. Although the MSOLA enter into the story of the White Fathers during these years and are frequently mentioned in this book, it must be stressed that this is not a history of their congregation and that they have their own history projects and historians.

The photographs in this book come from the Missionaries of Africa Photo-Archive, courtesy of its director Karl Stärk. I am grateful to Johannes

Tappeser and Julien Cormier for copying them. The maps are adaptations by Mr. William Hutt of originals in the Society's Archives, most of them sketch-maps made by former White Father archivist René Lamey.

In recent years the White Fathers have reverted, for general use, to their official name "Missionaries of Africa." However, the name "White Fathers" still sticks, and was, of course, generally used throughout the period under study, 1892–1914. The names "White Fathers" and "Missionaries of Africa" are therefore used interchangeably throughout this book.

The spelling of African personal and place names presents many difficulties in a book of this kind. In general the received spelling, as found in English publications, has been preferred, rather than the spelling used in the relevant countries or by purists of the vernacular. Thus: *Mutesa*, rather than *Muteesa*; *Wagadugu*, rather than *Ouagadougou*; *Lyons*, rather than *Lyon* etc. A special difficulty is posed by the prefixes of Bantu names. As a general rule, the root is used without the prefix; thus, the *Ganda* people, the *Ganda* language, *Ganda* culture, the *Bemba* people, the *Bemba* language etc. An exception is made for the kingdom of *Buganda*, and occasionally in context, for *Baganda* (people) and *Luganda* (language). The same for the *Bemba* and other ethnic groups. Readability and intelligibility are preferred to consistency. Since there are many vernacular terms, words in Latin and French and specialized expressions, a glossary is provided.

Some of the raw material of this book is appearing in articles written for the Dictionary of African Christian Biography (DACB), and the International Bulletin of Missionary Research (IBMR). I am indebted to the DACB Project Manager, Michèle Sigg, and the IBMR Editor, Dwight Baker for permission to use this material here.

I am also grateful to Joseph Vanrenterghem for providing translations of Flemish texts. Finally, a word of thanks goes to the members of my community in London, for providing a conducive working environment and much valuable support throughout the past two years.

CHAPTER ONE

The Legacy of Cardinal Lavigerie

A Missionary Society in Crisis

In the early hours of November 26th 1892 a small group of people gathered around a deathbed at Saint Eugène in Algiers. Charles Martial Allemand Lavigerie, Cardinal Archbishop of Algiers and Carthage, Primate of Africa, was about to render his soul to God. A great French churchman, a renowned anti-slavery campaigner and an international figure, Lavigerie was also "the most outstanding Catholic missionary strategist of the nineteenth century."[1] He was one of the few in history to whom it is given to influence large numbers of his contemporaries, as well as people of many generations to come. Among those at his bedside was Prosper-Auguste Dusserre, his coadjutor bishop in Algiers, representative of the North African church, the glories of which Lavigerie had striven to revive. Also present were the superiors of the two missionary societies he had founded, the Society of Missionaries of Africa or "White Fathers" and the Missionary Sisters of Our Lady of Africa, the "White Sisters." They were Bishop Léon Livinhac and Mother Marie-Salomé Roudaut. After Lavigerie's death, many predicted that his missionary societies would disappear.[2] As one French newspaper put it, "It can be forecast that most of the works which [the Cardinal] supported through his own ingenuity will not long survive him."[3] That his missionary societies survived, and even outlasted the structures of the revived North African church, is due in large measure to the ability and experience of the superiors he had appointed and the spirit he bequeathed them. In the final analysis, his hopes for the two missionary societies were justified and his posthumous reputation was due in large measure to their subsequent success. The White Fathers and White Sisters were "a missionary force of unsurpassed vigour and consistency in the interior of Africa."[4]

White Father novices kept vigil by Lavigerie's coffin before the funeral Mass in Algiers and the embarkation for Tunis. The arrival of the vessel carrying the Cardinal's remains was the occasion for an impressive Catholic demonstration at Tunis. "Religion triumphs," exclaimed an observer, "and France grows in stature in the eyes of the infidel, astonished by so much pomp and splendour."[5] After the *Requiem* in Tunis Cathedral, the *cortège*

1

proceeded by train to Carthage, where another vigil took place, with the White Father seminarians gazing on the "pale and calm face," and awestruck Arabs placed letters and petitions on the coffin. On December 8th the final *Requiem* was celebrated and the mourners departed, after which, in the empty cathedral, the Cardinal was laid to rest by bishops, family and missionaries in the small vaulted chamber he had prepared. The vault was closed with a marble slab. Barely seventy years later, Carthage Cathedral was secularized and Lavigerie's remains were transferred to Rome.[6]

The Tenth General Chapter, held at Algiers over a period of two years in 1889–1890, had elected Livinhac, at Lavigerie's suggestion, to be his vicar for the functions of superior general of the Society of Missionaries of Africa. At Lavigerie's death, he was to continue as superior general in his own right until the next General Chapter was convened in 1895.[7] Livinhac, therefore, took over sole direction of the Society in November 1892, but early in the following year, only two and a half months after the founder's death, he decided to convene an extraordinary General Chapter for 1894.[8] Lavigerie's hopes were well-founded, but it could not be denied that the Society, deprived now of its founder's guiding hand, was a society in crisis.

Among Lavigerie's earliest foundations were the two Christian villages he had set up in the Chélif valley for the baptized survivors of the 1867 Algerian famine. The thirty or so families who lived there made no Christian impact on the surrounding population, and the villages were, as the Cardinal himself admitted, costly and ineffective ghettoes.[9] In the mountainous region of Kabylia to the south, there were half a dozen mission stations engaged in educational and medical work. Constrained by the prohibition—and indeed the inherent imprudence—of open proselytism in a Muslim society, the White Fathers had so far failed to interest the Kabyles in Christianity.[10] All they could report was a tiny trickle of adult conversions and the silent opposition of the masses.

Lavigerie had been given responsibility by Pope Pius IX in 1868 for evangelizing the Sahara and French Sudan, and it was his dream, as well as the dream of the French authorities, to cross the desert and link Algeria to the sub-Saharan colonies then being established by France. In particular, he focussed on the legendary city of Timbuktu. In the fourteenth century, Timbuktu had been a centre of Islamic culture and a flourishing halfway house for the trans-Saharan trade in gold and salt. Now it was a bastion of the slave trade. The French military, however, had so far failed to reach the southern Sahara, and in 1892 had not yet entered Timbuktu from the Senegal and Niger Rivers, let alone from the desert. The White Fathers had established a handful of mission stations in the oases of the Mzab and the northern Sahara, and from there two groups of missionaries had set out in 1876 and 1881, only to be massacred in turn by Tuareg tribesmen. A French military expedition had been similarly annihilated in 1881. After withdrawing from the desert for several years, the White Fathers crept back to northern Sahara and founded, or re-founded, five mission stations.

With revolts and continued unrest in the Mzab, and the Saharan slave trade in full swing, Lavigerie was desperate to provide some form of security for his missionaries there. Having failed to persuade the European powers to act, he decided to create his own Catholic army, "The Armed Brothers of the Sahara."[11] It turned out to be a counsel of despair, and, when the French government withdrew its support, the bizarre experiment had to be abandoned shortly before the Cardinal's death. At the same time, in 1890, the Vicariate Apostolic of the Sahara and (French) Sudan had been created, with the Kabylian missions becoming ecclesiastically part of the Algerian littoral. As vicar apostolic, Lavigerie consecrated Joseph-Anatole Toulotte (1852–1907) as his coadjutor. Toulotte was a fastidious scholar and reclusive ascetic, but not a leader of men, and the Cardinal was forced to admit that his choice had been mistaken.[12] Nevertheless, at Lavigerie's death in 1892, Toulotte automatically became vicar apostolic of the Sahara and (French) Sudan, with five stations in the Mzab and no hint, as yet, of any attempt to establish a foothold in the Sudan itself.

In 1878, Pope Leo XIII had made Lavigerie responsible for the evangelization of the Great Lakes region of equatorial Africa, and by 1892 the White Fathers had managed to maintain a tenuous presence there for fourteen years. The most successful mission had been the Vicariate Apostolic of Nyanza, centred on the Kingdom of Buganda, where, after a brief period of persecution, relatively large numbers had been converted, and the king, the former persecutor, seemed likely to become a catechumen. In January 1892, however, the Catholic loyalist majority had been defeated in a civil war, in which the agent of the Imperial British East Africa Company, Frederick Lugard, had lent armed support to the rival Protestant minority. Catholic mission property had been destroyed and Catholics themselves driven into exile. Many had been killed or enslaved. The White Fathers had been forced by the British to give up two stations in the eastern part of the vicariate, as well as one in the Sese Islands. At the end of 1892, they were left with three mission stations in Buganda itself and two on the western and southern shores of Lake Victoria. Theoretically, the vicariate stretched northwards as far as the Bahr-al-Ghazal and eastwards as far as Lake Naivasha in the Great Rift Valley, but no attempt had been made to occupy these vast regions.

In the rest of the lake region, the Church was still metaphorically speaking "in the catacombs," with missionaries cooped up in mission fortresses, while freebooting slave traders ravaged the countryside. Three missionaries and an auxiliary had died violent deaths in the region, and altogether twenty-three of the fifty-one young missionaries who arrived between 1878–1888, including two bishops, had died within three years of arrival. The Provicariate of Unyanyembe had been created in 1886. It covered most of what is now west-central Tanzania, together with the Kingdom of Burundi, but in 1892 it had only one mission station, started the year before. The Vicariate Apostolic of Tanganyika and the Provicariate of Upper Congo each had two stations, while the Provicariate of Nyasa, encompassing two thirds of modern Zambia and the whole of modern Malawi, had one. In 1892, Upper Congo was experiencing the climax of the war against Afro-Arab slave traders that raged on the northern and western shores of Lake Tanganyika. It can truthfully be said, therefore, that in 1892 the five circumscriptions of the Great Lakes region were struggling for survival.

Lavigerie's great anti-slavery campaign of 1888–1889 had certainly re-awakened the conscience of Europe and stimulated the search for solutions, but it had also unintentionally fuelled the colonial "scramble" for Africa. Slavery remained a fact of life for the White Fathers in every corner of the continent in 1892, and would remain so for the next thirty or more years, often with the connivance of the very colonial authorities that had espoused the anti-slavery movement.

Finally, if there was a ray of light to pierce all this darkness, it was St. Anne's Jerusalem. In 1882, a major seminary had been added to the apostolic school, where White Fathers (since 1878) were training future priests of the Greek-Melchite rite. St. Anne's, however, was not only forming an indigenous clergy for the Near East. It was also initiating the White Fathers on its teaching staff into the running of seminaries. Among them were a number of influential African missionaries, including no fewer than five future vicars apostolic.[13] For the moment, however, the only seminary that had been started in equatorial Africa (by Livinhac himself) was in abeyance due to the Buganda Civil War.[14]

Léon Livinhac

This, then, was the parlous situation of the Missionaries of Africa when the torch was passed from its founder to his successor. Auguste-Simon-Léon-Jules Livinhac was born on July 13th 1846 in a small hamlet of the Diocese of Rodez, in the Midi-Pyrénées region of France.[15] He was the second of three children born to Antoine Simon and Marie-Aimée Livinhac. His father died when Léon was two years old, and his mother when he was five. Thereafter, he was brought up by a grandmother and aunts. He was a child of delicate health but a good student and a hard worker. After several interruptions due to ill health, he finally finished his schooling in 1867 and entered the major seminary of Rodez at the age of twenty-one. During the Franco-Prussian War, in which his brother Arsène was killed, the seminary became a hospital. Soon after this, Félix Charmetant, on behalf of the Missionaries of Africa, visited Rodez during an astonishing vocation tour of virtually all the seminaries of France. As a result, Livinhac, now a deacon, wrote to Lavigerie in 1873, asking to be admitted to the novitiate in Algiers. He entered the White Fathers' novitiate in the same year with a group of thirty-eight priests and seminarians, including six future bishops and two future martyrs. A similar group of twenty-seven had entered the previous year. Clothed as a novice by Lavigerie in April 1873, he was ordained priest by him in October.

Livinhac had been a novice for only six months when he was appointed professor of dogmatic theology at the scholasticate that had been opened in Algiers two years earlier. In this capacity, he completed his canonical novitiate. Livinhac, like many of those who joined the Society as priests or deacons, had virtually no formal training as a missionary. Instead, he learned "on the job," as it were, and from the lips of Lavigerie, who frequently sat in his classroom and presided over the examination of his students. The neo-scholastic revival had not yet taken place, and the nominalist, propositional theology of the day left much to be desired. The spirituality Livinhac had imbibed was that of the French seminary tradition, directed towards the interior life, with more than a hint of Jansenism. It valued austerity, with no concession to creature comforts. Livinhac frequently returned to this theme in his teaching and writing, and practised it himself. When he returned to Rodez as a newly consecrated bishop in 1884, the seminarian who woke him in the morning was surprised to find him sleeping on the bare boards of a window embrasure and not in the bed provided.[16]

Livinhac warmed to Lavigerie's emphasis on personal sanctification as the driving force of the apostolate. "Life in Africa," Livinhac told the novices in 1898, "is short, so live intensely and be saints."[17] Lavigerie saw this as a necessity not only for his missionaries, but also for their African neophytes. Their conversion was to be a conversion of heart and of morals, leading to a religion of personal devotion that would translate into an active apostolate towards their fellow Africans.

In the novitiate, Livinhac encountered a new spirituality, that of the Society of Jesus. Livinhac's novice master was François Terrasse S.J. (1852–1922), the last of three Jesuit novice masters, who were employed for practical reasons by Lavigerie. His predecessors had each lasted one year, but Terrasse, who was more discreet about Ignatian methods and more liberal in his interpretation of them, was allowed to remain for five years. Under his influence, Livinhac drew up the plan of life that became the basis of a rule he wrote for the scholasticate. He also learned the importance of the colloquy with God, the contemplative phase of Ignatian prayer.[18] Throughout his life, Livinhac yearned to repeat the experience of that short novitiate, and he managed to do so in 1884 at Carthage, before his episcopal ordination. It was a second novitiate of six months, incorporating a thirty-day retreat.[19] Livinhac was less successful in getting his fellow missionaries to follow his example. Although this idea of a second novitiate or tertianship was proposed by the General Chapter of 1900, the idea was rejected by the Vatican.[20] Years later, in 1915, Livinhac wrote to Terrasse: "Lavigerie was my father, but you were my mother."[21]

1874 saw Livinhac handling the young Society's meagre finances, first as Treasurer General, then as Procurator conducting mission appeals in France.

The following year he was sent as superior of a mission post in Kabylia where he lived in abject poverty and learned Kabyle. Recalled once more to the motherhouse in 1875, he became rector of the scholasticate. During his three years in this position, he worked on a Kabyle grammar and introduced this language for Gospel reading in the refectory. In his second year as rector, came the news that three Missionaries of Africa had been martyred in the Sahara desert. This event confirmed him in his missionary vocation. Indeed, it provoked in him, as it did in the minds of his confreres, a fascination with martyrdom. Lavigerie said of the Missionaries of Africa in 1885, "One could call it a society of martyrs," and he told its members that this ordeal awaited them all: "if not a martyrdom that was bloody and prompt, then a martyrdom that was no less true, the lengthy, everyday martyrdom of privation, sickness and premature death . . ."22

Livinhac welcomed his nomination as a member of the first caravan of White Fathers to equatorial Africa in 1878 in this spirit. A tall, serious young priest of thirty-two, whose health was not the best, he was made superior of the Nyanza mission. Of the eight priests and one brother who accompanied him, one would die of malaria on the journey and two would be speared to death at Rumonge by Bikari warriors three years later.23 Livinhac and two others reached the Kingdom of Buganda the following year, remaining there until 1882, when he judged it too dangerous to stay. During those three years the foundations of the Catholic Church in Buganda were laid. Moreover, Livinhac saw Lavigerie's missionary principles being put into practice—language study, the catechumenate, medical care, the evangelization of Africa by Africans themselves—and he became completely convinced of their validity. The enforced residence of the missionaries at the Ganda capital influenced the young aspirants for power at court. Their keen adherence to Christianity survived the temporary departure of the White Fathers from 1882–1885. Not only did converts increase from twenty-five to six hundred, but three Christian communities were founded at a distance from the royal palace. From the very outset, the Ganda had become missionaries to themselves.

In 1883, Livinhac was named vicar apostolic of Nyanza, the first member of the Missionaries of Africa to be raised to episcopal rank. Therefore he did not return to Buganda with the other missionaries in 1885, but went to North Africa, where he made his cherished second novitiate and was ordained bishop by Lavigerie in the seminary chapel at Carthage, Tunisia. He also worked on a Ganda grammar to be printed in Paris, and a dictionary of up to seven thousand Ganda words, with narrative texts, that was unfortunately lost at sea. Out of humility, he had wanted to refuse the episcopate and, failing that, the title of *monseigneur*, but Lavigerie and ecclesiastical custom prevailed.

Livinhac got back to Buganda in 1886, to find a persecution in full spate at the hands of the young king, Mwanga. Together with Siméon Lourdel (1853–1890), he instructed, baptized and confirmed many of the Catholics most in danger, and when he left Buganda again in 1887 to consecrate Jean-Baptiste Charbonnier (1842–1888) vicar apostolic of Tanganyika at Kipalapala, he took with him the first documented testimonies of the martyrdoms, on the strength of which Leo XIII consented to the introduction of the Uganda Martyrs' cause. His next visit to Buganda in 1888 was brief. The martyrdoms, as it turned out, were only the first stage in a Christian revolution.[24] Persecution had been a stimulus and Livinhac encountered an immediate growth in numbers and the formation of Christian factions at court. These joined with the Muslim party to depose Mwanga in 1888. Within a month the coalition broke up and both Christians and missionaries were expelled by the Muslims.[25]

Exiled to Ankole, politicized Christian parties came into existence in 1889, calling each other "English" and "French," a misleading national stereotype in the latter case, since the White Fathers in the vicariate included missionaries from Germany and Alsace (then in German hands).[26] These parties succeeded in restoring the now penitent Mwanga. In 1890 a struggle for power began between the Christian factions. Catholics outnumbered Protestants, and with Mwanga an intermittent catechumen who even took Livinhac's Christian name Leo, they could claim to be the loyalist party. The White Fathers had been given the site of the former royal palace at Rubaga for their headquarters, and between 1889 and 1892, it began to look as if a Catholic Kingdom might become a reality in Buganda. Such an idea was considered an anomaly by British Protestants when the establishment of a protectorate by Britain became likely.

Livinhac left Buganda forever in 1890, summoned by the tenth General Chapter to act as superior general of the White Fathers. Although his attempts to re-visit Buganda in 1892 and 1901 were frustrated, Livinhac remained in constant contact with his old mission field.[27] The Vicariate of Uganda, as it came to be called, with its mass conversions, the memory of its martyrs and its vocations to the priesthood and religious life, became a model for all other missions of the White Fathers. In 1905–1906, its eighteen mission stations averaged more than five thousand Christians each. This was more than the total Christian population of every other vicariate of the Society, in East or West Africa. Only Nyanza South, with its wave of conversions in the Kingdom of Rwanda, could reach six thousand, and this was far below the numbers in the mission stations of the Ugandan Buddu province.[28] Livinhac pressed forward with all the stages of the Uganda Martyrs' beatification, collecting documents and testimonials, and supervising at a distance the "primordial" sessions in Buganda itself.[29] He lived to see their beatification by Pope Benedict XV in 1920. Livinhac also corresponded with the first two Ugandan priests in 1913.[30] As Simon Moullec wrote in 1895, the Ganda were "the lamps placed on the lampstand" to enlighten others.[31] The Missionaries of Africa were indeed fortunate to have as their superior general the founder of their most successful and exemplary mission. Before leaving for the East African coast, Livinhac consecrated

Jean-Joseph Hirth (1854–1931) at Bukumbi, as his successor in Nyanza.

Livinhac did not have Lavigerie's creative vision or originality. He also tended to be pessimistic by nature. There had been occasions in Buganda when he felt its people were under God's curse, and when he left it in 1890 he now believed that his departure from the mission at this critical juncture of its history was nothing short of a catastrophe.[32] Moreover, he believed that his presence in the Society's general council also spelt disaster. On his way to the coast, he penned an extremely pessimistic letter to Lavigerie. "If they insist," he wrote, "that I enter the Society's Council, that is an infallible sign for me that it is cursed by God . . . I go like a deportee to Cayenne."[33] Further along the road, Livinhac met a missionary caravan with another letter from Lavigerie. Although he read the letter on his knees, he wondered how the Society could have two superiors general.[34] Livinhac's extreme reaction to his appointment is expressed in hyperbole that seems to go beyond the terms of conventional humility and suggests a serious lack of self confidence. After attending the Paris anti-slavery conference, and visits to Rome and Malta, Livinhac was installed by Lavigerie in his new functions, the Cardinal declaring that he had all the necessary qualities for the post. Lavigerie was to retain responsibility for administration, nominations, foundations, finances and discipline. Livinhac was to oversee the interior and regular life of the Society.[35] It was not the best formula for a working relationship, and Livinhac was "tortured by "repugnance, sadness, anguish and fear."[36]

Lavigerie had two more years of life and, sensing that his end was approaching, looked for a coadjutor to succeed him as Archbishop of Carthage. Without his being informed, Livinhac's name was put forward in 1891 and his nomination was approved by both Rome and the French government. Lavigerie had expected a refusal from Livinhac and hoped to present him with a *fait accompli*. When he came to hear of it by chance, Livinhac categorically rejected the nomination. This time he was not to be moved.[37] In spite of his attachment to the Cardinal and his fidelity to his ideas, Livinhac was his own man. There would be many new situations which even Lavigerie, in his wisdom, could not have foreseen, and Livinhac's obstinate allegiance to the Society of Missionaries of Africa was a good augury for the future. After his second stroke on November 23rd 1892, Lavigerie could no longer speak or recognize him. In a final filial gesture, Livinhac kissed the dying man's hand.

The Crisis in Uganda

Now Livinhac, at the age of forty-six, was left alone to govern the Society. He was to be confronted with several major questions during his tenure. The most urgent, which could not be held over to the coming General Chapter, was the 1892 crisis in Uganda. When Frederick Lugard entered Buganda at the end of 1890 to annexe the kingdom on behalf of the

Imperial British East Africa (IBEA) Company, the two Christian factions were poised on the verge of civil war. Unfortunately, Lugard was no peacemaker. The Anglican missionaries in Buganda were representatives of an established church headed by the British sovereign, and the extension of British protection to the kingdom was in their interest. When it looked as if the IBEA Company would run out of money in 1891, the Protestant Bishop Tucker raised £15,000 in Britain to keep it in the country.[38] Most of the Catholic missionaries were French nationals, and although they believed in the mission of France to spread her civilisation and (Catholic) religion, the Napoleonic concordat of 1801 had come under increasing threat from anti-clericals in the French Republic, until it was made irrelevant by the 1905 Law of Separation. Most of the French missionaries had monarchist sympathies, but they held no brief for a theocratic state, even if the king, Mwanga, were to become a Catholic. Mutesa I of Buganda had secretly asked the White Fathers for a protective alliance with France in 1879.[39] This request was dutifully passed on to the French consul in Zanzibar, and Lavigerie also informed Charles-Louis Freycinet, the French premier.[40] France, however, had no immediate interest in the region and nothing came of the request. In fact, with Lavigerie's encouragement, the Catholic missionaries offered support to Carl Peters, the German imperialist, to counterbalance Protestant backing for the Imperial British East Africa Company, but this move was overtaken by the Anglo-German Agreement of 1890 which placed Buganda in the British sphere.[41]

From his first arrival in the country, Lugard, according to Livinhac, treated the White Fathers as "men searching above all to establish the influence of France" and saw their presence in the region as "a great danger for Britain."[42] Already in 1891, Lugard ordered the closure of the Catholic missions in Busoga and the eastern provinces of Buganda. This part of the Nyanza Vicariate was too close to the upper Nile and its sources to allow Frenchmen in the vicinity.[43] "Is this country [Busoga] to be lost to Protestant England?," asked the Anglican missionary, Baskerville.[44] The fear was that the French might move from Brazzaville to take over the headwaters of the Nile and so threaten Egypt, but even Captain Jean-Baptiste Marchand's epic march to Fashoda on the Bahr-al-Ghazal, seven years later in 1898, was only a half-hearted challenge. There was never any serious French threat to British interests in the area.[45] After the Catholic defeat in 1892, the White Fathers were also forced to abandon their mission on the Sese Islands in Lake Victoria, as these islands were regarded as a strategic outpost for safeguarding shipping on the lake and guarding the route south. "Catholicism and anti-English are synonymous," declared Commissioner Henry Edward Colvile in 1894.[46]

As one historian has written, "Lugard's own share of responsibility for the civil war between Catholics and Protestants in January 1892 should not be underestimated."[47] Indeed, he admitted his bias towards the partisans of his "own creed."[48] When the moment of truth came in January 1892, his superior weaponry and his arming of the Protestant ("English") faction with precision rifles ensured the rout of the majority Catholic ("French") party and the flight of the king, Mwanga.[49] At Rubaga, the unfinished cathedral had been left a smoking ruin, and three orphanages, a school, a chapel and the missionaries' residence had also been destroyed. As Protestant adherents rampaged over the rest of the kingdom, the tally rose to sixty chapels and twelve schools destroyed, and an estimated five to six thousand Catholic sympathisers sold into slavery.[50]

News of the disaster reached Algiers in April 1892. Lavigerie had already corresponded with Cardinal Manning of Westminster in 1891, suggesting that the head of the British administration in Buganda should be an English Catholic, and this suggestion had been communicated to Lord Salisbury, the prime minister.[51] He also strongly refuted the accusation that the Missionaries of Africa were representatives of France. They were, he wrote, "the peaceful envoys of the Pope."[52] Cardinal Manning, however, had died in January and there was no one in England whom Lavigerie could now approach. He therefore composed an open letter to an "Eminent English Catholic" which was published in France, but made no apparent impact in Britain.[53] Lavigerie suffered his first stroke in May, and his death was approaching. On April 22nd, the General Council of the Missionaries of Africa discussed the sending of supplies to the beleaguered missionaries and Christians. Livinhac wanted to return to Buganda to negotiate with Lugard, but it was pointed out that if the Captain would not listen to Bishop Hirth, he was unlikely to listen to Livinhac. In any case, the latter would be too late to exert any influence. Furthermore, his health was bad, and, with the prospect of losing Lavigerie in the near future, Livinhac was needed in Algiers for the good of the whole Society.[54]

In May Hirth's correspondence with Livinhac and Lavigerie and articles by Livinhac began to appear in *Missions Catholiques*.[55] In them, the Battle of Mengo and subsequent massacre at Bulingugwe Island were described, as well as the unfair terms of Lugard's settlement, which allowed the Protestants to retain a political position far in excess of their local strength. In June, English translations of these letters and articles began to appear in *The Tablet*.[56] "How sad the fate of our poor Uganda [*sic*]," wrote Bishop Hirth, "A very little more and it would have become a Catholic kingdom, and now it has relapsed into error, perhaps even barbarism, for who knows how many centuries to come!"[57] But the Catholic Kingdom was not an "anti-English Kingdom," argued the White Father apologist, Joseph Mercui. It came into existence through "the free preaching of the Gospel."[58] As *The Tablet* hastened to explain, Hirth's yearning for a Catholic Kingdom was not political.[59] It was a question of using traditional social structures as a means to advance Christianity.[60]

With the return of Mwanga at the end of March 1892, his eventual identification with the Protestant faction and the massive migration of Catholics to the southwest of the kingdom, the province of Buddu became, in the

words of Hirth, "a new fatherland for us."[61] Indeed, Catholics were virtually confined to Buddu in Lugard's settlement of 1892.

Meanwhile, the French government pressed the administration of Lord
Salisbury in London to carry out an official enquiry. In June, Salisbury's
Tory government fell and Gladstone returned to power as prime minister
for the last time. Before this happened, Salisbury appointed a commission
of enquiry, headed by an engineer from the Uganda railway survey, Captain
James Macdonald. Its outcome, the Macdonald Report, sided in the main
with the White Fathers, placing the blame squarely on the shoulders of
Lugard; ". . . by adopting a high-handed policy and by injudicious man-
agement of the crisis, he precipitated civil war in Uganda."[62] This report
was never published; it was overtaken by events. In September, the new
British foreign secretary, Lord Rosebery, summoned Lugard to Britain to
give his version of what had happened. Meanwhile, he commenced a campaign in the press for the British retention of Uganda. Herbert Vaughan had
been enthroned as Archbishop of Westminster in May, and was to receive
the Cardinal's hat in December. His brother, Kenelm Vaughan, who had visited Africa and collected information about the Buganda civil war, wrote to
The Tablet, protesting about the unfair representation of the Catholic position in *The Times* and other newspapers.[63] Lugard arrived back in Britain
in October. His letters and articles in *The Times* and other journals precipitated an even stronger anti-French and anti-Catholic reaction. Even
Catholic opinion in Britain, as Livinhac bitterly lamented, was greatly
opposed to the White Fathers in this matter.[64] In December, Rosebery
appointed Sir Gerald Portal, the British Consul-General in Zanzibar, to be
imperial commissioner in Uganda, with the ulterior purpose of preparing
the way for a British protectorate. Portal met both Catholic and Protestant
Bishops at Kampala on June 28th 1893.[65] As a result, a fairer division of
the country was worked out, although the balance of power remained with
the Protestant minority. The White Fathers were allowed back to the Sese
Islands, but Buddu remained the centre of Catholic power. Portal returned
to Britain at the end of 1893 and his recommendations were accepted by
the British cabinet in March 1894. A British protectorate was proclaimed
in August.

During 1893, while Portal was in Uganda, Livinhac agonized over the situation and over how to ensure the survival of the Catholic mission in the
face of a hostile British government and adverse public opinion. His primary
concerns were the advocacy of the just rights of Catholics in Uganda and
their claim for compensation. In all of this, he was powerfully aided by a
prominent Catholic in Britain, Major Ross-of-Bladensburg, friend of the fifteenth Duke of Norfolk.[66] These two men, who had close relations with the
Vatican, were described by Livinhac as "the only two Englishmen who have
truly studied the (Ugandan) question and who do us justice."[67] John Foster
George Ross-of-Bladensburg (1848–1926) was an officer in the Coldstream
Guards and came of a well-known military family. His grandfather, Major-

General Robert Ross, was the victor of the battle of Bladensburg, Maryland, in the 1812 Anglo-American War and had the doubtful further distinction of sacking Washington D.C. and burning the White House. After his death in an ambush at Baltimore in 1814, his descendants received the privilege of adding "Bladensburg" to their family name.[68] Major Ross (as we shall call him) had served with the Guards in the Egyptian expedition of 1885 that failed to relieve General Gordon in Khartoum. A Northern Irishman, he had become a Catholic, following the example of his wife, and with the Duke of Norfolk became closely involved in Anglo-Irish politics, upholding the rights of Irish Catholics. He also served on two British missions to the Holy See in 1887 and 1889.[69] According to his biographer, Major Ross possessed "great political ability and knowledge of European problems," and had a "brilliant and versatile intellect devoid of arrogance."[70]

Livinhac went to Rome in February 1893 for Leo XIII's episcopal golden jubilee. In the same month, Major Ross accompanied the Duke of Norfolk on the British pilgrimage to Rome, and was entrusted with the official mission to congratulate the pope on behalf of Queen Victoria.[71] It may be that Livinhac made the acquaintance of the two men on that occasion. At all events, a correspondence arose between Livinhac and Major Ross during 1893. In early December, Ross wrote to Livinhac about Portal's return to London and the probability that he was favourable to the Catholic claims. He felt it important that a representative of the injured party should come to London and lay the Society's grievances in person before the English authorities. He added: "No one could better represent the mission than Your Lordship, because from your high position, and from the fact that you were yourself Bishop so long in Uganda up to 1890, it would seem to me that you would be the best person to produce the required impression, if such an impression can at all be produced."[72] Ross offered to set up the meeting at the appropriate time.

On January 10th 1894, Major Ross wrote to Livinhac that he had discussed the matter with the Duke of Norfolk and that both were in agreement that he should come to Britain in person to meet Lord Rosebery. Ross noted that the Missionaries of Africa had established a branch of the Society in Germany. Would it not be possible, he asked, to do the same in England? In the meantime, he suggested, Livinhac might recruit some priests of British nationality to work in Uganda. "This would do much to calm the prejudices which have done so much harm in the past."[73] In view of the urgent situation and of Lord Rosebery's movements, Ross thought that Livinhac should come to London as soon as possible.

Livinhac accepted the proposal and immediately embarked on a three-week journey to London. It is clear from his correspondence with Ross that the idea of Livinhac's visit to London did not originate with the British government. It is also clear from the correspondence, and from Livinhac's report on the journey to the General Council, that he did not go with the specific idea of inviting the Mill Hill Missionaries to Uganda.[74] Livinhac took with him, as interpreter, John Forbes (1864–1926), the first Canadian White Father. In Paris, they saw the secretary for foreign affairs and told him that, although they were leaving the Uganda affair and the demand for compensation in the hands of the French Government, they were going to Britain to solicit help from British Catholics in counteracting the widespread calumnies against the Catholic missionaries.[75] In London, where they took rooms in the Charing Cross Hotel, they visited the French ambassador before meeting with "our benefactors," the Duke of Norfolk and Major Ross. With the Duke and Major Ross, Livinhac and Forbes visited Cardinal Vaughan, who received them warmly, but who maintained a reserve over the events in Uganda. They then went to see Lord Rosebery, whose manner was almost insulting. He even went so far as to say that France had enough African countries under its protection and that the Catholic missionaries would do better to quit Uganda altogether. The attitude of Lord Salisbury, who had been prime minister when the Ugandan civil war broke out, and who was also present at the meeting, was more correct.

Livinhac soon realized that the Society would have to make concessions, if it was to be allowed to remain in Uganda. The first suggestion was that Livinhac should invite Cardinal Vaughan's Mill Hill Missionaries to Uganda and place them together with the White Fathers in all the mission stations. Livinhac regarded this idea as preposterous. Then Major Ross made "a truly wise suggestion" that the eastern portion of the Nyanza Vicariate, which Hirth had been forbidden by the British to evangelize, should be confided to Mill Hill as a separate vicariate. Livinhac at once saw the advantages of the proposal. It would save Catholicism in the region. It would co-opt British allies, including Cardinal Vaughan, in the tussle with the authorities. Finally, it would give the lie to those who said that Catholicism was an exclusively French religion. Livinhac undertook to approach the Cardinal Prefect of *Propaganda Fide* without delay.

Back at his hotel, before his departure for Algiers, Livinhac drafted several letters. To Vaughan, he once more explained his main purpose in coming to London, namely that the Catholics of Uganda and their missionaries should no longer be regarded as a danger to the British administration, and promised to follow up the division of the Nyanza Vicariate. To Mr. Gladstone, he regretted that they had not been able to meet, but enclosed his short report to Lord Rosebery. Lord Salisbury he thanked for the Macdonald Commission. In his report to Lord Rosebery, Livinhac once more rebutted the insinuations of Catholic disloyalty and outlined the proposal concerning Cardinal Vaughan's missionaries.[76]

Soon after Livinhac's return to Algiers in February, Major Ross wrote a lengthy letter urging him to press the French government to insist on compensation and not to give the impression that the White Fathers were waiving this claim. The letter demonstrates Ross's considerable diplomatic skills.[77] In March he wrote again, expressing his satisfaction at the progress being made.[78] Finally, in April, he forwarded Portal's Report to Livinhac, angry that it did not include Macdonald's findings. He and the Duke of Norfolk had been to see Vaughan about sending Mill Hill Missionaries to Uganda in the summer.[79] The division of the Nyanza Vicariate took place in July and the first Mill Hill caravan, led by Bishop Henry Hanlon, reached Kampala in September 1895. In 1898 Vaughan announced to Livinhac that, without accepting liability for the actions of the IBEA Company and its agents, the British Government had finally remitted £10,000 as an indemnity to the Uganda Catholic Mission. However, Vaughan claimed a share of this, since his missionaries were now working in part of the area for which the money was granted.[80]

Without Lavigerie's protection, Livinhac remained wary of Cardinal Vaughan and his influence in Rome. He was anxious about the delay in appointing Antonin Guillermain as Hirth's successor in Uganda, fearing that the Mill Hill Missionaries might step in and take "the best mission we have."[81] In 1897 he became convinced that Cardinal Vaughan had designs on this flourishing mission, and asked the novices to make a novena about "this grave matter."[82] As late as April 1917, Livinhac wrote to the Mill Hill Bishop John Biermans, complaining that Mill Hill Missionaries had publicly attributed to themselves alone the achievements of the Uganda Catholic Mission.[83] These fears probably say more about Livinhac's paranoia than about the real situation. Livinhac's London visit of January–February 1894, however, had certainly saved the White Fathers' mission in Uganda. But the jibe that "French" and "Catholic" were synonymous died hard. In 1900, Britain's Special Commissioner to Uganda, Sir Harry Johnston, briefly revived the deplorable stereotypes, and the Protestant Bishop Alfred Tucker, in his memoirs of eighteen years' work in Uganda, referred consistently to Catholics as French "intruders," never once acknowledging the presence of British Mill Hill Missionaries.[84]

The Anti-Clerical Crisis

The second great crisis which confronted Livinhac was in many ways more menacing than the aftermath of civil war in Uganda, because it threatened the very existence of the Society itself. This was the French government's anti-clerical legislation of 1901 and 1905. René Waldeck-Rousseau (1846–1904) became premier in 1899, and his government passed the Law of Associations in July 1901, effectively rendering Catholic religious congregations illegal because they were directed from abroad. Waldeck-Rousseau himself did not wish to treat the religious too harshly, and as long as he was in power there was some uncertainty about the law's application. However, he resigned in June 1902, and his place was taken by a militantly anti-clerical former seminarian, Emile Combes (1835–1921). Combes denied authorization to virtually all religious congregations and societies in France, many of which were forced into exile in Belgium or Britain. The cynical king of the Belgians, Leopold II, famously remarked: "Send them all (to Belgium).

We never have enough honest people in my country. Religious are kind to others and they pay their taxes—something which should not be overlooked. Send them all here!"[85]

Combes went on to draw up the Law of Separation, secularizing all church schools, hospitals and other institutions, thereby violating the Concordat with the Catholic Church and withdrawing French diplomatic representation to the Vatican. This bill became law in December 1905, after Combes himself had fallen from power.

Livinhac was filled with forboding and addressed a circular to the Society about the "terrible storm" of persecution that threatened in France.[86] The General Council at first thought it was not necessary to apply for authorization.[87] A government decree of August 31st 1878 had recognized the Society of Missionaries of Africa as an "establishment of public utility" for teaching purposes. However, Livinhac was told that this had no bearing on the law of 1901.[88] The White Fathers had houses outside France and its dependent territories, but a letter from Waldeck-Rousseau himself insisted that authorization must be sought for the whole Society.[89] Authorization was requested towards the end of 1901, but there was still no reply in January of the following year.[90] Meanwhile contingency plans were drawn up to move the Paris community into a hotel. In December 1902, the White Fathers learned that their demand for authorization had been only partially accepted. A draft bill in the Senate authorized twenty-one establishments in Algeria and French Sudan, having a maximum of four hundred personnel. In France only the procures in Paris and Marseilles were approved, not the three houses of formation.[91] The General Council suggested turning one of the houses into a sanatorium, and explaining to the government why a seminary was needed in France. There was not much hope of success, so a search was begun for a suitable house in Belgium to which the philosophy seminary of Binson could be moved.[92] Livinhac wrote to the Society in January 1903 that authorization was "still uncertain."[93]

Rumours circulated in Algeria and Tunisia that the White Fathers would be expelled, and caricatures of priests appeared on the walls of Carthage Cathedral.[94] As churches in Paris were trashed by thugs called "Apaches," Binson seminary closed its chapel as a precaution, and Livinhac sent Paul Voillard (1860–1946) to Paris to await the decision of the Senate.[95]

At this critical juncture help arrived from an unexpected quarter in the person of the Princess Jeanne Bibesco.[96] Jeanne was the daughter of a Romanian prince, her mother being a granddaughter of Napoleon's favorite general, Marshal Ney. Having become a Carmelite in Meyerling, Austria, she was invited by Lavigerie to found a Carmel in Algiers. In 1890, at the uncanonical age of twenty-one, she was elected prioress of her foundation with the approval of Lavigerie, who overlooked the impediment of her age. As Mother Bénie de Jésus, she ruled the Algiers Carmel in liberal fashion for the next thirteen years. In May 1903, at the age of thirty-four, she travelled to Paris with another Carmelite and the vicar-general of Algiers

Archdiocese. With the help of her uncle, Prince Alexander Bibesco, she secured a meeting with Emile Combes, who was immediately captivated by the vivacious young nun. She paid him a series of confidential visits, and Combes, then aged sixty-eight, was observed gallantly handing her into her carriage at the Quai d'Orsay. Correspondence followed on Christian name terms, and Jeanne paid two further visits to see him in Paris. In September 1903, the White Fathers sent a report on the Society's works to the Senate, and at the end of the year the government tabled a favourable report on the desired authorization.[97] The princess was also assured that her Carmel would not be closed. Livinhac was still on tenterhooks in January 1904, but at length a "significant letter" dated August 30th 1904 clinched the matter, and the draft bill before the Senate was pigeon-holed until it was finally withdrawn in 1920. "She saved the Church in Africa!" was the verdict of one White Father in Algeria.[98]

After Combes left office in 1905, Jeanne continued to correspond with him about the imminent enactment of the Law of Separation. Then, on Combes's advice, she sought, and obtained, a papal dispensation from her vows in 1912, and returned to Paris, where she resumed her title of Princess and continued living there until her death in 1943. Her friendship with Combes was, to say the least, surprising.[99]

Livinhac continued to share with his missionaries his apprehension about the 1905 Law of Separation. "The storm," he wrote, "is still suspended over our heads," but the major crisis was over.[100] It took some time for people in Algeria to be convinced that the White Fathers had obtained government authorization to remain in the country. It was also several years before the Law of Separation took effect. The closing of schools started in 1907 and most of the White Fathers' educational work was shut down by 1914.[101] Henceforth, missionaries were engaged in extramural and post-school formation. In French Sudan the law was unevenly applied. Government subsidies were withdrawn, but private or "free" schools were generally authorized, although new foundations were sometimes opposed. Chaplains and religious were obliged to leave hospitals. The anti-clerical legislation occasioned a certain measure of harassment, but missionaries remained on good terms with the administration and mission expansion continued as before. The great benefit of the Law of Separation was to end the equivocal situation of Catholic missionaries as agents of the French colonial administration.[102] However, this outcome may not have been immediately apparent. "Why aren't the White Fathers booted out like the others?" a child asked his teacher in a secular school near Binson. "Because," answered the teacher, "they are useful animals."[103]

The Problem of Internationality

The Uganda crisis and the crisis over anti-clericalism in France were dramatic examples of the uncertainties confronting the Missionaries of Africa in a continent on the threshold of the colonial era. Underlying them both was the fact that the White Fathers were an international society, supported by an international Vatican congregation, *De Propaganda Fide*, whose policy differed markedly from the aims of the colonial powers.[104] A major question confronting Livinhac was how to maintain this international character in the face of competing European nationalisms. Lavigerie had founded an international Society: "I purposely wanted all the nations whose interests confront each other in Africa to be represented in it," he said on one occasion.[105] However, the shape and pace of this internationalization were often dictated by the colonial powers themselves. Although at the Cardinal's death, there were eight nationalities besides the French, among the 234 White Fathers, these were only represented by 55 individuals. The Society was, and continued to be, massively French in nationality.[106] In 1885 Leopold II insisted that missionaries in the Congo Free State should only be Belgians. Lavigerie, who had foreseen this development, opened a house in Belgium in 1884. Three years later he was forced to accept a drastic reduction in the size of the area entrusted to him in the Congo region. Nevertheless, it was a welcome move out of the purely Francophone area.[107] When Livinhac took over, there were twenty-one Belgians and twenty-four Dutchmen in the Society. In 1895, Victor Roelens (1856–1947), a Belgian, became vicar apostolic of Upper Congo because of strong feelings in Belgium against the French.[108] But Belgians were not in a hurry to join a French Society. Roelens soon realized that excluding non-Belgians would doom his vicariate to extinction. The Congo administration, in any case, disliked the French character and French direction of the Society, whether it had Belgian members or not. Roelens urged Livinhac, for the sake of the vicariate and of the internal unity of the Society, to send him non-Belgians.[109] The 1894 Chapter granted this request.[110]

When Livinhac took charge in 1892, there were only five German members of the Society. As effective German administration became established in areas of East Africa where the White Fathers had been working for more than a decade, it was more than ever necessary to recruit German members. A postulancy and apostolic school had been opened at Marienthal in Luxemburg in 1890. In 1894 a seminary was started at Trier in Germany, and in 1903 an apostolic school was built at Haigerloch. These three houses became the nucleus of a German Vice-Province in 1905. There had already been requests in German East Africa for German White Fathers, and for the teaching of German in schools.[111] In 1907, Bernhard Dernburg, the Director of German Colonies, requested that the personnel of the Society in German East Africa become gradually German, and the Provincial of Germany went to Berlin in the following year to discuss the question with Governor von Rechenberg.[112] A German language school was started for young White Fathers at Marienthal in 1905, and there were trips to Trier for courses in German literature, politics and colonization.[113] In spite of these developments, Livinhac was still receiving complaints from the German colonial office in 1911 about the French nationality of White Fathers and their persistent use of the French language.[114] In response, the General Chapter of 1912 decided that German should be taught in the seminaries.[115]

Alsace-Lorraine had been in German hands since 1871, and many White Fathers were natives of the area. This made Franco-German relations in the Society somewhat sensitive. Bishop Jean-Joseph Hirth's birthplace was Strasbourg, and his fluency in German was a reason for his appointment to German territory when the Nyanza Vicariate was divided in 1894. Bishop Henri Léonard (1869–1953) of the Unyanyembe Vicariate came from Metz, and—until the end of World War I—was a German by nationality. Many French White Fathers found it difficult to be "good Germans" in "the new African Germany."[116] However, the German authorities were on the whole appreciative of their efforts, and, at a debate in the Reichstag, the White Fathers were hailed as the "principal agent of civilization in the German colonies."[117] On the eve of the First World War, the German resident in Rwanda even claimed that the Society of Missionaries of Africa had contributed to the "pacification" of the country.[118] With the outbreak of hostilities and the conquest of Germany's African colonies by the Allies, there was no further question of satisfying German colonial sensibilities.

The Uganda crisis of 1892 brought to Livinhac's attention the need for English-speaking missionaries in the British colonies. Sir Gerald Portal remarked in 1893, a propos of his meeting with Hirth and Tucker, "I don't wish ever again to have a three and a half hours' skirmish with two angry bishops, one not understanding English and the other knowing no French."[119] In 1892 there was only one British White Father, Henri Gaudibert (1863–1929), who was the son of a Frenchman but was born in England, and brought up there by his widowed English mother. Gaudibert went to Uganda in 1891 and was frequently an interpreter between the missionaries and the British officers. From 1903 he taught in houses of formation in Europe, and—after an unsuccessful trial of a monastic vocation—was appointed to Canada in 1907, where he edited an English language missionary magazine. He stayed there for the duration of World War I, after which he returned to Algiers. Arthur Prentice (1872–1964), an English priest who joined the Society in 1903, also went to Uganda and was involved in teaching in schools and seminaries. There were some French White Fathers who, like Auguste Achte (1861–1905), taught themselves English, and others who were sent to London to learn the language. However, it was not until 1912, when anti-clerical legislation made it impossible for the Society to open a high school in France, that the Priory, Bishop's Waltham, was acquired in England, and the study of English became more common in the Society. Pierre-Marie Travers (1874–1927), its first director, was a fluent English speaker and had made himself useful in the Nyasa Vicariate before coming to England. By 1914, the White Fathers were even ready to accept vocations from Britain at Bishop's Waltham.[120] After the 1914–1918 War, Britain administered the League of Nations' mandate in former German East

Africa, and a knowledge of English became even more urgent for the Missionaries of Africa. At Heston in 1927, the first steps were taken towards starting a British Province.

If the recruitment of missionaries in Britain was not yet thought a worthwhile project, there was the real prospect of finding vocations in the British dominion of Canada, where many Catholics were fluent in both French and English. The first Canadian White Father was John Forbes (1864–1926), who, as we have seen, accompanied Livinhac on his journey to London in 1894 and acted as his interpreter. A second Canadian joined the Society in 1897, and, under the impulse of Forbes and that of the rector of the Montreal seminary, the idea of a foundation in Canada slowly took root. The General Chapter of 1900 asked Forbes to open a house of recruitment in Canada, and this became a reality in 1901.[121] Livinhac realized the importance of this foundation and crossed the Atlantic in 1910 to visit Canada himself.[122] By the time of Forbes's departure for Uganda in 1914, he had received sixty-six Canadian candidates, more than half of whom persevered to become Missionaries of Africa.[123] Forbes himself went on to become the first of five Canadian bishops in Uganda, and this was the beginning of a long line of distinguished Canadian priests and bishops who served the White Fathers' missions, particularly in British Africa. It is difficult to exaggerate the importance of the Canadian presence in the Society. It was a Canadian, for example, Oscar Morin (1878–1952), who crossed from French Sudan into the British Gold Coast to found the first White Fathers' mission station there in 1906.

The First Caravan to West Africa and the Society's Organization

The General Chapter of 1894 realized Lavigerie's unfulfilled dream of reaching Timbuktu and the French Sudan, by sending the first caravan of White Fathers there, led by Augustin Hacquard (1860–1901). Hacquard consulted the Minister for Colonies, who welcomed him and his missionary caravan as agents of French influence and bearers of the values of French civilization. As long as the mission superiors were French, the government was prepared to give subsidies and even to bear the cost of missionary travel and the forwarding of supplies.[124] In fact, without the help of the French administration and military authorities, it would have been impossible to do missionary work and make long journeys in the French Sudan. Hacquard and his first companions sincerely believed in the compatibility of evangelization with French patriotism, but misunderstandings soon arose, aggravated, as we have seen, by anti-clerical legislation in France.

When Livinhac took over in 1892, the Society of Missionaries of Africa was loosely organized into "provinces," although this term was not precise, and the reality did not correspond to the juridical concept of the *Constitutions* as approved in 1908. Thereafter, they were frequently termed "circumscriptions." The Province of Europe centred on metropolitan France, with houses in Belgium, the Netherlands, Italy, and later on in Switzerland and Britain. It was led by Alfred Louail (1851–1921), who was its superior for thirty years (1888–1918).[125] As we have seen, a German Vice-Province was cut out of it in 1905. The work of the White Fathers was carried out mainly in countries where French was the official language, and their own membership remained massively French. It was not surprising, therefore, that French should have been accepted as the language of the Society. Moreover, in the minds of Frenchmen at the time, France was a global cultural and linguistic entity: *Francophonie*. Théophile Delcassé, who was foreign minister from 1898 to 1905, declared: "Whoever speaks French is not far from thinking and acting like a Frenchman."[126] However, there was no thought of French White Fathers "nationalizing" their non-French confrères, although it was not until 1947 that English was accepted as an official language of the Society.

After Lavigerie's death, Livinhac's first task was to separate the property and works of the Society from those of the dioceses of which Lavigerie had been bishop. This was sometimes a delicate and complex matter. Livinhac was also now on his own in his dealings with the Vatican Congregation *De Propaganda Fide*. As the vicariates apostolic increased, this congregation assumed ever greater importance, and Livinhac's hands were often tied. Usually, the episcopal nominations he made were accepted by Rome without demur, but he did not have it all his own way. In 1913, a request to divide the Vicariate of French Sudan, which was four or five times the size of France, was refused by *Propaganda*, because it only had 2,000 baptized Christians.[127] The congregation criticized both Bishop Hirth in Uganda and Bishop Lechaptois in Tanganyika for accepting agreements with Protestants that infringed their rights to evangelize the whole vicariate. When Bishop Joseph Dupont invited the Montfort Missionaries into his Vicariate of Nyasa, the General Council left it to the new arrivals to explain matters to *Propaganda*. Both Dupont and Livinhac incurred the Vatican's wrath over this affair, and the agreement was annulled by Rome, a situation that endured until the death of the Cardinal Prefect Ledochowski.[128]

After Lavigerie's death, his friend Cardinal Mariano Rampolla del Tindaro (1843–1913) became Cardinal Protector of the Society. Rampolla was a Sicilian who had been Leo XIII's Secretary of State and was briefly Secretary of the Holy Office in the pontificate of St. Pius X. Rampolla's support in Rome was valuable, but this was inevitably a poor substitute for the influence of Lavigerie himself. More important was the friendship of Giacomo Della Chiesa, who was Rampolla's secretary and confidant for twenty years, and who became Pope Benedict XV in 1914. It is interesting to speculate about the White Fathers' influence on the future pope, who produced the first mission encyclical, *Maximum Illud*, in 1919, and who beatified the Uganda Martyrs in 1920.[129]

Livinhac was assiduous in visiting the houses of Europe and he twice went to St. Anne's Jerusalem. He always travelled incognito, calling himself by an alias, such as "Père Auguste." He was present at Marseilles whenever caravans departed for Equatorial Africa, and, after 1910, his journeys were mainly to take part in the consecration of White Father bishops. Livinhac was not able to fulfil his cherished desire to revisit equatorial Africa in person; it was decided in 1904 to choose missionaries to conduct general visitations in the African provinces, and to send their reports to Algiers.[130] These visitations became the occasion for common retreats which were greatly appreciated by the missionaries. Lavigerie had carried out a copious correspondence with his missionaries in the field. Livinhac expanded this custom. Every missionary was required to write to him personally twice a year, and extracts from mission diaries were to be sent to Algiers on a regular basis for editing and publication in the quarterly *Chronique Trimestrielle*. This was effectively replaced by *Rapports Annuels* in 1905. An internal bulletin called *Petit Echo* was started in 1912. These publications encouraged a cross-fertilization of ideas and experiences among missionaries.

During his thirty year tenure of office, Livinhac addressed 134 circular letters to the Society. After his death, a selection of 77 of these circulars were republished, in whole or in part, as his *Instructions*.[131] The letters deal with an array of subjects: General Chapters and their decisions, explanations of the *Constitutions* and *Directory*, appointments, important events, reports from the provinces, crises such as those of Uganda and anti-clericalism, visitations, the correspondence required by the rule, spirituality and the missionary life, the Uganda Martyrs, the first African priests. The letters are a remarkable testimony to Livinhac's devotion to the Society and its work, as well as to the memory of its founder. Livinhac took a particular interest in the houses of formation and their syllabi of studies, and also in the earliest missions of the Society in Kabylia and the Sahara. The General Council minutes testify to his interest in these two areas.

General Chapters

Between 1892 and 1914, four General Chapters were held. At each of them Livinhac was re-elected superior general, in 1912 for life. The 1894 Chapter was the first to be held without the founder. Its importance lay in presenting the superior general and his council with an overview of the whole Society, its houses, its prospects and its temporalities. The 1900 Chapter dealt with the major question of the relationship between the vicars apostolic and the provincial superiors. It was decided that provinces should serve several vicariates, or several countries. They should not be identified with a single vicariate or nationality. Nor should a vicar apostolic be the superior of a province. All of this was to safeguard the independence of the Society without trespassing on the authority of the bishop in pastoral matters. In equatorial Africa, for example, the six (since 1894) vicariates were to be divided among two provinces, with three vicariates in each.[132] The main work of the 1906 Chapter was to prepare the final text of the Society's

Constitutions for definitive approval by Rome, while the 1912 Chapter concentrated on the details of the new *Directory of the Constitutions*. It also tried to anticipate the shape of the White Fathers' relationship to the native clergy who would be ordained before the next Chapter met.

The twenty-two years from 1892 to 1914 were years of upheaval and uncertainty in Africa. There were lingering effects and survivals of the slave trade, accompanied by the violence and intense competition of European colonial powers. Yet it was in these years that the lasting foundations of the Catholic Church were laid by the Missionaries of Africa in more than a dozen African countries. The lengthy tenure of Léon Livinhac as first superior general provided the solidity and guidance that was needed in a fluid situation. Livinhac helped the Society to achieve a juridical standing in the church, and was revered by his missionaries as a living link with, and authentic interpreter of, the founder and his teachings.

CHAPTER TWO

The Missions and the "Colonial Scramble"

The Missionaries of Africa and the Colonial Powers

1892—A High Point in the Scramble for Africa

"What can we missionaries do in the midst of all these alarms of war, but throw ourselves into the arms of God's providence, persuaded that God will turn all to our good?"[1] A White Father diarist wrote these anguished words on the shores of Lake Tanganyika in 1892. It was a year of increasing intensity in the violence that accompanied the "scramble for Africa." The phrase commonly refers to the carving up of the African continent into some thirty colonies and protectorates, that was a by-product of the aggressive competition between the European powers in the nineteenth century. From 1892 to 1914, the period covered by this book, the rivalry escalated, especially at the turn of the century when Germany's *Weltpolitik* began to speed up the tempo of international competition. The scramble gave European nations ten million square miles of new territory, but it helped to poison the political atmosphere of Europe. The rivalry became, in effect, a gradual slide into the First World War.[2]

The year 1892 witnessed several crucial moments in the scramble for Africa. Lugard had captured the Kingdom of Buganda, with immediate repercussions on the White Fathers' missions. French armies were well on the way to acquiring an immense West African empire, after the humiliating defeat they had suffered in Europe at the hands of Germany twenty years earlier. British and Belgian expeditions were staking their claims to the Copper Belt in Central Africa, and the Arab rising against the Belgians was reaching its climax in the eastern Congo. In East Africa the Germans were advancing, and their forces under Tom von Prince captured Tabora. In the newly declared protectorate of Nyasaland (1891), Sir Harry Johnston was pursuing the slave traders operating around Lake Nyasa. During the next twenty-two years, France, Britain, Germany and Belgium would consolidate their positions in the areas being evangelized by the Missionaries of Africa: the Sahara, the lake regions of East and Central

23

Africa, and the Niger basin of West Africa. It would not be a peaceful occupation. These areas of Africa were already a prey to violence and inter-ethnic conflict precipitated by the slave trade, but the colonial incursion roused strong resistance on the part of African rulers, and aggravated their domestic wars. In 1892 an already violent situation was being rendered more violent. Every step of colonial annexation provoked resistance, and the consequences of resistance were devastating. Although colonial rule eventually created a more peaceful environment for missionary expansion, the lengthy initial violence took its toll.

This chapter first describes the attitudes of missionaries and colonial administrators towards one another. Then it offers a brief sketch of the colonial scramble in so far as it affected the areas occupied by the Missionaries of Africa. Afterwards, it deals with missionary travel and deployment, paying special attention to the biographies of the principal missionary personalities. The history of the White Fathers' missions at this time is, as Adrian Hastings has underlined, a history of personalities. What was decisive for lasting missionary achievements was the quality of the missionaries themselves.[3]

The Cross and the Flag

In 1892, the Missionaries of Africa had been present in Kabylia and the northern Sahara for nearly twenty years. In the region of the Great Lakes, they had been present for some fourteen years, but they were still two years away from any presence in West Africa. With the exception of the territories administered by France, it is true to say that the flag followed the cross in the initial process of colonization. However, in the missionary expansion that took place within the colonies after annexation, the cross frequently followed, or accompanied, the flag. What was the attitude of the White Fathers towards the colonial powers? Were they the willing lackeys of colonialism, as depicted by some left-wing historians, in a partnership that was all the more devastating and insidious because of the missionaries' assault on the very soul of traditional Africa? Were they, in short, collaborators in Europe's rape of Africa?

The question is a loaded one and perhaps historically naïve, but the answer is far from simple. To begin with, the aims of the colonial powers were basically political and commercial, while the object of the missionary enterprise was "to establish Christianity in the African continent."[4] Although European governments were pledged to uphold religious freedom, in practice their attitude to the different denominations was often far from impartial. They certainly held no brief for Christian evangelization as such. The Missionaries of Africa, on the other hand, had little or no influence on the scramble itself, but simply found themselves in one or another colony as a matter of accomplished fact. Neither France in 1879, nor Germany in

1890, was able to take advantage of the political opportunity created by the presence of French Catholic missionaries in Uganda. The acceptance of Portuguese protection for a White Father foundation in Nyasaland in 1890 also turned out to be premature. Public opinion in Britain, however, could not allow the abandonment of its missionaries to the whims and vagaries of foreign overlords, and this made it easier for Britain to use the presence of British Protestants in Nyasaland and Uganda as a pretext for annexation. The White Fathers never provided such a pretext. There were virtually no British Missionaries of Africa to send to the British colonies, and the loyalty of those belonging to other nationalities tended to be suspect. In many cases also, anti-Catholic prejudice aggravated this suspicion, which only began dissipate during the First World War. In German East Africa, there were few German White Fathers, and the colonial administration found the French (who were the majority) even less congenial after the signing of the Franco-British *entente cordiale* in 1904. German criticism of their French nationality and language became increasingly strident.[5] In any case, the White Fathers felt that the administration favoured Protestantism and the 1914–1918 war confirmed the Lutheran Church as the bedrock of the German state.[6] In Belgium, especially among Flemish speakers, there was considerable hostility to the French, but the Vicariate Apostolic of Upper Congo managed to retain a number of non-Belgian missionaries, most of them from France.

It was only in Algeria and French Sudan that the preponderance of French White Fathers was welcome to the authorities, and indeed—on occasion—demanded. Yet even here, there were tensions when official policy was at variance with missionary goals. This was especially the case with regard to Islam. There was also the hostility, bred by anti-clerical legislation, among many—though not all—French colonial officials. This hostility was largely overcome by the *union sacrée*, the strengthening of domestic unity in France when confronted by the German enemy in 1914.[7]

The 1876 Brussels Conference

The ambivalent attitude of the Missionaries of Africa towards the scramble for Africa goes back to the international Geographical Conference of Brussels, convened in 1876 by King Leopold II. This conference was attended by thirteen Belgians and twenty-four foreign guests, among whom were a number of famous explorers.[8] Ostensibly, the conference aimed to exploit the recent discoveries in Africa for commercial and philanthropic purposes. Although Leopold gave no public indication at the time that the African International Association, created by the conference, was a cloak for his own imperialist intentions, Cardinal Lavigerie greeted the conference and its outcome with alarm.[9] Catholic objectives were absent from its conclusions, and, although there had been a noteworthy Protestant participation, the conference had virtually ignored the prospect of Christian evangelization. Lavigerie deplored its secular and commercial emphasis, while appreciating that Catholic missionaries might be able to make use of the organization and means of communication established by the Association. Lavigerie proposed a rapid deployment of missionaries to the African interior and offered his own Society for the purpose. This offer was accepted by Rome and led to the first caravan of White Fathers to equatorial Africa in 1878.

Missionary Attitudes

The first directory of the White Fathers' Constitutions, published in 1914, laid down the attitude that missionaries should adopt towards the colonial administration. It noted that "national honour" was a priority for colonial officials and that they were preoccupied with fear of the natives. Europeans, it went on, tended to believe that "missionaries encourage the natives to be disloyal." Missionaries were to advise natives but not intervene in their dealings with the European power. Discretion was recommended whenever accusations had to be brought against the colonial authorities.[10] The passage reflects the delicate position in which missionaries frequently found themselves.

The White Fathers had much to criticize in the policies and conduct of the colonial administrations. Although they accepted the assumption of the superiority of European culture and technology, ascribing this to Europe's Christian roots, and believed that contact with whites should be edifying for Africans, they nevertheless deplored the bad example given in practice by Europeans. In many cases, the immorality of European officials was a byword. In French Sudan, the missionaries were horrified to find that officers had harems of child concubines, and in Northern Rhodesia, that British officials travelled with African "wives."[11] Even Victor Roelens (1856–1947), Vicar Apostolic of Upper Congo, whose understanding of African psychology was almost entirely based on the assumed superiority of European culture, found the actual influence of Belgian officers dangerous.[12] The White Fathers also deplored the double standards which allowed European administrations to condemn and even abolish slavery in theory, while tolerating it in practice, or even conniving with the slave trade themselves.[13] They opposed the upholding of polygamy and child pawnship, which encouraged slavery, and condemned the general colonial tendency to resist cultural development in any form.[14] Colonialism had a vested interest in appearing to maintain the *status quo*. Missionaries everywhere sought the liberation of women, although with hindsight it must also be admitted that a considerable measure of discrimination was present in the church itself.[15]

In every country the colonial powers introduced taxation and forced labour. The White Fathers tried to reduce the burden these placed on the people by persuading the authorities to commute them. Forced labour took people away from catechism, and children from school.[16] The missionaries refused to become tax collectors for the administration and deplored the fact that the imposition of tax caused the dispersion of Christians from the vicinity of the mission stations. "We have not come here to facilitate tax-gathering," wrote a White Father at Ushirombo, German East Africa, "but to win souls."[17] "We do not want people to fall back into idolatry," wrote another missionary, "for the sake of three miserable rupees per hut per year."[18] If they were to attract people to the catechumenate and school, missionaries had to distance themselves from the tax business.[19] They were even successful in obtaining a respite from the rubber quotas imposed by the Congo regime, which in other parts of the country gave rise to the atrocities that were internationally condemned.[20]

The considered opinion of missionaries concerning colonialism was often more negative than positive. After the visit of a British district officer to Kayambi mission (in modern Zambia), a Missionary of Africa wrote that the first concern of the colonialists was to fill their pockets and that they were not loved by the people.[21] Colonial officials usually had short tours of duty that made it impossible for them to learn a local language, or familiarize themselves deeply with local custom, while missionaries, who spent virtually their whole lives in the field, were esteemed for their linguistic work and lived relatively close to the people.

White Father priests were obliged to wear their *gandourah* (cassock) and rosary at all times.[22] This certainly made them visibly distinct from colonial officials. However, in the minds of local people, they sometimes appeared to be one and the same, especially if they came into an area already occupied by the administration. When the Missionaries of Africa entered Rwanda in 1899, for example, they were assumed to be emissaries of the German colonial power.[23] In French Sudan there was a similar ambiguity between missionary and colonialist. They were of the same race and collaborated in the same work. The only difference was that the White Fathers were poorer and learned local languages.[24] When the missionaries went to Kupela in 1905, to make the first foundation among the Mossi (in modern Burkina Faso), they had a military escort and the people thought the missionaries were soldiers.[25]

In fact, there was something of a symbiotic relationship between the military and the missionary. All the colonial regimes went through a military phase, the army eventually handing power over to a civilian administration. The White Fathers had better relations with the army than with civilians.[26] Not only was the missionary ideal frequently couched in military metaphors of conquest, discipline and *esprit de corps*, but many missionaries themselves had had military experience. This was true of Théophile Dromaux (1849–1909) and Bishop Joseph Dupont (1850–1930), who had both fought in the Franco-Prussian War before joining the Society. It was also true of Bishop Prosper-Augustin Hacquard (1860–1901), who had been superior of the ill-fated Armed Brothers of the Sahara, and who was hailed by Governor-General Chaudie of French Sudan as emanating "from the phalanx of soldier-priests originating in the genius of Mgr. Lavigerie."[27] Many French White Fathers had been obliged to do military service and to register as reservists during their theology studies in North Africa. The general feeling was that they were happy to have "tasted" the military profession and to have successfully braved its dangers to body and soul. The superiors were very much alive to the moral dangers of military service. Not only were prayers and novenas offered on behalf of the soldier-students, but the General Council asked that they do their service in Tunisia and not undergo the depravity of barrack life in France.[28] However, where relations with the military were concerned, the effect of combining theological studies with military training should not be underestimated. As chaplains to military camps and barracks, the White Fathers were popular. In retirement, Bishop Dupont was quoted as saying: "Missionaries and the military understand one another, because they have the same heart. Sword and holy water sprinkler go together."[29]

The White Fathers believed in the humanitarian ideals of colonization, not to seek gold, but justice. However, when there were abuses, avoiding intervention between the colonizer and the colonized, as the Directory advised, was easier said than done. It was especially in German East Africa that people found it difficult to go directly to the administration for redress. Missionaries like Bishop François Gerboin (1847–1912), however, saw human development as the principal benefit of colonialism. It was a missionary task, he wrote, "to help Africans get out of the rut they are in and to teach them submission to the authority of the whites, without murmuring too much."[30] When Frédéric Salelles (1874–1956) visited the government station at Kasama (modern Zambia) in 1908, he was favourably impressed with its lawns and flower beds, its trees and pathways, its office, kitchen, prison, carpentry shop and workers' houses. "All breathes cleanliness and good order" was his verdict.[31] It was an example to be followed.

Following the instructions of Lavigerie and imitating the precedent of Buganda, the White Fathers, with varying measures of success, encouraged their neophytes to take upon themselves the work of evangelization. However, the promotion and empowerment of newly converted Christians to be catechists and auxiliaries did not always meet with the approval of colonial officials and chiefs, who tended to think it subversive.[32] The Missionaries of Africa attempted to transform whole societies by influencing their socio-political structures. They wanted to create a stable and relatively prosperous peasant society, comparable to the deeply Christian rural areas of France, Flanders or Alsace from which they themselves came. But the forces of change were not under missionary control, and the paternalism of such an ideal became apparent, in so far as it failed to reflect the scale and direction of socio-economic change in the colonial state.

Colonial Attitudes

What did the colonial authorities think about the Missionaries of Africa? A frequent justification for the colonial presence in Africa was to invoke its civilizing role, but in the period we are considering—1892–1914—it is abundantly clear that this role was exercised to a greater extent by missionaries than by colonial officers. The White Fathers maintained hundreds of mission and village schools, and at the behest of the government, opened *élite* schools to train the growing bureaucracy. Literacy was in the hands of the missionaries. In the Congo they were even asked to open military academies, though nothing came of it.[33] Secular government schools could not hope to compete with mission establishments, which often supplied them with pupils. Missionary brothers trained scores of builders, brick makers, carpenters and farmers. With varying degrees of success, colonial governments put pressure on the missionaries to grow the cash crops that were part of their development plans: coffee, cotton and rubber. They sought the help of missionary hospitals and dispensaries in combating epidemics, like sleeping-sickness, and in promoting their public health programmes.

Visiting officers never ceased to marvel at the mission stations and their achievements, and such visits were numerous. Distinguished visitors were brought to see them: Joseph Chamberlain, British Secretary of State for Colonies in 1902; Bernhard Dernburg, German Minister for Colonies in 1907; Winston Churchill, British Under-Secretary for Colonies in the following year.[34] Bishop Henri Streicher (1863–1952) was pleasantly surprised to receive a "thank-you" note from Churchill, ending "with every good wish for the continued success of your admirable work."[35] When Hesketh Bell was sent to govern the Uganda Protectorate in 1905, he received dire warnings from his colleagues in the colonial service about the refractoriness of Catholic missionaries. To his surprise he found them wholly admirable in their devotion to the people's welfare and in their co-operation with the administration. "No praise," he concluded, "is too high for the White Fathers."[36] An article he contributed to *The Times* of London contained a fulsome eulogy of the Society, which was reprinted in newspapers around the world.[37]

It was customary for colonial authorities to take a paternalistic view of the peoples in their charge, and missionaries tended to concur with this view. The Muslims of Algeria, said one, are "subjects in tutelage, children adopted by France."[38] The Malinke and Bambara (of modern Mali) were, according to Bishop Hacquard, "a band of big children, naïve, credulous, headstrong sometimes, but always reasonable."[39] However, the White Fathers at

Chilonga, Northern Rodesia (Zambia) were surprised when a colonial administrator went so far as to take a spiritual view of this tutelage. Collector Melland wrote to them: "The union of the two powers, spiritual and temporal is necessary for the civilization of the blacks and the good order of things . . . The work you do and the work I pursue here, are they not the same? Is it not all for God? He has entrusted the administration of this country to Britain, but, if we govern, we do so as tutors only."[40] The White Fathers, however, were not prepared to surrender the moral high ground so easily to the colonial power.

The "Scramble for Africa"

Algeria, Sahara and French Sudan

The French occupied Algiers in 1830 and their struggle to command a shallow inland corridor took thirty years. The Amir Abd-al-Qadir, the most powerful leader of the resistance, surrendered in 1844 and was exiled to Damascus. Resistance by the mountain-dwelling Kabyles was quelled in 1857 and 1871, after which French settlers came in greater numbers. Ten years later, an unimportant border dispute was used as a pretext for annexing Tunisia.

The French hoped to cross the Sahara and link Algeria to the colonies being established in the French Sudan. The area was geographically complex and peopled by a number of ethnic groups both sedentary and nomadic, all professing a form of Islam. Laghouat was occupied by the French in 1852. To the south lay the seven towns of the Mzab, where there was short-lived resistance in 1872.[41] In the southwest were the oases of the Tuat and the Moroccan border, while to the far south lay the mountains of Hoggar, the homelands of the warlike Tuareg and Ahaggar.[42]

It was only in 1894 that French armies from the south occupied Timbuktu. Expeditions to reach it by crossing the Sahara had all been wiped out by Tuareg.[43] Only the heavily armed expedition of Ferdinand Foureau and François Lamy got through to Lake Chad in 1899.[44] But it was not until the advent of Colonel Henri Laperrine (1860–1920) in 1901 that any lasting impact could be made. Laperrine had been appointed "Commander of the Oases," with orders to occupy the newly captured Tuat in the western desert and to create a force for controlling the southern Sahara. In 1904 he made an exploratory journey to the Hoggar, accompanied by the saintly hermit, Charles de Foucauld.[45] Laperrine reached the Sudan border in 1904, crossed it in 1906 and again in 1909.

From Algeria and the northern desert, the Missionaries of Africa were unable to penetrate the southern Sahara, as long as French armies failed to control the area. By the time this was achieved in the early twentieth century, the White Fathers were already in Timbuktu, and crossing the Sahara no longer held any practical interest for them.

Louis Faidherbe (1818–1889), who had fought in the Algerian campaign against Abd-al-Qadir, was responsible for the French advance to the upper Senegal and upper Niger Rivers in the 1850s and 1860s.[46] The chief obstacle to his progress was the empire of the Tukolors, set up by the Muslim revolutionary leader Al-Haj-Umar in the country of the Bambara. After Umar's death, his son Ahmadu and Samory-Toure, leader of the Malinke, were defeated by Louis Archinard in the 1890s. Eugène Bonnier occupied Timbuktu in early January 1894, but was killed shortly afterwards in a raid on a Tuareg encampment. Other French columns occupied Wagadugu in 1896, placing the Mossi and Gurunsi people under French protection. By the end of 1897, the whole of the Niger basin was in French hands, and the fugitive Samory was captured in the following year.[47] Spasmodic resistance continued in the Mossi Kingdom, and there were revolts or threats of revolt there, as well as at Segu and Kayes, in 1904–1909.[48]

The Missionaries of Africa entered French Sudan before the conquest was complete, and they were dependent on the French military authorities for the security of their movements and of their mission stations.

The Congo Free State

At the Berlin conference of 1884, Germany, with British and American backing, gave formal recognition to the creation of the Congo Free State. Leopold II hired the explorer, Henry Morton Stanley, who agreed to combine his Emin Pasha Relief Expedition of 1887–1888 with the foundation of posts along the Congo River. In the east, power lay in the hands of Hamed ben Mohammed el Murjebi, the notorious Afro-Arab slave trader from Zanzibar, known as Tippu Tip. Stanley was empowered to commission Tippu Tip to be governor of this region, a recognition of his *de facto* hegemony over the area.[49] The Brussels Anti-Slavery Conference in 1889–1890, one of the outcomes of Cardinal Lavigerie's anti-slavery crusade, gave Leopold the opportunity to sponsor expeditions against the Arabs, who revolted after Tippu Tip's final departure for Zanzibar in 1890. At the same time, a succession of expeditions won the race with the British South Africa Company (BSAC) for the Copper Belt and raised the Congolese flag in Katanga.

The Arab war in the east had been triggered by competition for ivory. It was a bloody affair, rendered more horrific by the cannibalistic practices of the armies on both sides. By 1893 the rebel headquarters of Nyangwe had been taken by Baron Francis Dhanis; while Ngongo Lutete, chief of the Tetela and former *protégé* of Tippu Tip, had been treacherously killed. This left Mohammed ben Kalfan, known as Rumaliza, in control of the northern end of Lake Tanganyika. Until German authority was permanently established on the eastern lakeshore, Rumaliza rampaged around the lake, conducting slave raids and holding the local population in terrified subjection. The Missionaries of Africa, who had been in the area since 1879, were caught up in the conflict. Captain Leopold Joubert (1842–1927), an armed auxiliary, had taken up the task of defending the mission stations and their dependent settlements in 1887. Until the arrival of the anti-slavery expeditions, he was left on his own, with the small army he had trained, to fight Rumaliza and his lieutenants. Captain Jules Jacques arrived at the end of 1891, and a second expedition, under Descamps, arrived in 1893. The slavers were defeated, and Rumaliza retreated northwards, finally escaping in 1894 to make his way back to Zanzibar.[50] In 1896 a mutiny of the Tetela and the Congolese *Force Publique*, involving literally thousands of soldiers, brought endless conflicts to the Upper Congo region. Joubert collected his forces once again to keep the mutineers at bay.[51] Defeated in several pitched battles, the mutineers began surrendering in small groups or crossing Lake Tanganyika to give themselves up to the Germans. However, they were still a force to be reckoned with to the south of Lake Tanganyika and in Katanga as late as 1907.[52]

In 1892 the Congo Free State became a state monopoly, with the land divided up between Leopold's private domain and that of concessionary companies in which the king had a controlling interest. The worldwide rubber boom placed a premium on the collection of wild rubber, and Africans in the Congo were forbidden to harvest it for themselves. Instead, in what came to be known as the "Rubber Terror," quotas or *prestations* of this valuable commodity were extorted under threat of torture, mutilation and death.[53] Although it purported to continue the anti-slavery campaign, Leopold's administration in the Congo simply magnified the methods of the slavers themselves. Villages were burned, hostages were starved and mutilated, and terrified refugees were witnesses to the atrocities. An authoritative estimate, based on local sources, is that between 1880 and 1920, the population of the Congo basin was cut by half.[54]

Edmond Morel, a businessman turned journalist, began a press campaign against the Congo atrocities in 1900, supported—after some hesitation—by British and American Protestant missionaries. In 1903 the British Government commissioned its consul in the Free State, the Irish patriot Roger Casement, to conduct an investigation. His findings led to the formation of Morel's Congo Reform Association in 1903, and two years later Leopold was obliged to set up the Janssens Commission which only confirmed Casement's conclusions. Under pressure from opinion at home and abroad, Leopold was forced to hand over the administration of the Congo to Belgium in 1908, though not without a handsome compensation. He died in the following year. The Belgian government implemented reforms, and the atrocities against rubber workers diminished. The Missionaries of Africa were not directly affected by the Rubber Terror, but lived in relative isolation from the Congolese administration which was slow to impose its rule on the area.

German East Africa

In 1885, after the close of the Berlin conference, Bismarck issued a charter to Carl Peters' German East Africa Company.[55] The sultan of Zanzibar, supported by Britain, exercised a shadowy dominion over the Arab potentates who organized the ivory and slave trade along the mainland trade routes and in the country surrounding the Great Lakes. However, the British needed German friendship in their rivalry with France, and they agreed to let Bismarck have a free hand in East Africa, as long as he had no designs on Zanzibar itself. The imposition of German rule led immediately to violent resistance on the part of African and Afro-Arab leaders at the coast, notably Bwana Heri and Abushiri. A small but formidable army of Sudanese, led by German officers, crushed the risings.

Hermann von Wissmann then set out to secure the caravan routes to the interior. The Chagga of Kilimanjaro were subdued in 1891. Emin Pasha, the eccentric Austrian doctor, blazed a trail to Tabora and Lake Victoria, founding stations at Mwanza and Bukoba. However, Isike, Chief of Unyanyembe, remained defiant at Tabora, and Lieutenant Tom von Prince, known to African posterity as *Sakalani*, the Germans' best fighting soldier, was sent to resolve the situation in 1892. Meanwhile, in 1891, a German column under Emil von Zelewski was annihilated by the Hehe resistance leader, Mkwawa, on the road to Iringa. The war against the Hehe occupied the Germans until Mkwawa's suicide in 1898. In 1897–1899 the Germans explored and occupied the kingdoms of Rwanda and Burundi.

The small kingdoms and chiefdoms of the ethnically fragmented peoples of the interior were easy to defeat, but difficult to rule. Like African war lords of the past, the Germans used bands of gunmen to maintain authority over compliant local leaders, and German conquest was often nothing more than an extension of tribal warfare itself. Force and compulsion were everywhere the order of the day. According to one historian, between 1901 and 1913 the government sentenced 64,652 Africans to corporal punishment, an average of five victims a week at every district office in the country.[56] Rebellions were endless, the most serious being the Maji-Maji rebellion of 1905–1907. This was an explosion of African hatred towards European rule which spread to more than half the ethnic groups in the country. Many people hoped the rebels would succeed in driving out the whites.[57] The German revenge was overwhelming. Villages were burned, populations driven out, farmland devastated. So ruthless was this scorched earth policy that whole areas of the southeast became uninhabited and marginalized, a situation that persisted after World War I and even after political independence in 1961. Apart from this major rebellion, local chiefs were continually rebelling. Between 1898 and 1909 the White Fathers recorded revolts in all of the areas in which they worked.[58]

The European invasion incorporated East Africa into the disease environment of the world.[59] Devastation and depopulation exposed whole populations to human and animal epidemics. In fact, the period from 1892 to 1914 witnessed an ecological catastrophe of enormous proportions. This catastrophe primarily affected German East Africa, but it also involved all the regions bordering the Great Lakes, including Congo, Uganda and Northern Rhodesia (Zambia). The most serious epidemic was that of sleeping sickness. Tsetse flies, the carriers of the disease, were endemic to the bush country and its wildlife, but the illness was dormant among humans until an infected traveller reached the area. Governor Hesketh Bell of Uganda believed it had been brought by Stanley's expedition from the Congo in 1889.[60] Certainly the devastation that followed the German incursion and the suppression of the Maji-Maji rebellion caused an increase in tsetse infested bush land. The epidemic reached enormous proportions and people died at the rate of some fifty thousand a year. In some places, up to ninety percent of the population died. After Mass one Sunday at Mwanza (Nyanza South) in 1908, some people questioned a missionary about the origin of all these epidemics. The missionary dismissed the idea that they had been brought by Europeans. However, the African questioner was nearer the truth.[61]

Like other colonial powers in what was then the railway age, the Germans embarked on railway construction, with lines to Kilimanjaro and Lake Tanganyika. The first locomotive reached Tabora in February 1912, but the line soon became a key target during the East African campaign of the 1914–1918 War.[62]

Although the Missionaries of Africa worked outside the areas involved in the Maji-Maji rebellion, they were affected in one way or another by the violence and unrest. They were also intimately concerned with the care and treatment of sleeping sickness victims.

Uganda, Nyasaland and Northern Rhodesia

On Livinhac's recommendation, following the upheavals attending the British annexation of Uganda, the Vicariate Apostolic of Nyanza was divided in July 1894. The eastern portion, stretching into British East Africa (Kenya), was entrusted to the Mill Hill Missionaries and became the Vicariate Apostolic of Upper Nile. The northern portion, stretching from Lake Albert to the Bahr-al-Ghazal, was joined to the old vicariate of the Comboni Missionaries in Anglo-Egyptian Sudan, archaically named "Vicariate Apostolic of Central Africa." The remainder was divided in two. North of Lake Victoria, the Vicariate Apostolic of Northern Nyanza (later called the Vicariate Apostolic of Uganda) comprised most of the Buganda kingdom, the kingdoms of Toro, Bunyoro and Ankole, together with the district of Kigezi and a considerable area of Congo beyond Lake Albert.

South of Lake Victoria, in German East Africa, the Vicariate Apostolic of Southern Nyanza comprised Mwanza, Bukoba and most of Rwanda.

In 1890, Captain Lugard installed Kasagama as king of Toro, to be a wedge against the more bellicose kingdom of Bunyoro. Between 1893 and 1895, the British led two expeditions against Chwa II Kabarega, king of Bunyoro, and, after his defeat and flight, placed his son Kitahimbwa I on the throne.[63] Both Kitahimbwa and Kasagama became Protestants, and used their conversion to consolidate their political position. Meanwhile, in the capital of Buganda, the White Fathers were still unrealistically hoping that Mwanga might return to his Catholic allegiance. The diarist of Rubaga pathetically described Mwanga's embarrassment and shame in 1896, as he read him a translation of passages from Canon Nicq's biography of Siméon Lourdel (1853–1890), describing the king's cruelties and vices.[64]

Then, after flirting with the Germans and attempting to smuggle ivory, Mwanga raised the standard of revolt against the British in 1897. This was the most serious challenge to the British in Uganda. Mwanga looked for support from the Catholic stronghold of Buddu and some chiefs joined him, notably the alcoholic Gabriel Kintu Mujasi. In 1898 Mwanga joined forces with the exiled Kabarega. At the same time, a mutiny took place in Busoga among the Nubian soldiers of the British army, the remnant of Emin Pasha's Sudanese force, a brutal and undisciplined horde that was responsible for much of the damage and destruction perpetrated on Catholics in the 1892 civil war.[65] Together with Mwanga, Kabarega and Mujasi, they now posed a formidable threat to the Uganda protectorate. At this moment, Mwanga's son, Daudi Chwa (1897–1939), was born in the house of the Protestant regent Apolo Kaggwa, and was proclaimed *Kabaka* (king) in his father's place by the British.

Buddu province became a battlefield, with rebels and pro-government forces pillaging missions and enslaving women. Mwanga at first took refuge with the Germans who held him prisoner at Mwanza. However, he escaped back to Uganda and, together with Kabarega, was captured at Bukedi on April 9th 1899. A Missionary of Africa described the scene, as the ex-king was led captive in pouring rain to a waiting boat on Lake Victoria. "What sad thoughts," he wrote, "must have gone through that evil head!"[66] Both Mwanga and Kabarega were exiled to the Seychelles where the former died in 1903, and the latter in 1923, on his way to repatriation in Bunyoro. Mujasi continued a desultory rebellion until 1901, when he was captured by the Germans and taken to Dar es Salaam with a band of followers. Thereafter, the Germans allowed him to settle with his companions in Burundi.

The Uganda Agreement of 1900 ensured that the Buganda monarchy would be Protestant, with two Protestant regents and one Catholic. Of the twenty senior chiefs, ten were to be Protestant, eight Catholic and two Muslim. Although in the following years, there were many disputes over appointments and especially over the right of Catholic children, adopted or inherited by Protestants, to keep their faith, the fact that Catholics were in the overwhelming majority ensured that freedom of religion was practised. On attaining his majority in 1914, Daudi Chwa was crowned by an Anglican bishop, but the Church of England establishment was not ulti-mately "for export."

The Uganda Railway, dubbed "the lunatic line" by sceptics in Britain, reached Kisumu on Lake Victoria in 1901, and Entebbe, laid out by Sir Harry Johnston, became the new capital of the protectorate. The defeat of the rebels enabled the British administration to occupy the remainder of the protectorate more peacefully. Buganda had always claimed suzerainty over its neighbours, and the British used Ganda imperialism, as well as Protestant Christianity, to extend their administration. The chiefs from Buganda were far from popular and revolts took place against them, as happened in Ankole in 1908. Sir Hesketh Bell, governor of Uganda from 1905 to 1909, was confronted by the sleeping sickness epidemic, and his drastic decision to clear the tsetse infested shores of Lake Victoria helped bring the illness under control. Bell, as we have seen, became an admirer of the White Fathers and a personal friend of Bishop Henri Streicher. On leaving Uganda in 1909 to become governor of Northern Nigeria, he visited Rome, where the White Fathers arranged an audience for him with Pope St. Pius X.[67]

In Central Africa, Cecil Rhodes' British South Africa Company (BSAC) had been given an imprecise area to explore north of the Zambezi.[68] The company was aware of the presence of minerals in the Katanga area, but its immediate aims in the north of the territory, which came to be known as Northern Rhodesia (Zambia), were at first unclear. In 1889, Sir Harry Johnston had been appointed British Consul in Mozambique for the pur-pose of strengthening British influence in the disputed area of the Shire Valley and along the western shores of Lake Nyasa. Although Portugal laid claim to the region, it was unable to put down the slave trade that operated there, or to safeguard the Scottish Presbyterians and the Anglicans of the Universities Mission to Central Africa that had founded missions in the region. Rhodes helped finance Johnston's treaty-making, and, after the Anglo-Portuguese Agreement of 1891, the British Protectorate of Central Africa (Nyasaland, later Malawi) was proclaimed. Johnston, from his base at Zomba, took responsibility for the country west of the Lwangwa valley on behalf of the BSAC, and continued the war with the Yao slavers along the lake, capturing their forts at Karonga and executing their leader, Mlozi, in 1895. In that same year he handed the administration of Northern Rhodesia back to the BSAC.

The BSAC, however, was slow to exert any authority there, and in the early 1890s the north was a prey to slavery and brigandage in which the Bemba played a major part. In 1893, Von Wissmann, from the German side of the frontier, defeated the Bemba chief, Sampa, and the BSAC founded a post (called Abercorn) at Mbala, south of Lake Tanganyika, supplying arms and ammunition to protect the people from Bemba depredations. The BSAC had its hands full to the south of the Zambezi River (Southern Rhodesia), and its agents eight hundred miles away on the borders of Bembaland had no power to impose their authority. It was this situation which allowed the Missionaries of Africa to pre-empt the presence of the BSAC among the Bemba and to forestall punitive expeditions against them. The company gradually imposed its rule during the first decade of the twentieth century and Britain took over the administration of Northern Rhodesia in 1911.

The foregoing historical sketch of the countries which were being, or were about to be, evangelized by the Missionaries of Africa in 1892–1914, shows the extent of the upheaval caused by the colonial scramble. These countries of north, east, central and west Africa were a prey to continuing violence and unrest. The people to whom the White Fathers came as missionaries were subjects of sweeping and unwelcome change, as well as victims of evils, both imported and endemic to the continent itself. It has been truly said that "Africans have been and are the frontiersmen who have colonised an especially hostile region of the world on behalf of the entire human race."[69] Africans have always had to co-exist with nature, a hostile environment that included poor soils, fickle rainfall, insect pests and the prevalence of disease. Worse than this, their first extensive involvement with the outside world was through the brutalities of the slave trade and the colonial scramble.

In the early days, Missionaries of Africa frequently passed harsh judgements on the "laziness," "instability" and "inconstancy" of the African.[70] However, they failed to take account of such inescapable social facts as the need for shifting cultivation and population mobility, for conserving strength in a tropical climate and for husbanding scant human resources.

African populations were culturally and politically fragmented. As such, they lent themselves to colonial manipulation. Most of the people evangelized by the White Fathers were organized into multi-chiefdom societies, but there were also centralized kingdoms like those of the Great Lakes and military empires, such as those of Samory or the Arab slavers. Whether or not they were recent constructs, kingdoms and empires were often aggrandizing, and represented an obvious threat to colonial domination. As a result of policy or practical necessity, colonial powers exercised a form of indirect rule, which they were ready to modify as circumstances demanded.[71]

Deployment and Modes of Travel of the Missionaries of Africa 1892–1914

In 1892, at the start of the period covered by this book, the Missionaries of Africa were responsible for seven ecclesiastical circumscriptions or vicariates: Northern and Southern Nyanza, Unyanyembe, Tanganyika, Upper

Congo, Nyasa and Sahara-Sudan. As a result of subsequent divisions, there were nine in 1914. The remainder of this chapter is concerned with the missionaries' modes of travel to these territories, and the biographies of their leaders. The story of missionary deployment is, in fact, best told through the lives of these remarkable people.

Until the Uganda Railway was completed in 1901, and even for a short time afterwards, due to the Nandi war which endangered the railway, the only way to reach the missions of the White Fathers in equatorial Africa was on foot from Bagamoyo at the coast.[72] Caravans departed by boat from Marseilles, where the Society maintained a supply procure, to Zanzibar where another procure had been established in 1882. After a short crossing to the mainland, the journey of 530 miles to Tabora was made on foot, sometimes partly by donkey or, when sick, in a hammock or litter. The first caravan of 1878 took three months, one week and five days to reach Tabora. The onward journey took two months to Lake Tanganyika and six weeks to Lake Victoria. The journey was made longer by frequent stops to negotiate the *hongo* or toll fee, charged by chiefs through whose territory the caravan passed, by the sickness of missionaries and by skirmishes with thieves or bandits. By the turn of the century, the journey was shortened to around two months, as missionaries became more experienced and harassment by local chiefs and bandits was reduced.

The first caravan hired some three hundred porters and, with the armed escort and bearers, numbered a total of four hundred and fifty individuals. The ill-fated second caravan of 1879, which lost eight out of a total of seventeen Europeans, hired six hundred porters. Later caravans were able to reduce the number to a hundred and fifty or less, but it was uneconomic to send many small caravans, rather than fewer large ones. The loads were sometimes carried as two bags tied to one piece of wood, or as a double load carried by two men. The articles taken with them included biscuits, tinned food, rice, salt, tea, coffee, sugar, cocoa, condensed milk, matches, flour, jam, curry powder, wine for Mass, live chickens and goats, cloth and beads for barter and for the porters' wages. Various medicines were recommended, among them the favourite "Cockles' Pills" for bilious attacks.[73]

The missionaries slept in tents along the way, rising at 4:30 a.m. After prayers, packing, feeding the donkeys and a substantial breakfast, the caravan set off at 5:45 a.m. A rest could be taken after three or four hours of marching, and camp was made after a maximum of six hours' march. A small meal was taken on arrival and a cooked dinner at 5:30 p.m. Missionaries were supposed to dress well for the journey, wear headgear and wrap themselves in a long flannel cummerbund. The theft and pilfering of loads was a constant nuisance. For example, Brother Justin Guitard (1855–1908) found in 1907 that the contents of his boxes had been removed and replaced with firewood and stones.[74] In 1894 the White Fathers lost the goods of an entire caravan.[75] The lake voyage from

Bukumbi to Kampala, by canoe or sailboat, took about two weeks, but storms could make the journey longer and even hazardous. During a memorable lake voyage in 1891, Bishop Jean-Joseph Hirth (1854–1931), Auguste Achte (1861–1905) and Jean Marcou (1867–1940) were forced to lighten their vessel in a storm by throwing overboard the new harmonium they were carrying to Rubaga.[76]

When a bishop was leading the caravan, elaborate arrangements were made for his reception upon reaching the destination. For example, when Bishop Adolphe Lechaptois (1852–1917) returned to Karema in 1902, a tent was set up a kilometre from the mission, so that he could wash, put on his episcopal robes and move in procession to the church.[77] Similar arrangements were made in 1907 for Bishop Victor Roelens (1858–1947), who went directly to Baudouinville cathedral for a solemn *Te Deum*, while a choir sang *Ecce Sacerdos Magnus*.[78] Roelens arrived on another occasion, riding a donkey, "which reminded us," remarked an irreverent missionary observer, "of the triumphal entry of Our Lord into Jerusalem."[79] The idea of a reception tent, however, was not always a success. When Bishop François Gerboin (1847–1912) arrived at Misugi, Burundi, in 1898, Antoon van der Wee (1871–1943) went out to meet him and found him struggling through a swamp. "This was scarcely the moment to throw myself at his feet and ask his blessing," wrote the missionary afterwards. They proceeded to the reception tent for the clean-up required for a dignified episcopal entry, but the porters carrying the bishop's robes were several hours behind, and Gerboin had to continue to the mission in his swamp-stained attire.[80] When he entered Tabora to open the first mission station there in 1900, Gerboin was welcomed by a military band and an immense crowd of well-wishers.[81] He himself enjoyed going out to meet approaching caravans, and in 1903 left Msalala to meet his fellow-bishop Lechaptois in the forest.[82]

François Gerboin, bishop of the immense Unyanyembe vicariate, was himself one of the great missionary travellers of the period and a popular travelling companion. After spiritual exercises, morning prayer and Mass, he would have his cup of coffee, and then take an active part in striking camp, folding the tents very carefully. Once the caravan had moved off, he would make his meditation *en route* and recite the Angelus. After this, he would break into hymns in honour of the Blessed Sacrament, the Sacred Heart and Our Lady. Finally, he would delve into his *repertoire* of secular, humorous songs and anecdotes.[83] Auguste Achte was another great traveller. He lived in considerable personal poverty, rejoicing that he shared so literally the Africans' condition of life. He walked everywhere, while praying his big Jerusalem rosary, and even climbed the Ruwenzori mountains in 1896 with Bishop Antonin Guillermain (1862–1896), to erect a cross on the summit.[84]

By the end of the nineteenth century, there had been no fewer than eighteen White Father caravans from the coast. Thereafter, although the grandiose term "caravan" was still used for parties of travelling missionaries, most of the journeys were made more comfortably by train and steamer. With the inauguration of the Uganda Railway, it was decided to move the Zanzibar procure to Mombasa in 1903.[85] Henceforward it was possible to reach Entebbe or Mwanza in twenty-five days, including four days on the train and two on the steamer.[86] Before long, the train journey was shortened to two days. Up to three meals were taken by the passengers at bungalows along the line. The rest were taken in the compartment. Spiritual exercises were made *en route* and for the rest of the time the missionaries could gaze at the enormous herds of wild animals that then roamed the plains on either side. As the train neared Kisumu, young White Fathers never failed to be shocked by the people of Kavirondo, and what was variously described as their "*nudité absolue,*" their being "*in puris naturalibus,*" or (as one diarist put it) their costume "too basic for description."[87]

Missionaries who arrived at Mwanza on the steamer *Winifred* travelled onwards overland with a small caravan of one hundred or so porters to Unyanyembe, Karema or Upper Congo. It was necessary to set up a procure for this at Mwanza in 1907, and to provide a missionary escort for new arrivals who did not know the language.[88] The whole journey from Marseilles to Karema on Lake Tanganyika could take as little as two and a half months.[89] The building of the central railway in German East Africa meant an even more rapid journey. Bishop Henri Léonard (1869–1953) made the journey to Tabora in 1913 in thirty-six hours.[90] Procures were set up at both ends of the line: at Dar es Salaam in 1911, and at Ujiji in 1913.[91]

In the Nyasa Vicariate, the usual route used by missionaries to reach the Bembaland missions was by boat to the Mozambique port of Quelimane, then overland to Lake Nyasa, whence they took a steamer of the African Lakes Company to Karonga. From there, it was a relatively short distance overland. In 1907, however, the railway line from Beira to Broken Hill (Kabwe) on the edge of the Copper Belt offered a new possibility.[92] Although the rail journey was lengthy and meandering, the distance overland from the Lake Bangweolo area to Broken Hill was around 250 miles. The journey was quicker and more economic than the route via Lake Nyasa. After the start of missionary work in Angoniland (Nyasaland, Malawi), and the building of the railway from Beira to Blantyre, it was comparatively easy, in 1913, to take the train and then travel overland, usually in a hammock.[93]

The first caravan to French Sudan, led by Prosper-Augustin Hacquard (1860–1901), left Marseilles on Christmas Day 1894. The boat journey to Dakar took eleven days. The caravan then ascended the Senegal River by river barge, reaching Kayes on February 12th 1895. From there, the missionaries travelled on horseback to Bamako on the Niger, moving again by river to Segu, which they reached on April 1st. The journey took the better part of three months.[94] The railway linking the two rivers came as far as Kita in 1903 and finally reached Bamako in 1904.[95] The mission stations founded along the river or the railway were easily accessible, but the White Fathers had to strike overland from the Niger to reach the country of the Mossi (in modern Burkina Faso). Everyone was astonished in 1908 when the *visitatrice* of the Missionary Sisters of Our Lady of Africa (White Sisters) arrived at Segu from Banankuru by car.[96] As a result of his journey to Segu and Timbuktu in 1896–1897, Bishop Toulotte recommended the overland route from Conakry in Guinée to Bamako for missionaries travelling without luggage.[97] However, the river route was not abandoned until railways were built from the coast to the interior.

Algeria and French Sudan

Kabylia and the Mzab

The oldest missionary foundations of the Society were the two Christian villages of the Attafs in northern Algeria and the mission stations of Kabylia, and the Mzab in northern Sahara. The villages had been populated by Lavigerie with the baptized survivors of the 1867 famine. By 1906, however, they only counted some 360 Christians in thirty-six families.[98] In Kabylia, the mission stations of the White Fathers had increased from two to seven in 1892. At the turn of the century, another two stations were founded in the Aurès, further south, in the Saharan Atlas. By 1900 there were thirty-nine Kabyle Christians, and ten years later just under three times that number.[99] These were grouped in tiny Christian communities at five of the mission stations. They were an outgrowth of the mission schools and had no influence on the wider community. In the Mzab, there were four mission stations in 1892, but one was suppressed ten years later. In Rome, *Propaganda Fide* regarded the work of the White Fathers in the Sahara as a "sterile mission," but over the course of time new understandings of the missionary presence in a Muslim milieu would develop.[100]

Joseph-Anatole Toulotte

In 1891 the Prefecture Apostolic of Sahara and Sudan was made a vicariate, and the province of Kabylia was attached to the dioceses of northern Algeria. At the same time, Lavigerie consecrated a coadjutor bishop, who became vicar apostolic in his own right when he died in November 1892. The coadjutor was Joseph-Anatole Toulotte (1852–1907). As we have seen, Lavigerie expressed misgivings about Toulotte after appointing him.[101] He was a refined scholar and by preference a solitary ascetic, rather than an active leader. His immediate task as vicar apostolic was to organize the first caravan to the French Sudan, through Senegal to the Niger in 1894. The General Council of the White Fathers had been made aware that the Senegal route was now open. "The brilliant campaigns of our officers during the last six years have placed the country under the exclusive influence of France," they declared with more than a hint of triumphalism. "Our flag flies at Timbuktu, and nearly all the country confided to us by the Sacred Congregation of *Propaganda* recognizes the French Protectorate."[102] The explorer-missionary Prosper-Augustin Hacquard, former superior of the Armed Brothers, was appointed its leader, but not before a seemingly point-less quarrel with Toulotte, who accused him of a lack of respect.[103] Toulotte led the third caravan to the French Sudan in 1896, but returned, broken in health and "aged by twenty years."[104] He resigned the following year, to be succeeded by Hacquard.

Toulotte lived another ten years, dividing his time between Rome, Algiers and Jerusalem. During that time, he lived the life of an anchorite, taking vegetarian meals alone, kneeling in his room and scourging himself daily. He never took wine, milk or coffee and slept on a bed of planks. Out of humility, he cultivated a deliberate lack of style in his scholarly writing in order to attract criticism, and destroyed much of his work. His delicate health could not stand up to the rigours of this chosen lifestyle. When he died of pneumonia in Rome, at the age of fifty-five, two hair shirts, four spiked chains and a discipline with eighteen bloodstained knots were found in his room.[105] The modern reader finds such eccentricities disturbing, but Toulotte's contemporaries were impressed, and he was widely admired. At that time, missionary life in the Sahara was associated in people's minds with the poverty and asceticism of the ancient desert fathers, and the asceti-cal practices of Charles de Foucauld, the hermit of the southern Sahara, were equally health-threatening.[106]

Prosper-Augustin Hacquard

Prosper-Augustin Hacquard was born at Albestroff in the French diocese of Nancy. In 1878, at the age of eighteen, he applied to join the newly founded Society of Missionaries of Africa (White Fathers) in Algiers, where he was ordained priest five years later by Cardinal Lavigerie. Hacquard was a romantic and heroic figure, a "bearded colossus" of pow-erful physique, with clear, frank eyes and a broad, intelligent forehead. Vivacious, fearless, with energetic gestures and precise words, he was a man who mastered himself and knew how to lead. He became a fluent Arabic speaker, who knew the language and its literature better than any *marabout*.[107] His first assignment was to the teaching staff of St. Eugène apostolic school in Algiers. He then became a "missionary soldier," as reli-gious superior of the Armed Brothers of the Sahara in 1891. Hacquard's caravan arrived at Segu in 1895, where he established a mission among the Bambara. Later in the same year he went to Timbuktu to establish a short-lived mission there. In January 1896, Hacquard achieved a master-stroke by accepting an invitation to accompany, as an interpreter,

Lieutenant Hourst's hydrographical expedition for mapping the Niger. Besides rendering an invaluable service to the explorers, this voyage of exploration gave Hacquard an immediate understanding of the prospects and possibilities of missionary work in the countries bordering the Niger river. French forces were then occupying the densely populated country of the Mossi, and Hacquard received a measure of criticism for the "Hourst escapade." However, he strongly repudiated any suggestion that he was an explorer, acting on behalf of the French colonial administration. "I am more ambitious than that," he said, "I am a missionary."[108] Hacquard's immediate impression of the Mossi was that they would provide "the finest mission field in the whole of the vicariate."[109] He hoped to found a "Christian empire" there that would block the advance of Islam from the north and east.[110] The Mossi were welcoming, hardworking believers in God. "They will do honour to our religion," wrote a missionary in 1903. "God will shine his sun of justice on this interesting country."[111] Hacquard also noted that his vicariate overlapped the northern territories of the British Gold Coast. These could provide a refuge if an anti-clerical administration made missionary work impossible in the French protectorate.

In 1898 Hacquard succeeded Toulotte as Vicar Apostolic of the Sahara and Sudan, and was ordained bishop in France. He returned to West Africa in the following year, explored the kingdoms of the Mossi and Gourma in 1899, founding mission stations there in the following year. In 1900 he even crossed into the Gold Coast to make contact with the British authorities.[112] His unexpected death on Holy Thursday, April 4th 1901 at Segu, was as spectacular as his life. After presiding at Mass, he spent an hour and a half before the altar of repose. He then went for a bathe in the Niger with some youngsters from the mission. He lost his footing on the river bed, was sucked into a whirlpool and drowned.[113] He was forty-one years of age and with him were lost his plans, projects and pioneering character. Eugene Konde (1877–1974), one of the youths who witnessed his death and had tried to save him, lived to be ninety-seven.[114]

Hippolyte Bazin

At Hacquard's death, the vicariate of Sahara and Sudan was divided, and Hippolyte Bazin (1857–1910) succeeded him in the Sudan. Bazin was a Breton from the Diocese of Rennes. After studies at the diocesan major seminary, he entered the novitiate in Algiers as a subdeacon in 1879. He took his oath and was ordained priest by Lavigerie in 1880. After appointments at the scholasticate and novitiate, he was made Rector of the scholasticate at Carthage in 1888 and held the post for thirteen years. Bazin was a scholar who was ill-prepared for practical leadership. Of middle height, he presented a stiff and cold exterior. He was what we would call today a "control freak." He did not like to be contradicted, and his powers of observation were limited. However, he exhibited a heroic humility, a remarkable personal austerity and a scrupulous fidelity to community exercises, but he was not a man for human relationships. Nor was he good at public speaking. At Segu, he was always the first person in chapel, and spent an hour of adoration every Wednesday. Although he studied the Bambara language, finalized its orthography and composed the first Bambara dictionary, he never preached or spoke publicly in the language.[115] Even though he was not a man of action, he took over Hacquard's projects, but the prevailing anticlerical legislation prevented new foundations. He was obliged to withdraw from Patyana and was refused permission to make a foundation at Kudugu. He was also handicapped by inadequate financing. However, in 1906, the year in which the mission station of Timbuktu was closed, he sent Oscar Morin (1878–1952) to found Navrongo, the first foundation made by the vicariate in the Gold Coast. Fortunately, a crisis plan to concentrate the personnel at Navrongo while leaving a skeleton staff at the other missions did not have to be implemented. Bazin inherited four mission stations among the Malinke, along the railway line that joined the Senegal and Niger rivers, and three among the Bambara. In the country of the Mossi there were two mission stations, and for the Gurunsi in Gold Coast (Ghana), the mission at Navrongo. It must be said that under the uninspiring leadership of Bazin the vicariate experienced a slowing down of development. He died on the way to hospital at Kayes in November 1910 and was succeeded by Alexis Lemaître (1864–1939). The Vicariate of French Sudan was four or five times the size of France, and included the modern countries of Mali, Burkina Faso and large portions of Niger, Chad and Guinea. Although the General Council in 1913 agreed with Lemaître's petition to divide it, *Propaganda Fide*, as we saw in Chapter One, refused on the grounds of smallness of numbers.[116] Lemaître founded mission stations at Reo, among the Gurunsi on the French side of the border with Gold Coast, and Toma, among the Samo, in 1912 and 1913 respectively. In the latter year, he also made a foundation in Guinea, at Nzerekore.

The Sahara

Charles Guérin and Charles de Foucauld

When, at the death of Hacquard in 1901, the Sahara was separated from the French Sudan, it became the Prefecture Apostolic of Ghardaia, with Charles Guérin (1872–1910) as prefect. At the time of his appointment, Guérin was only twenty-nine years old. The son of a Tunisian archaeologist, he had joined the White Fathers as a priest five years earlier. After novitiate, he spent a probationary year at Ghardaia and then taught Arabic to the novices. His extreme goodness and his attraction to asceticism were a recommendation. As Prefect Apostolic, he lived poorly, occupying two small rooms, surrounded by boxes and packages for forwarding. He slept on planks supported by tin trunks.[117]

Guérin's appointment coincided with the arrival in the Sahara of Charles de Foucauld (1858–1916). Charles-Eugène, Vicomte de Foucauld, had served as an officer in the French army in Algeria and Tunisia. In 1882 he resigned his commission and for two years explored Morocco in disguise. After receiving the first gold medal ever awarded by the Geographical Society of Paris, he crossed the Algerian Sahara from Morocco to Tunis in 1885. Back in Paris in 1886, he underwent a religious conversion and later became a Trappist monk, spending nine years in Palestine and Syria. He was ordained priest and returned to Algeria as hermit and missionary in 1901.[118]

Probably no other individual associated with the Sahara has so caught the public imagination as Charles de Foucauld, Brother Charles of Jesus. Guérin received him with joy and allowed him to establish a hermitage at Beni-Abbès in the Tuat, on the Moroccan border, where he was pastor to the military and spoke to the slaves about Jesus.[119] In 1902 Guérin approved his foundation of the Little Brothers of the Sacred Heart of Jesus, following the rule of St. Augustine and linked to the fraternity of Montmartre, Paris. They were to practise perpetual adoration of the Blessed Sacrament, poverty and solitude in a missionary environment.[120] Guérin was happy to have a missionary in the Tuat, as it had been an unfulfilled ambition of Toulotte to place a community there. De Foucauld's own aspirations fluctuated between active missionary work and the life of a hermit. He longed to evangelize Morocco and the Tuareg, but military pacification and French civilization were, he thought, necessary preliminaries. This was far from the approach of Lavigerie's missionaries, but he felt he could counterbalance the "base interests" of the heavy-handed military.[121] The White Fathers, however, believed that his contemplative tastes rendered him unfit for the life of an active missionary.[122] Guérin kept up a tireless correspondence with the hermit of Beni-Abbès, receiving 164 letters from him and writing 92.[123] He also managed to visit him in person in May-June 1903. He esteemed de Foucauld for the spiritual influence he radiated, rather than for any missionary enterprise. "His unalterable sweetness, his inexhaustible charity, taken with his joyful character, have absolutely won all hearts," wrote Guérin to Livinhac, the Superior General. "His solitude frightens me even more than formerly, for it seems to be part of God's designs. The oratory of Beni-Abbès is a precious treasure for us all."[124] To de Foucauld himself he wrote: "I count absolutely on the very abundant graces which flow to our Society from the blessed shrine of Jesus at Beni-Abbès."[125] In his report for 1903, Guérin called Brother Charles of Jesus a "true priest who possesses the spirit of Jesus" and wrote of the respectful admiration he received from soldiers and natives. "The marabout of Beni-Abbès is everywhere known."[126] His example of a holy life and the power of God's Word were said to have converted a young Kabyle from Islam.[127]

In spite of repeated efforts, seconded by Guérin and the White Fathers, to make converts and find members for his brotherhood, no one was prepared to share his austerities. De Foucauld, in his solitude, began to envisage his role as that of the "universal brother," united with Jesus in the Blessed Sacrament, in the midst of the Muslims. It was an apostolate of presence and spiritual encounter, an evangelization that renounced proselytism.[128] Guérin, in imitation of de Foucauld, made a retreat under canvas in the desert with three other missionaries in October 1903, and reported exultantly on the experience.[129] It was a view of de Foucauld's apostolate which came more clearly into focus at Tamanrasset, and Guérin worked hard to make it possible, by securing in 1907, from Pope Saint Pius X in person, the permission he needed to celebrate the Eucharist alone.[130]

In 1904 de Foucauld accompanied his friend Laperrine on an exploratory journey to the Hoggar, learning Tamachek in the process.[131] Guérin was at first doubtful, but soon saw the value of the information which de Foucauld could give him on the country and on the beliefs and customs of its inhabitants, with a view to founding possible mission centres.[132] De Foucauld founded a second hermitage at Tamanrasset in the heart of the Hoggar in 1905, and thereafter divided his time between the two. He translated the Bible into Tamachek and also created a Tamachek lexicon and dictionary. Guérin referred to him proudly as "(my) missionary in Tuareg country."[133] In February 1909 de Foucauld presented a proposal to the White Fathers for a mission station in the Hoggar. The proposal was rejected because of the current anti-clerical legislation.[134] Guérin died of typhoid in 1910 at the early age of thirty-eight.[135] De Foucauld was murdered at Tamanrasset in 1916 by a group of disaffected Tuareg and Harratin, who had joined Sanusi raiders from Tripolitania (Libya).[136]

Uganda

Antonin Guillermain

After the division of the Nyanza vicariate in 1894, Jean-Joseph Hirth, the actual bishop, was transferred to Southern Nyanza "*pour calmer les esprits*," as it was said.[137] Antonin Guillermain (1863–1896) was named vicar apostolic of Northern Nyanza and received episcopal ordination at the hands of Bishop Henry Hanlon MHM of Upper Nile on October 28th 1895. He died of blackwater fever scarcely nine months later, at the age of thirty-four.

In spite of the trauma following the British annexation of Uganda, one positive consequence was that Christianity spread beyond Kampala and even beyond Buganda, and the denominational spheres were no longer observed.

Moreover, at the very moment when Catholic missions were being pillaged by rebels in Buddu and Koki, and government forces were invading Bunyoro, a movement of mass conversion was gathering momentum. In the tradition of the Uganda Martyrs, this was basically an indigenous missionary movement emanating from Buganda, and in virtually every instance, the missionaries followed on the heels of indigenous evangelists. In 1895, mission stations had already been founded in Toro and on the borders of Bunyoro. Foundations in Ankole and Kigezi followed during the first decade of the twentieth century. By 1906 there were nineteen mission stations in the vicariate and six years later there were twenty-six.

Auguste Achte

The great apostle of western Uganda was Auguste-Armand-Aimé Achte (1861–1905).[138] Achte came from a farming family near Dunkirk in French Flanders. In 1881 he joined the Missionaries of Africa and completed his seminary studies at Algiers and Carthage, where he was ordained priest in 1885. Achte was first sent to Jerusalem as a teacher at St. Anne's seminary for Greek Melchite priests. Here his knowledge of Arabic, gained in North Africa, stood him in good stead. Then in 1889 he asked to go to Equatorial Africa and was appointed to the procure of the Missionaries of Africa on the island of Zanzibar. On the boat from Port Said he commenced his study of the Swahili language. Achte is remembered as a remarkable linguist. In addition to Flemish, French, Arabic and Swahili, he later learned Luganda, Runyoro-Rutoro and Kiziba, translating Gospel readings, catechisms, hymn books and devotional works into those languages. Achte also taught himself English in order to communicate with the British authorities in Uganda. At Zanzibar he taught a baptism class of ransomed slave children, and went to Bagamoyo on the mainland to meet the missionaries who had accompanied Henry Morten Stanley and Emin Pasha on the last stages of the Emin Pasha Relief Expedition. In April 1890, he and the German White Father Auguste Schynse (1857–1891), were allowed to join Emin's caravan to the interior and walked the eight hundred or so miles to the southern shore of Lake Victoria.

For several months Achte remained there at Nyegezi, recovering from the journey, rebuilding the mission station and teaching in Swahili and Luganda. In January 1891 he was ready to accompany Bishop Hirth across the lake to Uganda. Arrived in Uganda, Achte first helped to found a short-lived station in Kyagwe, east of the capital, and then travelled to the Sese Islands in Lake Victoria to claim the region allocated to the Catholics there. He was in Sese when the dramatic events occurred in the capital during January 1892. When Hirth arrived in Sese, he ordered Achte to minister to the Catholic refugees, massing in Buddu and across the border of German East Africa. Achte, a man of gentle disposition and infinite patience, was a born peacemaker. During his fourteen years as a missionary in Uganda, he made blood pacts with no fewer than eight African chiefs. He now took it upon himself to write to Captain Lugard, asking for fairer terms for the defeated Catholics. This letter was eventually instrumental in securing the return of the king and successive agreements giving better guarantees to Catholics.

In the midst of the turmoil, Achte managed to found the mission of Bikira (Buddu), build an elegant church, continue his linguistic work and instruct twelve hundred people for baptism and confirmation. In 1893, when Catholic missionaries were once more allowed to work outside Buddu, Achte—after a brief stay in Kiziba—was sent to found a mission station at Koki, where a flourishing community was established. During a week long retreat at Koki, Achte and two other priests heard the confessions of 3,286 people. Then in 1894, the British authorities launched their expeditions against Bunyoro, and Achte was asked to establish a Catholic mission on the Bunyoro border, under Kikukule, a local chief of doubtful loyalty. Although the Catholic position was fragile in the extreme, Achte repeatedly managed to assuage the chief's latent hostility and to build the mission of Bukumi. This mission survived in spite of being twice besieged by the rebels.

In 1895 Achte was asked to go to the Kingdom of Toro to found the mission of Virika near Fort Portal, at the foot of the Ruwenzori Mountains. He was the first foreign missionary among the Toro, and made his foundation in spite of considerable opposition from the king and native authorities. Mission buildings were completed, three schools started, and by 1897 there were more than three thousand catechumens. Achte continued his linguistic work, while teaching religion and giving medical treatment. The Toro version of his name was *Ati*, but his fellow missionaries jokingly called him "Father Act-ivity," such was his boundless energy. Early in 1897 Achte explored the region south of Lake Albert, with a view to a foundation at Katwe and in order to make contact with officials of the Congo Free State across the river Semliki. There, on one of his journeys, he and his small party fell into the hands of the dreaded Mulamba, leader of the mutineers from the *Force Publique* known for their cannibalistic tendencies. Achte was stripped and his life threatened. After three days without food, and several interviews with Mulamba in which his powers of reconciliation were put to their severest test, he persuaded his captors that he was a man of God, a Frenchman and not a Belgian, that he was unarmed and that he had never struck an African. At this, he and his companions were released.

In 1897 Achte was asked to return to the capital and take charge of Rubaga cathedral parish, where it was felt that his gift for reconciliation and good relations with the British would be put to good use. Besides his heavy pastoral duties at Rubaga, and in the midst of all the turmoil of Mwanga's rebellion, Achte became provicar for a year during the bishop's absence. He travelled far and wide to all the mission stations, calming and reconciling everyone, and helping in the work of restoration. In his spare time, he wrote a *History of the Ganda Kings*.[139] At the end of 1899, he went to Algiers to take part in the General Chapter of 1900, making a stopover in his beloved Jerusalem. He also went to Scotland to brush up his English.

Back in Uganda, he was again appointed to Rubaga from 1901 to 1902. He then asked to return once more to Virika in Toro, where he spent two very active final years. It was at Virika that he died, after a short illness, on February 2nd 1905, at the age of forty-four. It has been said that Achte's death marked the end of an era in Uganda. When he came in 1891 there were nine Catholic missionaries, three mission stations and a combined total of twelve thousand baptized and catechumens. When he died, fourteen years later, the Catholic Church in Uganda counted 72 male missionaries, 16 missionary sisters, 965 catechists, 19 mission stations, a junior seminary and senior seminary, 92,182 baptized Christians and more than 100,000 catechumens. An Anglican missionary friend, Archdeacon Walker, wrote that Father Achte devoted his life to God's glory. Nothing could be truer than this moving tribute.

Henri Streicher

Henri Streicher (1863–1952) was appointed vicar apostolic in succession to Bishop Antonin Guillermain in 1897.[140] He was born at Wasselonne in Alsace and joined the Society of Missionaries of Africa in 1884. During the Franco-Prussian War, his father was taken prisoner, and the family moved out of Alsace when the war was over. Streicher was small of stature and, as a young man, had rather effeminate looks. Hesketh Bell wrote of him: "His small, frail body seems very inadequate for the vigour of his spirit."[141] He was ordained priest in September 1887 and his first appointment was to teach church history and Bible for two years at St. Anne's in Jerusalem. Then, for another year he taught systematic theology at Carthage. This early experience of seminary teaching convinced him of the importance of training an African indigenous clergy, a conviction that he shared with other missionaries in Uganda, who had profited by the Jerusalem experience, notably Jean-Joseph Hirth, John Forbes, Joseph Mercui and Auguste Achte. Appointed to the Nyanza vicariate in 1890, he arrived at the beginning of 1891 and was immediately posted to Buddu where the Catholic loyalist majority took refuge in the following year. Streicher, who was called *Stensera* by the people, founded the mission station of Villa Maria in the same year and was put in charge of Hirth's seminary there in 1893. When Guillermain died suddenly in 1896, Streicher was nominated his successor, receiving episcopal ordination from Hirth on August 15th 1897 at Bukumbi. It is said that the two bishops had to share the only available crozier. Streicher was vicar apostolic of Northern Nyanza (later called the Vicariate Apostolic of Uganda) for thirty-six years, and made Villa Maria his headquarters. Intelligent, energetic, authoritarian and independent, Streicher was a superb organizer. His diocesan synods were meticulously prepared and all the resolutions were drawn up by him beforehand. Synodal participants were simply required to vote *placet* before being allowed to seek explanations from the bishop afterwards. Streicher travelled all over the vicariate by car to gain linguistic and ethnographic knowledge of the people, and by 1912 had founded a further twenty mission stations. Livinhac tried to get him to restrict the number of foundations and to strengthen existing stations, but the number of conversions forced the pace. Up to 1914, Streicher received ten new missionaries every year. Instrumental in obtaining the beatification of the Uganda Martyrs, the ordination of the first African Catholic priests and the first African Catholic bishop of modern times, Streicher was hailed by Mgr. Celso Constantini of *Propaganda Fide* as "certainly the greatest missionary of the twentieth century." Streicher himself was honoured by the pope, firstly in 1914 with the right to wear the *cappa magna*, and then in retirement with the personal title of archbishop and assistant to the pontifical throne. The French government made him *Chevalier* of the Legion of Honour, and the British government named him a Companion of the British Empire. He died on June 4th 1952.

Yohana Kitagana

Before the arrival of the White Fathers in Ankole and Kigezi, these regions of southwest Uganda were evangelized by an African lay missionary, Yohana Kitagana (c. 1858–1939), whose talents had been recognized by Streicher.[142] Kitagana was born in the Kingdom of Buganda, on the island of Busi in Lake Victoria. His mother was called Bwayinga. Kitagana belonged to the lungfish clan and entered the service of Madzi, chief of Koki. When the Catholic missionaries arrived in Buganda in 1879, Kitagana was in his twenties. By that time, he had amassed a small fortune for himself and had no fewer than five wives, as well as a slave girl concubine. In the civil war of 1892, he went to the kingdom of Ankole to help negotiate on behalf of the refugees. On returning to Buganda, Kitagana began to be interested in Christianity. By chance, he attended a Catholic catechetical instruction and was influenced by the example of the Catholic chiefs, especially by the conversion of Chief Kagolo. His interest in Christianity increased while working for Chief Jumba at Bunjako. One by one, his wives abandoned him and he gave the slave girl her freedom.

Up to the moment of joining the catechumenate in 1892, Kitagana was illiterate. As a catechumen, he learned to read and write. By the time he was baptized at Kisubi in 1896, he had decided to remain single for the remainder of his life. Kitagana's baptismal name was Yohana or John. In his late thirties, he was tall and thin of build, with an attractive personality. Moving to the mission of Mitala Maria, Kitagana was made a chief in 1900. However, during a retreat he made in Holy Week 1901, he felt the call to become a missionary, and giving up the post of chief, began to work as a catechist in Busoga and Teso in eastern Uganda.

Impressed by his dedication and the quality of his work, Bishop Henri Streicher sent Kitagana to Bunyoro, to work with the missionaries at Hoima. Meanwhile, a catechist training centre had been opened at Rubaga, and Kitagana was sent there for training. Kitagana's ardent preaching of Catholicism in Bunyoro was seen as a form of opposition to the colonial government and to the Protestant establishment. Kitagana was therefore sent to the kingdom of Ankole, to Bunyaruguru where the British had established an enclave under chiefs brought from Buganda. Kitagana began a medical apostolate, using both western and traditional medicines. Living in poverty, he cultivated his own food crops, and began to attract the youth of the area. Eighty people attended his first catechetical instruction. Abuses by the chiefs from Buganda led to his receiving death threats from the local population. When an Ankole rising against the chiefs took place in 1908, Kitagana's life was in danger, but his reputation saved him. Kitagana rebuked the Catholic chiefs for their abuses, while remaining on good terms with the Protestant chief, Kasigano. He also contested the influence of traditional healers and mediums.

In 1909 Catholic missionary priests finally joined Kitagana in Ankole and he asked to be sent to Kigezi in the following year. Kitagana settled at Kagamba in Mpororo under Chief Yohana Ssebalijja, formerly of Bunyaruguru. As was the custom, Kitagana taught religion at the chief's court. He also opposed the Nyabingi spirit possession cult, which exerted a strong influence in the area. For thirteen years Kitagana prepared the soil in Kigezi for the eventual coming of the missionary priests to Rushoroza, Kabale, in 1923. Once again Kitagana asked to carry out pioneering evangelizing work, this time in Bufumbira. After sixteen more years, often encountering life-threatening situations in a strongly traditional area opposed to the introduction of Christianity, Kitagana died and was buried in Kabale cemetery.

In his life work, Kitagana embodied the Ugandan experience of African lay evangelists, preceding the arrival of expatriate missionary clergy. The success of the Catholic Church in the areas of his primary evangelization is due in no small part to his piety, faith and hard work. Yohana Kitagana has been called a "true saint of God" and an "outstanding Catholic catechist."[143]

German East Africa

Jean-Joseph Hirth

The three White Father vicariates which lay in German East Africa were each led by an outstanding personality. Jean-Joseph Hirth was already forty when he became Vicar Apostolic of Southern Nyanza in 1894.[144] After his "baptism of fire" in Buganda, he now concentrated on developing the southern portion of his former vicariate. There were two mission stations, Bukumbi and Kashozi, near the new German towns of Mwanza and Bukoba respectively. These were, in effect, supply stations and refuges for Uganda, and they were situated among the fairly scattered local population of Sukuma, Haya and related peoples, organized in chiefdoms of varying sizes. In the undulating highlands southwest of Bukoba lay the densely populated, centralized kingdom of Rwanda. This was also part of his vicariate and presented a different demographic picture altogether.

Hirth was born in Alsace—since 1871 part of Germany—and the fact that he was fluent in German was an obvious advantage in German East Africa. A tall bespectacled young seminarian of twenty-one, he was admitted to the novitiate of the Missionaries of Africa in Algiers in 1875. He completed his theology under Livinhac, and was ordained subdeacon, deacon and priest by Lavigerie in 1878, all in ten days. After serving on the staff of the Brothers' novitiate, he went with Toulotte to Jerusalem in 1882, where for four years he was the first director of the junior seminary of St. Anne's. With him on the seminary staff was another future missionary to Uganda, Joseph Mercui (1854–1947). Hirth toured Syria for recruits and brought the number of students up to sixty.[145] In 1886, he was appointed director of the apostolic school of St. Eugène in Algiers, but was allowed to join Livinhac in Nyanza the following year. Livinhac appointed him superior of Bukumbi, where he opened a catechist school *cum* seminary. He was ordained bishop by Livinhac "in modest circumstances" at Bukumbi in 1890. After the civil war in Uganda and the flight of the Catholic population, Hirth took refuge in Kiziba and founded the mission station of Kashozi. As bishop in Southern Nyanza, he returned to live there after 1895, before moving to Rubya, where he had founded a seminary and was personally involved in the formation of the first priests from Bukoba and Rwanda. By 1906, he had five stations in the Bukoba area and three in the Mwanza region, two of them being foundations on the lake islands of Ukerewe and Kome. But it was in Rwanda after 1899 that he scored the biggest success, with the initial help of catechists from Buganda. There were six Rwandan stations in 1906, and ten by 1912, with a total of eighty-five hundred baptized Christians, almost equalling the number in the fourteen stations of the Bukoba and Mwanza regions. Of the twenty-four stations in the vicariate, all except Bukumbi had been founded by Hirth.

In 1910, Hirth was given a coadjutor, the Dutchman Joseph Sweens (1858–1950), who carried out the diocesan visitations for him. When Gerboin died in 1912, the six mission stations of Burundi (until then part of Unyanyembe vicariate) were added to those of Rwanda, to become the Vicariate Apostolic of Kivu, and Hirth became its first vicar apostolic. Sweens inherited the South Nyanza Vicariate, now comprising the Bukoba and Mwanza regions only. Hirth moved to Kabgayi with his Rwandan seminarians and eventually retired there in 1921. There were over thirty thousand baptized Christians in the vicariate at the time of his resignation. During the ten years of his retirement at Kabgayi Seminary, this "Father of the East African Seminaries" acted as spiritual director and organist, dying at the age of seventy-seven in 1931. Hirth was a "giant" of the African apostolate, and his name appears in every chapter of this book.

François Gerboin

The provicariate of Unyanyembe had been taken out of the Tanganyika mission at the end of 1886. Ludovic Girault (1853–1941), who had been a member of the first caravan to equatorial Africa in 1878, was named the first provicar. Suffering from river blindness, he was forced to resign and return to Europe in 1890. François Gerboin (1847–1912) was then named provicar in his place.[146] Gerboin came from Laval, France, and joined the Missionaries of Africa in 1872, at the age of twenty-five. He was ordained two years later. The first sixteen years of his missionary life were spent in North Africa and Europe, at mission stations in Kabylia, carrying out promotion work in France and serving as Secretary General of the Society in Algiers. Of moderate intelligence, he was nevertheless hardworking and immensely kind. He was loved by people in Africa for these qualities and for his good humour. He arrived at Bukumbi towards the end of 1890, at the age of forty-three. In his provicariate, there were no mission stations and no missionaries. In 1891, Gerboin, together with sixty catechists and Christians from Bukumbi, founded his first mission station at Ushirombo in the country of the Sumbwa, who welcomed missionary protection against the Ngoni invaders of the area. Although his resources were limited, Gerboin sought to lay effective claim to his vast territory by constructing mission stations at strategic intervals. These missions eventually formed an immense parabola from the north of Lake Tanganyika in the west to Lake Manyara in the east, taking in the region of Tabora to the south, at the bottom of the curve. Most of the vicariate was sparsely populated and the distances between the mission stations made communication difficult, if not impossible. Gerboin's annual visitation was a journey of over a thousand miles. The exception was Burundi, where a dense population made the foundation of many mission stations in relative proximity feasible. Gerboin's base was at Ushirombo, within easier reach of Burundi than the rest of the vicariate.

In 1897, with four mission stations already founded, Unyanyembe was made a vicariate, and Gerboin was its first vicar apostolic. He was ordained bishop by Hirth at Bukumbi and his title of *monseigneur* gave rise to his African name *Musenyela*. In 1907, with ten stations already established, Gerboin sent missionaries to found a mission among the Cushitic-speaking Iraqw in the extreme east of the vicariate. Here they found that a party of Spiritans, sent by the vicar apostolic of Bagamoyo, had arrived ten days before them, in the mistaken belief that it was Spiritan territory. The beginnings of the mission in Iraqw were difficult enough without a missionary "scramble," but, after consultation with higher authority, the Spiritans withdrew. Gerboin invited the Missionary Sisters of Our Lady of Africa (MSOLA or White Sisters) to the vicariate in 1893, and thereby became the first bishop in sub-Saharan Africa to have religious sisters working alongside the White Fathers. In 1900, the German Jewish psychiatric doctor, traveller and German Resident in Rwanda, Richard Kandt (1867–1918), donated a former Arab-owned plot, called Baharini, in Tabora for another mission.

Suffering from heart disease, Gerboin became bedridden in the last months of his life. In a long letter to Livinhac, he outlined the needs of the vicariate and asked for a coadjutor. Henri Léonard (1869–1953) was appointed on June 26th 1912, but Gerboin died the next day, and Léonard at once became Vicar Apostolic. With the six mission stations of Burundi given to the Kivu vicariate, Léonard moved his headquarters to Tabora and the focus of the Unyanyembe vicariate shifted from Burundi to the eight remaining stations. Gerboin's epitaph is the tribute to his goodness summed up in the Sumbwa proverb: "*Musenyela* is dead, there is no more mercy."

Adolphe Lechaptois

As a vicariate apostolic, Tanganyika had been in existence since 1886. In 1892 Adolphe Lechaptois (1852–1917) was already the third vicar apostolic.[147] Jean-Baptiste Charbonnier (1842–1888) and Léonce Bridoux (1852–1890) had died in swift succession, heading the vicariate for seven months and two years, respectively. Lechaptois was to be its bishop for twenty-eight years. In 1892, the vicariate lay along the eastern shore of Lake Tanganyika and carried further east across the Fipa plateau and the Rukwa plain to the Southern Highlands. It had a scattered population of some two hundred thousand people. Lechaptois had attended the seminary of Laval together with Gerboin. He entered the Society of Missionaries of Africa in 1872, and taught in the junior seminary at Algiers for two years before beginning his theology studies. He was ordained by Cardinal Lavigerie in 1878. For the next five years he alternated between teaching at the junior seminary of St. Eugène and assisting the master of novices at Maison Carée. Although he had not taught at St. Anne's Jerusalem, he came to equatorial Africa with considerable experience of seminary teaching. In 1883, he was briefly appointed an assistant general of the Society, but in the following year he became the master of novices. In 1886, he was appointed regional superior of Kabylia in Algeria, where he was active in the promotion of the Christian villages. Finally, after more than a decade of work in the formation centres and villages of North Africa, he received his first appointment to equatorial Africa in 1889. He was thirty-seven.

Portugal, at this time, was laying claim to the Shire Highlands of southern Nyasaland, and Lavigerie hoped to begin missionary work in the area under the auspices of this Catholic power. Lechaptois was appointed provicar of Nyasa and travelled to the southern end of Lake Nyasa (Malawi) via the Portuguese colony of Mozambique. Here he founded the mission station of Mponda in December 1890, beginning a medical and teaching apostolate among the Yao people. Within a very short time, he had 116 regular pupils at the mission. Instruction was given in the local language, not in Portuguese. This missionary initiative, however, was overtaken by events. The Anglo-Portuguese agreement of 1890 ceded the whole of Nyasaland to Britain, and a British protectorate was declared. In 1891, Lechaptois was obliged to close Mponda and move to Mambwe at the southern end of Lake Tanganyika, in the region that was the responsibility of the British South Africa Company.

In June 1891, Lechaptois was appointed vicar apostolic of Tanganyika and, until 1896, administrator of Nyasa (Mambwe). Lechaptois established himself at Karema, the former Fort Leopold, and carried out a visitation of the Upper Congo Mission on the other side of the lake, the superior having recently died. The whole area was then in turmoil, due to the Arab war and the depredations of the slave-trader Rumaliza. There was little that could be done other than to fortify the mission stations and to run orphanages for the ransomed children and other casualties of slavery.

In 1894, Lechaptois attended the general chapter of the Missionaries of Africa in Algiers and finally received episcopal ordination there from Archbishop Dusserre. He returned to Karema with a group of Missionary Sisters of Our Lady of Africa, the first missionary sisters to work in the vicariate. Between 1894 and 1896, he founded five more mission stations.[148] In 1895, Lechaptois accompanied Joseph Dupont to Mambwe as the new superior of the Nyasa mission. Two years later he ordained him Bishop of the Nyasa vicariate at Kayambi. On the eve of World War I, the Tanganyika Vicariate possessed thirteen mission stations covering some six thousand square miles. The stations formed a compact grid, each fifty miles from its neighbours. Mission stations had networks of ten to fifteen outstation chapel-schools with a resident catechist, extending as far as the outstation networks of the neighbouring missions. This was an extremely effective method of covering the ground and ensuring a "saturation" process of evangelization.[149] At the end of our period, Tanganyika vicariate counted the best part of ten thousand baptized Christians and half as many catechumens.

Expansion was partly spurred by Moravian incursions into the eastern part of the vicariate, in spite of the delineation of missionary spheres of influence by the Germans. Attempts by Lechaptois to enter the Moravian sphere were blocked by the colonial authorities. By and large, however, Lechaptois enjoyed the support of the German colonial government. In 1896, Mambwe was closed and Lechaptois moved the catechist-teacher training centre he had founded there to Utinta on the shore of Lake Tanganyika. It was moved again to Karema in 1899, where the teachers studied alongside candidates for the priesthood. In 1912–1913 the teacher-catechists were moved to Zimba and the Karema centre developed into a junior seminary.

Lechaptois, who was a good superior to his missionaries, visited every mission station annually. Possessing great zeal, transparent goodness and simplicity, he has been described as "a man of almost pathological humility."[150] He slept on a Swahili string bed, and the other furniture in his room consisted of two wooden chairs and two cupboards: one for his clothes and the other for the diocesan files. Although marked by the paternalism of the time, his love for his people and fellow workers was genuine. He was also a scholar who bought, read and wrote books. For his ethnography of the region, published as *Aux Rives du Tanganyika* in 1913, he received the Prize of the Geographical Society of Paris in 1912, and the Society's silver medal.[151] The work demonstrates his positive appreciation of the people of the region, their character, traditions, arts and organization. Lechaptois died of a stroke in 1917, after receiving news of a friend's unexpected death.

The Congo Free State

Victor Roelens

The mission of Upper Congo covered the watershed between the western shore of Lake Tanganyika and the Lualaba, the most important confluent of the river Congo. In 1886, when the territory on the other side of the river was entrusted to the Scheut Missionaries, Upper Congo was proclaimed a provicariate. Victor Roelens (1856–1947) arrived as administrator in 1892. There were three stations: Kibanga, Mpala and Joubert's village of Mrumbi. Besides being prey to the violence of the Arab war, the whole area was swamp-ridden and unhealthy. Kibanga was closed for health reasons in 1893, but in the same year Roelens laid the foundations of Baudouinville (Moba), the station which became the centre of his theocratic mission-state, which filled the power vacuum in the region.[152] Roelens was made provicar in 1893, and vicar apostolic two years later.[153] He was ordained bishop by Cardinal Goossens of Malines in 1896.

By nature, Roelens was authoritarian, pragmatic, hard and obstinate. His life-style was simple and he despised any trace of sentimentality or personal comfort. A Belgian, he was born in the Diocese of Bruges, western Flanders, and inherited his father's respect for, and love of, manual work. In 1880, as a seminarian, he entered the novitiate of the Missionaries of Africa at Algiers, and after theological studies at Carthage in Tunisia, was ordained priest by Cardinal Lavigerie. For seven years Roelens was employed in Europe and the Near East. He worked mainly in Belgium, setting up the anti-slavery committee there, and then taught at St. Anne's Jerusalem, where the students found him somewhat intimidating.[154]

Roelens took over Upper Congo at a difficult time. Although open, large-scale slave raiding finally ceased around 1893, the massive mutiny of the Congo *Force Publique* in 1895 continued to cause violent unrest in the area, and delayed the expansion of the vicariate in the northern Kivu region. In 1905, the White Fathers' General Visitor found it urgent to occupy the north of the vicariate, in case the region was given to another missionary society.[155] Roelens made an exploratory journey to Kivu travelling on a monocycle—a basket chair set on a single wheel between shafts drawn by six carriers—and in 1906 a first foundation was made there. Between 1903 and 1907 widespread epidemics caused thousands of deaths, and nineteen, out of forty-two, missionaries were among those who died. In the absence of effective administration by the Congo Free State, the missions continued for some years to be reception stations for orphans, ransomed slaves and other casualties of violence and epidemics. In fact, the mission in Upper Congo revolved around institutional orphanages and Christian settlements long after such things had disappeared in other parts of Africa. Another consequence of the initial ineffectiveness of the state administration was that the Catholic Church was in such a strong position when the colonial administration was effectively established that it virtually shared civil power with the state. The 1906 concordat with the Vatican allocated substantial areas of land to the church, as well as subsidies for Catholic schools.

The Rubber Terror did not reach the Upper Congo vicariate. At first, Roelens was inclined to defend the Belgian king against the "unproven" accusations, and Catholics were blamed for colluding with the Congo authorities.[156] The Janssens Report of 1905 even went so far as to accuse Catholic missionaries of sharing in King Leopold's exploitation of the Africans. In the wake of the Report, however, it was revealed that Catholic missionaries had given private accounts of horrifying abuses to Congo state officials.[157] Roelens set up the Association of Superiors of Orders and Congregations with Missions in the Congo to counter the accusations, and he addressed an open letter of protest to the commission.[158] The association met in January 1907 at the White Fathers' junior seminary in Antwerp, and again at Leopoldville (Kinshasa) in 1908, where it became the Plenary Conference of Mission Ordinaries.[159]

In 1906–1907, Roelens crossed swords in the press with Edmond Morel of the Congo Reform Association.[160] Morel had published posthumously letters from a missionary of Upper Congo, accusing the Congo administration of knowing connivance in slave trading in Katanga and Mtowa. The letters mentioned that the missionary in question, Bruno Schmitz (1872–1905), had alerted the vicar apostolic. Roelens' reply was prickly, and made much of the errors of detail in Morel's article. However, he made it known that, having failed to get redress from the Congo administration, he had taken the matter up with Brussels, and this had resulted in the sending of the Fontana expedition to put an end to the abuse. Roelens certainly did not see eye to eye with the Congo government, especially on the subject of military youth camps or children's colonies, and he was able to avoid any involvement in these.

In 1893 Roelens started a catechist training centre at Mpala, and this moved to his new mission station of Lusaka in 1905.[161] Under government impulse, it eventually became a teacher training centre. The schools and orphanages of Upper Congo remained firmly in the hands of the church, which attempted to shield the pupils from secular influences. Roelens drew up a catechism in Swahili and enunciated his missionary policies through rigid circulars and instructions, which were often racist in tone. A junior seminary stream developed alongside the catechist centre at Lusaka. In this, the students were allowed to learn French, as well as Latin, and to study classical authors such as Cicero. In 1907, a major seminary was started at Baudouinville, and this produced the first Congolese priest, Stephen Kaoze, who was ordained by Roelens in 1917. The success of the seminary and the perseverance of Kaoze probably owed more to the support of Roelens' auxiliary bishop, Auguste Huys (1871–1938) than to Roelens himself. Huys died in 1938 and Roelens received Urbain Morlion (1894–1985) as coadjutor in 1939. When Roelens resigned in 1941, after forty-six years as bishop, his vicariate had fifty-two thousand baptized Christians in twenty-eight mission stations. He spent his last six years of retirement in study and prayer. Dying at the age of eighty-nine, he had outlived forty-nine of his missionaries, whose names he had inscribed on a board, before which he prayed his daily rosary. Although he was a controversial, and in many ways an unattractive, character, Roelens was a major founder of the Catholic Church in Congo and its first bishop.

Northern Rhodesia and Nyasaland

Joseph Dupont

In 1895, Adolphe Lechaptois was still administrator of Nyasa, a provicariate that comprised half of Northern Rhodesia (Zambia) and all of Nyasaland (Malawi), a surface area of three hundred thousand square miles. On returning to Tanganyika after his episcopal ordination, Lechaptois summoned a council of missionaries to discuss the provicariate's future. The Bemba people in the north of the region had been notorious as raiders of caravans and neighbouring villages, making pacts with slave traders and showing hostility to Europeans. The provicariate possessed a single station, Mambwe, at the southern end of Lake Tanganyika, and the Bemba were effectively blocking any approach to more populous areas beyond. Cardinal Ledochowski, the Prefect of *Propaganda Fide*, had urged Lechaptois to go to the Bemba, adding that the most cruel people were sometimes the quickest to accept the Word of God. This advice coincided with the conquest of the Bemba, their effective containment by the German military, and an invitation from Makasa, whose chiefdom lay on the Bembaland border. The council of missionaries summoned by Lechaptois decided to close Mambwe and send Dupont to Makasa's as superior of the Nyasa mission. It was hoped that this would be a starting-point for the evangelization of the Bemba.[162]

Joseph-Marie-Stanislas Dupont (1850–1930) was a colourful and original personality, impulsive, energetic and adventurous.[163] Always optimistic and using superlatives, he displayed what some called *panache* and others saw as self-dramatization. In Tanganyika, his military manner and ceaseless activity earned him the Swahili nickname *Moto Moto*, "Man of Fire," the name that went with him later to Northern Rhodesia. Lechaptois reported to Livinhac that Dupont combined military virtues with the faith, zeal and piety of a priest. "His vivacity and rough exterior manner (were) tempered by a genuine kindness of heart."[164] A fellow missionary remarked that Dupont, like Achte in Uganda, had discovered the secret of perpetual motion.

Born in France at Geste, in Maine and Loire, he entered the diocesan college of Beaupréau at the age of fourteen. Dupont was very far from being an academic. Later, as bishop, he discouraged further studies for his missionaries and, in retirement, a characteristic saying of his was "(academic) discussion leads to division, not action." Dupont was twenty when the Franco-Prussian War broke out. Although, as a seminarian, he could have avoided conscription, his college director thought a military career might suit him better, and did not apply for exemption in his case. Dupont enjoyed his military service so much that, after the war, he offered to fight the Paris Commune. In this conflict he exhibited considerable bravery, personally disarming and capturing a Communard leader in the Père Lachaise quarter. Dupont, however, overcame the attraction of a military career, and, to everyone's surprise, returned to college in 1872 to complete his studies. Two years later he entered the major seminary of Angers. He experienced some difficulty in securing release from his diocesan bishop, but eventually in 1879 was admitted to the Society of Missionaries of Africa after priestly ordination and made his novitiate year at Algiers. After his missionary oath, he spent the next four years as a teacher at the College of Saint Louis of Carthage at Thibar in Tunisia. This was not a congenial posting, but it enabled Dupont to know his missionary society better.

Cardinal Lavigerie had been entrusted by Leo XIII with the evangelization of an immense territory west of the Lualaba-Congo, as well as the region of the Great Lakes. Anxious not to lose his claim to the Lower Congo region, he invited the Congregation of the Holy Spirit (Spiritans) to help him, while, at the same time, planning a mission of his own in the same area. In 1885, he sent Dupont and two other missionaries to found a station on the Congo above Stanley Pool, at Kwamouth in the country of the Bayanzi. Journeying up river by road and steamer, Dupont managed, with considerable difficulty, to begin work at Bungana in 1886. Meanwhile, the Spiritans lobbied *Propaganda Fide* in Rome to obtain exclusive jurisdiction for themselves. Leopold II was also anxious for Belgian, rather than French, missionaries. At length in 1887, the Pope consented to give the territory to the Spiritans and Dupont was obliged to withdraw.

With a heavy heart, Dupont returned to the uncongenial task of being a teacher again for four years at the apostolic school of Saint Laurent d'Olt in France. He was rescued from this servitude in 1891 to be made leader of the tenth caravan of the missionaries of Africa to Equatorial Africa, arriving at Karema on Lake Tanganyika in 1892. After three hyper-active years at Karema, he now found himself appointed provicar of Nyasa. The sociopolitical organization of the Bemba was complex and fraught with violent conflict. Dupont immediately founded Kayambi Mission at Makasa's and went on to become the first vicar apostolic of Nyasa in 1897, taking as his episcopal motto "Would that the fire be kindled" (Luke 12:49), a reference to his nickname *Moto Moto*. His titular see was none other than Thibar, where he had held his first appointment.

Dupont admired the intelligence and fine physique of the Bemba, and the fearlessness and proud independent spirit of their warriors. He adopted the social categories bestowed on him by the Bemba and responded to their expectations of him as priest, healer and diviner. The Bemba, for their part, admired Dupont's military bearing and authoritarian manner. Evangelization was geared to the rhythms of Bemba life, but depended almost entirely on the vivacity and personal magnetism of Dupont. After protracted negotiations with the effective Bemba paramount, Mwamba, Chief of Ituna, a mission station was eventually established in the Bemba heartland at Chilubula in 1899, where the British South Africa Company accorded him concessionary status as a native authority. Dupont's missionaries found his style decidedly military, issuing written orders and imposing strict discipline. Moreover, the bishop's predilection for the Bemba meant that the remainder of his vast diocese was neglected. When hepatitis and arthritis forced him to take sick leave in Europe in 1899, the vicariate consisted of three Bemba mission stations, with eight priests and four brothers.

Dupont was absent from his diocese for four years. In his absence, his administrator, Mathurin Guillemé, founded several mission stations in the country of the Ngoni and Achewa across the Lwangwa river in Nyasaland (Malawi).[165] For his part, Dupont in Europe arranged for the first Missionary Sisters of Our Lady of Africa (MSOLA, White Sisters) to go to Bembaland, and signed a contract with the Montfort Missionary Society to staff the extreme south of Nyasaland. This agreement was made with Dupont's usual impulsiveness, forgetting entirely to secure the prior approval of Rome. As a result, the Montfort Missionaries were recalled, and Dupont spent a fruitless time at the Vatican trying to secure approval for his *fait accompli*. The matter was only rectified after Dupont had been severely reprimanded, and the Cardinal Protector of the Montfort Missionaries had himself become prefect of *Propaganda Fide*.[166]

Dupont returned to his diocese in 1904. He was still a sick man. Moreover, he found that the large Bemba concentrations around his missions had dispersed. The Bemba were, after all, shifting cultivators and the *Pax Britannica* encouraged population dispersal. Many missionaries despaired of the Bemba altogether. They believed the future of the diocese lay in Nyasaland, and thought the bishop's preference for the Bemba misplaced. Dupont's faith in the Bemba was eventually justified, but not until he had set up a catechist training centre at Chilubula and espoused methods of evangelization that were more orthodox.

It was becoming clear that Bembaland and Angoniland would have to become separate jurisdictions. Dupont wanted to remain forever with his beloved Bemba. Theirs were the language and culture he knew. Bembaland was also his power base in the diocese. He therefore suggested that Nyasaland should become a separate prefecture apostolic. The anomaly was, however, that he was vicar apostolic of "Nyasa." His superiors at Algiers requested that he leave Bembaland and take direct responsibility for the rest of his huge diocese. This he felt unable to do. In 1910, Livinhac, the Superior General, requested his resignation. With a broken heart, he obeyed, his resignation being accepted by Rome the following year. "May God's will be done," he wrote to Livinhac, "the glory of God procured and souls saved. The rest is unimportant. I am surprised, however that such a decision was taken and delivered in public before any word was said to me . . . Let me be buried as quickly as possible, but may the missions live and save souls."[167] His last act was to consecrate at Chilubula the Montfort Missionary Auneau as vicar apostolic of Shire in southern Nyasaland. Dupont retired to Thibar, Tunisia, the place of his episcopal title. Here he lived out his exile from Bembaland, a venerable, if pathetic, figure until his death from double pneumonia on March 19th 1930 at the age of eighty. In 1997, the centenary of his episcopal consecration, his bones were taken to Kasama, Zambia, to be buried in the land of his beloved Bemba.[168] In the oral tradition and folklore of the area the love affair of *Bwana Moto Moto* and his Bemba warriors continues unabated to this day.

Dupont's vicariate was divided in 1911 between Mathurin Guillemé

(1859–1942), as vicar apostolic of Nyasa (Nyasaland), and Etienne Larue (1865–1935) as vicar apostolic of Bangweolo (Northern Rhodesia). Nyasa had five stations and just under thirty-five hundred baptized Christians. Bangweolo had seven stations, with just over seven thousand baptized Christians.

Conclusion

An attempt has been made in this chapter to do three things. The first was to describe in general terms the relationship of the Missionaries of Africa to the colonial powers and the views they held of each other. Secondly, the so-called "Scramble for Africa" was depicted in so far as it affected their mission territories. Finally, an account was given, in broad outline, of the missionary deployment of the White Fathers in these territories through the biographies of the outstanding personalities involved. The remainder of the book is a more detailed analysis of particular aspects of the process, beginning in the next chapter with the persistence of slavery, the role of traditional rulers and the occasional exercise of civil power by the missionaries.

CHAPTER THREE

Slavery, Missionaries and Civil Power

African Slavery and the Arab War of 1890–1894

Lavigerie's Anti-Slavery Campaign

"All I can add in my loneliness is, may Heaven's rich blessing come down on everyone, American, English or Turk, who will help heal the open sore of the world." David Livingstone (1813–1873) wrote those words in Tabora exactly a year before his death, and they were inscribed on his gravestone in Westminster Abbey.[1] The words were quoted by Cardinal Lavigerie in the address he delivered in London during his anti-slavery campaign in 1888: "I wished in my capacity of an old African to visit the tomb of the great explorer, the glory of this century and of your country, placed by you amidst your greatest men, beneath the vaults of Westminster. And it was with an emotion that brought tears to my eyes when I read the words written by him just before he died and which England has engraved upon his tomb . . ."[2] Many people in Europe believed that, with the ending of the Atlantic slave trade, the era of African slavery was over. The purpose of Lavigerie's campaign was to tell them that the "open sore of the world" was still open and needed healing. He wanted to make known the extent of the trade as revealed by the missionaries he had sent to equatorial Africa.

Lavigerie was successful in raising this awareness, although he failed to obtain any concerted, international action. The scramble for Africa had started, and every European nation wished to address the problem of slavery on its own terms. Lavigerie had long been aware of the trans-Saharan trade, operating out of Timbuktu and the (French) Sudan. Around 1900, five years after the Missionaries of Africa penetrated the region, it is estimated that there were more than a million slaves in the French Sudan, out of a population of five million.[3] In 1870, the East African trade brought 35,000 slaves annually to Zanzibar. After 1873, when the Royal Navy began its blockade of coastal waters, the caravans of slaves were absorbed by plantations at the coast or further up-country. Livingstone had witnessed a massacre in the market place of Nyangwe, Manyema, in 1871, carried out by the slave trader Dugumbi. Lavigerie therefore made Nyangwe a destination

63

for his first caravan to equatorial Africa in 1878.[4] Besides the work of evangelization, Lavigerie wanted his missionaries to show kindness and compassion to the victims of the slave trade, but he knew full well that the trade
itself must somehow be stopped. In his eyes, the slave trade was nothing less
than war—a war waged on peaceful populations in order to obtain captives.
Armies were needed to defeat such aggressors, and these could only be provided by the European powers, either through the armed expeditions sent
by national anti-slavery committees, or by the occupying forces of coloniz-
ing nations.

African Slave Societies in 1892

In 1892, Lavigerie's anti-slavery campaign was a recent memory, and even
though the scramble for Africa was now under way, the slave trade could
not be abolished overnight. In one form or another, the trade would survive
until World War I in all the territories of the Missionaries of Africa. Worse
still, slavery would penetrate and distort African socio-cultural institutions
for a long time to come. The regions to which the White Fathers came were
slave societies, in which a constantly expanding servile class supported the
merchants and their armed men.[5] In a commercialized economy that
included labour intensive plantations, slavery was assumed to be a necessity. In Tabora (German East Africa), slaves were even owned by other
slaves. The terrible social and psychological effects of the trade were such
that for a long time to come, many Africans would suffer from an ingrained
slave mentality. Nearly one hundred years later, villagers still discriminate
against the descendants of slaves in Congo and the Sahara, and in the 1970s
families in Tanzania still pursued feuds that originated with disputes over
slave ownership.[6] Slaves were in demand throughout Arabia well into the
twentieth century, and slavery remains an accepted way of life today in
places such as Northern Nigeria, the Sudan and Mauritania.[7] Sexual slavery and the enslaved condition of some African domestic servants in Europe
are still social facts in the twenty-first century.

The Arab War around Lake Tanganyika

When Tippu Tip signed the contract with Leopold II in 1887, he agreed to
prohibit the slave trade between Stanley Pool (Kinshasa) and Stanley Falls
(Kisangani), and to concentrate solely on the trade in ivory.[8] Apart from the
fact that Tippu probably did not seriously intend to oppose the slave trade
at all, Leopold and Stanley failed to realize the extent to which the ivory
and slave trades depended on each other. Hunters were needed to collect the
ivory and hundreds of porters were required to carry the tusks to the coast.
If the enterprise was to be profitable, both hunting parties and porters had
to be slaves. Not only did they require no remuneration, but they themselves

would bring in income. Wherever the long-distance trade in ivory continued, the slave trade was not far away.

In 1892 the Arab War was reaching its climax in the Congo Free State. Lake Tanganyika was a strategic area, and the slavers had to be defeated there if any impact was to be made on the East African slave trade as a whole. The revolt was caused by government competition in the ivory trade, with which the slave trade was connected. Until the arrival of the anti-slavery expeditions which followed upon Lavigerie's campaign, Joubert, the armed auxiliary of the White Fathers, together with his small militia, carried the whole burden of the war with Rumaliza and his allies.

Captain Leopold Joubert

Captain Leopold-Louis Joubert (1842–1927) was a Frenchman. At the age of eighteen, he had left school in order to join the army being raised by Pope Pius IX for the defence of the Papal States. He served for eleven years in the pope's Franco-Belgian battalion. Wounded at the battle of Castelfidardo in 1860, he spent time in a Piedmontese hospital, but returned to Rome in 1861. He was on garrison duty until 1865, and chose to remain in Rome as a papal Zouave when the French left Italy in the following year. He saw action at the Porta Salaria when the Piedmontese marched on Rome in 1870. Then, after the disbanding of the Zouaves, Joubert sailed to Algiers in 1880 and offered his services to Cardinal Lavigerie. In 1887, he was on his second tour of duty in equatorial Africa. He was to stay for another forty years, until his death in 1927. For in 1888 he married Agnes Atakao, a native of Congo, and settled at Mrumbi with her and the ten children she bore him.[9]

In 1889 Joubert drove off the slaver Mohamadi. Then, in early 1890, after a terrible slave raid by Katele, Joubert launched an attack on the slaver's fortress, and drove him away also.[10] As their "secular arm," the missionaries felt that Joubert should not be too closely identified with the mission at Mpala, so he moved south and built himself a fortress at Mrumbi. During 1890–1891, Joubert divided his time between Mpala and the Mrumbi plain, the only two areas that he could keep relatively free from Rumaliza's unwelcome attentions. Even then, he had a major engagement on land and lake with Rumaliza's lieutenant, Rajabu, and an enemy force of four hundred. Joubert, on this occasion, was helped by a storm that wrecked Rajabu's flotilla.

The Paris anti-slavery conference, chaired by Lavigerie in 1890, voted to send an expedition to the aid of their "heroic" compatriot, but Leopold II had no intention of allowing an armed French expedition to be let loose in Belgian territory. The idea of a Franco-Belgian expedition also turned out to be a non-starter. So it was left to the Belgians alone to take action.[11] The anti-slavery expedition of Captain Jules Jacques arrived in the region at the end of 1891. Joubert joined him in another lake battle in 1892 and an unsuccessful assault on the fortress of Toka Toka. Jacques requested urgent reinforcements from the Belgian anti-slavery committee, and the expedition of Descamps arrived in 1893, bringing relief. In the meantime, Rumaliza's forces took the initiative in April 1892. In a retaliatory skirmish, Jacques' young lieutenant Vrithoff was captured, killed and—apparently—eaten by Rumaliza's cannibal followers.[12] When the reinforcements came, the slavers were defeated, and Rumaliza, as we saw in the previous chapter, escaped back to Zanzibar in 1894.[13] Large areas of the Upper Congo Vicariate had been devastated and the northern mission station of Kibanga had been virtually abandoned. It was closed in July 1893. Famine reigned in the Marungu plain to the south, and between March 1891 and March 1893, Théophile Dromaux made three expeditions across the lake from Karema, rescuing and ferrying back more than two hundred victims of slavery and starvation.[14]

Slavery and the Anti-Colonial Revolts

Mwanga's Revolt and the Congo Mutiny

Slave raiding was not necessarily synonymous with anti-colonial rebellions, but it was one of their side effects. During Mwanga's revolt in Uganda in 1897–1898, and its continuation after his capture in 1899 by Gabriel Kintu Mujasi, the missionaries recorded that hundreds of women and children were snatched by the rebels. In 1898, 300 women, captured by Muslim rebels, were liberated by Catholics.[15] The following year, 220 Catholic women were captured and enslaved by rebels in Buddu.[16] Casualties, like the little Toro slave, wounded in the rebellion and entrusted by a British officer to the White Sisters (MSOLA), were numerous.[17] In Burundi, as late as 1909, the White Fathers ransomed thirty-three girls and three boys, taken as booty in a recent revolt against the Germans.[18] The mutiny of the Congo *Force Publique* and Tetela Revolt in 1895–1908 also included slave-raiding. From the missionary point of view, "rebel" and "slaver" were one and the same.[19] The mutiny involved thousands of soldiers, and thus brought endless conflicts to the Upper Congo region. In November 1896, these rebels forced the abandonment of Lusaka mission south of Baudouinville, and Joubert collected his forces again to oppose them.[20] Although the rebels were defeated and large numbers surrendered, they retained control in southwest Katanga during the first decade of the twentieth century. The missionaries recorded the slaving activities of the Congo mutineers and Tetela rebels in 1898 and 1902.[21]

Bishop Roelens' polemic with Edmond Morel in 1907 shows that the slave trade in Congo was continuing with official tolerance or even connivance in 1905–1906, and that salt, rubber and ivory were being smuggled and exchanged for slaves. In the Katanga area Lupungu, the Congo agent at Kabinda, was directly involved. A few miles from the Congo government's headquarters at Mtowa (Albertville), Sefu, the son of Tippu Tip and former Arab rebel, was conducting this trade with the knowledge of the authorities. As we have seen, Roelens got nowhere with the local officials until he took the matter to Brussels.[22] As a result, the Fontana expedition was dispatched to the Katanga area.[23]

Slavery and Resistance in French Sudan

In French Sudan, slave trading continued to be a profitable enterprise among the Tuareg at Timbuktu and in the so-called Bambara and Malinke "empires" of the Tukolor, Ahmadu, and Samory-Toure. These were military adventurers who represented a popular type of Islam, and who resisted the French occupation towards the end of the nineteenth century with very considerable bravery and skill. Samory's empire was unique, in that he managed to move and re-found it further south. The less attractive aspect of these resistance leaders was that they were pillars of the slave trade, selling or distributing among their followers the war captives they took.[24] It is reckoned that more than two hundred thousand captives resulted from the wars of Ahmadu and Samory. Men, women, boys and girls who were sold at Timbuktu could raise more than twice the sum if sold in the oases of the Saharan Tuat.[25] As long as such disparity of prices continued, slavery was definitely a commercial proposition. Pawnship, or the loan of children, was practised among all the ethnic groups of French Sudan, and the sale of family members to buy food in times of famine was but a further step in the same direction. Domestic slavery was widely practised, and even the Mossi (of modern Burkina Faso), who were never large-scale commercial slave traders, sold slaves to one another.[26] Slavery was a means of production, supplying cultivators, porters and herders.[27]

Slave Trading in the African Interior 1892–1914

The Continuing Trade in Slaves

When the wars waged by the slave raiders were brought to an end, the commerce in slaves continued virtually everywhere in the missions of the White Fathers. In equatorial Africa, the traditional routes taken by the slave traders passed through German East Africa (modern Tanzania) and most of the trade was still oriented in this direction. In 1894, the missionaries noted that many of the "brigands" and slavers in German territory came from Uganda, and four years later a Ugandan was seen at Ndala with four slaves for sale.[28] In Ushirombo, missionaries reported several slaving incidents between 1895 and 1902. In the latter year, they noted that local chiefs were taking a cloth tax from slave traders, instead of handing the culprits over to the Germans. The missionaries denounced the practice, and five traders were immediately arrested and punished at Tabora with twenty-five lashes each. "May this example be followed everywhere," wrote the diarist, "so that vestiges of the slave trade will not fail to disappear from our equatorial regions."[29] Large numbers of slaves were being sold at Msalala in 1898, and two years later, a missionary in Kashozi saw "many slavers in chains" after their capture by the Germans.[30] Even in 1907, a missionary in the same station complained that "slavery still causes us headaches."[31] Slave traders were active in the kingdoms of Rwanda and Burundi, which were then part of German East Africa. The trade was in full swing at Bujumbura in 1898 and the ill-famed Bikari (who massacred the White Fathers at Rumonge in 1881) were also implicated.[32] In Kissaka in 1906, the slave trade was far from abolished. A band of twenty slave merchants was reported by a missionary in the neighbourhood of a Burundi mission in 1907.[33]

It was in Tanganyika Vicariate and the southern end of Upper Congo Vicariate that the slave trade was most openly practised. In the late 1890s slave caravans were still observed in the vicinity of Karema, and bands of *ruga-ruga*, or mercenaries, were carrying off women for sale. Chief Katunka was named as a notorious slave trader and "lake pirate."[34] There were bands of freebooting slavers in Upper Congo, and traders from Goma were dealing in ivory, rubber and slaves at Lukulu in 1906.[35] Wherever Arabs settled, it was noted that slavery continued to flourish. People sold them children to become "soldiers and servants" of the slave trade.[36] It is obvious that the presence of slave traders in a neighbourhood was a continuing incentive to raise money by selling a relative or neighbour to a passing caravan.

Kidnapped—The Story of Alfred Diban

Kidnapping was a time-honoured means of acquiring slaves in the era of the trans-Atlantic trade, but it continued everywhere after the abolition of the sea trade, and as a more discreet alternative to the slave wars of the African interior. A Missionary of Africa at Kupela, in the Mossi kingdom of French Sudan, wrote in 1904: "The slave trade continues—not through razzias, but through isolated kidnappings and the selling or pawning of children for food in time of drought."[37] Bishop Roelens found the buying and selling of children prevalent in Upper Congo in the 1890s and described how small children were seized from the fields when cultivating or herding.[38] Even newly baptized Christians were tempted to kidnap children. In 1898 scandal was caused at Ushirombo when Alphonse Mupipi stole and sold a mission girl. He was forced to return her and do public penance.[39] The story of the centenarian Alfred Simon Diban (c. 1875–1980), hailed today as Burkina Faso's first Christian, is typical. Diban, a Samo, was between sixteen and eighteen years old when he was taken from the fields, where he was looking after the family herds in the 1880s. After a struggle, he was knocked out and gagged. Sold for several bars of salt in a village near Timbuktu, he made three unsuccessful attempts at escape, during one of which he was severely wounded.

He finally managed to make his way to the Niger, where he was picked up by some fishermen. These took him to a nearby camp of the White Fathers. Jean-Marie Garlantézec (1871–1929) brought him to Segu, and Victor Ficheux (1866–1901) took him to Banankuru mission where he was baptized in 1901. Four years later he rejoined his family in Samo and was eventually posted there in 1913, as a catechist at Toma mission.[40]

Colonial Complicity in the Slave Trade

Policy and Practice—Britain and Germany

Colonial administrations inherited a fluid situation and were inevitably compromised from time to time. The British prided themselves on their anti-slavery tradition and forced the sultan of Zanzibar to close the island's slave markets in 1873. The institution of slavery, however, continued. In 1892, the White Fathers reported that twelve slaves had been recaptured from the sultan's boat, among them two school children who took refuge with the fathers at the procure. The sultan, however, succeeded in repossessing and selling the children. "Thus does slavery flourish under the British flag!" was a missionary's bitter comment.[41] Slavery was officially abolished in Uganda in 1896. However, the Protestant chiefs retained their slaves and the buying and selling of slaves continued.[42] The British were more immediately successful in ending slave trading among the Bemba (modern Zambia) in 1905, and in abolishing domestic slavery in Mombasa (modern Kenya) in 1908.[43] An amusing anomaly, however, occurred in 1909, when Andrea, a slave ransomed in Burundi, accompanied a White Father to Uganda and was arrested and imprisoned. He managed to escape from Kampala Fort, but, like the young man in Mark's Gospel (Mark 14:51–52), lost his loin cloth in the process. With great presence of mind, he snatched the Union Jack from its mast and wore it instead.[44]

In German East Africa, slaves from the Congo continued to be absorbed along the trade routes. It was estimated that slaves constituted seventy-five percent of the population of Unyanyembe. In fact, according to Francis Nolan, slavery was nothing less than a form of controlled immigration.[45] The Germans tolerated slavery, fearing that abolition would cause an economic revolution. However, slaves could be freed if they were maltreated, and, after 1905, all children of slaves were legally born free. Freedom could also be bought. In 1900, 150 certificates of freedom were issued, and by 1912, the number had risen to 591. It was left to the British to abolish slavery in the country altogether in 1922.[46]

French Sudan

The administration was committed to anti-slavery measures in French Sudan, but it could only be effectively prohibited in areas where French power was fully established. French administrators inspected and controlled caravans, issuing trade licences for commodities that included "captives." Thus, although the slave trade was officially prohibited, it was in fact authorized and taxed by the administration. Timbuktu remained the biggest slave market in the colony, and in 1897 a caravan of more than one hundred slaves left for the north. French officials even possessed their own slaves at Timbuktu. Attempts were made to stop the trade and prevent slaves leaving the colony, but this proved impossible. So the administration turned a blind eye, while officially prohibiting the trade.[47] Decrees of abolition were issued at various times, but even after 1905 when universal liberation became legally definitive, such decrees were only locally effective, and the possibility of manumission varied in practice. When abolition was decreed at Banankuru in 1907 most of the war captives returned home, but the rest just put as big a distance between themselves and their former masters as possible for fear of reprisals that could include poisoning and magic spells.[48]

The Sahara

In the southern Sahara, which was the immediate destination of the slave caravans from the French Sudan, the French military had no interest in emancipation, and tended to believe that slavery was an economic necessity for the survival of the oases. Charles de Foucauld was aghast at the military's tolerance and complicity. He complained bitterly to Guérin in 1902 and even sent ransomed slaves to Algiers.[49] Guérin's response was pragmatic: de Foucauld was to take no official action in the matter on behalf of the church until the question had been more fully studied. Moreover, the prefect apostolic could not finance the sending of ex-slaves to Algiers. Guérin deplored slavery as a social evil, but, in the climate created by the current anti-clerical legislation, prudence demanded that there be no public denunciations.[50] In any case, slavery was officially abolished in Algeria two years after this exchange.

Ransoming Slaves

A Humanitarian Practice

That the Missionaries of Africa did not have the power to end slave trading by force was proved by the failure of the Armed Brothers of the Sahara, discussed later in the chapter. Their most characteristic response to the problem was the humanitarian practice of ransoming the victims, particularly when they were young children. The practice of ransoming slaves was begun by Cardinal Lavigerie, and he dealt with the subject in considerable detail in his instructions to his missionaries.[51] The diaries and correspondence of the period we are considering, 1892–1914, are filled with references to the ransoming of slaves, and it would be impossible to reproduce all those references here. It is clear that relatively large numbers of slaves were involved. In May 1898, there were already five hundred ransomed children at Karema in German East Africa, and in the following year twenty-six slaves were ransomed at nearby Kirando.[52] Bishop Lechaptois of the Tanganyika vicariate estimated that between 1885 and 1910, 1,804 slaves were ransomed at Karema.[53] At Ushirombo in 1898, runaway slaves were being ransomed every day, and at Lukulu in Upper Congo in 1906, missionaries were ransoming ten slaves a year and feeding thirty-five on a daily basis.[54] Bishop Toulotte, on his journey to French Sudan in 1897, saw sixty children—mostly ransomed slaves—at the two existing stations of Segu and Timbuktu.[55] The missionaries did not have to go out of their way to look for slaves to ransom. Most of them sought asylum at the mission of their own accord. Very occasionally, missionaries would follow a slave caravan to save the small babies or visit a slave market in order to ransom little children. In 1907, for example, missionaries at Lukulu sent their village headman across the Lualaba river to buy little slaves who were known to be very numerous in the area.[56] Ransoms were financed by subsidies from *Propaganda Fide*, and more especially from the French anti-slavery society, but there was a limit to what could be afforded. Bishop Hacquard, who ransomed Mossi captives in 1900 for 30–150 francs each, would not allow his missionaries to buy slaves in the Sahara, where the price ranged from 600–1,000 francs.[57] Ransoms enabled the missionaries to help parents recover kidnapped children or to redeem pawns, when this was possible. Alfred Simon Diban was eventually reunited with his family, as we have already seen. Félix Payete, a Mossi from Kuritenga, near Kupela, was ransomed by White Fathers at Ghardaia in the northern Sahara. He was eventually brought back by the missionaries to his home village in French Sudan.[58]

To the children and young adults ransomed by the White Fathers were added large numbers of liberated slaves, often of very young age, brought to the mission by the colonial administration. When slave traders were caught or rebels conquered, their human merchandise—slaves and war captives—were brought to the fathers to be cared for. This was normal practice for the Germans in East Africa and for the French in the Sudan. In 1902 for example, the French resident at Wagadugu brought thirty-one liberated children to the Missionaries of Africa, some of them as young as four or five years old.[59] In the space of five weeks in 1902 the mission of Wagadugu received more than one liberated slave every other day.[60]

There were a number of ambiguities associated with the ransoming of slaves.[61] The White Fathers were strongly criticized by the British at the coast for "buying" slaves, and the British consul, Sir John Kirk, complained about it to his French opposite number. Where the law against slave trading was enforced, ransoming slaves could even be regarded as illegal. The feeling was that ransoming slaves, so far from solving the problem, contributed to it. The Missionaries of Africa, however, were motivated by compassion and anxious to prevent loss of life, especially among the very young victims who could not survive the hardships of the slave caravan. Moreover, the number they ransomed was relatively insignificant compared to the total number of slaves sold. Acutely aware of the suffering caused by the slave trade and unable to prevent the trade itself, they opted for the next best course of action, which was a rescue operation. Protestant missionaries were divided on the issue. Some regarded ransom as, to all intents and purposes, co-operation in sin. Some also felt that consciences would be more effectively shocked by the refusal to show compassion. Others, like Edward Coode Hore of the London Missionary Society, who knew the extent of the misery caused by slavery, shared the compassionate attitude of the White Fathers, and himself ransomed slaves or received them as gifts. As one author has written, "A great love lay behind the ransom policy."[62] For the White Fathers, it was an important means of demonstrating the love towards Africans which Lavigerie required of his missionaries. As one missionary in Tanganyika Vicariate wrote, after negotiating the ransom of a young slave, "It is moving to see the liberty of someone being disputed for the sake of a few pence, more or less."[63]

Having said that, it must be admitted that the policy could be equivocal in other ways. Lavigerie stressed that ransomed slaves should not be exploited, but treated as sons or brothers.[64] The missionaries were interested in the ex-slaves for themselves and not as a means to an end. They were to be remunerated for their work. Ransom was to be a final liberation, with no prospect of re-selling. Where possible, the ex-slaves were to be immediately or eventually reunited with their families. However, finding their families and places of origin over vast distances was seldom possible. What the freed slaves needed in the first instance was medical care, food and, above all, love. Refuges had to be created for them, orphanages and Christian villages that were safe havens. Not being in their home area, it was usually not possible for the ex-slaves to abscond, and they were very much in the hands of the missionaries, who educated them, taught them trades such as carpentry, masonry, brick-making or tailoring, and who helped arrange their marriages when they reached marriageable age. Slavery conferred a social stigma that was difficult to avoid, and it was not surprising that the children and young people in the mission orphanages and villages should sometimes be called the "slaves of the fathers."[65] Missionaries were equally regarded as a threat by the slave traders, or in competition with them. Misunderstandings of this kind contributed to the disaster at Rumonge, which is described later in the chapter.

Orphanages and Freed Slave Villages

There were many ambiguities concerning the orphanages and villages which the Missionaries of Africa set up. Although it was hoped that some of the ex-slaves would become Christians and even auxiliaries in the task of evangelization in their home area or other parts of Africa, Lavigerie and his missionaries had few illusions. Many ex-slaves were in fact baptized, and some eventually became catechists and teachers. Indeed, the candidates sent to Lavigerie's Malta institute for training as doctor catechists were mostly ransomed slaves. Some of these, like Adrian Atiman, were outstanding. However, Lavigerie's experience of Christian villages in Algeria taught him that they were marginal and could exercise no influence on society.[66] Indeed, the effect of large freed slave villages has even been described as "disruptive."[67] The freed slaves were of course foreigners with little or no experience of family life. Moreover, they did not share the cultural background of the local inhabitants. They were rootless, restless individuals, who could even, on occasion, lapse into savagery.[68] In 1899 ransomed slaves on Ukerewe island in Lake Victoria fought for three days with the mission's catechists and burnt down their house.[69] Freed slaves who became teachers or catechists were notoriously unstable. In 1906, at Mkulwe mission in Tanganyika vicariate, the teachers, who were all ransomed slaves, left in a body, hoping to make money from government employment. Orphanages also proved to be a drag on educational development. It was noteworthy that when they came to an end—as in Uganda, under Bishop Hirth—there was an immediate expansion in the number of schools. One of the reasons why secondary education developed so late in French Sudan was the fact that the anti-clerical colonial administration continued to encourage and even subsidize orphanages, while discouraging mission schools and failing to make a success of its own secular schools. The very first secondary school in the region was the junior seminary of Pabre (Burkina Faso), founded in 1922. With the growth of a local Christian population, it became possible to send orphans to Christian families for foster care. This was already beginning to happen in Hirth's Vicariate of Southern Nyanza in 1906.[70]

The White Fathers had little experience of running orphanages in which children of disparate ages boarded together. Apart from the major problem of discipline among the young ex-slaves, the missionaries were surprised to encounter a problem of homosexuality, even among those who had been baptized.[71] The Missionaries of Africa however had known the junior seminary of St. Eugène in Algiers, and some had taught there. It was not surprising therefore that this model was reproduced in the orphanages of equatorial Africa and French Sudan. A rigorous timetable was introduced at Bukumbi (Southern Nyanza), for example. The children rose at 5:45 a.m. and recited morning prayer. Those who had been baptized then attended one or other of the (private) Masses celebrated by the missionaries, while the non-baptized swept the dormitories and compound, and carried water. Manual work took place from 6:45 until 10:30, when there was a half-hour break followed by catechism at 11 a.m. At 2 p.m. there was a singing class or time for reading, followed by three more hours of manual labor. At 5:30, there was recreation, followed by evening meal and bed after sundown.[72] At Kita mission in French Sudan, "orphans" rebelled against the severity of the missionaries, and there were even complaints to the French administration about lack of care and clothing and insufficient food.[73] Orphanages were discussed at the Leopoldville (Kinshasa) meeting of Catholic Mission Superiors, convoked by Bishop Roelens in 1907. Although there was lively criticism of these institutions, Roelens felt that, in the Congo situation, the *régime* of the orphanages was infinitely preferable to the traditional upbringing of children.[74]

Religious Sisters and Female Orphanages

The White Fathers concentrated at first on boy "orphans" but, as time went on, more and more girls were entrusted to them. This posed a problem until Sisters were available to run female orphanages. The Missionary Sisters of Our Lady of Africa (MSOLA, or "White Sisters") began to arrive in the sub-Saharan missions in the 1890s. Until then, they had operated hospitals, dispensaries and workshops only in North Africa. Bishop Gerboin, at Ushirombo, was the first to bring MSOLA to equatorial Africa in 1893. In 1897, Bishop Toulotte invited them to Kati in French Sudan. Bishop Roelens welcomed them to Upper Congo in the following year, and Bishop Streicher brought them to Uganda in 1899. Running female orphanages was only a part of their work, which included staffing hospitals, and the evangelization, education and promotion of women. African Sisters also played a part in staffing the female orphanages. The first Religious Sisters of St. Peter Claver made their temporary vows at Karema early in 1908, and a novitiate was opened by the MSOLA at Villa Maria in Uganda for the Bannabikira towards the end of the same year. Until sisters were available, female orphanages were run by elderly Christian women, as in the French Sudan, or Christian widows as at Buhonga in Unyanyembe.[75] At Rubaga, Uganda, the remarkable Maria Machtilda Munaku, sister of Saint Noë Mawaggali, began taking care of the girl orphans there in 1886.[76] Her story belongs with those of the women catechists and first women religious described in later chapters. In 1888 she made a private vow of virginity and has been called the first Ugandan religious sister. At Ushirombo (Unyanyembe), the girls' orphanage was run for a time by Paulina, widow of the Hausa doctor-catechist, François Gogé, who was killed in the defence of Rubaga mission in the Ugandan civil war of January 1892.[77]

Liberty Villages

The Christian villages were an outgrowth of the orphanages and of the policy of ransoming slaves. For example, at Ushirombo (Unyanyembe) in 1905, the Christian village contained 192 homesteads, and twenty-two new families emanating from the two orphanages were installed there during the year. In 1880, the colonial authorities started so-called "Liberty Villages" in the French Sudan, with money donated by the French anti-slavery society. There were three such villages in the Segu area when the Missionaries

of Africa arrived (Segu, Banankuru and Patyana). Freed slaves were placed
in the villages as a pool of workers for government forced labour projects.
Inevitably, the inhabitants were dubbed "the district's captives." Bishop
Hacquard told Livinhac that these villages were exceedingly unstable.[78] Not
only did the villagers frequently abscond in order to avoid forced labour,
but the villages lacked structure and organization, and even food was a
problem. The Missionaries of Africa began evangelization in these villages,
and the government entrusted them with responsibility for the villages situated near the mission stations. Understandably, the missionaries preferred
to found their own liberty villages. At Kita, the White Fathers inherited the
liberty village of St. Isidore the Farmer from the departing Spiritans.[79] At
Kupela, the liberty village of St. Leo was started near the mission, and at
Wagadugu, the liberty village of St. Eugene.[80] The MSOLA started a workshop in the latter village, in which cotton-spinning and weaving were taught.
It became renowned throughout the colony and even exhibited artefacts at
Marseilles in 1919.[81]

A few liberty villages survived even to the beginning of World War II, but
most began to disappear with the approach of World War I. In 1913 Bishop
Lemaître was one of the severest critics of the system. He believed that the
orphanages and liberty villages were undermining the family and traditional
society. Raising so-called "orphans" at great expense to be married and
installed in costly villages away from their parental families was reprehen-
sible. Only genuine orphans should be taken and they should be fostered.[82]
Bishop Roelens, in his instructions to the vicariate of Upper Congo of 1920,
was more nuanced. He believed that mission villages were still desirable,
but that orphanages were definitely not a strategy of evangelization, let
alone embryonic seminaries. They were a humanitarian expedient to provide family education where it was lacking.[83]

Traditional Forms of Slavery

Chiefs and Slavery

As long-distance slave trading diminished, traditional forms of local or
domestic slavery gained importance. Slavery and the slave mentality were
deeply embedded in traditional institutions, especially chiefship and polygamous marriage. Throughout the period 1892–1914, chiefs continued to
have retinues of slaves. At Ndala mission in Unyanyembe the local queen
had her own slaves in 1897, and in the following year at Ushirombo a
crowd of slaves took part in the traditional installation of the first Christian
chief of the Basumbwa, Constantine I Makaka.[84] At the same time, another
member of the chiefly family lost eleven of his slaves, acquired originally
from Rumaliza.[85] At Bukoba (Kashozi), the chief was reported as having
many slaves in 1907. They were mostly women who had been bought,
donated, kidnapped, inherited or acquired as the result of a lawsuit.[86] The

same chief claimed a deceased slave's child, who had to be ransomed by the missionaries so that she could continue her preparation for baptism.[87] At Mpimbwe in Tanganyika Vicariate, Chief Kalulu was reported to have re-sold one of his slave concubines in 1907.[88] Chiefs exercised power over the marriages of their slaves and the lives of their offspring. Many kept a pool of slave girls, who could be given in marriage to anyone they wished to favour. Usually, they demanded that a daughter from the marriage be given back to them. This was a sort of "rolling slavery," passing from one generation to the next. When ritual murders accompanied the funeral of a chief or a member of his family, the victims were taken from among his slaves. Thus, Mawaza, an important chief of the Manyema in Congo, was arrested in 1908 for killing a white officer and for having slit the throats of twenty slaves on his brother's grave.[89]

Slavery and Polygamy

Most slaves were essentially female sex-partners, and in some areas it was the first ambition of every young man to acquire a slave concubine. Buying a slave was simpler than undertaking protracted negotiations for a marriage alliance. A man could acquire many such wives to "cultivate" for himself and re-sell them, if necessary. At Mkulwe in Tanganyika Vicariate, the Missionaries of Africa found that small girls aged seven or eight had already been bought and paid for by adult men.[90] This was not the classic plural marriage of African tradition, but a perversion of the institution. It is small wonder that the White Fathers became convinced that polygamy was not merely opposed to the Christian ideal of monogamy and exclusivity in marriage, but that it was linked to immoral practices associated with female slavery.

In French Sudan, missionaries reached a similar conclusion and fought a long-drawn out battle against polygamy and forced marriage. As in East Africa, they gave refuge to a growing number of girls, fleeing their own parents and families. For these girls, becoming a Christian was a passport to freedom and human dignity. The girls were cared for by the sisters and prepared for baptism in the special catechumenate, which became known as the *sixa* (from "sister"). Inevitably, this led to conflicts with parents and chiefs who fought hard to prevent the Christian education of girls and their consequent loss of control over the institutions of marriage. It also led to occasional disputes with the French colonial authorities who tended to cling to an unchanging view of African marriage custom.[91]

The tradition of pawning children has already been mentioned. At Banankuru in 1903, the Missionaries of Africa redeemed pawns that were brought to them and gave them a Christian education.[92] Enslavement was the traditional punishment for certain crimes or forms of anti-social behaviour, especially the unauthorized practice of sorcery or evil magic. At Lukulu in Upper Congo, the chief of Ngoyabondo brought a small girl to the mission in 1909. She had been enslaved along with her mother and uncle, after they had been accused of sorcery.[93] Slavery was part of the larger question of how the Missionaries of Africa related to chiefs and traditional authorities, and the rest of the chapter is concerned with this problem.

Buddu in Uganda

The Concept of the Christian Kingdom

In his detailed instructions to the First Caravan in 1878, Cardinal Lavigerie stressed the importance of winning over chiefs. The conversion of a single chief, he believed, would do more for the advancement of the mission than the conversion of hundreds of isolated individuals.[94] Lavigerie, as a church historian, was fond of citing precedents like the conversion of Constantine in 313 or Clovis, king of the Franks, in 496, and he knew that much of Africa was parcelled up into larger or smaller chiefdoms. In the first place, there were the centralized, interlacustrine kingdoms of Buganda, Toro, Bunyoro, Ankole, Rwanda and Burundi, and secondly the multi-chiefdom societies which lay to the south. Some of their chiefs, like Rumanika, Mirambo and Nyungu-ya-Mawe, were war lords in their own right who had subjugated surrounding rulers. There were also the Afro-Arab slave traders, such as Tippu Tip and Rumaliza. In West Africa, there were the "empires" created by Islamic adventurers, such as Ahmadu and Samory-Toure, and there were multi-chiefdom "pyramids," with a divine king at the summit, such as the Mossi kingdom. Finally, there were societies without chiefs, such as the autonomous villages of the Bobo (modern Burkina Faso), and the Luo (modern Kenya), as well as unstructured pastoralist societies like those of the Masai and the Peuhl. Lavigerie's missionaries were poised to enter a volatile, pre-colonial situation, and he advised them to seek the support of whatever stable rulers could be found.

Lavigerie was aware of the explorer Stanley's eulogy of Mutesa I, *Kabaka* (king) of Buganda, as a potential Christian convert, and his suggestion that (Protestant) missionaries evangelize his kingdom.[95] In 1877 Anglican missionaries of the Church Missionary Society (CMS) arrived in Buganda and were disappointed that Mutesa held them at his capital as a potential source of arms and ammunition, and as levers with the British government against the threat to his independence posed by General Gordon, Governor of Sudan. When three more CMS missionaries entered Buganda in February 1879, following the northern Nile route instead of coming across Lake Victoria, Mutesa was deeply suspicious of their intentions. He welcomed Lavigerie's White Fathers in the same month, on learning that their nationality and religious denomination differed from that of the Protestants.[96]

Mutesa kept both sets of missionaries at court, where they were assimilated into the hierarchical Buganda society and accorded the position of senior chiefs.[97] Although Lavigerie wanted his White Fathers to influence

Mutesa, he was not happy about their polemics with the Church Missionary Society.[98] Protestant missionaries tended to insist on exclusive spheres of influence, and the CMS regarded the White Fathers as intruders. Catholic mission policy accepted no such limitations; indeed, Lavigerie wanted to counteract Protestant influence. However, he had no wish that missionaries of different denominations should tread on each other's toes. In his instructions of 1878, he insisted on a distance of eight to ten kilometres from Protestant stations.[99] In the instructions of 1880, he increased the distance to twenty-five kilometres, having heard of the altercations at Mutesa's court.[100] In reality, the Buganda missionaries had no choice in the matter.

Meanwhile, in his 1879 instructions, Lavigerie elaborated a plan for a "Christian Kingdom." This entailed the identification and empowerment of an African "Constantine," but the (future) cardinal was already sceptical of Mutesa as a possible candidate.[101] In spite of this, the enforced residence of the missionaries at the Buganda capital, which was the only focus for political ambition in the kingdom, began to bear fruit in the emergence of a young Christian elite. When the White Fathers returned to Uganda from exile in 1885, they found that the young Mwanga II, who succeeded Mutesa at the end of 1884, was nervous about both the German activities at the East African coast and the British domination of coastal waters that culminated in the occupation of Mombasa. He was also struggling to achieve absolute power in the kingdom. His nervousness prompted the murder of the Anglican Bishop, James Hannington, who attempted to enter Buganda from the east, and the persecution of Christians as "disobedient subjects" in 1885–1886. The new religion, however, was far from being annihilated, and the martyrdoms were only a first reaction to the ongoing Christian advance.[102]

A Virtual Catholic Kingdom

After the civil war of January 1892 and Mwanga's identification with the Protestant faction, Buddu became the centre of Catholic power. In spite of having been suspected by the British of wanting to set up a rebel kingdom with Mwanga in Buddu, most Catholics showed no hostility towards the Protestant kingdom, even when Mwanga rebelled against the British in 1896 and attempted to rally Buddu to his cause. Although some Catholic chiefs were implicated in the rebellion, they were all excommunicated by the church. At one point the Catholics had even gone so far as to ask Lugard for a British resident.[103] However, they resented the uneven sharing of power.[104] It was in this situation that a "virtual" or "heavenly" Christian kingdom came into existence in Buddu, a paternalistic politico-religious system designed to guarantee the Christian moral order. The Upper Nile Vicariate included two and a half senior chiefdoms of Buganda, while Buddu, in the Vicariate of Nyanza North, was the focus for the remaining five and a half. Bishop Henri Streicher (1863–1952) made Villa

Maria, the principal mission station of Buddu, which he himself had founded, his headquarters.[105]

Until Streicher was appointed and could consolidate his rule, the Catholic Church in Buddu was organized by the African laity in the persons of the officially appointed Catholic chiefs. These chiefs, most of whom had been royal pages in their youth, became catechists in the tradition of the martyrs. They sent their sons and other trusted followers to be instructed by the missionaries as auxiliaries in the work of evangelization. The chiefs built the mission stations, copying the ground plan of the traditional royal palace, with the church taking the place of the king's house, surrounded by "audience halls" for the instruction of catechumens, and duplicating the various royal departments.[106] The chiefs' houses surrounded the "mission-palace." At Villa Maria, there were three hundred houses, and at Bikira Mission two hundred. All the traditional reverence for the Buganda kingship was transferred to the missionaries and especially the bishop, as earthly representatives of the divine King of Kings. Sons and daughters of chiefs were placed in the "king's service," as seminarians and religious novices, in the tradition of the former royal pages and servants. Even chiefs knelt to greet the White Fathers, as they had formerly greeted the *Kabaka*. Streicher himself posed for the photographer enthroned on the royal leopard skin rug, or wearing the black Arab *joho* over his white cassock (*gandoura*, or *kanzu*) like the *Kabaka*, and the royal princes or officials.[107]

By 1896, many chiefs had begun to rebel against missionary discipline and some joined Mwanga's revolt against the British.[108] Streicher declared that there was now less need for the help of these chiefs and he attempted to control them through a "pious association of chiefs" under the "flag of the Sacred Heart." This signalled a clericalization of the church in Buddu, with the initiative passing to Streicher and the missionaries.[109] It also entailed the gradual abandonment of the Catholic Kingdom idea. The principal Catholic chiefs held a meeting with the missionaries at Rubaga in 1899, and, as late as 1908, conferences were given to more than fifty Catholic chiefs at Villa Maria.[110]

In the centralized kingdom of Buganda, the important chiefs were appointed by the king or his regents, and it was a case of *cujus regio, ejus religio*. The chief saw it as his duty to promote among his subjects the form of Christianity to which he himself subscribed. Thus when Kamswaga of Koki returned as a Protestant from Kampala in 1894, many Catholics in his chiefdom surrendered their Catholic medals and declared "We must pray where the king prays."[111] The Protestants went so far as to ordain large numbers of chiefs as deacons and priests, although they received little or no training for ministry. In general, chiefs who became Protestants tried to impose uniformity on their subjects, and used their religious denomination as a means to consolidate their political power. The presence of Catholics in the chiefdom could even be interpreted as a rebellion against their authority.

Catholics, however, with far bigger numbers, had a vested interest in religious freedom. Some Catholic chiefs actively assisted catechists in their chiefdom, offering them a lodging and a plot for cultivation, and even building a chapel for them. Others merely welcomed catechists who were supported by the mission.[112] In the early days, some Catholic chiefs took it upon themselves to act as catechists, giving instructions and leading prayer. Catholic chiefs were encouraged to evangelize villages where Protestants were already numerous, and catechists were sent to contact chiefs in provinces assigned to the Anglicans and to make converts in their villages, especially those of Bulemezi, Singo and Kyaddondo. In 1897, there were seventy such frontline catechists in these areas.[113] When a Catholic mission station was founded in Protestant Gayaza in 1908, the chief of the province tried to obstruct the missionaries and their catechists, believing in common with many Anglicans that their aim was political.[114]

In all the Ugandan kingdoms the king and most of the royal family became Anglicans. Political opportunists tended to become Protestants and the dissidents and peasant classes, Catholics.[115] However, this pattern was repeatedly broken. Although Protestant rulers felt too politically insecure to encourage religious freedom, some of their chiefs did become Catholics, and those who did not were unable to prevent their subjects from doing so.

The Kingdoms of Rwanda and Burundi

Aristocrats and Serfs

As vicar apostolic of Nyanza South, Jean-Joseph Hirth was impressed by the kingdom of Rwanda, whose *Mwami* or divine king, Yuhi V Musinga, was the absolute ruler of two million subjects. Rwanda lay in Hirth's vicariate, and he saw it as a more favourable mission field than the multi-chiefdom societies, with their scattered populations, that surrounded the southern and western shores of Lake Victoria. Unlike Buganda, Rwanda had not been traumatized by civil and religious wars, and there were as yet no Protestant missionaries in the kingdom. A dense population ruled by an absolute sovereign—could not this be the African Christian Kingdom of Lavigerie's dream?[116] The German administration penetrated and occupied Rwanda in the 1890s, and, with its blessing, Hirth sent his first caravan of missionaries, catechists and porters in December 1899. The White Fathers were allowed to found a mission on the Save plateau, five hours' march from the Tutsi royal capital at Nyanza. In fact, the kingdom of Rwanda was not as centralized and unified as that of Buganda. Its structure was largely the result of Kigeri IV Rwabugiri's conquests in 1860–1895, and in 1899 the Tutsi occupation of the country was far from complete. Besides internal rivalries among themselves, the Tutsi pastoralists were in the process of displacing the monarchies of the agricultural Hutu whose lands they continued to pillage, and on whose sub-chiefs they imposed quasi-feudal rights in cattle. This legal system was itself in a state of flux. There were also turbulent Hutu (or Hutu-related) chiefs on the Uganda border, who were not yet fully subjugated by the Tutsi. The German administrators of the country found it expedient to work with the Tutsi and to help them consolidate their power over the Hutu, who constituted more than eighty percent of the population. Musinga, king of Rwanda, had no aspiration to become another Constantine. He and the Tutsi pastoralist aristocracy remained aloof and impervious to Christian evangelization until the "tornado" of conversions that took place in the 1920s.[117] Instead, the missionaries—often in the face of Tutsi opposition—addressed the subservient Hutu peasants, the poor, orphans, abandoned children and ransomed slaves.[118] There was no top-down movement of evangelization in the Rwandan kingdom. When the Tutsi eventually turned to Christianity, substantial numbers of Hutu had already become Christian, and the Tutsi conversion sowed seeds of ethnic conflict in the church itself.

In the meantime, the Missionaries of Africa were in the ambiguous position of being accepted by the Tutsi as emissaries of the Germans, while appearing also as rival patrons of the Hutu peasants and the poor. The Germans, for their part, had an ambivalent attitude towards the missionaries. They were jealous of their influence with the ordinary people, and, at the same time, expected their support in handling the king and chiefs. They pressured the king to accept a mission station at Kabgayi in the centre of Tutsi country and a school at court, and they allowed the White Fathers to settle in other areas which they found difficult to administer.[119]

The Murder of Paulin Loupias

Although the murder of Paulin Loupias (1872–1910) at Rwaza on April 1st 1910 was untypical, it nevertheless illustrates the delicacy of the missionaries' position in Rwanda, and the fact that their presence was being used to further the progress of German control. Loupias was superior at Rwaza mission on the northern border. Lukara, the rebel Hutu chief of Barashi, had been deposed by King Musinga, who sent a Tutsi chief to communicate the unwelcome decision. The envoy brought a letter from Musinga asking Loupias to protect him, and accompany him to face Lukara. Loupias was reluctant to go, but realized that to refuse the king was dangerous. The following day he set out with the envoy, accompanied by four dependable Christians, one of whom had a rifle. Lukara surrounded by his warriors refused to listen to the envoy, or to other complaints brought against him by the Tutsi, and made as if to leave the meeting. Loupias tried to persuade him to stay. With one hand he took the rifle from his companion, and with the other clutched the chief's toga. The gesture, which was interpreted as an attempt to kill the chief, prompted his warriors to let loose a shower of spears, one of which struck Loupias in the forehead and entered the brain. Lukara and his men fled the scene, and the dying Loupias was carried back to Rwaza mission. He was the first European to be killed in Rwanda, and the Germans, fearing another Maji-Maji rising, arrived several days later to make a show of force against Lukara.[120]

There was a sequel in the following year. German officers, with one hundred native soldiers and three thousand Tutsi warriors, stormed Lukara's hiding place, captured him and took him to Ruhengeri to be tried and hanged. Two Missionaries of Africa were obliged to witness the proceedings. After the trial, Lukara was taken in chains to the gallows by an armed escort. Suddenly, the prisoner seized the sergeant's machete and drove it into his back. He was shot on the spot and, with this final act of defiance, entered the realms of Rwandan legend.[121]

Burundi

The kingdom of Burundi was similar in structure to that of Rwanda, with a majority Hutu population under a Tutsi monarchy, and a substratum of chiefs jealous of their authority. After an early period of violence and uncertainty, in which the White Fathers opened and closed several mission stations, the political situation in Burundi became more stable than that in Rwanda. In 1906, Kisabo became king, having been helped by the Germans to achieve effective paramountcy. The German resident at Bujumbura expected the Missionaries of Africa to help him counsel and control the king, while co-operating with him and upholding his authority.[122] By 1912, when Burundi was detached from the Vicariate Apostolic of Unyanyembe and joined with Rwanda to form the Kivu Vicariate, six mission stations had been founded. After World War I, when the Belgians replaced the Germans as administrators, Burundi was again detached from Kivu in 1922 with Julien Gorju (1868–1942) as "Vicar Apostolic of Urundi." Gorju noted that the Tutsi were still uninterested in Christianity, and that the Belgians had the unenviable task of supporting Tutsi authority, while attempting to curb their abuse of the Hutu.[123]

The Pyramid Kingdom of the Mossi

The "New Abyssinia"

Bishop Hacquard made an exploratory journey into the Mossi Kingdom of French Sudan in 1899, and returned in the following year to make a foundation there, as well as in the neighbouring kingdom of Fada N'gourma. In contrast to the confused political situation of the Bambara, Malinke and Songhay regions, the Mossi Kingdom appeared to Hacquard an oasis of calm and good order. It possessed a hierarchical authority structure. Its homesteads and villages were neat and clean, with an abundance of livestock and food reserves. Moreover, Islam was virtually absent. Hacquard's ambition, following Lavigerie's idea, was to create a Christian kingdom like that of Ethiopia.[124] "The Mossi," he wrote, "must become the Abyssinia of our Sudanese empire."[125] The kingdom was a pyramid, with a divine king, the Mogho (or Moro) Naba at the summit. He was, in the words of Hacquard, a "*personnage fêtiche*," a ritual figure, who held the protective talismans of the kingdom, and in whom the talismanic power resided.[126] The Mogho Naba was also the focus of a solar cult, performing ceremonies at sunrise and sunset.[127] However, there was no state religion as such. The whole country lay under the authority of the Mogho Naba, who ruled much of it directly. In addition, there were five great Nabas who ruled their provinces more or less independently. Within the provinces were further subdivisions or cantons, which were rationalized by the French administration and which were ruled by lesser Nabas.[128] At every level, the Naba had an advisory council.

The Mossi kingdom was conquered in 1896–1897 by Captain Paul Voulet, whose name is still remembered in West Africa as a byword for sadism and brutality. Voulet drove the reigning Mogho Naba Wobgo into exile in British territory, and installed his brother Sigri in his place. He then carried out the exemplary executions of prominent people, whom he suspected of being under the ex-Mogho Naba's influence, and defeated and killed another Naba whose pretensions threatened to divide the kingdom. Finally, he negotiated with the British the ending of an incipient civil war. The Mossi were thus conquered by superior weaponry and through their own dynastic and political rivalries.[129] Hacquard deplored Voulet's reign of terror, and wrote to his sister saying that nothing could justify it.[130] However, on his first journey in 1899, he met the new Mogho Naba at Wagadugu, and won approval from the French military by celebrating a Requiem Mass for an officer who had been killed in a skirmish with the Mossi. Hacquard realized at once that the Mogho Naba was not likely to become a catechumen, let alone an African Clovis. He did not nourish any ambition to Christianize the political structure of the kingdom, but simply welcomed it as a framework within which the evangelization of individuals and villages could take place. He and his missionaries were also prepared to be "re-invented" according to Mossi categories, as experts who made rain and offered sacrifices.

When Hacquard returned in 1900 with missionaries for the Mossi, he decided against an immediate foundation in Wagadugu itself. In a letter to a friend, he explained his reasons. The French resident there, a Captain Amman, had no confidence in the Mogho Naba whose political power was being progressively eroded. Hacquard would have had to seek the Mogho Naba's protection, and would thereby have alienated the resident. The mission would have been "between the hammer and the anvil."[131] He therefore sent his missionaries to the independent Naba of Kupela, while he himself went on to found the short-lived mission of Fada N'Gourma in Upper Dahomey. Kupela was 150 kilometres from the French fort at Wagadugu, but enjoyed the protection of a nearby French military detachment. On June

21st 1901, with the co-operation of a more benevolent military resident, a second group of White Fathers, led by Guillaume Templier (1865–1906), inaugurated the mission station of Wagadugu itself.

The Missionaries of Africa still needed the good will of the Nabas, who on more than one occasion were jealous of the missionaries' growing influence with the people. At Kupela in 1905, the fathers and their Christians suffered a persecution at the hands of the local Naba which lasted ten months. The chief waged a violent campaign against schoolchildren and catechumens, and even on one occasion threatened to position soldiers at the mission to shoot anyone wearing a medal around their neck. In fact, the attempt to make the people boycott the mission was counter-productive, and more catechumens were enrolled. At length, the Naba capitulated and gave permission for Sunday catechism and the visits of the missionaries to the villages.[132]

The White Fathers' closeness to the people benefited the French during the Mossi revolt of January 1908. The revolt was led by a *marabout*, who planned to massacre all whites and install a pretender as Mogho Naba. Wagadugu was partially evacuated and armed guards were posted at the mission. Luckily for the French, the *marabout* was killed in a skirmish early in the rebellion. The French administrator, a freemason named Carrier, asked the missionaries to find a trustworthy political advisor and an interpreter for negotiations with the rebels. As a result, the revolt failed and the ringleaders were arrested and imprisoned.

Multi-Chiefdom Societies

German East Africa

In the so-called multi-chiefdom societies of German East Africa, the Missionaries of Africa had to deal with relatively insignificant local rulers who were being transformed into agents of the colonial administration. The White Fathers were regarded as a "third political force," but they never received the full endorsement of the government or the full confidence of the chiefs.[133] Tensions arising from the triangular relationship of the chiefs, the German administration and the missionaries were perennial. The White Fathers depended on the good will of the local chief to set up their mission stations and to evangelize the chief's subjects. Missionaries were welcomed by the chiefs when the latter felt they could gain some advantage from the proximity of the missionaries. On occasion, the chiefs denounced the missionaries to the Germans for infringing their prerogatives or undermining their authority in matters of taxation and forced labour, but more frequently it was the missionaries who denounced the chiefs, or who intervened with the Germans in succession disputes or on behalf of rulers threatened with dismissal.

In the Vicariate Apostolic of Nyanza South, the chiefs on the shores and islands of Lake Victoria tended to be minor despots. "We are afraid of the chief," the people told the White Fathers at Kashozi in 1894, "He does not want us to pray."[134] In 1898 the chief's son, Kartasigwa, burned the Christian villages, and the missionaries reported him to the Germans. Bishop Hirth interceded for him and he was pardoned. The chief, himself, however, remained hostile, and in 1903 Christians were beaten "because the chief does not pray."[135] It was only when the advantages of literacy were understood that the chiefs in the Kashozi area evinced "a frenzy for reading and writing," and encouraged attendance at the mission school.[136] On Ukerewe Island, the chief denounced the missionaries to the Germans and embarked on "an unheard of persecution."[137] Eventually, the missionaries supported a Christian candidate for chief, who was successfully appointed in 1910. Often the chiefs appeared to be on good terms with the White Fathers on the surface, but they wanted to keep their people, body and soul, in their own hands. The mission, they felt, was "stealing" their country from them.[138]

In the Vicariate Apostolic of Unyanyembe, the Sumbwa chiefs welcomed Bishop Gerboin to Ushirombo in 1891 to provide a protective umbrella against the invading Ngoni. The German administration at Tabora was too far away to give effective assistance. The mission station and Christian village were constructed on a scale not seen elsewhere in the region. Physically and psychologically, they overshadowed the local chief and his headquarters. The Missionaries of Africa were masters of the country and Bishop Gerboin was *de facto* king. In this situation, a Christian kingdom emerged, with Robert Munesi and Constantine Makaka as its first baptized chiefs. At Msalala, Chief Hwimu, on the brink of a local war, invited the missionaries in 1893 to give him material and moral support, but the relationship deteriorated and Bishop Gerboin denounced the disaffected chiefs of the area to Tabora. By 1905, Hwimu was openly hostile, ordering the people not to sell goats to the mission. He was rebuked by a Catholic German officer and thirty goats miraculously appeared at the mission on the same day. Two years later, the White Fathers secured the removal of the hostile Chief Mgobole, who was paraded by the Germans around his chiefdom in chains, to identify the people he had robbed and driven from their homes.[139]

At Ndala mission, founded by the White Fathers in 1896, Queen Matolu had less authority than most other chiefs. Moreover, she needed the missionaries to help her maintain order in her chiefdom and to keep her heterogeneous population together. Ndala was strategically placed on the caravan routes in the vicinity of Tabora, and both mission and chiefdom prospered. At Iraqw (Iraku) in the far east of the vicariate, the Missionaries of Africa received a frigid reception in 1909. Chief Ishara placed them in quarantine and the new mission was deserted by the local people. At length, the Germans advised the missionaries to move the mission to another chiefdom.

When the Catholic chief of Ukerewe, King Gabriel Mutehengerwa, was appointed, he was solemnly blessed in the mission church. At the altar, he was asked: "From whom have you received the dignity of kingship?" And he replied: "I have received the dignity of kingship from God." "Why have you received this dignity?" "That I may rule my people with justice and so care for them that they may gain heaven . . ."[140] The ceremony expressed, albeit on a small scale, Lavigerie's ideal of the Christian kingdom, but, in the first quarter of the twentieth century, the role of the colonial power could not be ignored. The Christian Kingdom of Ushirombo was ultimately a failure. Although it flickered into life again in 1914, and Bishop Henri Léonard (1869–1953) installed the new king Mpipi in a church ceremony, like that of Ukerewe, Mpipi fell foul of the British authorities, was dismissed by them and flogged on the church steps in view of a cheering crowd of his own subjects. By that time, traditional chiefs, whether Christian or not, were fast becoming an anachronism.[141]

Armed Auxiliaries and the Theocratic Mission State

Corporal Punishment

In 1878 Lavigerie was acutely aware that he was sending his missionaries into a violent and unstable region with no immediate prospect of colonial "pacification." The very journey into the interior of equatorial Africa held its dangers. The first caravan of White Fathers had been attacked on August 30th 1878 in the Lake Chaya area by sixty of Nyungu-ya-Mawe's *ruga-ruga* (professional warriors), who made off with three bales of cloth and the contents of some twenty other loads.[142] The White Fathers were lucky on that occasion. There was also the problem of the discipline and defence of missionary caravans, as well as the maintenance of law and order in mission stations and Christian villages. Siméon Lourdel had been shocked to witness the public flogging of an absconding soldier in July 1878.[143] This was a commonplace of African travel and exploration. In his manual for the traveller in "wild countries," Francis Galton, Honorary Secretary of the Royal Geographical Society, laid down the principles and scale of such punishments.[144] Lavigerie regarded the occasional corporal punishment of adults as a necessary evil in the circumstances, but he strictly forbade his missionaries to carry out such sentences themselves.[145] Indeed, he had deprived a missionary sister of Eucharistic communion for two weeks for having beaten a young woman in one of the Algerian Christian villages in 1874.[146]

The White Fathers generally shared Lavigerie's views on this subject. For example, when the German imperialist Carl Peters was accused in 1906 of brutal floggings, he was strongly condemned by a German White Father, who nevertheless believed that moderate punishment and "striking arguments" were necessary in Africa.[147] Such punishment was, in fact, traditional. At Bukumbi mission, situated on the southern shore of Lake Victoria, young men and women from the orphanage were settled in a Christian village where the missionaries were occasionally obliged to cope with criminal behaviour. There was no local authority available, and in the ten-year period between 1883 and 1892, the year when German administration began to be effective, corporal punishment was ordered on only seven occasions.[148] This was certainly far from excessive. Nor was it only Catholic missionaries who were confronted with this problem. In 1898, the London Missionary Society was obliged to prohibit its missionaries in Bembaland (Zambia) from "taking any responsibility in passing sentences or administering punishment," after a missionary had complained of "the abominable practice of whipping natives."[149]

The Papal Zouaves

Lavigerie felt that some kind of Catholic army was necessary to protect missionary caravans, organize the defence of mission stations and strengthen the position of a possible Catholic prince. He even went further and suggested that, if no African prince was forthcoming, "a brave, Christian European" soldier could fulfil that role and organize a Catholic state in the heart of pre-colonial Africa.[150] He therefore set about recruiting armed auxiliaries.[151] Two Scotsmen, Oswald and Stewart, answered the advertisement he placed in *The Tablet*, and accompanied the White Fathers' second caravan in 1879. Oswald was repatriated after a hunting accident and Stewart, at the southern end of Lake Victoria, found he had nothing to do. A group of nineteen former papal Zouaves was prepared in Algiers. Eight of these—French, Belgian and Dutch by nationality—were ready to join the third caravan in 1880. Among them was the renowned Leopold Joubert (1842–1927). He and two others went to Lake Tanganyika. The other six were concentrated at the short-lived mission station of Mdaburu on the Ugogo border in 1881–1882, after a coast man, Mwenye Mtwana, had established a fort there with the blessing of the Sultan of Zanzibar's, and had ousted Nyungu-ya-Mawe's puppet ruler with the help of two European expeditions. It was a precarious situation, with Nyungu's warriors still counter-attacking.[152]

The Rumonge Incident

The armed auxiliaries did not prevent the murder of Brother Max Blum (1847–1880), in a party travelling to Lake Victoria and Buganda in 1880, nor yet the ugly incident at Rumonge Mission at the northern end of Lake Tanganyika in 1881. On this occasion, the missionaries, one of whom had himself been a papal Zouave and afterwards fought in the Franco-Prussian War (Théophile Dromaux, 1849–1909), were involved in a show of force with the Bikari over the abduction of a ransomed slave. The Bikari were well known for their warlike propensity and had shown hostility towards Stanley and Livingstone during their joint exploration of Lake Tanganyika in 1872.[153]

Years later, before he died, Brother Jerome Baumeister (1831–1898) unburdened his conscience about the incident in a long letter to Livinhac, the Superior General. His story differs substantially from the official "sanitized" accounts. Two missionaries and an armed auxiliary attempted to scare the attacking Bikari with rifle shots. This provoked a fire fight in which eight Bikari were killed. The missionaries foolishly followed the retreating Bikari who easily ambushed them, killing the two White Fathers, Toussaint Deniaud (1847–1881) and Joseph Augier (1851–1881), and the auxiliary Félix D'Hoop. Jerome praised Augier as a soldier, but not "as a priest."[154] Lavigerie thereafter forbade his missionaries to bear arms and to fire a shot even in self-defence. He declared that those at Rumonge had been "not apostles, but anti-apostles."[155] Two other armed auxiliaries died, and, while Joubert and Visser remained another year in the Tanganyika area, all the others went home. The experiment had not been a success. The armed auxiliaries were adventurers, not missionaries, and many White Fathers distrusted them as untrained, uncommitted and inexperienced lay men.[156]

Mission City States—Mpala

After the recognition of the Congo Free State in 1884, Leopold II's African International Association withdrew from its stations of Karema and Mpala on the eastern and western shores of Lake Tanganyika. The king offered them to Lavigerie, who immediately sent missionaries to occupy them in 1885. In both places, the White Fathers inherited a political, and in the case of Mpala a war situation from the Congolese agent, Captain Emile Storms (1846–1918). In July 1885, Auguste Moncet (1849–1889) and Isaac Moinet (1849–1908) took over Mpala. They found an immense *tembe*, or flat-roofed, square fort of sun-dried brick, sixteen feet high, built on a promontory in the lake, and surrounded by rows of houses. Around Mpala was a confederation of villages extending over three thousand square kilometres. These counted on the protection of the fort. Storms handed over stores consisting of seventy-seven rifles, seven barrels and ten boxes of gunpowder, as well as stocks of lead, copper wire, cloth, cowries and beads. Twenty-five soldiers were left to guard the fort, together with rations to feed them. Storms then departed to induct Jean Randabel (1852–1905) and Gerard Mertz (1909–1850) into Karema (Fort Leopold) on the other side of the lake. Here the White Fathers found another *tembe* in the form of an irregular hexagon, with a storied residence in the centre, situated on a small hill in the midst of a vast plain abandoned by the lake. After making an inventory of stores, Captain Storms departed with a caravan of seven hundred people, leaving ninety men, women and children, and thirty Remington rifles. Unlike Mpala, peace reigned at Karema for the time being, and the local villages were situated at some distance from the fort.

Joubert had been occupied in fortifying and organizing the defence of Mulwewa and Kibanga missions, but these were eventually both abandoned after the acquisition of Mpala and Karema. He went back to France in 1885, but was persuaded by Lavigerie to return and police Mpala and its dependencies, administering justice, preserving law and order and organizing defence against Rumaliza's slave-raiding activities northwest of the lake. He was to defend this "little kingdom" without necessarily consulting the missionaries.[157] He returned in 1886. Joubert was a man of deep faith and an experienced soldier, who was in Lavigerie's eyes the ideal leader of a Christian kingdom. As we have seen, he was to live, marry and die in the church's service in Africa.[158] While Lavigerie conducted his anti-slavery campaign in 1888 in the capitals of Europe, Leopold was organizing his Congo Free State. As we have already seen, he hired the services of the notorious slave trader, Tippu Tip, as governor at Stanley Falls (Kisangani) in 1887. Technically therefore, Tippu Tip was Joubert's superior. However, Tippu departed from the scene in 1890, leaving the field to Joubert's foe, Rumaliza.

At Mpala, barely a month after his arrival, Moinet was faced with an embarrassing punitive raid by a party of mission *ruga-ruga*, who murdered a farmer and captured four slaves. The culprits were punished with a flogging. Throughout 1886 a series of cases were heard and punishments decreed by Moinet.[159] Joubert arrived in May 1887 and took over the civil administration, presiding over the judicial cases. Flogging was decreed for manslaughter, for administering the poison ordeal, for seduction and adultery. Capital punishment was reserved for murder and the theft of firearms. Joubert, with two missionary assessors, passed the sentence of death on a fire-arms thief. For priests to impose a death sentence was contrary to Catholic canon law. Lavigerie was displeased and decreed the removal of Moinet from Mpala.[160] Until the arrival of the anti-slavery expeditions which followed upon Lavigerie's campaign, Joubert was left on his own, with the small army he had trained, to fight Rumaliza and his lieutenants. As we have seen, from 1889–1891 he battled on land and lake with the slavers Mohamadi, Katele and Rajabu.

Among the White Fathers there was a growing feeling that Joubert should not exercise civil power or indulge in military activities in an area now claimed by a European power, but in the circumstances, Leopold II had no choice but to tolerate Joubert's informal command. The position was regularized by making him a citizen of the Congo and appointing him anti-slavery commander. Joubert accepted the status reluctantly, but flatly refused to acknowledge either Tippu Tip as his superior, or the authority of the Belgian anti-slavery committee, which was a cover for Leopold's colonial activities in the Congo.[161]

Mission City States—Baudouinville and the Theocracy of Roelens

In the midst of the hostilities around Lake Tanganyika, Victor Roelens (1858–1947) arrived as administrator of the Upper Congo mission in 1892 and started missionary work at Joubert's village of Mrumbi. In the following year, he founded the new station of Baudouinville (the modern Moba) on the lake, a mile or two from Mrumbi, for refugees from the slave raids.

Baudouinville became a large and flourishing town, a virtually independent mission city-state like Mpala, and the centre of the Upper Congo Vicariate of which Roelens became the bishop in 1897. By 1911, there were around two thousand inhabitants at the station, which effectively controlled a further twenty-seven thousand people in the immediate neighbourhood.[162] Roelens wrote exultantly to Livinhac: "This colony should constitute a small republic and I will be its president. All temporal and spiritual matters must be regulated for the greater well-being of souls . . . Non-Christians and Christians alike are subject to the laws of our little colony."[163] Roelens favoured strong-arm methods and his favourite Arab proverb (learned in North Africa) was: "The rod was born in paradise."[164]

Joubert was now only allowed to handle minor cases. Serious offenders had to be sent on to the Belgian station of Mtowa for sentencing. Thus, in October 1896, he sent a man accused of murder to be executed at Mtowa.[165] Missionaries found that European justice was slow and unsatisfactory, with malefactors often going free.[166] However, the peace which followed the retreat of Rumaliza did not last long. In 1896, the mutiny of the Congolese *Force Publique* brought more conflicts to the Upper Congo region. In November 1896 Joubert was forced once more to take the field.[167] And in spite of widespread defeat and surrender, the mutiny smouldered on until 1907.[168]

Roelens extended his political sway to the whole area that lay between Mpala, Baudouinville and Lusaka (Upper Congo), and ruled this triangle with little or no reference to the Congolese administration.[169] The Congo's foreign minister, Baron van Eetvelde, was not happy about Roelens' vicariate being called "Upper Congo" and thought it should be called "Western Tanganyika"; however, he granted the bishop an extraordinary concession of five thousand hectares of land at Baudouinville. This land was never surveyed, but it was a symbolic acknowledgement of Roelens' private province and of its limits. Roelens, notwithstanding, was eager to extend his civil authority to other regions of his vicariate, in particular to Manyema and Urua, where there was nothing but "the anarchy that reigns everywhere among Africans."[170] Roelens obtained from Brussels the free transport of goods and materials to his new mission station in Manyema, but he was not allowed to extend his political power beyond the triangle.

Within the triangle, the Congo Free State exercised no authority whatsoever. Besides enjoying exemption from all taxes, Roelens minted his own currency, called *pesa*, a coinage of zinc that could be exchanged in the mission shops. He owned all the available lake transport, and he presided over a system of justice, with its own police, courts and prisons. All the roads, bridges and hospitals were built by Roelens and belonged to the mission. The African population within the triangle enjoyed a standard of living superior to that found anywhere else in the Congo, and was completely devoted to the mission. They had no experience of the Congo Free State or its administration. The triangle was the proverbial state within a state. In 1907, however, new legislation in the Congo deprived Roelens of his police force.

Finally in 1914, Roelens clashed again with the minister of colonies over his private currency. The minister was Jules Renkin, who was briefly prime minister of Belgium shortly before the Second World War. The Congo Free State had belatedly begun minting its own money in 1909, and Roelens was asked in 1911 to abolish the *pesa*. He argued that the official money was of no use to the people in his area of jurisdiction, so long as there was no outside commerce. Moreover, he claimed that for his missionaries to handle real money would flout canon law. It was not until Renkin had recourse to *Propaganda Fide* in Rome that the dispute ended and the *pesa* was eventually superseded.

The visitations carried out by the White Fathers were also evidence of Roelens' ruthless regime in the triangle. When the regional visitor, Mathurin Guillemé (1859–1942), visited Baudouinville in 1905, he found that there was too much corporal punishment and that too many fines were being imposed.[171] At Mpala it was the same story. Fines and punishments were being imposed on the inhabitants of the plain, and the whipping of women, which even the government had abolished, was being practised.[172] Two years later, at Baudouinville in 1907, Guillemé found no improvement in the matter of corporal punishment.[173] However, in 1920, by which time his theocracy had been dismantled, Roelens published his *Instructions for Missionaries*, in which he strongly forbade such punishments, despite his earlier draconian predilections. Missionaries were not to execute justice, and criminals were to be handed over to the local chiefs. Even these were forbidden to whip women and children. School teachers also were forbidden to beat, bind or lock up their children, but the incorrigibles were to be sent to the superior for a "paternal correction."[174] In Nyanza South, Bishop Hirth's regulations for the apostolic school at Rubya were altogether modern by comparison. Hirth forbade all forms of exterior punishment, humiliation and ridicule.[175]

Mission City States—Karema

By comparison with Upper Congo, Karema on the eastern side of Lake Tanganyika was a paradise. The slave raiders operated at a considerable distance from the mission, and Karema, in fact, became a haven for refugees from the famine and rapine that raged across the lake. On the whole, civil power was exercised somewhat leniently. For example, a woman who strangled her little daughter and cast the blame on a neighbour was merely given an exemplary caning.[176] Adolphe Lechaptois (1852–1919) was appointed vicar apostolic of Tanganyika in 1891. In the following year he appointed Joseph Dupont (1850–1930) superior of Karema.

Dupont immediately set about rebuilding and fortifying the mission station, including a stone-built "castle" that was the admiration of visiting Europeans.[177] Dupont's civil authority was recognized by the German officer at Ujiji, and he played a part in suppressing the local slave raiders, while securing the goodwill of the chiefs, some of whom were appointed by him. Under Dupont, the execution of justice escalated somewhat. A man who murdered his wife in November 1893 was handed over to a council of elders who promptly sentenced him to death. The missionaries obtained a stay of execution until the unhappy man had been instructed and baptized.[178] As the mission diarist explained, "in this country there are no official police, no prisons, no homes for the criminally insane."[179] This exercise of civil power, however, was shortly afterwards surrendered to the Germans, who established a colonial administration in their territory sooner than did the Belgians in the Congo Free State. Some of the chiefs became Christians, and Adolphina, sister of King Kapufi of Ufipa, became the first religious of the vicariate. When Kapufi himself began to show a lack of fervour in 1900, a missionary exclaimed: "We must hope that Divine Providence will not allow any shadow of separation between Church and State in Ufipa!"[180]

Bishop-King of the Brigands

Until their defeat by the Germans on the East African border, the warlike Bemba in the north of present day Zambia (then Northern Rhodesia) effectively blocked any approach to the peoples further south. In 1891 Lechaptois had been named administrator of the vast Nyasa Mission, its only station being Mambwe at the southern tip of Lake Tanganyika. As we have seen, with the encouragement of Cardinal Ledochowski, Prefect of *Propaganda Fide*, and after an invitation from the Bemba chief Makasa, it was decided to close Mambwe and send Dupont to Makasa's as superior of Nyasa, thereby starting the evangelization of the Bemba.[181]

We have already noted that Dupont founded Kayambi Mission at Makasa's and went on to become the first vicar apostolic of Nyasa in 1897. After protracted negotiations with the effective Bemba paramount, Mwamba, chief of Ituna, a mission station was eventually established in the Bemba heartland at Chilubula in 1899. Mwamba died in the previous year, confiding to Dupont that he wanted him to inherit his chiefdom. Kayambi Mission Diary states tersely: "We receive a letter from Monseigneur. Mwamba is dead and Monseigneur is King of Ituna."[182] Dupont, in characteristic style, made the most of his chiefly status, declaring that he was the inheritor of the dead chief's widows and father of their children. Probably, Mwamba had merely intended Dupont to be the interim regent and protector of his chiefdom, until an African successor could be installed without the customary bloodshed and upheaval. This was, in fact, what happened. Bembaland lay in Northern Rhodesia (Zambia), the sphere of the British South Africa Company, but the company's administration had not yet reached the area. It had been intended to crush the Bemba and dismantle their political structure, but Dupont's intervention ensured the chiefdom's survival. His pre-emption of power was at first unwelcome to the local

British authorities, who disliked being upstaged by a French Catholic missionary. However, the governor, Sir Robert Codrington, supported Dupont, and realized that his presence and that of the White Fathers in Bembaland helped to guarantee the *Pax Britannica*.[183] Dupont, in fact, secured the allegiance of Mwamba's thirty-three junior chiefs. In 1899, the British conferred on Dupont the authority of a native chief in the Christian villages surrounding Chilubula Mission, a concession of some four square miles. He was allowed to execute justice and could sentence offenders to a maximum of ten lashes or a ten shilling fine. Dupont used his powers to punish pagan survivals. In 1904, for example, a diviner received eight lashes.[184] After Dupont's resignation in 1911, the autonomy of the mission villages was eroded, and the concession of land was rescinded by the British administration on the eve of World War I. It had been an exception at a time when there was no colonial administration in the area.[185]

Such a concession was also an anachronism in a pluralist society. As in Rwanda, Upper Congo and Karema, the White Fathers in Bembaland at first had no Protestant competition. When missionaries of other denominations appeared, the administration strove to maintain separate spheres of influence. Not only did Catholics oppose such a division, but Bemba mobility rendered it unworkable. Catholics and Protestants penetrated each other's areas and were forced to abandon any ideas of creating a homogeneous Christendom.

The exercise of civil power by a White Father was recorded also in French Sudan, at the start of the very first Mossi mission. Jean-Joseph Pierry (1868–1953) at Koupela was given permission by the French military administrator, Captain Lorillard, to act as a judge in local cases. This concession only lasted from 1900–1901, but it was not well seen by his superiors. It was judged unseemly for a missionary priest, and it was also thought imprudent that he should have accepted a judicial role without a written mandate.[186]

The Armed Brothers of the Sahara

A Religious and Military Order

With the outstanding exception of Joubert, Lavigerie's experiment with the Armed Auxiliaries had not been a success. The Cardinal then conceived the idea of arming the missionary brothers. The General Chapter of the Society of Missionaries of Africa which met in 1885 discussed the proposal. It asked who would give the order to open fire, if the occasion arose, and who would give the brothers weapon training? Above all, it asked whether the European powers would approve of such a Catholic army?[187] During his anti-slavery campaign in 1888, Lavigerie tried in vain to persuade the powers of Europe to create a co-ordinated, international force against the slave trade. After two groups of White Fathers had been massacred in 1876 and 1881, missionaries had been temporarily withdrawn from the Sahara, and even French exploration and occupation were at a standstill. Although he had given up the attempt to penetrate as far as French Sudan, Lavigerie wanted to restart the Sahara mission, but there were revolts and continued unrest in the Mzab, and the Saharan slave trade was in full swing. The Cardinal determined to create an armed troop which would protect missionaries on journeys and in their houses, and help bring about the suppression of the slave trade. It would attempt to recapture slaves and eventually man a chain of posts leading to the French Sudan.[188]

Inspired by the example of the medieval military and religious orders, Lavigerie tried first to interest the Knights of Malta in his scheme and to create an order of "African Knights" or "Knights of the Sahara." The ambitions of the Knights of Malta at the end of the nineteenth century, however, centred on peaceful and philanthropic objectives, rather than on military ones.[189] Faced with this rebuff, the Cardinal decided to create his own military order, and in 1890 sent a printed circular of fifty-two pages to volunteers of the anti-slavery movement, inviting applications to join the "Association of Pioneers or Brothers of the Sahara." It was to be a religious society, placed under the direction of the White Fathers, without vows, pursuing the perfection of its members, the abolition of slavery, the care of the sick, agriculture and the use of arms. Lavigerie worked out every detail of their life, including the daily timetable and a diet that included a breakfast of black coffee, bread and dried dates. More than seventeen thousand enquiries were received by the Paris Anti-Slavery Committee.[190]

The Rise and Fall of the Armed Brothers

Lavigerie received 365 applications to join the Armed Brothers from all over Europe, including Britain, and from Canada and the United States. Candidates had to be Catholics, with an irreproachable past, of good health, and with no family dependants; they had to be over twenty-five and to have seen active military service. Ninety five postulants were admitted, forty-six of whom were later withdrawn or departed of their own free will.[191] The novitiate opened at Biskra in June 1891 with the White Father, Prosper-Augustin Hacquard (1860–1901), as Superior. By the end of June 1892 there were thirty-five novices. Lavigerie wrote their Constitutions and designed their costume. The full dress included a cloak and plumed pith helmet.[192] Lavigerie entered into correspondence with the French and Algerian authorities. The project was welcomed in Algeria and by the French Minister for Foreign Affairs in Paris. The Minister for War, however, was slower to give his approval, but eventually Lavigerie was permitted to buy sixty rifles, fifteen carbines, twelve muskets and ten thousand rounds of ammunition from arms dealers in Paris.[193]

On July 12th 1891, Lavigerie consecrated Joseph-Anatole Toulotte as his coadjutor for the Vicariate of the Sahara and Sudan. The ceremony took place in Algiers and the Armed Brothers made their first public appearance.

The Cardinal's homily included the following words: "In opening to Monseigneur Toulotte's apostolic zeal this immense field dominated by barbarism, I have wished to give him an army, and you will see him surrounded on the day of his consecration by the first fruits of these Brothers of the Sahara. The world has never seen a more disinterested, more noble, more patriotic, more Christian enterprise." The Armed Brothers duly paraded in their comic opera white uniforms, a red cross on their breast and a gold cross, surmounted by a red plume, on their headdress. An observer reported: "They marched modestly, but firmly, escorting the consecrating prelates and the newly consecrated bishop, proudly bearing the weapons which they must only use, as we know, for the defence of slaves they have liberated and received under their patronage."[194] The Cardinal and his project received a great deal of vituperation in the French press. La Vigie referred to the brothers as the "Catholic brigands of the Sahara" and Le Figaro called them "a raggle-taggle of adventurers without resources or morality," the fear being that Lavigerie was raising conflicts in the Sahara into which France would be drawn. Lavigerie wrote to Le Figaro, explaining that the brothers were not an army of combat.[195]

The final blow fell in October 1892 when the French government withdrew its support and Lavigerie was obliged to abandon the project altogether.[196] There were only 22 members remaining and some of these applied to become brothers in the White Fathers society.[197] The most famous ex-Armed Brother was the colonial governor of French West Africa, the ethnologist and linguist, Maurice Delafosse.[198] Lavigerie wanted to go himself to Biskra to announce the disbandment of the Armed Brothers and to thank them personally. However, by this time the Cardinal was dying, and the disbanding of his bizarre "Catholic Army" was the last act of his extraordinary life.

We have now concluded an account of the social conditions obtaining in the territories occupied by the Missionaries of Africa at the commencement of their mission. These were principally the slave trade and its aftermath, relations with traditional rulers and, where the colonial power was not yet installed, the need to supply some measure of civil power. We can now turn to the main purpose of their coming to Africa: evangelization.

Léon Livinhac

Jean-Joseph Hirth

Henri Streicher,
seated on his leopard skin

Augustin Hacquard

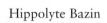
Hippolyte Bazin

Charles Guérin

Yohana Kitagana

Auguste Achte with catechists and children

Adolphe Lechaptois

François Gerboin

Joseph Dupont

Victor Roelens

Leopold Joubert and family

Mpala fort and church

Baudouinville in 1918

Maurice Bellière

Chilubula cathedral with the added clerestory

Dr. Adrian Atiman

Caravan of 1896 — Jean-Baptiste Sambateshi with flute, centre, front row

Machtilda Munaku

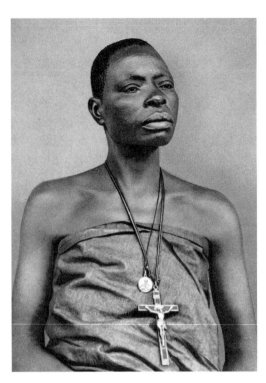

Ushirombo with its wall and gate

Basil Lumu and
Victor Womeraka

Stefano Kaoze

Prosper Kamara

CHAPTER FOUR

God's Work in Africa

Survival

From One Mission Station to Another

"It is all God's work. Our role is to write the names."[1] A Missionary of Africa wrote this in 1907, at an isolated mission station in German East Africa. Although in this instance it was a reaction to the religious indifference of the local people, the words reflected a deep-seated conviction that, whatever the exertions and emotions of the missionary, the mission of the church in Africa belonged to God and was ultimately under God's control. The missionary's task of teaching, baptizing and recording was secondary to the action of God's grace. Missionaries wrote the names, but it was divine grace that made people into disciples of Jesus Christ. According to Cardinal Lavigerie, founder of the White Fathers, successful missionary work depended on such a conviction, born of personal holiness. In one way or another, this conviction was shared by his missionaries in all the different circumstances of their mission. This chapter is concerned with the processes, content and agents of evangelization—in other words, the task of creating the tangible conditions for the intangible operation of God's grace.

The Missionaries of Africa came to evangelize and serve the peoples of that continent. But, as Adrian Hastings has pointed out, they had first to survive. They needed to create the material setting in which to carry out this work, and this meant that, in the first place, "the mission had to revolve around the needs of the missionaries themselves."[2] They had to be housed, to be fed and to look after their health. The period 1892 to 1914 was one of colonial expansion and consolidation. Against this background—favourable or not as it might be—the White Fathers laid the foundations of the Catholic Church in some fifteen African countries. Missionary goals at that time were frankly concerned with converting individuals, creating viable communities and setting up ecclesial structures. This was best done from a mission station, a strategically-placed operational base, at which the missionaries themselves resided and from which they penetrated the surround-

106

ing settlements. The mission station was, therefore, the all important unit of survival and effective action.

Just as monasteries have founded daughter houses, so mission stations multiplied by making new foundations. The mission stations sent out advance parties. Missionaries and their auxiliaries migrated from one station to the next. In many instances, Africans themselves took the initiative in preparing a new foundation. We have already noted the example of Yohana Kitagana. When the first Missionaries of Africa reached Mbarara, Uganda, in 1903, they found six catechists from Buganda at work there before they came.[3] Three of them had been working there for eight months.[4] In the 1880s, many Christians in Buganda became spontaneous catechists, and this zeal was channelled by Bishop Hirth and Bishop Streicher, who sent catechists out as ambassadors and contact people to chiefs in other provinces and regions. Such emissaries were sent to places south of Lake Victoria, in German East Africa, as well as to the kingdoms of Toro and Ankole and as far as Congo.[5] Frequently, local chiefs or headmen invited the missionaries to make a foundation in their area. Sometimes, the missionaries found that people already knew the precepts and principal truths of Christianity, before they had spoken to them, or that they had learned the basic prayers on their own initiative.[6] In 1891, Bishop Gerboin set out from Bukumbi (Nyanza South) with sixty Christians and a number of catechists to found the mission station of Ushirombo (in Unyanyembe).[7] In December 1899, Alphonse Brard (1858–1918) set out from Kashozi (Nyanza South) with two other Missionaries of Africa, a dozen catechists from Buganda and 150 porters from Sukumaland, to found the mission of Save, the first in Rwanda.[8] Four years earlier, Joseph Dupont had moved with a party of Tanganyika Christians and catechists from Mambwe mission to Kayambi in Bembaland (Northern Rhodesia).[9] At Save, Brard continued to receive auxiliaries from Buganda. In 1903, he had no fewer than twenty-one such catechists, who arrived in groups to work for a year at a time.[10]

In 1896, a station was founded in Burundi at Misugi, which was obliged to move two years later to Muyaga. In 1897 Bishop Lechaptois of the neighbouring Tanganyika Vicariate sent supplies to help the new foundation. These arrived by boat on Lake Tanganyika and included clothes, a *Rituale* for blessings, books for spiritual reading, paper, ink, envelopes, wheat, potatoes, seeds, and a mould for making roof tiles, together with tile samples. The missionaries of Misugi sent the good bishop palm oil in exchange.[11] In 1907, Théophile Dromaux (1849–1909) at Galula (Tanganyika) was able to supply the confreres of neighbouring Urwira with goats, and Likuni Mission in Angoniland (Nyasa) embarked on raising livestock the following year in order to help other stations in the area.[12] These are all practical examples of how mission stations helped each other. More importantly, they learned from each other's pastoral experience. In this, the quarterly chronicle from Algiers, *Chronique Trimestrielle*, which published extracts from the mission diaries and reports from the vicariates, played a major role, help-

ing to consolidate the pastoral strategy of the entire Society in the various
African regions.

Choosing Sites

In his instructions to the missionaries, Cardinal Lavigerie gave much practical advice about choosing the sites of mission stations. The missionaries
were to take into account various factors, particularly the density of the
local population and the health of the missionaries. The site should be ele-
vated and salubrious, and the definitive installation should only take place
after a lengthy study of all the advantages and disadvantages. Humid and
swampy terrain was to be avoided at all costs, but the ground should be sufficiently fertile for the growing of food crops, so that the station could
become self-sufficient as soon as possible.[13] The geological condition of
Upper Congo, with its swamps, shallow soil, stagnant water, heavy rain,
heat and humidity, rendered it extremely unhealthy and was responsible for
the deaths of many missionaries and for devastating epidemics. Kibanga
Mission had to be abandoned in 1893 for health reasons, but Bishop
Roelens looked forward to a time when more intensive cultivation in the
vicariate would improve conditions.[14]

Missionaries were not always entirely free to choose their mission sites.
Permission had to be obtained from the local chief, with the approval of the
colonial administration. However, the officers were often reluctant to put
pressure on the chiefs and declined to intervene when permission was
refused. It was sometimes in the missionaries' interest to distance themselves
from the colonial administration, as happened at Ushirombo (German East
Africa) and Kupela (French Sudan). The friendliness or hostility of the chiefs
was dictated by the calculated advantage or disadvantage to themselves, and
by the perceived relationship of the missionaries to the colonial power. For
the most part, chiefs valued their own freedom of action, and sought to
avoid competition. However, there were occasions when the protection or
support afforded by the missionaries was welcome. Many mission stations
had a difficult beginning, moving from site to site. This was especially the
case in Burundi (German East Africa), where the Tutsi rulers were exceptionally hostile. Very occasionally the administration itself invited or prohibited the founding of a mission station. Kati Mission was founded in 1897
at the behest of the governor of French Sudan, who wanted the MSOLA
(White Sisters) to staff the military hospital there, but in 1904 the enforce-
ment of anti-clerical legislation obliged the sisters to leave, and in 1910 the
missionaries were ordered to quit the vicinity of the military camp at Kati.
The administration also found reasons to prohibit the projected mission station at Kudugu. When Bishop Hippdyte Bazin sent the Canadian Oscar
Morin to make the first foundation in the Gold Coast in 1906, he had hoped
to make a start at Tamale. The British, however, for security reasons, wanted
the mission to be near their own station at Navrongo. In German East

Africa, Bishop Gerboin had no wish to place his mission stations near German military posts, but the German administration invited the White Fathers to Tabora, and Richard Kandt, the German Resident in Rwanda, gave them a large property which Gerboin personally took over in 1900.[15]

On arrival at a new site, the missionaries pitched tents, while provisional buildings went up. "We are tired of tents," complained a diarist at Kyanja (Nyanza South) in 1904.[16] While Bukalasa Seminary (Uganda) was being built in 1905, the staff lived in tents, like other missionaries on a new site. The provisional buildings that followed the tents were sometimes rondavels, or small round huts, as at Navrongo (Gold Coast), Wagadugu and Kati (French Sudan). Or they were cottages made of wattle and daub, or sun-dried brick, with a thatched roof. At Marangara (Rwanda), the provisional mission house was made of straw and had six compartments. Sometimes, as at Marienseen (Burundi) or Iraqw (Unyanyembe), a fortified house or *tembe* was put up, with a flat earth roof. But such a house was not always watertight and missionaries had recourse again to tents, spreading them over the roof. It was while they lived in the provisional structures that materials were collected for more permanent buildings.

Finding Materials

Bishop Lechaptois built stone churches at Kala and Kasakula (Tanganyika) in 1905 and 1907, but, although stones were ordinarily used in the foundations, buildings of stone masonry were rare.[17] Churches and mission houses were usually built of either sun-dried mud brick (adobe), or preferably of burnt brick. Burnt bricks, however, were made of clay, and suitable clay was not always available. At Mibirisi (Rwanda), excellent clay for burnt bricks and tiles was discovered in 1908, but in 1907 at Chilubi on the shores of Lake Bangweolo (Northern Rhodesia), the firing of bricks failed because of bad quality clay, and the missionaries continued in vain the search for a better material. Adobe was more suitable for a dry climate, as long as there were no termites in the offing, but a building method employed in both East and West Africa was to cover the adobe with a skin of burnt brick. Brickmaking was a major activity in the early stages of the mission and enormous quantities were produced. At Kashozi (Nyanza South), three hundred forty thousand bricks and one hundred seventeen thousand hollow tiles were produced in 1905; at Narozari (Nyanza North) seven thousand bricks in the same year; at Marangara (Rwanda) two hundred thirty thousand bricks in 1907.[18] At Usui (Nyanza South), one hundred forty thousand bricks were made, of which half were fired, and at Navrongo (Gold Coast), twenty-four thousand bricks were needed in 1908.[19]

Making, carrying and stacking bricks on this scale required a considerable labour force. On Kome Island (Nyanza South), every Christian was required to make a thousand bricks in 1904. At Kayambi (Northern Rhodesia) in 1906, three teams of workers made seventy-five hundred bricks. In the following year, men were engaged to carry 250 bricks a day, while women carried 150. They were paid in fish-hooks.[20] A similar rate of production was achieved at Patyana (French Sudan), where twelve workers made thirteen hundred bricks in a single day.[21] At Marangara, already mentioned, there were 150 workers, making and firing twelve thousand tiles and five thousand bricks.[22] Sometimes, the people gave their labour freely. At other times, they earned their government tax money by working for the mission. Occasionally, the administration exempted them from government forced labour if they were working at the mission. Local chiefs also sent workers. The White Fathers were happy that the building operations attracted so many people, because it was an initial contact with the local population that could later bear fruit in evangelization.

All this labour had to be supervised by lay brother auxiliaries. Lay brothers constituted more than a third of the membership of the Society of Missionaries of Africa throughout the period 1892–1914.[23] In 1892, they numbered 69, as compared to 165 priests. In 1914, there were 241 lay brothers, in comparison to 658 priests. Today (2006), lay brothers are barely ten percent of the Society's total membership.[24] The years we are considering were the Brothers' heyday. Brothers were the mainstay of the mission. After postulancy and novitiate, the favoured place for them to acquire professional skills was at St. Joseph's agricultural colony and model farm at Thibar in Tunisia, a project that had been started as a source of income for the Society after Lavigerie became Archbishop of Carthage in 1884. At any one time some thirty brothers were engaged there in the workshops, fields, pastures and vineyards, teaching and gaining experience. Carpentry was a major specialization of the brothers, and this skill was essential for making the roof frames, windows and furnishings of the new buildings in sub-Saharan Africa. At Thibar, Arab students followed a four-year apprenticeship, but it proved difficult to get African apprentice masons to persevere in the new mission stations of the south. There is no doubt, however, that the brothers gave a major impetus to material development in equatorial Africa and the (French) Sudan.

Brick-making sometimes had its problems. At Villa Maria (Nyanza North), the brick kiln exploded in 1899.[25] But the more usual problems were caused by rain. An unexpected downpour could easily destroy ten to twenty thousand bricks drying in the sun. At Mua (Nyasa) in 1909, the diarist recorded that a storm reduced fifty thousand bricks and ten thousand tiles to "marmalade."[26] Early rain also damaged the buildings themselves if they were not roofed in time, as happened at Mugera (Burundi) in 1908.[27] Two other important building materials were chalk and timber. Chalk was needed for mortar and whitewash, and it was in short supply. Where no chalk deposits could be found, the brothers resorted to crushing or burning shells from the lakeshore.[28] Assembling sufficient timber depended on the good will of local rulers to permit logging in the neighbouring forests and woodlands. Bamboos were also necessary for making ceilings. At Marienseen (Burundi), the chiefs themselves sent beams in 1907, and at Marangara (Rwanda), large numbers of workers came, singing as they carried the wood.[29] At Nya Gesi, in the Kivu region of Upper Congo Vicariate, the chiefs were ordered by the administration to provide five hundred trees and one thousand bamboos.[30]

Building and Re-building

Although the drawings made by the brothers were far from elaborate, many different kinds of building were planned. Ideally, the missionaries' residence contained a bedroom and office for each individual, a community dining room, kitchen, store and verandas. Houses had to be built for the catechists, class rooms, hangars to accommodate the regular influx of catechumens, a dispensary and eventually a convent to accommodate sisters. Surrounding the site—and absorbing an enormous quantity of bricks—was the perimeter wall. The glory of every mission station, however, was the church, the focus for a liturgically-based catechesis. Churches were continually being enlarged or replaced as congregations grew in size, and the missionaries proudly recorded their growing dimensions and measurements. These were the first notable buildings of the African interior and their builders were understandably appreciative when they were praised by visitors. "Mpala church is the most beautiful building in Central Africa," declared a British hunter in 1895.[31] The new church at Rukwa (Tanganyika) was regarded as "one of the most considerable monuments in the country."[32] A German officer admired the roof structure and carpentry of the church at Nyundo (Burundi), and other church buildings were said by colonial officers to be "splendid" and "pretty."[33] At Msalala (Unyanyembe), after the completion of the bell tower, a missionary described the church as "a true little cathedral, half Gothic and half Romanesque."[34] Government officers were frequently helpful in obtaining labour and materials for building, as at Nya Gesi (Upper Congo) and Navrongo (Gold Coast), where the Catholic district commissioner went so far as to donate the harmonium.[35]

In spite of the missionaries legitimate pride and well-deserved praise, not a few of these fine buildings collapsed. The brothers' building experience was limited and they were using unfamiliar materials. Moreover, they were often unaware of climatic and geological factors. Most of the collapses were caused by hurricanes and storms, or else by subsidence and earth tremors. Rubya Seminary was especially unlucky, having buildings collapse in two successive years. At Ukerewe (Nyanza South) in 1898, a roof collapsed on top of a missionary in the midst of a catechism class. One of the seventy pupils died on the spot, after receiving baptism.[36] Luckily, on such occasions the fatalities were few.

The most spectacular collapse was that of Chilubula Cathedral (Northern Rhodesia) in 1906. The building was the work of Brother Optat (Louis) Pelet (1867–1911). Earlier in the year, it was decided to transform the first church into a cathedral for Bishop Joseph Dupont. To give the building a more elegant look, the roof was demolished and the walls increased in height. Internal columns, Romanesque windows and a new tile roof were added. Christmas Midnight Mass in the newly refurbished cathedral was a splendid occasion, with 260 people receiving communion and 101 adult baptisms. Five days later, during the night of December 30th, an internal column gave way and a third of the building collapsed. No one was injured. Brother Optat, who began the work of restoration in the New Year, died of cancer four years later in January 1911. His funeral took place in the cathedral he had built and twice rebuilt.[37]

Bishop Joseph Sweens (1858–1950) of Nyanza South was the remarkable survivor of two church collapses. In 1928, he was saying his breviary at Rutabo when the church collapsed on top of him. With considerable presence of mind, he saved his life by ducking under the *prie-dieu* at which he was kneeling, and emerged unscathed from the wreckage. Five years earlier, in 1915, he was at the door of Bukoba church, when a British gun-ship on Lake Victoria fired a shell through the roof. The shell exploded in the church on the exact spot where he had been saying the rosary a minute earlier.[38]

The most frequent threat to the new buildings was fire. Arson was responsible in a few cases, notably at Muyaga (Burundi), where repeated fires were part of a concerted campaign to drive the missionaries away after 1899. In many cases, buildings were struck by lightning. Accidents in the kitchen or the sacristy, and bush fires on adjoining land, were also responsible for fires. Large numbers of people gathered to put the fires out. A crowd of two thousand, for example, helped contain a fire at Baudouinville (Upper Congo).[39] At Narozari (Nyanza North), a remarkable discovery was made in 1905. Provided it was available in sufficient quantity, the most effective fire-extinguisher was banana beer.[40] On several further occasions, it was used to dowse fires in Buganda.

Food Crops and Livestock

Every mission station had a vegetable garden, as well as fields or banana plantations for the staple food crops of the area. The missionaries grew maize, potatoes and groundnuts. In addition to the fast-growing eucalyptus and casuarinas, grown as an easier source of timber, the missionaries planted fruit trees, such as mangoes, figs, almonds and palms. Mission stations had many hungry mouths to feed: orphans, auxiliaries, servants and other dependants. There were also feeding programmes for hundreds of victims of famine. The mission stations also made a great effort to grow wheat in order to have flour with which to make altar breads. Nearly every vicariate had highly successful wheat harvests, and there was only an occasional failure due to rust or rats. Although Cardinal Lavigerie had been optimistic about planting vineyards in equatorial Africa, vines were an almost universal failure in the sub-Saharan territories of the White Fathers, and, from time to time, a scarcity of altar wine threatened the frequent celebration of the Eucharist. A drastic reduction in the amount of wine used at Mass was imposed at Mpala (Upper Congo) in 1898 and at Wagadugu (French Sudan) in 1907.[41] White Fathers, however, were lucky to have sources of wine in Algeria and Tunisia, which could be imported through their procurator at Zanzibar, Mombasa or Marseilles. The missionaries participated in government programmes for planting rubber trees, cotton and coffee, and these were an expected source of income.

Livestock-raising was another important activity of the mission stations. At Rubya (Nyanza South), there was a herd of 82 cattle, and Bishop Streicher (Nyanza North) kept a herd of 350 cows in South Buddu, for the sale of meat and dairy products as a source of income for the vicariate. At Kayes in French Sudan there was an ostrich farm for the export of feathers.[42]

Health and Sickness

Health—both the health of the local people as well as their own health—was a major preoccupation of the Missionaries of Africa during this period. Ministry to the sick was one of the priorities of mission work, and it was closely linked to evangelization. Cardinal Lavigerie saw it as an apostolate of compassion that continued the mission of Jesus himself: "Cure those who are sick, and say, 'The kingdom of God is very near to you'" (Luke 10:9). The ministry of healing underscored the ministry of the Word.[43] In Kabylia, people came by the thousands every year for treatment at mission dispensaries. The same was true in equatorial Africa and French Sudan, even when the dispensary in question was no more than a box in the superior's office containing a few simple remedies. Africans, at this time, were experiencing imported diseases and epidemics on a scale unheard of hitherto. The White Fathers shared in this experience themselves and contributed significantly to the processes of healing. There was a quantum leap in the quality of medical care when the White Sisters (MSOLA) joined them in the 1890s to run hospitals, dispensaries, leprosaria and hospices.

Sickness was part of the missionary vocation, and at times every member of the mission staff was sick in turn. "May this suffering," wrote a missionary at Ulungwa (Unyanyembe) in 1909, "become a blessing and a grace of conversion for our dear Africans."[44] Although the missionary death rate levelled off during this period, the rate of mortality was still high. Between 1892 and 1914, the society averaged ten deaths a year, which was between three and four percent of an average total membership of three to four hundred. In 1899, the figure was as low as five deaths, but in 1906 there were nineteen.[45] By far the most common cause of death was blackwater fever, a usually fatal complication of malaria producing the massive destruction of red blood cells. It was sometimes caused by an overdose of quinine, especially by those unaccustomed to this prophylactic. Gustave Debeerst (1865–1896) died of blackwater fever at Lusaka (Upper Congo) at the age of thirty-one. Louis Loonus (1864–1897) was a victim at Kilimatinde (Unyanyembe) aged thirty-three. Other victims were: Willibrord (Louis) Flappers (1864–1897) at Mpala (Upper Congo), also aged thirty-three; Joseph van den Biesen (1869–1898) at Bujumbura (Burundi), aged twenty-nine; Pierre Koolen (1871–1899) at Ushirombo (Unyanyembe), aged twenty-eight; Arthur Herman (1847–1902) at Kirungu (Upper Congo), aged fifty-five; François Monneraye (1873–1903), aged thirty and Paul Sieffert (1878–1907) at Kala (Tanganyika), aged twenty-nine. There were many other blackwater deaths, including numbers of the MSOLA (White Sisters). In 1905, Mother Marie Claver Eprevier, assistant to the MSOLA superior general, died at Mpala during a general visitation of her sisters.[46] Towards the end of the first decade of the twentieth century, deaths from blackwater fever began to diminish, but before doing so, the disease made an appearance at Wagadugu (French Sudan) in 1904.[47]

Advances in medical knowledge were responsible for the virtual disappearance of blackwater fever. When the Missionaries of Africa first entered equatorial Africa, they believed that malaria was caused by "miasmatic vapours" emanating from swamps.[48] In 1897–1898, the mosquito was identified as the carrier of the disease, and it was only five or six years later that missionaries began to take precautions. The first missionary caravan to bring mosquito nets arrived in 1904, and the utility of such nets was demonstrated for the first time at the London School of Tropical Medicine in the following year.[49]

West Africa is the home of another major killer, yellow fever. This acute and infectious tropical disease is also transmitted by the mosquito, and was responsible for the deaths of a number of White Fathers during this period. Guillaume Templier (1865–1906), founder of Wagadugu mission and general visitor of the French Sudan province, died of it at Kita in 1906. Within a few days, two other missionaries also died of yellow fever at Kita: François Ménoret (1859–1906) and Mathurin Guidrais (1872–1906).[50] Four years later, Bishop Bazin (1857–1910) was visiting victims of the disease at Kayes, when he also died on the way to hospital.[51] The diarist of Kita Mission, who had fever at the same time as the yellow fever victims of 1906, took preventive measures that were highly original. He dressed "like a Siberian," drank an entire pot of tea and sat reading Racine throughout the night.[52] Apparently, it worked. In addition to disease, accidents and encounters with wild animals were also causes of missionary deaths. There were several, besides Bishop Hacquard, who drowned. The Sahara Desert does not sound a likely scenario for a drowning, but André Vellard (1865–1906) and Stanislas Comte (1868–1906) were caught by a flash-flood in the *wadi* Biskra on their way to Wargla. Paul (Maurice) Hamey (1880–1908), a young brother, was drowned in the Mediterranean off Carthage. Gustave Castelyn (1857–1903) was taken by a crocodile at Galula (Tanganyika). Antoine Rigouste (1875–1903) attempted to separate two fighting horses at Kati (French Sudan) and was felled by a kick from one of them. Finally,

Nicholas Hoscheit (1878–1908) died at Zimba (Tanganyika) after being mauled by a leopard. The only casualty of human violence during this period (1892–1914) was Paulin Loupias (1872–1910), whose murder in Rwanda has already been described. Successive deaths could cripple vicariates that were already short of personnel. In 1907, for example, seven missionaries died in Upper Congo, which represented more than half the deaths in the whole society that year.

In combating epidemics, the missionaries collaborated with the medical services of the colonial administration. Mission stations became vaccination centres for measles and small-pox, and especially, when it made its appearance, sleeping sickness. Sleeping sickness is carried by the tsetse fly and affects the brain, inducing fever, extreme lethargy and mental dullness, coma and eventually death. It is a slow, progressive condition, and in the early years of its appearance in equatorial Africa it was always fatal in spite of recommended vaccines. The disease appeared in Uganda in 1903 along the shores of Lake Victoria, and spread to the whole of the Great Lakes region in the years that followed. In 1905, fifteen victims of the epidemic died at Mpala (Upper Congo), and in 1906, Lusenda in the same vicariate was abandoned because of the disease. At Kisubi (Nyanza North), the mission and junior seminary became a hospice for those dying of sleeping sickness. By 1909, Mpala had ceased to be a flourishing mission and had become a hospital and a cemetery. The colonial administrations set up isolation camps and quarantined areas. The White Fathers built chapels in the camps and founded hospices of their own. They also collaborated in the administration of atoxyl, an early arsenic-based drug of uncertain effect. The epidemic was the occasion for a marked increase in religious faith and fervour. Bishop Streicher ordered a three-day fast in Uganda to implore relief from the epidemic. In 1905 at Mpala, Christians held a *triduum* of prayer and vowed to build a hill-top shrine to Our Lady. At Baudouinville, a lady chapel was dedicated in 1906 in thanksgiving by those who had escaped infection.[53] The great sleeping-sickness epidemic was a medical crisis, comparable in many ways to AIDS in our own day. It was also truly a partnership in adversity for the missionaries and their people. "As our founder foresaw," wrote a missionary in Uganda in 1908, "medical treatment is an evangelization."[54]

Finances

If the vicariates apostolic were beset during this period by a lack of personnel, their financial resources were also scanty. During most of the time, the Society maintained four procures in Europe and one at the East African coast. In Rome, the general procure of the Missionaries of Africa had dealings with the congregation *De Propaganda Fide*, from which it received funds, and also did business with other Vatican departments. The principal centre for receiving donations was the procure in Paris, but there had also been a postulancy at Gerra in the Netherlands since 1889. This was joined to a procure, occupying rented premises at Boxtel in 1896. The principal procure for supplying the missions in Africa was Marseilles, and beginning in 1878 there was another procure at Zanzibar, which was transferred to Mombasa at the end of 1902. Mission aid societies, from which the Society and the vicariates received funds, were not then unified under the aegis of Rome, but operated from different European centres. Of these, Lyons, headquarters of the Association for the Propagation of the Faith, was the most important. On several occasions Cardinal Lavigerie had been a candidate for the archiepiscopal see of Lyons, and he had preached a mission appeal there in 1885. In 1898 the Society agreed to a proposal from the Lyons Association to send two missionaries to help establish its work in South America.[55] Thereafter until 1934, a community was maintained at Buenos Aires to solicit funds in Argentina and neighbouring countries.

The motherhouse in Algiers supplied White Fathers with stipends and personal allowances. It also responded to requests for funding special projects. For example, in 1908 François Ménard (1862–1927) asked for a Kirundi dictionary to be funded, and Célestin Dupupet (1876–1949) asked for money to build a staff house at the Rubaga English School. Both were referred to their bishops. However, bishops did not necessarily fare any better. Bishop Bazin's request in the same month—for money to buy a house in Bamako (French Sudan)—was also turned down as "inopportune."[56] *Propaganda Fide* sent subsidies to the vicariates, but these depended on the regular submission of statistics to Rome.[57] In 1896, for example, Bishop Dupont received the generous subsidy of one hundred twenty thousand *francs* towards the foundation of his mission to the Bemba (Nyasa), and in 1900, sixty thousand *lire* were received at Zanzibar as subsidies for the Vicariates of Nyanza North, Unyanyembe and Nyasa.[58] After 1907, subsidies from Rome diminished considerably.[59]

In spite of the subsidies, bishops were in a continual state of penury. In 1906 and 1907, the Vicariates of Nyanza North and Nyasa recorded deficits and were forced to limit their expenditure while looking for other sources of income.[60] Bishop Streicher encouraged the growing of cash crops at mission stations, and Dupont found some generous private benefactors to place his vicariate on a sounder financial footing. By 1910, Streicher was able to report that his receipts just covered the expenses.[61] Bishop Gerboin funded three mission stations with donations from an American benefactor, and a leprosarium with the help of a benefactress in France.[62] Bishop Hirth also found a benefactor for his new church at Mwanza (Nyanza South).[63] As a result of the financial difficulties of Nyanza North, the General Council of the Society insisted that the vicariates overhaul their finances, that each should appoint a treasurer-general, that the budget of each mission station should be regulated, that no disbursements should be made without the bishop's permission and that twice-yearly statements of account be produced.[64]

Mission Training and Spiritual Formation

Training for Africa in Africa

The White Fathers, at this time, were among the best-trained missionaries in Africa. This was true although Catholic missiology had not yet been born, and the infant social sciences, with their secular bias, were understandably absent from seminary curricula. The crucial factor in the White Fathers' training was that the spiritual and theological formation of these future missionaries took place in North Africa, at Algiers and Carthage. They were formed in Africa for the African mission. The content of the teaching in the novitiate and scholasticate did not differ in essentials from courses given to Catholic seminarians and religious elsewhere in the world, but for the White Fathers it took place in a mission environment. Novices and scholastics usually finished their studies with more than a smattering of Arabic. Consequently, they were already convinced of the need to be good linguists. They also possessed an elementary acquaintance with Islam and had experienced a culture different from their own. Above all, they had mingled with the poor and cultivated a lifestyle of poverty themselves. In their holidays, for example, they were sent out to visit the mission stations of Kabylia.[65] They had trained together over a number of years and understood the value of community life. They were not strangers to each other, as many missionaries were, who were "parachuted" from an individualistic bourgeois environment in Europe straight into the materially undeveloped communitarian societies of Africa. Instead, they came to their task with many African insights and experiences. They already belonged to Africa, and were prepared for a dialogue of life with African people.

The relevance of military service to the self-discipline of these theology students has already been mentioned. At Carthage there was another influence and this was the work of Alfred Louis Delattre (1850–1932), archpriest of Carthage Cathedral and archaeologist, who spent a lifetime recovering the history and architecture of ancient Christian Carthage. Seminarians helped him in his excavations and took part in the celebrations that he organized of the early African martyrs. These, together with his flow of publications and the museum that he created, gave the students the sense of belonging to an African Christian tradition, the church of Augustine, Cyprian and Tertullian. The benign spirit of Lavigerie, whose tomb lay in the precincts of Carthage Cathedral, also overshadowed the scholasticate and its inmates.

Lavigerie's instructions, in the collection published in 1884, were available to his missionaries, with all the practical wisdom they contained. The quarterly *Chronique*, with its unfolding picture of contemporary missionary life in Africa, was also accessible. To these must be added the continuing series of circular letters from Bishop Livinhac, the superior general. These letters, with their repeated emphasis on missionary spirituality, obedience, personal austerity and the importance of learning languages, set the tone for the whole Society, and their themes were taken up in the instructions which the vicars apostolic published for their own personnel.[66]

Apostolate and the Rule

A historian has described the legalism of the White Fathers' constitutions as "grotesque," comparing their psychological importance to that of British colonial administrators wearing dinner jackets in the bush.[67] There is no doubt that the first constitutions of the Society belong to a mindset altogether different from our own. It is also true that the routine engendered by a set of rules inculcates a sense of security for people in unfamiliar, and even hostile, surroundings. The constitutions had, however, a much more profound importance for the Missionaries of Africa in the period we are studying. They were a guarantee of personal holiness, which—according to the thinking of that time—consisted primarily in fidelity to a rule. They were also a guarantee of fidelity to the purpose of the Society, as conceived by the founder. This purpose was also personal holiness. Article two of the first constitutions, approved in 1908, reads: "The purpose of the Society is the glory of God, through personal sanctification and apostolic life, having as object the establishment of Christianity in the African continent."[68] The *Directory of the Constitutions*, which was approved in 1914, was a practical manual designed to help the missionary to be faithful to the constitutions, and so acquire holiness. Although there was a hierarchy of importance among the documents of the Society, to be a "perfect missionary" one had to follow all the prescriptions, without making any practical distinctions between them.[69] According to the thinking of the founder, all apostolic success derived from the personal holiness of the missionary. Only the holy missionary could bring forth holy Christians.

Emphasis was laid on community life, characterized by fraternal charity among the missionaries and a family spirit. There was to be a gentle, friendly approach to the Africans, devoid of all harshness and constraint. Human contact and personal relations were at a premium. The "precious treasure of the interior life" was to be nourished by spiritual exercises carried out in community: morning prayer, meditation, particular examen (examination of conscience or review of the day), short visits to the chapel after the two main meals, spiritual reading, a fifteen-minute evening visit to the Blessed Sacrament, night prayer and general examen. Apart from parish Masses, the daily Eucharist was celebrated privately, and recitation of the breviary, like the rosary, was also in private. Lay brothers were to receive communion on Sundays and feast days. Although it inhibited initiative in various ways, community life provided a "framework for harmony and survival."[70]

Certain aspects of this common life appear alien to the modern reader.

These were due to two major influences. The first influence, frankly admitted by the directory, was the application by the Holy See to the Missionaries of Africa of various new dispositions intended to regulate religious congregations with simple vows.[71] This was in spite of the fact that the Society was not a religious congregation, but an institute of secular priests and lay auxiliaries, and that Lavigerie's original constitutions were of a markedly different character. There were several monastic practices in the 1908 constitutions. One was the recitation of the penitential Psalm 50 (51), *Miserere mei Deus*, while moving from dining room to chapel after dinner and supper. This procession was one of the "sights" in every mission station. Another practice was the maintenance of silence all day "apart from breakfast, recreation and work requiring speech."[72] Yet another was the custom of reading during meals, at least for a quarter of an hour, excerpts from the Bible, *The Imitation of Christ* or the martyrology. Several petitions were made to the General Council for exemptions to this rule, especially when one of the three community members was absent. However, Livinhac and his council were inflexible on the point. One missionary must read aloud, while the other ate. Another characteristic custom of religious life was the need to be accompanied by a confrere when visiting outside the community. Given that White Father communities were small, and that visiting villages and homes was the principal method of evangelization, this was an unrealistic requirement, and the directory itself envisaged the substitution of a "person of confidence," approved by higher authority. Most missionaries were accompanied on their pastoral journeys by a trustworthy catechist. The visits usually took place in the afternoon, followed by language study, translations and the preparation of instructions back at the mission station. It must be admitted that the tension between community life and active apostolate was certainly aggravated by practices suited to a religious congregation.

The other influence was that of the French seminary, with its traditions of austerity and clerical etiquette. "The life of the missionaries," said the *Constitutions*, "should be by itself a rough and continual penance."[73] Early rising was a *sine qua non* of the missionary vocation. A threefold failure to rise on hearing the regulator's *Benedicamus Domino* at 5 a.m. was a ground for dismissal.[74] There were to be no luxuries and, although a third of a litre of wine could be drunk at meal times (presumably in France and North Africa) in an equal measure of water, spirits and tobacco were strictly forbidden except for medicinal purposes. A small flask of spirits might be carried on journeys as "a praiseworthy precaution" against indisposition or great fatigue, and to purify brackish and unhealthy water.[75] Tobacco was allowed in cases of "real utility" and not for sensual satisfaction, "in the measure in which each one judges it truly useful for his health or for the better accomplishment of his duties."[76] The modern reader might be surprised to find that tobacco could be judged good for one's health, but it would appear that this refers to the usefulness of tobacco smoke in keeping away mosquitoes and flying insects. It was also recommended for neutralizing the stench when cleaning wounds.[77]

The etiquette for external modesty is frankly hilarious by modern standards. The head was to be held high, but the eyes lowered when speaking to superiors and persons of the opposite sex. The missionary should have a serene, calm and open expression, redolent of joy, rather than sadness. His posture should be upright. His hands should not be in his pockets or dangling negligently. His walk should be natural and poised, but not heavy or precipitate. His tone of voice and gestures should be moderate. He should avoid coughing, spitting, nose-blowing or touching his head or face.[78]

Livinhac exhorted his missionaries to "crush under foot the enjoyments and conveniences of life."[79] But however desirable it might be in itself, austerity could certainly be justified by an aspiration to share in the simple lifestyle of the African poor. In fact, conditions of life in tropical Africa were sufficiently rough and penitential in themselves, without the need for much further mortification. The capital means of sanctification, however, was obedience to the superior, and on this point the directory was eminently sensible. Superiors were to treat confreres as "intelligent collaborators" and to involve them with the supervision and direction of the work. There was to be a cordiality of relations at all times.[80] This common-sense approach to the virtue of obedience differed in spirit from the more traditional concept of "blind obedience" enshrined in the *Letter on Obedience* of St. Ignatius Loyola, which was obligatory reading during monthly recollections.

Spirituality and Relaxation

Weekly confession, together with monthly recollection days and annual retreats, were all required means of sanctification for the Missionary of Africa. However, the constitutions only recommended, but did not impose, the long retreat after ten years of missionary life. This was called the "second novitiate" and consisted of the "spiritual exercises in complete silence for one month."[81] The reference was to the method of St. Ignatius, although the saint was not mentioned by name. Surprisingly perhaps, St. Ignatius did not figure among the authors recommended by Livinhac for spiritual reading. These included: St. Francis de Sales, St. Alphonse Liguori, Frederick William Faber, St. Vincent de Paul, St. John Mary Vianney, John Croiset and St. Thomas à Kempis.[82] In 1908, common retreats were introduced in the missionary provinces, and they were an immediate success. They took place on the occasion of a general visitation and the retreat preacher was usually the visitor himself. They were held at seminaries like those of Rubya, Kabgayi or Bukalasa, or at mission stations with large enough premises. Frequently, the vicar apostolic took advantage of the occasion to hold a diocesan synod. "These common retreats," wrote a missionary from Burundi in 1908, "are an excellent idea and a great grace from God, in spite of the inconvenience caused by the absence of two missionaries from a single station, the journey, the expense etc."[83] "One would have thought we were at the mother house," remarked Bishop Lechaptois approvingly.[84] The long retreats took place at Algiers and were usually directed by Paul Voillard (1860–1946), Livinhac's eventual successor as superior general.

The hour-long recreation after dinner was usually curtailed by the need for a *siesta*. The evening recreation lasted half an hour and took place by candlelight between supper and night prayers. The *vade mecum* of the Society states that it usually consisted of conversation between *confreres*, while sitting or walking. If there were games, they were not to be strenuous, but confined to those that provided a real refreshment of mind and body.[85] Card games and indoor board games were nowhere mentioned, but some missionaries undoubtedly played a musical instrument. Some costumed Luba dancers entertained the missionaries at Lusaka (Upper Congo) during an evening recreation in 1899, and everyone was delighted when Brother Hubert Metzels (1864–1907) produced his accordion. The evening ended with dancers and missionaries saying night prayers together.[86] Early forms of the wind-up gramophone began to make their appearance in the first years of the twentieth century: in Kabylia in 1904, in Nyanza South at Katoke in 1905 and Bukumbi in 1907, and in Tanganyika at Galula and Kirando in the same year. Called variously "graphaphone" or "phonograph," the early models used cylinders, rather than flat records. They were used to great effect in public sessions with the local people, but they may also have contributed to the evening recreation.[87] The same may be true of the magic lanterns, stereoscopes and projectors, which also made their appearance at this time. These were first used at Galula (Tanganyika) in 1905, at Marangara (Rwanda) in 1907, at Rubya (Nyanza South) in 1908 and at Banankuru (French Sudan) in 1909.[88]

Maurice Bellière and Thérèse

The year 1898 saw the publication of *Histoire d'une âme*, the spiritual autobiography of a twenty-four year old Carmelite, Thérèse of the Child Jesus, who had died of tuberculosis at Lisieux in France the year before. The book took the Catholic Church by storm, and her canonization in 1925 led to a worldwide devotion.[89] She had wanted to be a missionary, but her poor health made this impossible. Instead, she offered her daily renunciation of little things within the convent for the mission of the church. The White Fathers were convinced, as we have seen, that their mission was under God's control, but they shared the pessimistic view of salvation that was common at the time. According to this view, the salvation of non-Christians was not only uncertain without the intervention of the missionary. It was, to all intents and purposes, impossible. In this theology, Satan and the stranglehold of sin loomed large. In her writings, Thérèse presented the image of a God who is sheer merciful love. She believed that even without becoming active missionaries, people could participate in Christ's salvific presence in the world through prayer and suffering in this life, and through the power and love of the risen Christ in the next. Her teachings sowed the seed of a more positive missionary outlook, and she was declared patroness of the missions by Pope Pius XI.

In the year before her death, she corresponded with a young Missionary of Africa, and her letters to him contain some of the finest expressions of her teaching. Maurice Bellière (1874–1907) was twenty-one, a year younger than Thérèse, when he wrote to the prioress of the Lisieux Carmel in 1895, asking for a nun to pray for him so that he might overcome "the assaults of the world."[90] Bellière also came from Normandy. His mother had died in giving him birth, and he had been brought up by an aunt. His father took no interest in him, and it was only when he was ten or eleven years old that he was told about his biological mother. In 1895, he was a student in the Bayeux diocesan seminary of philosophy, aspiring to become a missionary and dreading the mandatory year of military service that was imminent. He was a student of average ability and has been described as a "weak, needful man, sensitive, impressionable and keenly aware of his sins."[91] While waiting for a place at the seminary of the Paris Foreign Missionary Society, he was called up for military service. In October 1896, he completed what was, for him, a "distressing military year," and wrote again to the Carmel. The prioress was Thérèse's elder sister, Pauline, who promised to give him as correspondent "a saint among saints." Bellière was back in the seminary facing an uncertain future when Thérèse wrote him her first letter on October 21st, telling him that even the worst blunder of his life should be regarded as a grace.

By November 1896, it was clear that Bellière did not qualify for the Paris seminary, and he applied to join the Missionaries of Africa. Thérèse wrote in December about the immense power of suffering to win grace for others, and enclosed a poem, "To live by Love." In February 1897, she wrote again, hinting at her impending death. Her letter of April 25th addressed him as her "brother" and set out her doctrine of the "Little Way." His past sins, she told him, should be seen as an encouragement, because "God loves the littlest ones." In June, Bellière reported to her that he had been released by the diocese and that the way was open for him to join the White Fathers. Although Thérèse drafted a more explicit letter about her imminent death on June 9th, the letter was never sent. Instead, on June 21st she sent him a further instalment of her doctrine of God as "merciful love." Then on July 13th she told him in no uncertain terms that she would not recover from her illness and that she sought union with the risen Christ in heaven, where she would share in his active presence in the world and in his mission to souls.

Bellière was thunderstruck by the news and told her that in heaven she would learn of his faults. Thérèse replied that Jesus had forgotten those faults long ago. She sent him her photograph. By now he was completely at ease in his correspondence with her. They wrote to each other like brother and sister. On August 5th 1897, he wrote the simple words: "I found Jesus in you." For her part, she loved him for his frailty. He was "the quintessential little soul" to whom she was attracted.[92] After beginning the correspondence with Bellière, Thérèse also corresponded with Adolphe Roulland of the Paris Foreign Mission Society, a missionary in China, but there was never the deep personal friendship with him that developed between her and Bellière. The latter had been accepted by the Missionaries of Africa and was preparing to travel to Algiers. In her last letter to him Thérèse promised to bequeath him a reliquary and a small crucifix. Bellière wrote three more letters. The last, dated October 2nd, she never received. On September 30th, as Bellière was crossing from Marseilles to Algiers, she died with the words, "How I love you, O my God, how I love you," on her lips. Bellière's final letter told of his happiness at arriving in Africa for the novitiate. His first day as a Missionary of Africa was her first day in heaven. With her first missionary, Thérèse began her own mission to the world.

Although he found the life spartan, Maurice Bellière fell in love with Africa and was eager to do his best as a White Father. In 1898, he began theology studies at Carthage. He was ordained to the priesthood on June 29th 1901 and celebrated his first Mass at the Algiers Carmel. For a year, he acted as English secretary to Livinhac, who became fond of him, and in this capacity Bellière met Charles de Foucauld, who was on his way to found the hermitage of Beni Abbés. Then in July 1902, Bellière was posted to the Nyasa Vicariate, where he served in several of the Angoniland stations, finally becoming superior of Likuni. In 1903, he survived the dreaded blackwater fever, but a year later his behaviour began to give cause for concern. His inconstancy, astonishing flightiness, apparently purposeless journeys and visits to administrative officers, coupled with continuing fevers and a dispute with a confrere, Jean Louveau (1871–1906), who had wounded his sensitive nature, made the missionaries at Likuni believe he had contracted sleeping sickness. The lengthy incubation of this disease meant that his behaviour was affected before his condition was diagnosed. He had probably contracted it on a journey with Bishop Dupont in 1904.

Dupont did not believe Louveau's impassioned denunciations, but he was at a loss to explain Bellière's behaviour.[93] The latter left for France without authorization and was summoned to Algiers by the General Council of the Society in December 1905. The Council found Bishop Dupont's letters obscure and Bellière's own explanations unsatisfactory. It was felt that there were extenuating circumstances and that the missionary should return to Nyasa in a subordinate capacity.[94] Bellière's bouts of fever continued and his departure for Central Africa was delayed. Eventually he was admitted to the White Fathers' sanatorium at Autreppe (Belgium), where he was judged to have lost his mind. It is probable that he was advised to join the diocese of Bayeux. However, on June 8th 1907, he was admitted to the Bon Sauveur Psychiatric Hospital at Caen—the very same hospital to which St. Thérèse's own father had been taken—and he died there on July 14th at the age of thirty-three, without having formalized his departure from the Society. He was buried at his natal village of Langrune, his epitaph proclaiming that he was the "spiritual brother and protégé of Saint Thérèse." Patrick Ahern summed up his story thus: "If his achievements were not heroic and if his life seems to have ended in disappointment, his ideals were great and his dreams could soar. When all has been truly said, his end was no disaster." He achieved another kind of martyrdom.[95]

The Transformation of Africa by Africans

Saving Africa with Africa

"Missionaries should above all be initiators. The really lasting work must be accomplished by Africans themselves who have become Christians and apostles."[96] Cardinal Lavigerie wrote these words in 1874, but the idea had been planted in his mind ten years earlier. In 1864 Daniel Comboni (1831–81 who was canonised on 5 Oct. 2003) had produced his *Plan for the Regeneration of Africa*, the theme of which was to "save Africa with Africa."[97] Lavigerie met Comboni in Paris in 1865, and this theme became a major objective of his missionary policy. It took pride of place in his "Secret Memorandum" to *Propaganda Fide* of 1878, in which he gave Comboni credit for the idea.[98] However, Lavigerie elaborated the concept, trying to discover the means of carrying it out in practice. In the first place, he believed that baptism made Christians into apostles. Baptism imposed the obligation to proclaim and promote the faith, and this was the duty of ordinary African Christians. Secondly, he explored ways in which some of these Christians could become effective auxiliaries of the missionaries in the work of the apostolate. From the outset, the Missionaries of Africa sought to convince their neophytes to become apostles to their fellow Africans. Socio-political factors helped to make this happen spontaneously in Uganda, and this mission subsequently became a model for others. The most striking examples recorded are those in Buddu (Uganda): for example, the case of the Catholic who undertook service as cook to a Protestant chief in order to instruct his people, and who brought forty of them to the mission. Another was that of the old blind flute player at Villa Maria, who wanted to become a Christian and who brought along with him thirty-two men.[99] At Mugera (Burundi) in 1905, missionaries reported a similar snowball effect, by which those attending catechism brought others to the classes.[100] At Kissaka and Save (Rwanda), it was a rule in 1906 that a person who wanted to be baptized must first instruct others.[101] At Mpimbwe (Tanganyika), when the Christians went on their annual fishing trips, they invited the local people to join them at morning and evening prayer.[102] And at Baudouinville (Upper Congo) and Chilubula (Nyasa), Christians and catechumens were zealous in baptizing the dying.[103]

However, the missionaries were not always successful in imbuing their neophytes with the apostolic spirit. At Kashozi (Nyanza South), it was said that Christians were rarely apostles, and at Virika in the kingdom of Toro (Nyanza North), a missionary lamented that Christian families were inward-looking, with no spirit of proselytism as in Buganda.[104] At Msalala (Unyanyembe), a missionary complained that the converts were not energetic or ardent, and that they did not understand the need for proselytism. Whether others believed in Christianity or not was not considered their affair. He put this down to a spirit of independence and a traditional apathy in religious matters, which missionaries could not overcome.[105] By contrast, at Segu (French Sudan), the Bambara neophytes were real "catechists," doing their utmost to interest the youth in Christianity, and the same was true of the Mossi at Wagadugu, who possessed a genuine spirit of proselytism.[106]

The Project for Doctor-Catechists

Cardinal Lavigerie's intuition concerning the relationship of medical care to evangelization has already been mentioned. In 1881 he began to realize a plan that had been maturing in his mind for several years: the foundation of an institute for training ransomed African slaves as doctor-catechists. In African tradition, religion and health are connected, and the project appealed to Lavigerie because, without professionalizing medicine, it allowed the graduates to exercise the greatest possible influence on their compatriots.[107] The Cardinal wanted the candidates to retain their African way of life, even though the training would not be available in Africa itself. He chose Malta as the place for this experiment as a kind of "halfway house" to Europe, and especially because the island provided a strongly Catholic environment.[108] Lavigerie believed that the project was a practical way to "save Africa with the Africans."

The Cardinal's enthusiasm was not shared by all his missionaries. Some of them, especially Livinhac and others working in the Nyanza Vicariate, were pessimistic. Livinhac suggested, as a cheaper and less risky alternative, that lay brothers could teach the children technical skills in their own country.[109] The missionaries thought that uneducated African boys would find a university course too difficult, that the journeys involved would be too expensive, that their future work would depend on a continuous supply of expensive European medicines, and that as laymen they would be independent of church authority and a possible cause of scandal. However, Lavigerie railroaded the project through the Society's General Council, objections notwithstanding, and the Apostolic Institute for Young Africans was opened near Valetta in July 1881 with sixteen ransomed slaves as students. They were divided between three sections, according to age and experience. Only the first section attended a university. They did this as "free students," with no ultimate right to the title or diploma of a doctor.

The others received the equivalent of a primary and secondary education at the Institute itself.

The atmosphere of the Institute was that of a junior seminary, with spiritual exercises, a brass band and occasional amateur theatricals. Students had to buy their own textbooks, which were in English, but courses at the university were in Italian. Several of the students travelled to Paris and Rome. Further intakes of ransomed slaves and freeborn youth from different parts of Africa were received by the Institute over the years, eventually reaching a total of forty students, with twenty-four in residence at any one time. Only eleven attended the university medical courses. Three of these were posted to Tanganyika: Adrian Atiman, a Songhay from French Sudan, together with Louis Coro and Augustine Mechire, also from French Sudan. Four were posted to Upper Congo. They were Charles Faraghit, a Bambara from French Sudan; Joseph Gatchi, a Hausa from Kano (in modern Nigeria); Andrew Mangwe, who was himself from Congo; and Chelula, who had been ransomed in Ugogo (German East Africa). Two were sent to Nyanza (Uganda): Francis Gogé and Michael Abdu, both Hausas from Nigeria. Charles Mudu became "the black doctor" of Carthage, and Marie-François Nazara Yanaba, a Mossi from Kupela (French Sudan), who had not followed the full course of medical training, was posted to successive mission stations among the Malinke of French Sudan.[110] The most renowned and best documented of the doctor-catechists was undoubtedly Adrian Atiman.

Adrian Atiman

Adrian Atiman (c. 1866–1956) worked for sixty-seven years until his death, in and around Karema, western Tanzania.[111] He was born at Tundurma on the river Niger, in what is today Mali. His father was called Jucda and his mother Tandumosa; they were probably Muslims. He was less than ten years old when he was captured and enslaved by Tuareg raiders, who sold him to an Arab in Timbuktu. In 1876 he was ransomed for three hundred francs, along with five other African children, by a Missionary of Africa who found him in a slave market in northern Algeria. He was taken to Algiers where he met Cardinal Lavigerie, who arranged for his education. Lavigerie himself baptized the teenager in 1882. Shortly afterwards, he was sent to the Malta institute to study medicine. Although he was at first uneasy in the dissection room, and there were no women to help in the maternity section, Atiman succeeded in his studies and spent seven years in Malta, after which he made a pilgrimage to Rome and had an audience with Pope Leo XIII.

In 1888 Atiman, now aged 23, and two other Malta graduates, Joseph Gatchi and Charles Faraghit, joined the seventh caravan of the Missionaries of Africa to equatorial Africa. From Zanzibar, they crossed to the mainland and accompanied Charles Stokes, then still a member of the Anglican Church Missionary Society, to Tabora, and thence proceeded to Lake

Tanganyika. At Karema, formerly known as "Fort Leopold," Atiman was given a room near the door of the fort. Barely six months after his arrival at Karema, Atiman married Agnes Wansahira, daughter of Mwami Mrundi, chief of the Bende tribe, on September 5th 1889. This marriage, which was seen as a political alliance between the Catholic mission and the Bende, was not an entirely happy one, but to the great joy of his parents, the couple's only child, Joseph, was ordained a Catholic priest in 1923, the first of Tanganyika Vicariate. Agnes died in 1939.

Although Atiman began his medical apostolate within days of his arrival at Karema, he was obliged to join the Christian militia which was being organized by Joseph Dupont (*Moto-Moto*). Dupont's authority was recognized by the German authorities, and his small force counted twenty men, including Atiman, armed with Greek rifles. For his first five years at Karema, Atiman was caught up in skirmishes with slave traders and their Bende supporters. In 1894 he personally welcomed the White Sisters (MSOLA) to Karema, and worked closely with them in the medical apostolate thereafter.

In 1897, Atiman had to leave Karema because of his wife's adultery, and was posted to Zimba where he helped to found the Catholic mission. While at Zimba, he resisted the efforts of some Nubian soldiers to make him a Muslim by force. Two years later he returned to Karema, and was asked to start a catechist training centre at nearby Usoa. This school had an eventual enrolment of sixty pupils. He also trained nurses to help him in his Karema clinic. Atiman used western medicine, but also experimented successfully with traditional remedies. During 1907 he was involved in the treatment of victims of sleeping sickness, and a year later cured Brother Antoine (Joseph) De Leyer (1874–1953).[112] In the same year, he gave eye treatment to Jean-Marie Robert (1879–1966).[113]

On the silver jubilee of his arrival at Karema, Atiman was awarded the papal medal *Pro Ecclesia et Pontifice*. In his old age Atiman was much decorated, receiving the Legion of Honour from the French government, the papal *Bene Merenti* medal, and several British awards, among them the Wellcome Medal in 1955, with which he was the first African to be honoured. At Karema he was hailed as "our devoted and learned doctor catechist."[114]

Little is known about Atiman's companions, Coro and Mechire. Coro was sent to Kala, where he started a school with an enrolment of fifty-four students in 1895. Besides being a skilled carpenter, he was also a musician and choirmaster. He married the daughter of a chief near Kala. After medical work at Kala and Kasanga, he retired to Mwazye and died there. Mechire married Maria Wamwina and the couple were sent to Mambwe to help start a catechist school. This was moved to Utinta and later to Karema. At Utinta, Mechire became the village headman, levied taxes and judged cases. At Karema, the school included a junior seminary stream. Mechire taught first aid and hygiene. During the East African campaign of the 1914–1918 War, he served as doctor to a German column and was shot dead by a Belgian patrol.

Joseph Gatchi

After teaching for a time at the catechist training centre of Mpala, Joseph Gatchi arrived at Kibanga (Upper Congo) in 1889, where he carried out apostolic and medical journeys, in addition to acting as a catechist, musician and literacy teacher at the mission itself. He even ransomed slaves. Gatchi married a Congolese wife, Emma Kabwe, who bore him a daughter, but died in childbirth. His second wife, Judith, bore him three more daughters. Gatchi was put in charge of the military post at Kibanga, and helped repulse the Arab attack of 1890, for which he earned the praise of the Belgian officer Deschamps. His complaints about the unhealthy climate of Kibanga led to its closure in 1893, and he was posted to Joubert's village of St. Louis, Mrumbi. There he acted as catechist and visited the surrounding villages. He had nearly two thousand pupils for catechism. In 1898, he saved Adolphe Claeys (1869–1900) from blackwater fever. After the outbreak of sleeping sickness, he was forced to move to Misembe, but in spite of the move caught the disease himself and died on July 11th 1912.[115] Joseph Gatchi was remembered as an intelligent, cultured and outspoken man.

Charles Faraghit

Charles Faraghit (c. 1870–1931) was born in French Sudan (Mali), and was a member of the Bambara tribe.[116] In childhood he was captured by slave raiders and taken across the Sahara desert. He was ransomed from slavery in Algeria by the Society of Missionaries of Africa. After education and baptism, he was sent as a teenager to study in Malta. On finishing his medical training in 1888, he travelled to Lake Tanganyika in the caravan of the newly appointed vicar apostolic of Tanganyika, Léon Bridoux, in the company of his fellow Malta graduates, Adrian Atiman and Joseph Gatchi. Atiman remained on the eastern shore of the lake, while Faraghit and Gatchi crossed to Upper Congo, where they became religion teachers at the catechist training centre of Mpala. While at Mpala, Faraghit tended those who had been wounded after Jules Jacques' defeat by the Arab slavers.[117] Afterwards, Faraghit became the resident doctor-catechist at the outstation of St. Michael's Kipongwe. In the confused situation of Upper Congo caused by the activities of Afro-Arab slave raiders, Catholic authorities, as we have seen, exercised civil power in their stations. Consequently, Faraghit became the headman of Kipongwe, and was renowned as a hunter.[118] Meanwhile, his community scarcely grew. Bishop Roelens believed that Faraghit was bored by his catechetical and teaching duties, and remarked that "he does not have the sacred fire."[119] In 1907, he was moved to Baudouinville, where Albert Smulders (1880–1957) was asked to oversee his medical practice.[120]

Faraghit married the niece of a local chief, who bore him twelve children, only four of whom survived. One of them, Joseph Faraghit, became the second Congolese priest to be ordained, on November 1st 1921. Two years after his arrival at Baudouinville, Charles Faraghit entered government medical service at Mpweto, and not long afterwards settled in the Tanganyika vicariate (German East Africa), where he became a trader at Kirando and Karema. "May God keep him a good Christian" was the fervent wish of the diarist in 1909.[121] In his last years he returned to Congo and died at Baudouinville (Kasongo) on April 24th 1931. Andrew Mangwc worked in Baudouinville before becoming a trader in his turn, while Chelula, who came to Baudouinville in 1893, remained there as organist and nurse till the end of his life.

Charles Mudu made a name for himself at Carthage, treating literally thousands of sick people there, and baptizing the dying in 1898–1899.[122] In 1900 he continued his medical work at Thibar and died there on April 27th 1903.[123] Francis Gogé and Michael Abdu, the two Hausas from Nigeria, arrived at Bukumbi, on the southern shore of Lake Victoria, towards the end of 1890, having already practised their medical skills en route. They reached Rubaga (Buganda) on February 21st 1891, and their medical assistance was immediately requested by both King Mwanga and by Lugard for his soldiers at the Kampala fort. Bishop Hirth did not favour this medical practice and expressed an intention of employing them as catechists or teachers only.[124] Gogé, who had already married, caused a scandal by petitioning the king for a high office at court, and Abdu was judged a failure as a teacher of catechism.[125] Gogé was shot through the heart in the attack on Rubaga Mission on January 24th 1892, and his widow, Paulina, as we have seen, was placed in charge of the girls' orphanage at Ushirombo (Unyanyembe). Abdu continued to teach in the catechumenate at Rubaga and in the junior seminary that had been started there. After 1897, he became a government medical officer, and finally went to live at Kagasa, near Villa Maria, where he organized elephant-hunting expeditions.

Marie-François Nazara Yanaba

Marie-François Nazara Yanaba, the Mossi from Kupela (French Sudan), had been ransomed by Lavigerie and baptized at Malta on December 24th 1889. He was confirmed by Livinhac in the chapel of the Institute on January 29th 1892.[126] A man of small stature, he travelled back to French Sudan with Bishop Toulotte, was posted to Kisidugu in Guinea and later to Dinguira and Diamu near Kayes (modern Mali). He was employed as a catechist and health worker until his death at Diamu in 1950.

Travelling back to French Sudan in 1897 with Bishop Toulotte and Nazara Yanaba were four other Malta graduates.[127] Alexander Hippolyte Kirsy, a Mossi from La, had been ransomed by the White Fathers in the Sahara. On his return from Malta, he served as a school monitor at Kissi, Banankuru and Wagadugu, and travelled on the first caravan to the Mossi Kingdom in 1900. He was reunited with his family and died at La in 1906.

Felix Alexis Payete, from Kuritenga, had been ransomed at Ghardaia. After Malta, he accompanied the Missionaries of Africa to Kupela and his nearby natal village. Peter Joseph Badwa (Badoa or Badoi), another ransomed captive, became a teacher at Segu, but was dismissed for misbehaviour. He became a government interpreter. Another ransomed captive on the first caravan to the Mossi Kingdom was a certain Philip, who still remembered the language of the Mossi (Moore).

Ugandans in Malta

Several groups of boys went from Uganda to the Malta Institute. There were five in 1884: Charles Buzabaliawo, Venant Kibi, Leo Ngongo, Charles Mugoya and Fortunat Kwatoti. The last named joined the Missionaries of Africa as a lay brother, but did not make a final profession. Buzalabiawo, Kibi and Mugoya worked for a time as catechists in Uganda, Mugoya teaching music at the junior seminary in Villa Maria. Ngongo worked in German East Africa. In 1890, six more Ugandans, who had been members of a party of fourteen travelling with Livinhac to Europe, arrived in Malta. Three of these joined the Missionaries of Africa as lay brothers. Of these, the most well-known was Toby Nabuga Kizza (1873–1961). One of the others, Karoli Nampagi, did not persevere, and the third, Paulo Kiwanuka, died on his return to East Africa in 1894.[128] Of the three others who remained at the Malta Institute, Stephano Kiwanuka is known to have worked for a time as a catechist on his return to Uganda. Stephen Mugoya's name appears with that of Nazara Yanaba on a document of 1894–1895, but there is no information concerning his further activities, nor those of John Baptist Kaluzemo.[129]

   In 1891, Livinhac visited the Institute in Malta and decided to put an end to the medical training that was given there. Henceforward, the students were to receive catechetical training only. Of those who graduated as catechists after this change of orientation, a dozen are little more than names to us and there is no information about the rest. An exception is Jean-Baptiste Sambateshi (c. 1878–1972), whose biography has been extensively researched.[130]

Jean-Baptiste Sambateshi

Jean-Baptiste Sambateshi was born near Bagamoyo on the East African coast, around the year 1878. He was about five years old when he was kidnapped and enslaved. Taken to Zanzibar, he was ransomed by a Missionary of Africa and attended catechism classes for four years as a boarder at the procure. He was baptized at the age of twelve on April 13th 1890. In September of that same year, he accompanied Livinhac to Europe, together with the thirteen other young Africans already mentioned. They went first to Paris, where they were present in the church of St. Sulpice for Cardinal Lavigerie's opening sermon of the Paris Anti-Slavery Congress. Then, after a visit to Lyons and an audience with Pope Leo XIII in Rome, Sambateshi and five others travelled to Malta via Carthage. In 1896, after his catechetical training, Sambateshi left Malta, in the final group of graduates from the Institute. He was taken to Kayambi (Nyasa) where he began teaching at the orphanage school. After building himself a house in the nearby village of Ilondola, he married a Bemba girl called Kanyapa on January 25th 1898. When the orphanage was replaced by a day school in 1900, Sambateshi continued as the teacher of its top class. An important aim of the school was to train the most promising pupils as catechists. In 1901 an adult catechist school was opened at Kayambi, and Sambateshi was placed in charge of religious instruction there. During this time, he also taught catechism in the villages. By January 1910 he had left his job at Kayambi, probably because of the low salary, and settled at Chilubula, where he played the harmonium on Sundays. When World War I broke out, he moved to a village near Kasama and became a government interpreter. Between the two world wars, with government assistance, he became a full-time farmer and eventually died in April 1972. He is pictured in a photograph of 1896, holding a flute, indicating his talent as a musician.

John Baptist Limongo from Buganda and Leopold Kizibao, a Congolese ransomed at Tabora in 1882, served as catechists at Ndala (Unyanyembe).[131] A certain Victor (possibly Jean Victor Mhoro), "one of our Malta children," enchanted everyone with his harmonium playing at Msalala in 1900.[132]

Closure of the Malta Institute

Barely two and a half months after Lavigerie's death, the General Council of the Society discussed the closure of the Malta Institute. However, it was decided to leave the decision to the 1894 Chapter, so as not to give the impression that the Council was in a hurry to abandon the Cardinal's cherished project.[133] The Chapter decided that it should continue because it had been established by the founder himself.[134] When the Chapter ended, the suggestion was made that the Institute should be moved to either Egypt or Tunisia, but financial reasons led to the abandonment of this idea. The Institute was finally closed in 1896 for all the reasons that had been voiced against it in the first place.

The general impression has been that the doctor-catechist project was a failure. Certainly, the medical training was haphazard and inadequate, and only ten of the forty students took the full course that was offered. Of these ten, only half were given the opportunity to practice their medical skill. Teacher-catechists, trained in their own vernacular or vehicular languages and working in their home vicariates, were ultimately more useful than doctor-catechists, who were mostly foreigners, trained in a foreign country. Moreover, missionaries did not want auxiliaries who functioned more or less independently of their control. When slave trading began to diminish, the possibility of ransoming captives for the project also ceased, and it did not really make sense to send free children, like many of the Ugandans, for training abroad. The White Sisters (MSOLA) took over the medical apostolate, and were considerably more effective than the medical graduates from Malta. Nevertheless, Lavigerie's daring plan had a limited success. Some of those trained in Malta were outstanding personalities, who made an important contribution to the teaching of religion and the formation of catechists.

Local Catechists—Travelling and Residential

Lavigerie had said that the lasting transformation of Africa would be the work of Africans themselves. If they were honest, missionaries admitted that this prophecy was fulfilled in their catechists. "The good done by the cate-chists is immense," wrote Bishop Auguste Huys (1871–1938). "Without them, it would be impossible for missions to grow and to assure a future for our holy religion in these countries."[135] In spite of the fact that mis-sionaries sometimes saw them as competitors and were often hard on them, Joanny Thévenoud (1878–1949) at Wagadugu believed that catechists were more effective apostles than the missionaries were.[136] A missionary at Kyanja (Nyanza South) confessed in 1905 that the catechist relieves the mis-sionary of half his work.

In the period 1892–1914, the White Fathers were laying foundations of the church in the vicariates they controlled. These years also witnessed the rise of the catechists: the recruitment and training of these catechists, and the impact they made on the pace and extent of evangelization that had been started by the missionaries, were important developments in this period.[137] At the beginning, as we have seen, missionaries relied on spontaneous cat-echists and contact people, sent out in advance. They also brought newly baptized Christians from one mission station to another to help with the catechism; there were no professional catechists. At Kissaka (Rwanda), intel-ligent local youths were enrolled in 1903—after three or four months' instruction—as "pro-catechists," presumably on the analogy of "provicars apostolic."[138] They simply repeated to others the catechism lessons they themselves were learning. At Nyundo (Burundi) in 1904, there were no cat-echists, just "advanced children" selected for the task, and at Msalala (Unyanyembe) "untrained children" were employed to teach the little cate-chism by heart.[139] At Kayambi, Dupont had founded a boarding school, which he called rather grandly his "college." It had a large, floating enrol-ment of free-spirited young Bemba, but a rather poor record of attendance. This was partly because Dupont, unlike Roelens in Upper Congo, believed in the positive value of African traditional upbringing, and encouraged mutual visits between the pupils and their families. Over a period of three years, some eight hundred Bemba youth passed through Dupont's college, attracted by the kindness and generosity of this stranger who loved them. Dupont and the pupils went on hunting expeditions together during which

Dupont would give them catechetical instructions. Some of the youngsters joined the catechumenate, and others were expected to influence their families at home. The experiment depended entirely on the personal magnetism of Dupont, and it did not survive his departure in 1899.[140] The "college" was closed in 1900 during his absence in Europe. Such informal catechists achieved rather little. As a missionary remarked at Save (Rwanda), "our improvised catechists are not prophets on their own hills."[141]

Visiting villages and homesteads was a major component in the White Fathers' strategy of evangelization. "We have learned this method of visiting villages from other stations," wrote a missionary at Msalala in 1904.[142] People came to the mission for casual employment, but they did not necessarily come spontaneously to the catechism classes—they had to be visited in their own homes. However, the missionaries' time was limited. Mornings were spent in the classroom or supervising construction. It was only in the afternoon that they could go visiting, and, until the arrival of the first bicycles in 1908, journeys were made on foot. This meant that visits were restricted to a fairly small radius. The first catechists were itinerant and assisted them in this work of visiting. Until catechist training could be organized regionally or at the vicariate level, promising neophytes who could read and write were formed at the mission station. Living at the station or nearby, they visited the nearest villages in the evenings. In Ukerewe (Nyanza South) in 1901, the trainees visited fifteen villages after their classes, and in Bunyoro (Nyanza North), where 116 catechists were recruited in 1905, each visited five to ten villages. At Kita (French Sudan) in 1906, either a missionary or a catechist was visiting the villages about every eight days. At Mpala (Upper Congo) in 1904, catechists were trying to cover all the villages, including important ones not previously visited. Although Dupont's "college" at Kayambi had been closed in 1900, a "small college of catechists" was functioning there in 1906 after the bishop's return, and its trainees were reaching some ten thousand people.

By 1912–1913, Bishop Lemaitre (French Sudan) found itinerant catechists expensive and ineffective. He thought it better to have a few good volunteers living permanently in the villages. Nevertheless, at Chilubula (Nyasa) during the same years, there were still travelling catechists going out in pairs to the villages every three weeks. Jules Keita, who became a catechist at Kati (French Sudan) after the Second World War, was an itinerant catechist for thirty-six years, visiting the villages on a bicycle and setting up catechumenates. By this time, of course, there were also residential catechists.[143] The goal of the early travelling catechists was to invite people to catechism classes at the mission station, or to assemble them for catechism in their own villages. Sometimes, quite large numbers were sent out. At Ushirombo (Unyanyembe) in 1899, eighty-four catechists were sent out ahead of the missionaries, and at Kashozi (Nyanza South) in 1905, twenty-one were sent out. At Galula (Tanganyika), a catechist was sent out on Sundays in 1907, to give catechism to people kept at home during the season of cultivation.[144]

In Uganda, residential catechists became the norm much earlier than elsewhere. This was largely because of the territorially-based political structure. Ambassador catechists were sent out to befriend the chiefs. Where accepted, they stayed, built a chapel and began to gather sympathisers. Other catechists were installed when visiting missionaries found a receptive chief. It then became possible to establish a network of catechists across the political map of the vicariate. The White Fathers built large mission stations in which at least three missionaries resided, and these—unlike the stations of the Mill Hill Missionaries, which were usually staffed by one priest—were fewer and further apart. In the "Catholic provinces," nearly every village had a chapel. For example, at the end of 1894, there were 122 chapels in Buddu and 25 each in Rubaga, Sese and Bukumi. During Mwanga's revolt of 1896–1898, 148 out of 166 village chapels were burnt down. In 1912, there were 45 outstation chapels in Villa Maria, 43 in Mitala Maria, 35 in Busubizi and 50 in Koki.[145] In the other vicariates a conscious decision was taken to change from itinerant to residential catechists. In 1908 the missionaries at Ushirombo (Unyanyembe) decided to install married catechists in fixed village posts. This was also done in Nyasa Vicariate, Upper Congo and especially in Tanganyika, where villagers and their chiefs asked for catechists, and were prepared to build a classroom, a catechist's house and a lodging for the visiting missionary.[146]

The duties of the village catechist were virtually the same everywhere. They were the leaders of the local Catholic community. They taught by their own example, gave advice and assisted the sick and dying. They were the points of contact between the village and the mission station. On Sundays, they led community worship in the absence of the priest, reading a homily composed by the missionaries. They helped prepare the catechumens for baptism, and were responsible for running the residential catechumenates when these were established in the villages. They also prepared children for reception of the sacraments and accompanied them to the mission station for this. They demonstrated new agricultural methods and crops, and lived in large well-built houses. They were effectively the principal agents of religious and social change, the representatives of a new society and a new authority. Inevitably, they came into conflict with the traditional authority of the chiefs.

Catechists and the Chiefs

We have seen that several doctor-catechists married into the families of local chiefs, and even exercised the functions of chief or headman in the Christian villages. The professional, residential catechist, who was responsible to the mission and not directly to the administration, appeared as a rival to the traditional chief. Such catechists lent support to those who criticized traditional practices such as divination. Chiefs were often unpopular as tax collectors and organizers of forced labour, but catechists refused to be involved in such unpopular measures and were accused of disloyalty. In Unyanyembe, a newly appointed chief arrested three catechists and took them to Tabora, where they were released by the German administration and absolved from road work. A similar dispute took place with the chief at Gayaza (Nyanza North).[147] At Segu (French Sudan), a campaign was launched in 1906 against a zealous catechist called Eugene. His mare was poisoned and his goats began to disappear mysteriously. Native administration police mocked and ridiculed him and other catechists in the villages around Segu.[148] One catechist died at the hands of a chief. This was Toby Kibati, an exemplary catechist in Rwanda, loved for his gentleness, fairness, affability and dignity. He died of wounds inflicted by the emissary of a Hutu chief, Ngomba Yombi, in February 1901. His murderer had threatened and then pierced him with a spear while demanding food supplies, and Toby became a "martyr of charity."[149] It was important in such potentially hostile situations to appoint catechists from the area itself. Although the expertise of catechists from Buganda was appreciated in Bunyoro, there were places like Usui (Nyanza South) where the catechists' authoritarian attitude made them and the missionaries who employed them unpopular.[150]

Catechist-Teachers

Initially, the catechists' teaching role in the villages was limited to religious instruction and reading. From about 1908, the more educated catechists in Uganda were encouraged to add writing to the programme, and small groups of children were taught arithmetic, geography and history by catechists at the mission station itself. The catechists in the central mission stations assisted the missionaries in preparing catechumens during the final phase of preparation for baptism, and in the education of Catholic children who came for residential courses before making their first communion. No distinction was made, or indeed thought desirable, between catechists teaching religion and schoolmasters teaching secular subjects. However, the popular demand for education led to a growth in the number of catechists and schools, and aspiring teachers saw the role of the multifunctional catechist as the first rung on the ladder of opportunity. Funds were limited and catechists were poorly paid. The poverty of the catechists did not impress people at Save (Rwanda), and at Mkulwe (Tanganyika), five catechists left in a body in 1905. Streicher, who had no fewer than 965 catechists in his vicariate, was obliged to halve their pay in 1906, and many left. In the following year, all the catechists of Chilubula (Nyasa) went on strike for higher pay, threatening to go work in the South African mines. There was a standoff with Dupont, who dismissed several on the spot, but no one resigned. At Wagadugu in 1908 two of the best catechists resigned because the salary was too meager.[151] As improved training became available and education began to be reorganized after 1910, better opportunities presented themselves to those who wished to leave.

Catechist training centres began to be established in the vicariates.[152] Although the aim was to train mature, married men as catechists, these centres resembled junior seminaries and many included a seminary or "Latin" stream, which eventually became a separate entity. At Mitala Maria (Nyanza North), which had sixty boarders, there were nine houses for families and a dormitory for single men, as well as a classroom and study room. At Kagondo, there were thirty children in the catechists' school, who were taught Swahili, Latin, geography, arithmetic and music.[153] The centres attended to the spiritual and intellectual formation of the catechists, using all the spiritual exercises of the White Fathers. Streicher instructed his missionaries on how to use these auxiliaries when they graduated. They were to be dressed "in printed cloth," not bark cloth, and if married, paid one *rupee* per month. The effectiveness of the residential catechist depended, to a great deal, on maintenance and networking. Missionaries paid them regular visits and the mission stations held meetings of catechists and updating sessions. The sacramental life of each individual was also closely monitored.

Machtilda Munaku and the Women Catechists

Very early on, women catechists were employed for teaching catechism to young Catholic children and preparing them for the sacraments. This was especially the case in Uganda, where the very first and most remarkable female catechist was Maria Machtilda Munaku (c. 1858 to 1934).[154] Munaku was born and brought up at Mityana in Singo County, Uganda. She was the sister of St. Noë Mawaggali, who was brutally martyred at Mityana on May 31st 1886. Mityana was the headquarters of the chief of Singo County and the focus for a remarkable Christian community, led by St. Mathias Kalemba Mulumba and St. Luke Banabakintu, the other two martyrs from Mityana. Munaku was taught the catechism by her brother and St. Mathias Mulumba. On the day of her brother's martyrdom, she boldly came out of hiding and offered to die like her brother for the Christian faith. The king's messenger, Mbugano, who had come to attack the Christians of Mityana, took Munaku captive, intending to make this young woman of twenty-eight his wife. Munaku courted martyrdom again by refusing to accompany Mbugano. However, although she was cruelly treated and bravely resisted his advances, she soon realized that Mbugano had no intention of killing her.

Baffled by the young woman's constancy, Mbugano, on arriving at the Ganda capital, decided to offer her to the missionary Father Siméon Lourdel for a ransom. A gun and some ammunition were handed over, and Munaku was freed. Baptized in July 1886 by Lourdel at Rubaga, she took a personal vow of virginity on her own initiative, promising never to marry anyone except Jesus Christ. Soon, other girls joined her at Rubaga, and together they accompanied the missionaries to Bukumbi on the southern shore of Lake Victoria during the civil war of 1888, where Munaku helped to found and run an orphanage for girls.

In 1890 she returned to Uganda, shortly after the death of Lourdel, her patron and saviour. When the seminary was started in January 1891, Munaku was put in charge of the material needs of the boys. Gathering together an association of unmarried women to help her, she moved with the seminary to Bukalasa in 1903 and then to Katigondo in 1911. Known as the "Mother of the Seminary," she continued to supervise the seminary kitchen until 1924, when this responsibility was taken over by the newly founded female religious order, the Bannabikira sisters. "I have no money to give the future priests," she is recorded as saying, "but I work for them with my hands." In fact, she gave an edifying example to the seminarians and even offered them timely advice on occasion. She died on April 7th 1934, aged 76, and was buried in Bukalasa cemetery.

In 1895, ten women catechists were at work at Villa Maria, and there were others at Bikira and Rubaga. Some of them are known by name because they afterwards joined the Bannabikira Sisters. In 1898, Streicher took four of them to Ushirombo, the first mission station of Unyanyembe. The MSOLA (White Sisters) arrived in Uganda in 1899. Under their direction, a "novitiate" for twelve women catechists was opened in 1901. Four of these went to work at Rubaga in 1902, two each to Nandere and Bujuni, and two went to Villa Maria, where a second novitiate for women catechists was started in 1905. These developments were overshadowed by the opening of a religious novitiate at Villa Maria in 1908. All of the religious novices were chosen from among the nearly one hundred women catechists already at work in the various stations. This was the beginning of the Bannabikira Sisters, or Sodality of the Daughters of Mary, which had more than fifty professed members by 1914. These continued their catechetical work alongside laywomen. A similar development, but on a smaller scale, took place in Tanganyika Vicariate. The novitiate of the Religious Sisters of St. Peter Claver started at Karema in 1907, and in the following year a house was opened by them at Zimba. By 1909, they were already teaching catechism to one hundred girls, and were joined there by three more novices.

The Catechumenate

The Importance of the Catechumenate

"We do not believe in baptizing people who will continue living like pagans," wrote Bishop Lechaptois in 1906.[155] The catechumenate was intended to ensure that this did not happen, and that conversion to Christianity was profound and lasting. It is difficult to exaggerate the importance of this institution in the history of the White Fathers' missions during and after this period. Not only did the catechumenate guarantee individual faith conviction; it transformed African society itself. It did this by creating structures analogous to the traditional African systems of social classifica-

tion based on age, and by producing a new vision of society. People instinc-
tively made comparisons between the Catholic Church and Africa's own cultural associations. The Church was an alternative version of their own
society, with new names and external signs, such as crosses, medals and
rosaries. It had a new calendar, a new set of ceremonies and new sets of relationships. The structure of the catechumenate was such that over four years,
groups of initiants came together in the villages with their catechists and visiting missionaries, or made the journey to stay for long periods at the central mission station, creating lasting ties among individuals and communities.

The catechumenate of the early church was the primordial form of
Christian teaching. It offered a framework within which, over a period of
time, new Christians were introduced to Christian doctrine and morality.
The context in which it took place was liturgical. During the eighth and
ninth centuries, the catechumenate vanished altogether, to be replaced by
the elementary religious teaching given to children by parents and sponsors,
and by the more formal catechism that appeared in the age of printing. As
a church historian, Cardinal Lavigerie knew of the catechumenate and
decided that his missionaries would revive it. Already in 1869, with the
approval of Rome, he decreed the establishment of catechumenates for the
instruction of Arab children in his North African orphanages. Ten years
later, he ordered their creation in equatorial Africa. This decision was
enshrined in the juridical documents of the Missionaries of Africa, approved
in 1908 and 1914.[156]

Lavigerie's Restoration of the Catechumenate

As he devised it, the four-year catechumenate was divided into postulancy
and catechumenate proper. For two years, postulants were to learn only the
natural truths of religion: the goal of life on earth, God, creation and the
fall, the commandments, sin and forgiveness, reward and punishment after
death, good and bad angels and the power of faith against demons. During
this period they were not to attend any public worship in a sacred building.
After due examination of their knowledge and way of life, they could be
admitted to the catechumenate proper, in which they were introduced to the
person of Jesus Christ and the mysteries of the Holy Trinity, the incarnation, the redemption and the sacrament of baptism. There was a great insistence on the supernatural, on miracles and the marvellous efficacy of prayer
and the sacraments. These catechumens could attend Mass up to the end of
the service of readings. They were not allowed to be present for the
Eucharistic sacrifice itself, or to attend Benediction of the Blessed Sacrament.
The catechumenate ended with baptism if the candidates were judged ready.
Otherwise, baptism could be postponed, if need be, even to the hour of
death. The baptized were the "faithful" who could be taught about, and
receive, the other sacraments, and for whom there were no more secrets.

The early printed catechisms produced by the Missionaries of Africa, and

used by their postulants and catechumens, scrupulously observed this programme of teaching. The Little Catechism of Algiers, translated into Swahili
in 1884, introduced the student to *Isa Kristu* after 53 questions; while the
Swahili translation of the Kabyle Catechism in 1885 introduced the
redeemer after 102 questions, out of a total of 250. Even the abbreviated
version of this catechism, designed for those in danger of death, ploughed
through 92 questions before reaching the incarnation.[157] Modern catechetical authorities recommend that the student be introduced to the person of
Jesus Christ as soon as possible, but quite apart from this, practical difficulties arose in Africa when Catholic postulants heard about Jesus for the
first time from the Protestants and Muslims among whom they lived, rather
than from the missionaries and catechists themselves. In 1908 Bishop Hirth
in Rwanda broke with Lavigerie's instructions regarding the postulancy. He
regarded the Gospel as the "heart" of the whole catechumenate and ordered
that the person of Jesus Christ and the Christian mysteries be taught from
the beginning.[158]

Cardinal Lavigerie was sceptical about African traditional religious
beliefs, and knew little about them, but the missionaries soon found that
their postulants were not a *tabula rasa*. On the contrary, they came to the
catechism class with a great deal of religious "baggage" concerning God,
spirits, the creation, and good and evil. Much of this could be exploited in
a section dealing with the truths of natural religion. This was especially the
case with the missionaries' teaching about good and evil spirits and the
power of demons. Although there was usually no personalized Devil in their
religious tradition, Africans were keenly conscious of evil and evil forces.
This corresponded to the emphasis on Satan and his kingdom in missionary soteriology. "The Devil is very strong here in Ubungu," wrote Théophile
Dromaux (1849–1909) at Galula (Tanganyika) in 1902. "The most terrible
wild beast here is the Devil," wrote Augustine van Waesberghe (1870–1934)
from a neighbouring mission station in 1903. Cannibalism, sorcery and
secret societies convinced Bishop Roelens that Urua (Upper Congo) was the
"citadel of the Demon." The diarist of Mugera (Burundi) wrote in 1907:
"Here the Devil has long claws and also a long tail. Many old recalcitrants
cling to it and will not let go." When a beam fell on a lay brother's head at
a building site at Nya Gesi (Upper Congo), the reaction was predictable:
"Satan is furious to see the reign of God established here."[159] The White
Fathers were convinced they were engaged in an apocalyptic struggle
between the forces of good and evil. "The Catholic Church enters the utter-
most fortress of the Devil," remarked a missionary in Mbarara (Nyanza
North). Even in North Africa, missionaries were conscious of the Devil's
presence. A missionary at Bou Noh (Kabylia), for example, wrote: "The
relentless struggle between the city of God and the city of the Devil continues here, as elsewhere." At Katoke (Nyanza South), there was a "hand-to-
hand fight with the Devil."[160] In their preaching, and especially in the Lenten
retreats that were held in parishes, missionaries laid emphasis on this strug-

gle. In 1900, Streicher announced as the subjects for the Holy Week retreat: salvation, sin, death, judgement, hell, the prodigal son, the Eucharist, sacrilegious communion, contrition and perseverance.[161] At Kashozi (Nyanza South) in 1906, the retreat conferences dwelt on the goal of man, salvation, mortal sin, death, judgement and hell, while a missionary at Ulungwa (Unyanyembe) wrote with satisfaction in 1908: "Hellfire is beginning to arouse disquiet in their minds."[162]

A Religion of Personal Devotion

Much more is known today about the early catechumenate, and especially its liturgical context, than was known in Lavigerie's day. In his restored catechumenate, there were no rituals other than the bestowal of a cross or a medal. Godparents played an important role in the ancient catechumenate, but there was no mention of them or where they were to come from in Lavigerie's instructions. The focus was almost exclusively on baptism, with no catechesis on confirmation or Holy Communion, which should normally accompany adult baptism. In fact, there was no detailed post-baptismal catechesis provided.[163] There was, however, a welcome emphasis on prayer, and this was nourished in practice by paraliturgical devotions. Besides the traditional liturgical year, with its seasons of Advent, Christmas, Lent and Easter, the Missionaries of Africa celebrated the month of St. Joseph (March), the month of Mary (May), the month of the Sacred Heart (June), the month of the Rosary (October) and the month of the Holy Souls (November). These months had their own characteristic devotions. Many celebrations took place outside the church building, for example, the rogation processions, the Palm Sunday procession, processions to Marian shrines and chapels on major Marian feasts, the splendid Corpus Christi procession, the Stations of the Cross and visits to the cemetery to pray for the departed. There were also the sacramentals and ritual blessings of fields and seeds, prayers for rain and the intercessions against plagues such as locusts or caterpillars. Every aspect of African rural life was sanctified by the church. These popular devotions compensated for the lack of a strictly liturgical spirit.

In 1911, Streicher decided to advance the date of baptism to the middle of the final, intensive, six months of the catechumenate, which took place at the mission station. This was so that the newly baptized could receive a catechesis on the Eucharist and acquire the habit of frequent communion.[164] It was a decision inspired by St. Pius X's "Instruction on Frequent Communion." Throughout 1908, a Eucharistic *Triduum* was celebrated in one mission station after another to introduce the people to frequent communion.[165] The missionaries were very happy with the new practice. Not only did it nourish the people's devotion and spiritual life, but it bound them more closely to the mission station itself.

Catechisms, Sacred History and Bible Stories

Another problem with the syllabus of the catechumenate and the catechisms that were used for it was that they were too notional and cerebral. The catechisms, it has been said, were excellent *resumés* of bad seminary theology.[166] The teaching had to be made more attractive. In 1906, the *Chronique Trimestrielle* published a catechetical article advocating a more personal and positive approach, and two years later a missionary from Kaliminwa (Nyasa) quoted Bishop Dupont in the same sense. "He recommends that we love the Africans sincerely and attract them with interesting catechisms and classes."[167] Lavigerie, as a historian, had realized the importance of "sacred history" in catechesis, and authorized its use in 1886.[168] The 1914 *Directory of the Constitutions* also spoke of the need for a "simple historical method."[169] The first book ever printed in the Rwandan language was by Alphonse Brard: *How God has Spoken to Human Beings*, published in 1902. It told the stories of the principal events of the Old and New Testaments, the life of Jesus and the founding of the church, the history of the church under persecution and confronted by heresies, finally the expansion of the church among the nations. The book contained beautiful, coloured pictures. Large wall pictures and magic lantern slides were also used to great effect.

The religion taught by the Missionaries of Africa was not a religion of the book, but a religion of personal devotion, and this was the secret of its success. In Uganda, the Anglican George Pilkington and a committee of Ganda translators produced a whole Bible in Luganda in 1897, translated over a five-year period mostly from Steere's Swahili Bible.[170] The Moravian Missionaries, present in the White Fathers' vicariates of Unyanyembe and Tanganyika, produced a translation of the whole New Testament into Nyamwezi in 1909 only twelve years after their arrival, but the White Fathers, who had been thirty years in the area, had no mandate, nor indeed ability, to undertake Bible translation.[171] The sole translations of the four Gospels to be produced by them during this period were in the Berber dialect of North Africa in 1900 and 1907, in Luganda and Rutoro in 1905 and in Swahili in 1913. It was only after 1920 that translations of the Gospels began to be made in earnest by White Fathers in the vernaculars of sub-Saharan Africa.[172] Catholic missionaries, of course, had no intention of encouraging the private interpretation of Scripture, but there was a danger that their converts would be biblically undernourished. Until they entered the field of Bible translation, the White Fathers preferred to use books of Bible stories, and had no wish to emulate the Anglican missionaries whom they had seen in Uganda, struggling to communicate a heavy-going exegesis of difficult texts from the Old Testament and the Book of Revelation.[173] Jacob Ecker's German *Bible for Schools*, published at Trier in 1906, was translated into the Rwandan language by Paul Barthélemy and Léon Classe in 1911. It had 245 pages with illustrations by Philip Schumacher. It was a beautiful book, in constant use until the 1930s, and was rapidly translated into all the languages of Nyanza South. Containing one hundred stories from each of the Old and New Testaments, it was easy reading, without any account taken of the literary genres.[174]

The Catechumenate and Movements of Mass Conversion

Although Lavigerie's insistence on a four-year catechumenate was loyally upheld by Livinhac and his Council, vicars apostolic were flexible in practice. This was nowhere more evident than in Uganda.[175] Up to 1892, there had been a rigorous four-year catechumenate, with all the instructions being given at the mission station itself. After 1892, the two-year postulancy took place in the villages, with regular instructions by the catechist. This was followed by an intensive residential course of six months at the mission station, with two instructions a day given by the missionaries, leading up to baptism. Numbers had a great deal to do with this change. By the turn of the century, Uganda had eighty percent of all the catechumens in the White Fathers' vicariates; and even on the eve of World War I, it had more than fifty percent of all the catechumens. In 1893 intakes for the residential course were restricted to three hundred catechumens. These were taught in batches of one hundred, a new group starting every six or seven weeks. It was judged physically impossible for the missionaries to give a full two years of instruction. Moreover, the logistics of housing and feeding hundreds of catechumens in and around the mission station presented a problem. Avenues of huts were constructed, and banana groves and vegetable gardens were planted. Fortunately, the banana or plantain, the staple food in much of Uganda, was a steady crop that was not subject to seasonal availability or variability like maize or millet. From 1910, another change was introduced. Residential catechumenates of five to six months were started in some of the major outstations. These were run by the catechists themselves. The catechumens only went to the central mission station for the final few weeks before baptism. In 1901, when Livinhac insisted that the full four-year catechumenate should take place in the villages, Streicher refused to comply.[176] In 1908–1909, the General Council noted Streicher's modification of the four-year catechumenate, but allowed a dispensation in individual cases only. A general concession was refused.[177] In 1912 however, despite Livinhac's misgivings, the General Chapter of the Society upheld the right of vicars apostolic to make modifications and exceptions to the four-year catechumenate.[178] The Ugandan practice, however, seems not to have been extended to other vicariates where conversions were not so numerous.

Liturgical Catechesis

Baptism was conferred at Easter or on other major feasts, such as Christmas, the Assumption or All Saints. These and other celebrations—confirmation, which involved a visit from the Bishop, the solemn communion of children and above all *Corpus Christi*—were days of unaccustomed joy. Because there were large numbers of Christians and a scarcity of missionaries, the task of founding and serving a sacramental church involved some problems. At Easter, priests spent days in the confessional. At Rubaga in 1904, five priests spent an entire day hearing the confessions of confirmation candidates, and in 1907, Christmas confessions took eight whole days. On the Saturday before Palm Sunday seven priests heard the confessions of twenty-five hundred people. At Entebbe (Nyanza North), a missionary was ordered to rest on account of "paschal fatigue."[179] Streicher was worried that the confessional could undermine the time available for spiritual direction, but when time did allow, conversations in the confessional were better than any catechism. A missionary from Ukerewe (Nyanza South) gave an example of such a conversation in 1901: "Where will these sins take you?" "To hell!" "Do you want to go to hell?" "No!" "Well, these sins want to take you there. Do you still love them? Do you not hate them? Do you still want to commit them?"[180] Occasionally, there were instances of misplaced zeal, as when a group of Christians at Nazareth (Nyanza North) celebrated Good Friday by beating each other "for Jesus" in a nearby banana grove like Spanish flagellants, or when two altar-boys fought at Nsasa (Rwanda), because one had "stolen" the other's indulgences by usurping his place as a Mass server. There was also the choice of unacceptable or unrecognizable baptismal names, such as *Peccatorum, Haricot* (Henriko) and *Goligoli* (Gregory).[181] But these were the occasional hazards of the very genuine religious devotion created by the catechumenate system.

Christian Presence in the Muslim Milieu

Lavigerie's Approach to Islam

Members of the Society of Missionaries of Africa have lived for more than 130 years as a Christian presence in a Muslim milieu. This has been a unique experience and it has resulted in their developing a distinctive approach to Islam. They are still working in the Maghreb and the Sahara, and also in sub-Saharan Islamic countries such as Mali, Niger, Chad and Sudan, as well as in the Near East, in Jerusalem. Lavigerie's interest in Islam began in 1860, when, as Director of the Work of the Eastern Schools, a French association for the support of missionaries in the Near East, he visited Lebanon and Syria to bring relief to the Christian survivors of a massacre carried out by the Druze, with Turkish complicity. His first impressions of Islam and of a Muslim *jihad* were inevitably negative, and he was forced to realize the coherence and the intransigence of Islamic society. On the other hand, he was favourably impressed by the humanity and culture of the exiled Algerian leader, the Amir Abd-al-Qadir, whom he met on this journey. It was about the same time that Lavigerie met the Abbé F. Bourgade, who had established a college for Muslims, Jews and Catholics in Tunisia. Bourgade was the author of three books on Islam which proposed a formal dialogue in narrative and Socratic form.[182] Opinions differ about the value of these works, but such efforts seem to be more than mere Christian apologetic.[183] In fact, they envisage Islam as a preface to the Gospel, which left to God's providence, would eventually bear fruit in Christian truth.[184] Although he appreciated the religious sentiments of Muslims, Lavigerie did not favour such a Socratic dialogue himself, but he recommended Bourgade's writings to his missionaries.[185] He probably thought that, given the right circumstances, a religious encounter between Christianity and Islam would eventually be possible.

A year after becoming archbishop of Algiers in 1867, Lavigerie founded the Society of Missionaries of Africa. They were to disarm Islamic disdain for Christians by adopting their external manner of life, their clothing, food, language, poverty and nomadism.[186] As it turned out, the Algerians abandoned the *gandourah* (tunic) and *burnous* (cloak) before the White Fathers did, and there was consequently the danger of clinging to an anachronistic folklore in the matter of clothing.[187] In 1868 Pius IX made Lavigerie apostolic delegate for the Sahara and (French) Sudan, and fifteen months later named this region a prefecture apostolic. This meant that Lavigerie's responsibilities extended to the enormous territories that lay beyond the diocese of Algiers.

Lavigerie's approach to Islam was far from bookish or theoretical. It derived from his ongoing experience of the Muslim milieu. From the outset, he claimed the right to love, and pray for, the Muslims of Algeria, not merely to be a chaplain to French settlers, soldiers and officials. His presence as a Catholic archbishop among the Muslims of North Africa was to be an active presence. Soon after his arrival in Algeria a succession of calamities occurred: an earthquake, followed by drought, a plague of locusts and a cholera epidemic, accompanied by famine. Refugees poured into the towns. Some ninety thousand people died of cholera, and another twenty thousand died of starvation. The French administration took no extraordinary measures to deal with the crisis, but Lavigerie set up camps and took in nearly two thousand orphans, eight hundred of whom died of cholera.[188] The anti-clerical administration suspected Lavigerie of proselytism and feared a fanatical Muslim reaction. Lavigerie, however, with the support of Napoleon III and French public opinion, took his stand on freedom of conscience and the freedom to practice charity. He forbade any of his refugees to be baptized, except babies in danger of death, and he was able to claim in a letter to Marshal MacMahon, governor of Algeria, in 1868, that not one of the eleven hundred children in his care had been baptized.[189]

This policy, however, was soon overtaken by events. Lavigerie remained responsible for a large number of children when the famine was over, and requests for baptism grew. Lavigerie acquiesced for those he considered most worthy, and the first baptisms took place in Rome and Marseilles.[190] About one thousand of these children were eventually baptized. From among these young neophytes, sixty or so were educated in view of the Arab minor seminary at St. Eugène. The others were to populate the Christian villages which Lavigerie established in the Chélif Valley, St. Cyprien des Attafs in 1872 and Ste. Monique des Attafs in 1874. Lavigerie saw these young Algerians as a Christian elite for the evangelization of the whole continent, the nucleus of a new African church, but the Christian villages were a disappointment and had no religious impact on Islamic society.[191]

The Mission to Kabylia

From his first arrival in Algeria, Lavigerie was attracted by the mountainous region of Kabylia, as a place he thought more likely to respond to the Gospel. This was because of the so-called "Kabyle myth" that the area had once been Christian, and that its people might be disposed to return to the religion of their ancestors.[192] In fact, these mountain dwellers had been virtually untouched by Roman civilization, let alone by Christianity. Although they disliked the Arabs and were slow to accept Islam, the Kabyles had developed their own amalgam of Islam and traditional beliefs, and had no desire to be Christians. Lavigerie's missionaries went to Kabylia in 1873, and twenty years later the White Fathers' mission stations in Kabylia had increased from two to seven. They were to remain at that figure for some years to come. At the turn of the century, another two stations were founded further south.

In order not to play into the hands of the anti-clericals, as well as to avoid offending Muslim susceptibilities, Lavigerie forbade any open proselytism. There were to be no boarding schools and no public catechumenates. Small day schools could be started and a small number of boarders allowed at the mission stations, but religion was not to be taught in school. Instead, there was to be a solid moral formation implicitly inspired by Christian principles. Catechism could be given to those who requested it, but there were to be no baptisms without the authorization of the parents and of Lavigerie himself.[193] Babies, however, could be baptized at the moment of death. "We talk as little as possible about religion," wrote a missionary in 1892.[194] In addition to the schools, the missionaries also opened dispensaries and hospitals. This social and humanitarian action was motivated by Christian love and compassion, while creating a favourable climate for eventual conversion to Christianity in the far distant future. Only in proximity to a military barracks, such as at Fort National (Tagmount Azouz), did the missionaries have a substantial church attendance of French soldiers. It was a long-term strategy which Lavigerie believed would take at least a hundred years to bear fruit.

The White Fathers in Kabylia aimed at the eventual conversion of individuals, but they had no intention of turning them into Frenchmen. In spite of this, they and their students encountered considerable hostility, as well as a measure of sympathy, from parents, *marabouts*, and village authorities. The mission diaries are filled with stories about the heroism of orphans, boarders and would-be catechumens under persecution. Although the missionaries felt that they were appreciated, it was sometimes said that the moral education they gave in school was put better in the Qur'an.[195] The missionaries' primary contact was with children and young people outside of the parental culture. Very few adult baptisms took place. It is fair to say that, although the missionaries had been inserted into Kabyle society, they failed to interest it in Christianity.[196] Instead there was a silent opposition.

Although adult conversions were few, there were many baptisms of dying babies. For example, between September 1904 and September 1905, only thirteen adults and thirty-five children of Christians were solemnly baptized in the whole of the Algerian Province, but there were nearly a thousand baptisms of infants in danger of death.[197] "Our neophytes are the dying," wrote one missionary in Kabylia.[198] The surreptitious baptism of dying babies was not merely an exigency of the pessimistic salvation theology then in vogue, but was seen as the creation of a "Kabylian Church Triumphant." These "Holy Innocents" were now intercessors for Kabyles on earth. That the White Fathers sometimes felt isolated in the midst of millions of Muslims is beyond doubt. They were also envious, as a visiting journalist discovered, of the thousands of converts being made by their confreres in equatorial Africa.[199]

"No one desires the conversion of African infidels more than me," Lavigerie was reported as saying, "but I only want it in conformity to the rules of wisdom."[200] As they saw it, the missionaries' first aim was to "destroy Muslim fanaticism," to undermine faith in Mohammed and, even more implausibly, "to detach North Africa from the Arabs and Islam."[201] Although they were forbidden to indulge in polemics themselves, polemical literature was recommended reading, such as Michel Nau's *The Qur'an against the Qur'an*.[202] The first edition of the *Directory of the Constitutions* in 1914 had few references to Islam, but the advice it gave was positive. Missionaries, it said, "are not there so much to destroy and risk creating a powerful party of opponents, as to build by a friendly exposition of the truth." Habitual criticism of Islam was not the right method to follow.[203] The missionaries, in fact, had no preparation for the encounter with Islam. They did not know classical Arabic and could not read the Qur'an, even with the permission from higher authority that was then required. Even their knowledge of the Kabyle language was far from perfect.[204]

French anti-clerical legislation threatened the mission schools in Kabylia in 1904. Without government support, many schools were forced to close. At length, in 1913, a ministerial decree closed all the remaining mission schools and the White Fathers began to concentrate on pastoral and social ministry.[205] Henceforward, with Henri Marchal as superior, there was more of a religious encounter with the Kabyle community. "The missionaries are filled with joy. We talk of God to people of good will. We encourage a real prayer of the heart . . . Many souls are uneasy with their (Muslim) religion, but we do not imagine they will come to us."[206] Religious conversation was now seen as the instrument of conversion, but conversion required a persevering and progressive action.

Lavigerie believed that God was positively at work among Muslims, but he still thought baptism necessary for salvation. However, he was not in a hurry to baptize individuals. Individual need was to be subordinated to that of the collectivity. To this extent, his salvation theology was less pessimistic than that of his missionaries.[207] Lavigerie was implacably opposed to Jansenism, and he must have been aware of the church's condemnation of the Jansenist proposition: "Outside the Church there is no possibility of grace."[208] Nevertheless, the theological climate of the time would not have allowed him to reflect very profoundly on this truth with reference to Islam.

The Mission to the Sahara

The White Fathers were establishing posts in the northern borderlands of the Sahara, and opened a station in the Mzab at Metlili in 1874.[209] From there, a party of three missionaries set out to cross the desert in January 1876, only to be massacred by Ajjer Tuaregs near El Golea, a few days out of Metlili. Seven years later, a second party of White Fathers took a different route, from Ghadamès in December 1881, and were massacred two days into their journey by a coalition of Tuareg tribesmen. Lavigerie had hesitated to send them out, after the annihilation of a French expedition led by Colonel Paul Flatters in February of the same year, but allowed himself to be persuaded that it was safe.[210] After this disaster, the Sahara was abandoned for several years. Gradually, as the French army moved south, the White Fathers returned to the Saharan oases in the 1880s and 1890s, re-opening mission stations at Ghardaia, Ouargla, El Golea (which became a military headquarters), and El Abiod Sidi-Cheikh. As French armies conquered and occupied the western—and eventually the southern—Sahara, the White Fathers in the oases of the northern desert pursued, with tireless devotion, the same evangelization policies as their brothers in Kabylia, in education, medical work and the avoidance of overt proselytism. As we saw in the previous chapter, Lavigerie recruited the so-called Armed Brothers of the Sahara to guard their stations and escort missionaries on their journeys, but was obliged to disband the force in 1892, after only eighteen months in existence.

In 1891 the Prefecture Apostolic of Sahara and Sudan was made a vicariate, and the province of Kabylia was attached to the dioceses of northern Algeria. Anatole Toulotte became vicar apostolic of the Sahara and the Sudan at Lavigerie's death in 1892, but resigned five years later. Meanwhile, Prosper-Augustin Hacquard, who would be Toulotte's successor in the vicariate, was dispatched on the first caravan to French Sudan and the famous city of Timbuktu. This was a holy city of eight thousand inhabitants which had been a centre of Islamic culture in the fifteenth century, and which had acquired in French minds a mystique that far exceeded the reality. Hacquard and four White Father companions set off for West Africa on Christmas Day 1894, and having reached Timbuktu in May 1895, founded St. Mary's mission. Very soon, the missionaries were asking themselves what they were going to do there.[211] In fact, the mission in Timbuktu settled down to being a carbon copy of mission stations in the northern Sahara, engaging in education, medical work and the ransoming of children enslaved by the Tuareg. The school was a failure, but the orphanage overflowed.[212] It was even suggested that Timbuktu should be joined to the ecclesiastical circumscription of Ghardaia, if a trans-Saharan route was opened.[213]

The "White Monk" of Timbuktu

One of the White Fathers, Auguste Victor Dupuis (1865–1945), was strongly attached to Timbuktu and became deeply immersed in its languages and cultures. He knew Arabic, Songhay, Tamachek (Tuareg), Bambara and Peuhl. By 1900, he had, together with Hacquard, produced four books on the Songhay language alone, and others were to follow.[214] However, in the midst of this erudition, and in a milieu that precluded open evangelization, he seems to have lost sight of his priestly role. Hacquard feared he was "going native" and that he was overly familiar with the people.[215] Known as "Yacouba," it was said that his reputation had spread along the whole course of the Niger.[216] Unfortunately, Yacouba's familiarity developed into what we would call today "inappropriate relationships," and in 1904, when faced by superiors with the order to leave Timbuktu, he decided that another vocation was calling him. Soon afterwards he married a Peuhl wife, a Muslim, and raised a family of seven children. He became a government interpreter, adviser on native affairs and even, for a short time, Commandant of Goundam, but his main claim to fame was to have founded a native faculty of higher studies at Timbuktu. Yacouba remained a legendary figure, the benevolent patriarch of the holy city. Always loyal to the Christian faith, he attended Mass celebrated by visiting missionaries, and even practised his priesthood by legitimately giving absolution to the dying. In 1945, he himself died in silent prayer, his wife and daughter at his side.[217] Although bishop and missionaries remained on good terms with him after his defection, it was felt necessary to close the Timbuktu mission in 1906.[218]

De Foucauld—Evangelization without Proselytism

When Hacquard died in 1901, the Sahara was separated from the French Sudan, and again became a prefecture apostolic, with Charles Guérin (1872–1910) at its head. As we saw in a previous chapter, Guérin's appointment coincided with the arrival in the Sahara of Charles de Foucauld (1858–1916). As Brother Charles of Jesus, de Foucauld became a hermit in the western and southern Sahara, practising perpetual adoration of the Blessed Sacrament in poverty and solitude.[219] Unable to make converts or find members for his brotherhood, de Foucauld in his solitude saw his work as an apostolate of presence among the Muslims, an evangelization that renounced proselytism, and a spiritual encounter with Islam.[220] After Guérin's death in 1910 and de Foucauld's murder in 1916, the latter's life and witness gave rise to a renewal.[221] Not only was his spiritual message the inspiration for new religious congregations, it also had an impact on the Missionaries of Africa and their thinking about the Christian presence among Muslims. The ideals he proclaimed were a life of poverty and service, a silent presence in the midst of a human group, love expressed through daily occupations, adopting the way of life of a people and enjoying friendship with them.[222] De Foucauld wrote many letters to other missionaries besides Guérin, among them seven to Henri Marchal (1875–1957), whom he met personally in 1913.[223] We do not have Marchal's letters to de Foucauld, but it is probable that de Foucauld was an influence on the new pastoral strategy towards Muslims which Marchal introduced in the Society of Missionaries of Africa.

Henri Marchal

Marchal joined the Missionaries of Africa in 1893, and, after his ordination in 1900, taught Arabic and other subjects at their seminary in Carthage, Tunisia. In 1905 he was appointed to the Sahara, where he joined Guérin at Ghardaia. There he came to the conclusion that missionaries, with the best will in the world, would never make progress in their knowledge of Arabic and Islam without the benefit of qualified teachers.[224] From 1909 to 1912, Marchal was regional superior of Kabylia where he emphasized the need for missionaries to be men of God, while carrying out a relatively open form of evangelization.[225] Then in 1912, he was elected Assistant General of the Society, a post he occupied until 1947, and in that capacity met Charles de Foucauld at Algiers in July 1913.[226] De Foucauld's practice of being spiritually united with Muslims at their Friday Prayers was in line with Marchal's own developing ideas. Muslims, he argued, should be kept open to the action of God's grace, but that grace should not be anticipated, and defiance among the masses should not be provoked. This implied that salvation did not depend on membership of a visible church. The economy of salvation was on a larger scale.[227] In fact, Marchal distinguished between conversion to God, conversion to Jesus and conversion to the church. The Christian missionary had first to invite people to be converted to God. Among these some might feel the inner call to discover Jesus. Finally, in very rare cases, they might accept the social consequences of this faith by joining the church.[228]

In 1927, Marchal was instrumental in implementing the decision of the 1926 General Chapter to found an *Institut des Belles Lettres Arabes* (IBLA). Established finally at Tunis, it taught Arabic and the Qur'an, as well as Islamic theology, law and history. Fifty-one Missionaries of Africa were admitted as students between 1927 and 1949. They were joined in 1932 by de Foucauld's Little Brothers of Jesus.[229] After the Second World War, the General Chapter of 1947 created two centres: IBLA at Tunis remained a centre of research and publications, while the formation programme moved to La Manouba. In 1960 the latter was formally recognized by the Vatican and became the *Institut Pontifical d'Etudes Orientales* (IPEO). When all non-Tunisian organizations were nationalized in 1964, IPEO moved to Rome, where it became the present *Pontificio Istituto di Studi Arabi e Islamici* (PISAI).

In 1937 the Bou Nouh Conference was held under the inspiration of Marchal, and attended by all the mission superiors of Kabylia, as well as by André Demeerseman (1901–1993), director of the IBLA. The conference produced some important conclusions: The goal of the missionaries' educational establishments was not proselytism. The importance of learning Kabyle and of studying Islam was stressed. Missionaries were to be primarily men of God, but there should be no haste in promoting individual conversions.[230] During his long life Marchal published more than thirty works, but probably none were so important as *Les Grandes Lignes de l'Apostolat en Afrique du Nord* (GLANA), which appeared in its final form in 1938, and *L'Invisible Présence de l'Eglise* (1950).

These works contain a pastoral reflection that both has theological implications and is a logical development of Lavigerie's principles.[231] Like Lavigerie, Marchal was a pastoral realist, and he was convinced that the starting point for any missionary work among Muslims was a profound knowledge of the cultural milieu. According to Marchal, the first priority for missionary work among Muslims was not to prepare individuals for baptism, but to promote the essential religious truths. Baptism was not to be conferred except after a prolonged catechumenate and under conditions that ensured perseverance. No specific Christian instruction was to be given outside the catechumenate. There should be a general religious education of the whole people, not of any particular group. Marchal believed that God is positively at work among Muslims and that their religious culture should not be destroyed. There should be no more denigration of Mohammed or demonstration of the falsity of Islam. The aim was not primarily to administer baptism but to save souls. For Marchal, there were many salvific truths from the Bible also found in Islam, and Muslims, he believed, could be saved through these truths if they were understood in the light of supernatural faith. The errors of their religion did not outweigh these truths. The duty of the missionaries was to awaken consciences, to generate a sense of sin, contrition, humility and conversion of heart. They were to invite Muslims to greater confidence in God's mercy, and to lead them patiently into the love of God, of which interior prayer is the sign and the instrument. Concretely, he hoped that Muslims themselves would be apostles to their fellow Muslims. In short, Muslims would become Christians without knowing it.

This was not to say that Marchal was a syncretist, or that he wanted to leave Muslims on their own to become "good Muslims." Nor did he advocate a borrowing from Islam of the "essential truths." For Marchal, the Qur'an was not a *praeparatio evangelii*, a "preparation for the Gospel," in the way that Bourgarde had suggested. The essential truths cannot be understood in a merely Muslim sense. Rather, they must be endowed with supernatural and salvific power. The missionary task was to influence the family and social milieu through kindness, service and Christian witness.

After Marchal

Although there were critics who did not believe that a Christian spirit could be injected into a Muslim community without its knowing, Marchal's reflections became the official policy of the Missionaries of Africa at the time, and were a stimulus for the dialogue of life and spiritual encounter espoused by the Missionaries of Africa after the Second Vatican Council. The White Fathers identified with the legitimate aspirations of the Algerian people in their rebellion against the French colonial authorities in 1946–1962, and ten White Fathers (out of nineteen people—bishop, priests, religious) gave their lives during and after the conflict in 1956–1994.

After political independence, the departure of the French settlers and administrators and the dismantling of church structures, the Catholic mission in Algeria deepened its spiritual relations with Muslims. The larger concept of a two-way dialogue implied that the faith of Christians could also develop through the encounter with Islam, and acknowledged the challenges that Muslims posed as interlocutors. Not only have "underground" Catholic communities of young Algerians, disgusted by the violence perpetrated in the name of Islam, come into existence in the cities, but Muslims themselves have begun to create structures of dialogue with Christians. The *raison d'être* of the Algerian church is now simply to be in relationship with Muslim society, and to be a "covenant of love between the God of Jesus Christ and (this) particular people."[232]

The next chapter studies the relationship between the Missionaries of Africa and African cultures. It considers the development of mutual understandings between the missionaries and the people. Not only did the White Fathers "invent" Africa, but as will have been apparent already, Africans reinvented the church.

CHAPTER FIVE

Africa Re-invents the Church

Re-inventing the Church

Invention and Convention

Culture, as Roy Wagner demonstrated twenty years ago, is a mixture of invention and convention.[1] Human beings engage actively with their own culture, appropriating it and making it their own. What is shared—the convention—has to be invented anew by individuals and groups in the process of living a culture. In this manner, cultural traditions develop and make progress over the generations. Human beings do not inherit a fixed cultural text which they learn by heart. On the contrary, they are given a dynamic and historically specific cluster of concepts and norms, within which they "play the game" of culture. Culture offers a certain perception of reality to which people subscribe creatively. In this activity of invention, they are influenced historically by an intercultural process that can be both local and global. Missionary evangelization is such a process.

Wagner further demonstrates that we can only learn other cultures as extensions of our own: we cannot wish away our own cultural coding. However, through self-criticism and a conscious effort of psychological approximation, we can achieve a relationship with an alien culture that is more or less objective, but the fact remains that we invent or re-invent other cultures, even more than we do our own. The Missionaries of Africa "invented Africa," to use the phrase of V.Y. Mudimbe.[2] That is to say, they formed their own understanding of African cultures. In the discussion about the extent to which such an understanding lacked objectivity, two facts generally receive little emphasis. First, Africans also invented or re-invented the culture of European missionaries, and this African understanding had to be taken into account by them. Second, the missionary understanding of African culture was dynamic, not static. It developed and became more objective as time passed, and as missionaries evinced a greater desire to know these cultures.[3] Their psychological approximation became more conscious and more accelerated. It was inevitable, in such a situation, that the church which missionaries came to found should have been in some sense a re-invention, arising from the complex, but complementary, interaction of evangelizers and evangelized, whatever inequalities were inherent in the process.

Overcoming Ignorance and Prejudice

The White Fathers in equatorial Africa started from a position of ignorance, and even scepticism, where African religion and culture were concerned. Before arriving in 1878, they had only the notorious cultural agnosticism of the explorers to rely upon, travellers whose experience of African ideas and behaviour was cursory and superficial. In the fourteen years of the missionary presence before 1892, much had occurred to dispel this ignorance. The missionaries had discovered that, by and large, Africans believed in a creator God. During the subsequent twenty-two years with which this current study is concerned, the missionaries' knowledge was enhanced, as more of them came to the field and more ethnic groups were engaged. The basic work of evangelization required the missionaries to make judgements about traditional beliefs and about theological vocabulary, especially in choosing a name for God. In opting for the vernacular, missionaries were operating in a medium in which Africans possessed "the first and last advantage."[4] Africans, for their part, were almost completely ignorant of Europeans and their way of life, let alone the explicit message of the Gospel. Both missionaries and Africans learned from the encounter.

However, the will to dispel the initial ignorance of the missionaries had to be established. When given the opportunity, Africans were on the whole eager to learn. The White Fathers, on the other hand, were not at first convinced that they had anything to learn from Africa. In fact, they laboured under several major handicaps. Most, if not all, were unable to distinguish clearly between faith and culture in their message. This was not a meaningful distinction for them. In order to be understood and lived, faith must be inculturated, and it was impossible for them to conceive of the faith they sought to spread as other than the faith they themselves knew and lived. Moreover, the White Fathers transmitted their faith, less by preaching and teaching, than by the "cumulative influence of the dialogue of life."[5] Catholic mission theology scarcely existed, and it would not have occurred to them to make the kind of distinctions we make today. The Missionaries of Africa came to the continent with a strong sense of cultural superiority. According to their understanding, the superior technology of Europe had developed within a Christian civilization, and it was difficult for them to concede that Africans, who were technologically inferior, were actually or potentially their intellectual, moral or spiritual equals. Everything that was unfamiliar to them as Europeans became an object of derision and distaste—even of demonization.

Nevertheless, the White Fathers exhibited a love and compassion for Africans, which, although it was couched in terms of condescension and pity that are distasteful to modern ears, proved to be entirely genuine. Not only did this love enable them to cope with initial culture shock, it became a driving force in their ongoing discovery and appreciation of African ways of life and thought. The White Fathers' missionary vocation was based on a strong faith conviction, but this was founded in turn on a pessimistic theology, which had no place for salvation outside the visible confines of the Catholic Church. It was the missionaries' ongoing discovery of African virtues and values that eventually transformed this outmoded theology of salvation. Signs of this development already begin to appear before the end of our period, with the first mission encyclical, Pope Benedict XV's *Maximum Illud* of 1919, which emphasises the relevance of language and culture for missionary work.[6] It is also true that missionaries shared to some extent in the power and authority of the colonial administration, even if their aims were different and their internationality transcended national frontiers.

Language—The Vehicle of Culture

Cardinal Lavigerie accepted the distinction, current in the nineteenth-century church, between customs and traditions that belonged to the religious sphere and those that belonged to the civil sphere. The first were essential and unchanging, as far as Christianity was concerned. No compromise could be entertained by Christian missionaries in matters of religion, morality, theology or public worship. However, civil customs and the exterior manner of a people's life could and should be retained by those who became Christians. The Cardinal envisaged a Catholic Church in which its members were distinguished from one another, according to different nations and races, by their external habits or conditions of life. He was opposed to the imposition of uniform externals. He resisted what he called the "Italianization of the Church," as well as every tendency to turn Africans into "black Frenchmen."[7] For Lavigerie "external habits" included clothing, food, sleeping arrangements and language. These his missionaries were expected to safeguard and even adopt. Although he was mistaken about the external or contingent nature of language, Lavigerie placed great stress on linguistic studies and even the collection of oral literature. As a result, the Missionaries of Africa became notable linguists, recording and using the African vernaculars to a greater extent than colonial officials and many other missionaries, Catholic or Protestant. Language, unbeknown to Lavigerie, is the central organ of culture, the grid that connects experience to thought. Languages carry with them, as the philosopher Ludwig Wittgenstein demonstrated, a whole system of meaningful forms, an entire design for living. In studying and recording African vernaculars and in rendering them literate, the White Fathers acquired a profound understanding of African thought and behaviour. The service they rendered thereby to African culture far outweighs any manipulation or bias that accompanied their work, as well as any negative approaches towards other aspects of culture.[8] Language study was the saving grace of the White Fathers' missionary project and a key to its success.

The Missionaries of Africa had to create theological and catechetical vocabularies as tools for evangelization. This involved inventing new words and bestowing new meanings on old ones. The process was a constructive engagement with the systems of meaning and forms of expression they encountered, a focused acculturation. As time went on, they acquired African helpers who entered into the spirit of this enterprise.

Cultural Marriages

Whatever their initial distaste for, or unfamiliarity with, African culture, the White Fathers were not passive observers. A real communication of meaning occurred between them and the African people. At times, this amounted to what may be called a "cultural marriage." Connections fell into place, and both African and missionary felt that they were on the same wavelength, as it were. This happened with individual missionaries, like Joseph Dupont, Henri Streicher, or Augustin Hacquard, but it also happened with nationalities, such as the French in Uganda. This was not just a happy accident or a "working misunderstanding," but a genuine marriage of cultural meaning. Africans understood the White Fathers according to their own socio-cultural categories, and these were frequently accepted, not always cynically, by the missionaries themselves.

At times, the Missionaries of Africa—rightly or wrongly—disapproved of what they saw. They encountered customs and beliefs which they judged incompatible with the Gospel. If the missionaries were successful in opposing such things, it was often because Africans themselves had an equivocal attitude towards them, and ultimately accepted that their tradition was flawed. At other times, Africans strongly resisted missionary pressure to bring about changes in their practices. There were many occasions when missionaries were forced to bow before the strength of public opinion. It was very far from the case that Africans were helpless victims of missionary ascendancy. Frequently, the White Fathers, if they were not simply "innocents abroad," realized the strength of the opposition that faced them.

Socio-Economic Development

The Missionaries of Africa felt that they represented modernity, especially with regard to health care, the educational skills of literacy and numeracy and the practical skills of a superior technology. In this they were not wrong, although the conviction made them slower to appreciate the traditional skills of Africa. Medical care, basic education and the teaching of practical skills were closely associated with evangelization, not always as a deliberate bait for potential converts, but as aspects of pre-evangelization or concomitant aspects of evangelization itself. The White Fathers wanted their neophytes to enjoy a better standard of living, and they hoped to recreate the kind of

Christian rural society with which they themselves were familiar in Europe. Such a goal smacked of paternalism and lack of realism, since it took scant account of either African aspirations or colonial priorities. The missionaries had great difficulty in accepting the growing phenomenon of migrant labour, let alone of adapting their own structures and ministry to it.

In spite of this, an African Church was "invented," with its own characteristic structures and ministries, as we have already seen in examining the role of catechists and the working of the catechumenate. Moreover, before the end of our period, 1892–1914, the first painful steps had been taken towards creating and integrating an African clergy, who would eventually take over the leadership of this church before the last quarter of the twentieth century. In this chapter and the next, the themes outlined here are illustrated and further explored.

The Missionary Appreciation of African Culture

Recovering from Culture Shock

On Cardinal Lavigerie's funerary monument in Rome are inscribed words from the spiritual testament he drew up in 1884, and from the dedication to a collection of his own writings, published in the same year. "It is to you that I now come, O my beloved Africa. Seventeen years ago I sacrificed all to you, when, driven by a palpable force from God, I renounced everything to devote myself to your service . . . I have loved everything about Africa, her past, her future, her mountains, her clear sky, her sunshine, the great sweep of her deserts, the azure waves that bathe her coasts."[9] Lavigerie exhorted his missionaries to love Africa and her peoples. He took the word *charitas*, "love," as his episcopal motto, and he harshly upbraided any White Father whose letters or reports bore traces of revulsion or disdain that appeared to belie such love.[10] Missionaries came prepared to love Africans, and—in most cases—this sentiment eventually triumphed over their prejudice, their ignorance and their fear.

This did not mean, however, that they were immune to culture shock. Philippe Déchaume (1879–1947), travelling by train from Mombasa to Kisumu on June 10th 1907, was shocked by his first sight of a Maasai warrior standing at the side of the track. The warrior's head and semi-naked body were smeared with red ochre, and the missionary had difficulty in recognizing him as a member of the human race. "And yet," he reflected, "these are the souls that call us to Africa."[11] In the bosom of this French White Father, supernatural love was wrestling with natural aversion. No doubt, ignorance and unfamiliarity played a part in such repugnance, but culture shock also stemmed from contemporary salvation theology. To the newly arrived missionary, uncouthness was the flip side of paganism. Cleanliness was definitely next to godliness.

In most cases it did not take long for missionaries to become accustomed to, and even to appreciate, the African way of life. A missionary at Rukwa (Tanganyika) noted in 1899 that the local people were "ignorant of the vices of corrupt civilization" and possessed "precious natural qualities."[12] Another in Burundi wrote, after seeing a husband treating his wife's ulcerous leg, "It is said that there is no conjugal love in Africa. That is untrue."[13] The non-Christians "are not so far from the Kingdom of God, as one might think," wrote a White Father in West Nile (Northern Nyanza) in 1912.[14] But it was not only the Africans' goodness which appealed to the missionaries. They were also impressed by their mental abilities and ingenuity. A leopard trap struck the White Fathers at Mkulwe (Tanganyika) as an "ingenious" invention. At Zimba, in the same vicariate, they found the people putting lion- and leopard-fat on the village palisade to scare away wild pigs. "Africans have good ideas sometimes; some excellent solutions to teach us," confessed the diarist in 1909.[15] Three years earlier, after severe floods at Galula in the same vicariate, Théophile Dromaux (1849–1909) noted that Africans extricate themselves from disasters much better than the inhabitants of developed countries.[16] In Ukerewe, a teenager helped a missionary translate a Bible story into the vernacular early in 1901. The missionary was astonished. "This shows that there are more resources in the heads of Africans than I believed!"[17]

There were also discoveries of another kind, as missionaries overcame their repugnance to African culinary delicacies. Albert Ducourant (1875–1925), at Chilonga (Nyasa), would not have eaten elephant meat if he had known what it was, but in the event found it "delicious."[18] At Baudouinville in 1900, Joubert was the guest when the White Fathers dined off warthog. Although ugly to look at, its meat also turned out to be "delicious."[19] Bishop Roelens brought a "superb" and "succulent" wild boar to Mpala (Upper Congo) in 1899.[20] Hippopotamus hunts are mentioned at Bumangi (Nyanza North), Rubya (Nyanza South) and Ngumbo (Nyasa).[21] At the last-named mission, the hippopotamus provided the missionaries with fat for six months. White Fathers were not excessive in their hunting, only dealing with animal intruders and occasionally shooting for the pot.[22]

On the shores of Lake Victoria, missionaries initially dreaded the seasonal swarms of flying grasshoppers, which were a source of protein prized by the local population. The swarms arrived unexpectedly and people stayed away from church to harvest them. The Fathers could not understand the people's craving for this outlandish delicacy, and they also disapproved of the magical practices used for predicting its arrival. On a Sunday in November 1908, the church at Kome (Nyanza South) was almost empty because of the grasshoppers, but it was not long before the missionaries themselves acquired the taste. They found them "delicious when fried in butter and sprinkled with salt."[23]

Africans are famous lovers of music and dance, but their musical idiom was not at first appreciated by the Missionaries of Africa. Little by little, however, African music began to make an impact on the strangers. At

Marangara (Rwanda), the local people came singing as they brought wood to the mission for building in 1906. "They serenade us," wrote the diarist, "in a more agreeable manner than people might imagine."[24] At Mwazye (Tanganyika) in 1908, the missionaries were fascinated by the dancer who led the children in a singing procession that brought earth for brick-making.[25] At Marienseen (Burundi), the missionaries welcomed dancers who came to thank them after the Germans restored some forty impounded cows at the end of 1907.[26] And it was at the same mission that Chief Muhini and his warriors performed a dance in honour of Bishop Gerboin, which the Fathers found "truly imposing and of an almost wild beauty."[27] In 1908, the people performed a dance after Mass to celebrate the opening of the new chapel at Kaliminwa (Nyasa). "The spectacle," confessed Frédéric Salelles (1874–1956) with notable understatement, "is not without interest."[28]

Whether or not they came from the rural areas of Europe, the White Fathers found themselves among rural dwellers in Africa, people whose oral traditions were interwoven with references to the flora and fauna of the African countryside. In equatorial Africa they soon heard the legend of the pied wagtail and learned its lessons. The African pied wagtail is the friendly little bird that is the symbol of hospitality and of the welcoming house-mother. The missionaries at Zimba (Tanganyika) welcomed, as a sign of good luck, the wagtails that settled on the roof of their new mission. "We also love the wagtails," they wrote, "and will never attack these birds, which entertain us with their song."[29] At Banankuru (French Sudan), during the annual three-day feast of the Bambara in 1909, the missionaries at first deplored the excessive drinking and frenetic dancing, but on the final day a well-known storyteller from Patyana visited the mission and entertained them with folktales in the local language. Crowds attended the recitation of these fables about monkeys, dogs, hyenas, frogs and all the creatures familiar to the Bambara. The verdict: "a charming evening in Bambara."[30]

As a matter of course, the White Fathers collected sacred myths about creation and the fall of man, but they also noted etiological "just-so stories," the legend that turned Darwin upside down by claiming that baboons descended from humans, and the African version of the pelican feeding her young with her own blood, which was also the Eucharistic symbol chosen by Cardinal Lavigerie for his episcopal coat of arms.[31] At Navrongo (Gold Coast), the missionaries had the brilliant idea of organizing an archery competition on their patronal feast day, and after Antoine Salle (1870–1945) commenced a study of traditional herbal medicines in Uganda, Bishop Streicher decided to set up a school of native arts and crafts at Villa Maria (Nyanza North) in 1908.[32] Little by little, the Missionaries of Africa, who already had had a brief experience of the Maghreb, were drawn into the unfamiliar material and mental world of sub-Saharan Africa. Most managed somehow to cross the cultural divide, but there were a few who failed. Prominent among these was Victor Roelens, vicar apostolic of Upper Congo.

Chronic Culture Shock—The Case of Victor Roelens

"Of all the White Father Vicars Apostolic of the time, Monsignor Roelens seems to have been the one most inclined to describe Africans in an unfavourable light." Such was the verdict of a historian, studying education in the White Fathers' missions in Central Africa.[33] It is also the verdict of other historians and social analysts.[34] Roelens' views about the African character and psychology are contained in his numerous writings.[35] The impression they give is one of ineluctable white racial superiority that makes the modern reader cringe. Roelens was obsessed with understanding the African character, because the reality so often contradicted his own prejudices. Instances of African intelligence continually surprised him. Somehow he had to integrate these "exceptions" into his own *a priori* pessimistic theory. Roelens was essentially an educator who saw his task as one of reforming Africans, strengthening their will and teaching them the good habits of white civilization as a foundation for lasting Christian conversion. Africans, he claimed, were impulsive and lazy. They resisted any intellectual effort, being dominated solely by the imagination. They were totally devoid of logic, incapable of abstraction from sense experience. Their motivations were chiefly pride, fear and self-interest. They were thoughtless, inconstant and improvident. Even their virtues of patience and natural affection were more apparent than real. Their vices and degradation excited a patronizing pity. What was needed, thought Roelens, was a gradualist programme of reform, following a European model, that would allow them to use their undeveloped faculties. It was a didactic strategy for domesticating their minds. Yet even this would not enable them to aspire to a "perfection of life that was found in the lower ranks of (European) civilized society."[36] That remained unattainable for them in a world of cultural inequality.

Roelens had only contempt for the African way of life. African traditional rulers were brutal extortionists like the Biblical Achab, the evil king of Israel. African parents brought up their children like animals, leaving them free to roam naked and to fend for themselves. Roelens constructed a missionary theocracy to replace the rule of the chiefs, and he removed African children from the influence of their homes. When Placide Tempels' famous *Bantu Philosophy* was published in 1945, two years before the death of Roelens, he hailed it, not because he agreed that the Bantu had a faculty for logical thinking, but because the book was a useful tool to cure their minds of ignorance and error.[37]

Roelens' attitude was a caricature of the European superiority complex. It contained many of the negative stereotypes common at the time among white colonials, but it went much further. How did he fail to cross the gulf between Europe and Africa that many, if not most, other missionaries succeeded in crossing? In many ways this failure was due to the socio-cultural vacuum in Upper Congo when Roelens took over. The area was prone to endemic disease, slave-raiding and warfare. The positive aspects of African culture and tradition were far from obvious. Roelens, as we have seen, created and constantly desired to extend a missionary theocracy. He was by no means consistently sympathetic to the colonial regime of the Congo, but he had created his own autonomous colonial regime, a colony within a colony, and his ideas were, if anything, more extreme than those of the Belgian colonial project.

In addition to being a towering figure of both church and state, Roelens was an intellectual and a philosopher. He came to Africa with a sophisticated, ready-made theory, and, once there, developed a scheme of social engineering in accordance with the theory. This is why, after a lengthy experience in Africa and many perceptive observations about missionary work in the Congo, he had little interest in, or sympathy for, the African way of life. This was in marked contrast to the attitude of his brother bishops in Uganda, Tanganyika and Nyasa. Although Roelens' aim was to assimilate Africans within a "superior" Christian, Belgian culture, he reiterated Lavigerie's caution against creating "black Europeans," and converted it into a denial of eventual social equality. He also believed in strong-arm methods, using a system of rewards and punishments to ensure that parents sent their children to his schools. Roelens, like many of his Belgian compatriots, desired to dominate through civilization. He wanted to create a "purified Africanity" that remained perpetually subordinate to Europe. This was very far from the Catholic implications of Lavigerie's missiology.

The Missionaries of Africa and Language

The Emphasis on Language

The Missionaries of Africa were outstanding linguists. Learning and recording languages were high priorities in Cardinal Lavigerie's instructions to his missionaries, and the control of language was for him a matter of mission policy. No interpreters were ever to be used. Without a language policy, the establishment of Christianity would have been impossible. The need for learning language was drummed into the White Fathers during their training in North Africa, sometimes by quite extraordinary measures, such as reading the New Testament in Kabyle in the refectory or reciting the psalm *Miserere* in Arabic after meals. In Algeria, Lavigerie imposed the speaking of Arabic or Kabyle among the missionaries themselves under pain of mortal sin, and he expected the missionaries of equatorial Africa to speak only the local vernacular among themselves not later than six months after their arrival.[38] It goes without saying that there was a measure of idealism in these instructions, but they left no doubt about the priority to be given to language. Lavigerie also laid down rules for composing a dictionary and a small catechism as soon as possible when missionaries began work in a new linguistic setting.[39] Although he desired the missionaries to collect historical narratives and other forms of oral literature for catechetical and apologetic purposes, the use of language as an entry into an understanding of whole ethnic cultures was a consequence that he did not explicitly envisage. However, it soon became apparent that ethnography was the logical concomitant of linguistics.

Language recording took place, according to Johannes Fabian, in two phases, passing from "descriptive appropriation" to "prescriptive imposition and control."[40] In the first phase, useful words and phrases were collected from native speakers and a few grammatical observations were made. After this initial phase, the missionary embarked on detailed regulations contained in vocabularies and grammars. These were followed by translations of liturgical, doctrinal and Biblical texts. All of these took the shape of small booklets, which were aids to oral evangelization. The 1914 *Directory of the Constitutions* reiterated Lavigerie's insistence on learning local languages, which were to be used by the confreres among themselves, except during recreation.[41] After this first phase, attention could be paid to the classification and standardization that were entailed in the production of dictionaries. The growing rate of literacy demanded the creation of more reading material and the production of small books, comparable to the creation of mass literature for the working class in Europe.

The White Fathers produced vernacular dictionaries and grammars for all the regions in which they had a professional interest. Apart from Arabic and Swahili, there was no pre-existing material. Between 1892 and 1914, nearly fifty vernacular dictionaries and grammars were printed at the White Fathers' headquarters in Algiers. Another one hundred doctrinal, Biblical, devotional and liturgical books were printed there, together with manuals of geography, arithmetic and agriculture for use in schools. These represented virtually all the languages in the regions of North Africa, equatorial Africa and the French Sudan where the Missionaries of Africa were working. Some works were printed elsewhere, such as Bishop Bazin's dictionary of the Bambara language, produced in Paris by the French government in 1906, and Jean-Martin-Michel Van der Burgt's (1863–1923) linguistic and ethnographic works, published between 1903 and 1921 at s'Hertogenbosch and Boxtel in the Netherlands.[42] After Julien Gorju (1868–1942) started operating the printing press at Bukalasa (Uganda), many such works were produced there. One of the earliest was a Runyoro prayer book printed in 1907.[43]

The linguistic map of equatorial Africa was far from simple. At Usambiro (Unyanyembe), for example, three languages were in common use: Rundi, Sumbwa and Swahili; and at Navrongo (Gold Coast), there were two totally different dialects: Nankana and Gurunde.[44] Missionaries in Nyanza North (Uganda) were surprised to find that there were considerable differences between the Ganda, Nyoro and Kiziba languages.[45] In equatorial Africa, however, the White Fathers were mainly oriented towards the Arab-dominated, Swahili-speaking area of Lake Tanganyika. Swahili, dubbed by one diarist "the Esperanto of equatorial Africa," was being extended and standardized by the Germans to the east of the lake, but west of the lake there were several varieties of the language: Congo Swahili, Shaba or Lubumbashi Swahili and the so-called Kingwana, a kind of "pidgin" Swahili. The Missionaries of Africa had a vested interest in Swahili and in this region, a virtual monopoly of Swahili vocabularies, primers and grammars. The most influential was Emile Brutel's (1874–1919) *Vocabulaire français-kiswahili et kiswahili-français*, printed in Brussels in 1911.[46] All of these publications rightly acquired a scholarly reputation.

Inventing Language

The White Fathers certainly made many African vernaculars literate, and this was a substantial contribution to the preservation and appreciation of African culture. However, their work was not a simple matter of collecting, recording and translating these languages. Following Lavigerie's instructions, they had to create a tool for evangelization and worship, and this was a work of invention. As Fabian points out, maintaining purity of doctrine and expressing its subtleties of meaning were activities intrinsically related to regulating the correctness of grammar and orthography.[47] More than this, missionaries had to create a specialized theological and liturgical vocabulary, completely unknown to the ancestors of their catechumens. At Katoke (Nyanza South) in 1904, the missionaries desperately sought help in translating the Apostle's Creed. How did one translate into Suwi such difficult words and phrases as "Almighty Father," "conceived by the Holy Spirit," "under Pontius Pilate," "descended into hell," "communion of saints," "remission of sins" and "life everlasting"? This was not merely a problem of transverbalization. The Fathers suggested a pooling of ideas at the motherhouse in Algiers, so that comparisons could be made, and translators could learn from each other's experience.[48]

The White Fathers were obliged to teach Latin in their seminaries, according to the requirements of the time. This resulted in the linguistic curiosity of Latin-African vernacular lexicons and grammars. The earliest to be printed appeared in Uganda in the years 1912–1914, but the bulk of them were published after World War I, when the seminaries got into their stride in all the regions where the Society was at work.

Nothing was more fundamental than choosing the right name for God. Africans already believed in the existence of the Supreme Being, upon whom they bestowed many names and attributes. Adopting an ethnic name, such as Imana, Lesa, Mungu, Katonda, Ruhanga, or Wende entailed a dialogue with the doctrine of God found in African tradition. This dialogue was far from being an unequal contest between the missionary and the African, between a linguistic manipulator and a "passive object of literacy."[49] It often took considerable time for missionaries to acquire an accurate idea of African traditional religion. A missionary at Urwira (Tanganyika) complained in 1907: "In the four years we have been here, we have not obtained any idea of the people's beliefs. The Africans evade our questions or pretend not to know. Our young catechists, who are more confident and enlightened, now give us information." From the catechists, the missionaries learned that the Sun was the creator, that there were inferior gods such as Katabi, that there had been an original disobedience on the part of human beings, that power was exercised by the shades of the dead and by witches, and that there was a giant monster that lived in the forest.[50]

In other cases, when missionaries were too cautious about naming the Supreme Being, the people put pressure on them to choose the correct name. This happened in Rwanda, where the missionaries decided to use the Swahili name for God, Mungu, instead of the Rwandan name, Imana. Although the name Imana was everywhere prevalent and appeared in countless personal names, proverbs and other literary contexts, the White Fathers felt that it was too tribal, and that the more universal Mungu would help transform the concept of Imana itself.[51] This situation lasted for ten years, after which popular pressure forced the missionaries to adopt Imana.[52] Language being a living entity, the people had the last word, despite linguistic regulations imposed by missionaries.

Moreover, the missionaries did not work alone. Catechists and others helped them with their compositions and translations, a process that culminated in the creation of a vernacular liturgy by African clergy sixty or seventy years later, after the reforms of the Second Vatican Council. Corneille Smoor (1872–1953) composed an Easter poem in the Rwandan language at Save in 1904; and at Karema in 1908 Théophile Avon (1870–1953) produced a French symbolist play by Baju, translated into Swahili.[53] Everywhere, much-loved French hymns and Christmas carols were translated into local languages. One hymn, beloved of French missionaries, without which—in their eyes—Christmas would not be Christmas, was *Minuit Chrétiens* ("O Holy Night"), set to music by Adolphe Adam, the composer of the ballet *Giselle*.[54] This hymn was translated into virtually every vernacular known to the White Fathers. At Kayambi in 1903 its Bemba translator was the Malta-trained catechist, Jean-Baptiste Sambateshi.[55]

The first vocabularies and dictionaries produced by the Missionaries of Africa were often far from perfect, but they were working documents that called for improvement as missionaries came to know the language better, and as native speakers made their own contributions. Jean-Martin-Michel Van der Burgt's French-Kirundi Dictionary, for example, appeared in 1903, but already in 1905 it was the subject of widespread criticism among White Fathers in the Rwanda-Burundi region. The Luxemburger Félix Dufays (1877–1954), one of the founders of Mulera mission station (Burundi) in 1903, was himself an ethnographer, and reported an extensive disapproval of Van der Burgt's work.[56] African linguistics was, in the hands of the White Fathers, the outcome of a widespread and ongoing collaboration among and between missionaries and native speakers.

Missionary Linguistics and Colonial Power

The exercise of power plays a role, as Fabian points out, in the social history of language.[57] Language policy was a high priority on the colonial agenda. It was an instrument of pacification and unification in a multi-ethnic population. It was a matter of colonial prestige, but more importantly, it was a vehicle of communication between colonial rulers and their subjects. Language was necessary to transmit the imperatives of colonialism and to turn native Africans into docile citizens, wage-earners and tax-payers. The so-called Congo Free State provides an object lesson. In eastern Congo, the administration espoused Swahili for this purpose, but the White Fathers were there before them, and they were the acknowledged Swahili experts. The government needed the help of the missionaries to implement their language policy, especially when it came to choosing the medium of education. Whether they liked it or not, the Missionaries of Africa became involved in the colonial regime's linguistic decisions.

However, the missionaries operated from a position of strength and their aims were not identical with those of the government. Broadly, the colonialists were "assimilationists" and the missionaries were "indigenists." This became apparent when a missionary watchdog body, the Committee for the Protection of the Natives, was taken over by the Congo regime in 1911 and given a new colonial objective.[58] Missionaries were enlisted to teach Swahili to the colonial officials and to provide manuals for this purpose, but the White Fathers insisted on maintaining a high standard of linguistic purity. When the administration attempted to take a short-cut by introducing Kingwana or "Kitchen-Swahili," the White Fathers resisted this deformation of the language, and promoted an exclusively literary Swahili. The colonial administration favoured a form of "pidgin" or "baby-talk" Swahili, because for them the language was nothing more than a vehicle for one-way communication between master and servant. The Missionaries of Africa, on the other hand, wanted the voice of the native speakers to be heard.[59]

Lavigerie refused to allow his missionaries to teach European languages to Africans, but he had not lived to see the full extent of the colonial scramble. As the colonial powers established effective rule in one country after another, they insisted on the teaching of their national languages. It was clear that educational policy and future development depended on the existence of an elite, that would speak English, French or German. In spite of anti-clerical legislation in the French Sudan, the major reason for continuing to tolerate private mission schools was that they taught French.[60] A missionary in Timbuktu, who had no particular wish to further French colonial aims, asked in 1906, "The inhabitants of Timbuktu have no enthusiasm for learning French—are they wrong?"[61] At Navrongo (Gold Coast), the district officer explained to the local chiefs that if they sent their children to the mission school, they would learn the language of the whites and could become salaried interpreters.[62] In German East Africa, the White Fathers were reluctantly obliged to start teaching German in 1898, and by 1902 Bishop Hirth reported that it was being taught in every mission station of his vicariate.[63] Even chiefs appeared at the mission to learn a smattering of the official language.[64] Schoolchildren and seminarians were regularly brought out to offer greetings or give recitations in German when official visits took place.

The alienation brought by colonialism was caused in part by a "redrawing" of the map and the changing of names. Lakes, mountains, rivers, towns and peoples were given new names of European origin. This process was resisted by the Africans, who not only remembered and used the traditional names, but who conferred their own names on the European strangers and the places they came from. This was especially true of the African names given to missionaries and their residences. The missionaries were closer to the Africans and more conspicuously part of the local landscape than distant and transitory colonials. The names given to the missionaries—such as Ati, Stensera, Musenyela or Moto Moto—were a sign of African cultural reinvention, as well as of affectionate familiarity.

Art and Worship

Language and Worship

During the period under study, 1892–1914, the church's liturgy remained in the inflexible idiom of post-renaissance, Tridentine Catholicism. Although there was a praiseworthy effort to record African vernacular languages, to create a published literature in these vernaculars, and even to move towards a dialogue with African religious ideas, the missionaries had no other practical goal, as far as public worship was concerned, than to replace traditional cults with the church's liturgy and seasonal devotions. Since the liturgy was always and everywhere in Latin, there was no strictly liturgical scope for the vernacular or for the arts and symbols of Africa. Such a development was beyond the imagination of missionaries at that time in any case. As we have seen in Chapter Four, the only possible margin for innovation lay in paraliturgies and informal devotions outside the liturgical framework itself.

At Mass, there were preparatory and thanksgiving prayers in the vernacular, consecutive vernacular Sunday readings and, of course, the homily in the vernacular. Apart from these, all was in Latin. It was very rare for vernacular hymns to be sung during Mass, but an exception was made at Beni-Mengallet (Kabylia) in 1905, when French and Kabyle hymns were sung during the Eucharistic liturgy.[65] However, the Roman liturgy appealed to all the senses. It was a visual performance and a ritual action in which people could participate. At Bujuni (Nyanza North), as elsewhere, there were liturgical ceremonies classes.[66] The as yet unrestored ceremonies of

Holy Week spoke to Africans on the symbolic level. "Now, they are beginning to understand better," wrote a missionary from Ushirombo (Unyanyembe)
at Easter in 1906. The Solemn High Mass with deacon and subdeacon,
although rarely celebrated, also never failed to impress. African personifi-
cations were introduced to refer to sacred seasons. In Uganda, Lent was per-
sonified as *Basibie* (literally, "they fast"). "*Basibie* has arrived, let us do
battle with him!"[67] When, according to custom, the church bells were
silenced during the Easter Triduum, people at Banankuru (French Sudan)
remarked: "The bells are making their annual retreat!"[68]

The liturgical arts in these early years depended almost entirely on
European imports. Vestments, statues, sacred vessels, linen: all came from
abroad, being laboriously carried in the caravans from the coast. Africans
marvelled at these things. At Msalala (Unyanyembe) in 1904, the wax crib
figures imported from Brittany and dressed in clothes made by French
Carmelites, were much admired. Interest centred especially on the black
king.[69] When Gerboin started a mission among the Cushitic speaking Iraqw,
in the extreme east of his Unyanyembe Vicariate, people flocked to see the
pictures the Fathers had put up. They were especially attracted by one of
the infant Jesus. "Father," they exclaimed, "I want to see your child. Show
me your child."[70] However, the imported pictures were not always understood. An Anglican chief, visiting the White Fathers in Mbarara (Nyanza
North) in 1908, inquired on seeing a picture of Christ crucified: "What is
that wild beast?"[71]

The evening service on Sundays was customarily the Second Vespers of
Sunday in Latin. Although the people came to enjoy singing the *Magnificat*
and hymns such as *Ave Maris Stella*, the recitation of the divine office in an
unknown language held less attraction for them than the Mass, and it was
virtually impossible to maintain the custom. Bishops Bazin and Gerboin
were prepared to replace Vespers with the recitation of the rosary in the
local language, and this was usually followed by Benediction of the Blessed
Sacrament at which vernacular hymns were allowed.

Music and Worship

The Missionaries of Africa quickly realized the importance of music and
song in Africa. Traditional music could be heard everywhere, from the songs
of the Bafuvo society, with their costumes made of leaves, at Kashozi
(Nyanza South) in 1902, to the performance of "our dear Gurunsi" at
Navrongo (Gold Coast), with their drums, horns and whistles in 1909.[72]
Young men were everywhere to be seen with musical instruments in hand,
usually a lyre, fiddle or hand piano. It was not long before the missionaries
formed their own bands and choirs. In some cases it was a "native band,"
as at Bwanja (Nyanza South), with various types and sizes of drum and cal-
abash shakers. "It is a little wild for ears newly arrived from Europe,"
remarked a missionary apologetically, "but when one is accustomed to it,

the sounds are harmonious."[73] Mostly, the bands that formed in schools and seminaries followed European conventions and had at least some European instruments. These bands played for important visitors, as happened in 1907, when the Duke of Meklenberg-Strelitz dined at Kashozi. During dinner the seminary band "did not cease to make heard superb pieces of music, both instrumental and vocal, with words in German."[74] Some choirs, such as François Tessier's (1879–1949) *chant nègre* at Kaliminwa (Nyasa), carried out a dual function, performing both traditional songs and Christian hymns in Bemba. "Tessier," said a condescending missionary admirer, "has smoothed these uncouth voices."[75] At St. Anne's, Jerusalem, the seminary band was invited by the celebrated Dominican Bible scholar, Marie-Joseph Lagrange, to play at his Church of St. Stephen's in 1908.[76]

In church, the choirs attempted ambitious choral pieces on feast days. A favourite in all the White Fathers' missions was the French Baroque "Royal Mass" by the seventeenth-century Walloon composer, Henri Dumont. One of St. Pius X's first projects on becoming pope was the restoration of Gregorian chant, and this was put into effect throughout the church. By 1908, the White Fathers were everywhere introducing the chant, accompanied by the ubiquitous harmonium also imported from Europe. In 1908, Michele Franco (1874–1955) introduced Gregorian chant for the first time at Bukalasa Seminary (Nyanza North), and it was also performed for the first time at Kirando (Tanganyika) and Baudouinville (Upper Congo) in the same year.[77] The music was not less strange to Catholics in Africa than elsewhere, but they came to like the melodies of the *Missa de Angelis*, which remained a staple of Catholic liturgical music up to the reforms of the mid-1960s.[78] In 1914, the General Council of the Society ordered that the *Liber Usualis* of Gregorian chant be used at the generalate and in all houses of formation.[79]

Drum and Dance

In sub-Saharan Africa, the White Fathers from Europe had the unfamiliar experience of living among people for whom music and song were invariably accompanied by dancing and drumming. Dance and drum were interwoven with life itself. It could be justly said that African societies were "dancing societies." Dance accompanied almost every aspect of individual and social life. This was a novelty that missionaries had difficulty in understanding. A missionary at Bukumbi (Nyanza South) sourly remarked in 1905 that dancing was a major waster of time and an obstacle to conversion.[80] It is a common axiom that missionaries waged a relentless war against dancing as a savage or immoral practice, or that, having forbidden dancing, they introduced football to take its place.[81] It is not true that the White Fathers made a sweeping condemnation of dancing, although they certainly introduced the game of football, founding clubs and starting teams in many African countries. A football stadium was even named after a White Father in Mali, Georges Bouvier (1905–1952), and when it was renamed

Almadi Konate Stadium, after a speaker of the National Assembly, Malians wrote to the newspapers, attributing their defeat in the Africa Cup of Nations to the anger of Bouvier's spirit.[82]

As matters stood in the years 1892–1914, there was no way that dancing could take place in church, or that the drum could occupy the honoured place of the harmonium. However, the mission station had its drums, and dancing took place in religious processions and festivities outside the church building. Drums were used to call the Christians to Mass, especially at outstations. They were also used to welcome visitors. For example, at Kagondo in 1909, drums were beaten to welcome a party of newly arriving Missionaries of Africa. When the local chief visited the same mission with his own drummers, the three great mission drums beat out a responding welcome.[83] Dancing accompanied processions to local shrines, calvaries and outdoor altars. It also took place in the forecourt of the mission station after important liturgical celebrations. The blessing of the outstation church at Mwila (Zimba Mission, Tanganyika) was typical, being followed by drumming, dancing, feasting and beer-drinking.[84]

Nevertheless, there were certainly dances which the missionaries judged incompatible with Christian morality, and they imposed sanctions on catechumens and neophytes who participated in them. They were usually dances that already had an ambiguous reputation among the people themselves, and the prohibition was far from being indiscriminate or unilateral. On the contrary, the missionaries were very discerning. Jean-Marie Robert (1879–1966), the ethnographer of the Fipa people of Tanzania, described in detail two dances that were generally regarded as extremely immoral, and which were seldom danced because of this.[85] The *Kilangwa* dance involved female striptease and nudity, while the *Mitete* dance included explicit sexual abuse, and was designed to induce sexual arousal in dancers and bystanders. Dances connected with the rituals of twin birth involved transvestism and obscenity, and parents of twins commonly sought to escape the embarrassment caused by them. There were also spirit mediumship dances which the missionaries opposed on religious and health grounds, as they did the dances of the girls' nubility rites. Finally, there were the dances of secret societies, which provoked feuding and violence, and the dances of societies that were widely believed to practise ritual murder. It goes without saying that genuine war dances were also banned for Christians.

As a rule of thumb, the White Fathers discouraged nocturnal dancing and dances that ended in brawling and violence. The sanctions for Christians included a greater or lesser measure of excommunication. It was rare that the Fathers slit the drums used by the offending dancers, as happened occasionally at Ushirombo (Unyanyembe), or that the father superior leapt among the obscene dancers brandishing a cane, as happened once at Kashozi (Nyanza South) in 1897.[86] The dances that fell under the ban did so, not because they were dances, but because they involved activities that contradicted Christian faith or morality.

The Missionaries of Africa were not merely tolerant of African dancing, they were perceptively and positively committed to it. Let the last
word be given to Bishop Jean-Joseph Hirth, who—to his everlasting
credit—actually proposed in 1902 that liturgical dancing take its place
inside church! Writing to his brother, his only proviso was that obscene
dances be given up by Christians. Referring to the dancing procession in
honour of St. Willibrord at Echternach in Luxemburg, he wrote: "We
should have dared to keep certain dances in our religious ceremonies, like
the good Luxemburgers do at Echternach. A religion in which one can
dance would draw more people to baptism."[87]

Missionary Afro-pessimism

Migration and Mobility

In 1906 a missionary at Kisaka (Rwanda) painted a picture of African society that was dire. It was an example of Afro-pessimism at its worst, blaming
the African poor for their own poverty and rivalling—in its negativity—the
opinions of Bishop Victor Roelens in Upper Congo. The following is a summary of the passage: The people of Rwanda live in miserable huts. Because
of this, they catch colds and fevers, whereas missionaries, who have blankets
to cover them at night and whose houses are less draughty, enjoy better
health. Africans are profoundly lazy. Their houses are badly built and their
land is badly cultivated. Their bodies are not properly clothed. Intellectually,
they are uncouth. They make no effort to reflect. Their lack of property and
lack of any other incentive encourages vice. Their land and its produce are
at the mercy of the chiefs. All of this denotes the presence of sin. If the
Rwandans become Christians, our religion will give them humanity, and the
enjoyment of their private property will be guaranteed.[88]

This is an early (Catholic) example of the "prosperity Gospel" according to which health and wealth depend on acknowledging sin and embrac-
ing the Gospel. It is also a judgement based on European cultural constructs
such as the work ethic, the notion of private property and the need for stability and for material incentives. Apart from pointing an accusing finger at
the chiefs, this portrayal makes no attempt to identify the ultimate cause of
poverty. In the diaries and correspondence of the White Fathers during this
period, it is rare to find as devastating an indictment as this. However, there
are many complaints about laziness, inconstancy and instability, and little
about the fragility and volatility of a life confronted by disease, ignorance
and the natural adversities of climate and terrain.

One of the most frequent complaints made by the missionaries was about
the Africans' lack of stability. Problems would be solved, they believed, if
people would only stay put, in the vicinity of the mission station, and let
the missionaries help them raise their standard of living through work on
their own land. The wish was naïve and took no account of the developing

opportunities and pressures of colonial society. As Bishop Gerboin pointed out, it was also illogical to accuse Africans of both indolence and instability. They were inveterate and energetic travellers and there was nothing apathetic about their journeys.[89] The truth was that Europeans did not appreciate the working conditions or the pace of life in rural Africa.

In many of the White Fathers' vicariates, the predominant economy was one of shifting cultivation, with farmers rotating their fields every five or six years because of poor soil fertility. This was especially the case in Upper Congo, Tanganyika and Nyasa. In an effort to concentrate the population for closer administration, the colonial government of Northern Rhodesia in 1907 ordered that fields for cultivation should not be further than two miles from Kayambi village.[90] This was an early example of the fruitless policy of "villagization," pursued over the years by colonial and independent governments in African countries. The church also wanted to put an end to "slash and burn" agriculture, and Bishop Roelens was predictably and crudely critical of the system. Writing on this subject in 1905, he commented: "We are called to draw these people out of their idleness and brutishness."[91]

Long-distance migration was even more unacceptable to missionaries. There were both push and pull factors in long-distance migration. In some cases, it was due to food shortages or agricultural distress at home. The end of slave-raiding meant that it was now safe to travel, and that there was no longer any need to find security in concentrated village settlements. Moreover, the imposition of taxation by the colonial administrations encouraged people to migrate in order to look for salaried work. New opportunities for increasing incomes were now emerging. Deep water harbours were developing at Mombasa and Dar es Salaam. The laying of the telegraph, as well as railway construction and maintenance in British and German East Africa, the Rhodesias and the French Sudan attracted many labourers. There was work to be had in the French railway workshops and in the early workings of canals and waterways on the Niger River system. Sisal was the only commercial crop in German East Africa that grew in quantity in the years 1912–1914, and labour was needed for the coastal plantations.[92] There was also work available in the mines of the Transvaal, Southern Rhodesia and Katanga in the Congo Free State. All of these were magnets attracting the rural population. In addition, there were commercial prospects in towns both near and far. Nearby Tabora town was an attraction for the inhabitants of Ndala (Unyanyembe), while Kabyles in Algeria were drawn to Tunis, "the Babylon of North Africa."[93] Finally, there was what Bishop Bazin of French Sudan called "the world of the demi-civilized," domestic employment offered by European settlers and colonials, though it must be said that they tended to favour Muslims rather than Christians.[94]

Although Africa remained essentially rural, and although the migrant's focus in the last analysis was always on the rural homeland, these beginnings of socio-economic development in the colonies were part of an ongoing trend. It was a trend that would take a different course in the First World War, but it was not one that would go away, for all the wishful thinking of missionaries. The Catholic Church in Africa, as elsewhere, was basically a territorial church. It needed stable populations gathered around the mission centres, for regular instruction and reception of the sacraments. Labour migration and the scattering of the Christian population made evangelization and pastoral care more difficult, and pastoral journeys longer. The White Fathers praised the introduction of frequent Holy Communion as a counterweight to migration.[95] But migration threatened the viability of some mission stations, and these had sometimes to be closed or moved because of population mobility. Mitala Maria (Nyanza North), Lusenda (Upper Congo) and Msalala (Unyanyembe) were all missions that were severely affected in one way or another by population movement.[96]

The missionaries feared for the marriages and for the faith and morals of migrant labourers. They expected them to return disillusioned and corrupted, perhaps bringing the sleeping sickness with them, and in any case needing a major effort of reintegration within the Christian community at home. It was a surprise when a young Christian returned to Banankuru (French Sudan) in 1909, from working on the Mauth Canal, with his faith and morals intact.[97] Bishop Henri Léonard noted in 1909 that, on the whole, this was the case with most migrants, and he added in 1913 that the railway was simply a fact of life that had to be accepted.[98] Bishop Etienne Larue of Bangweolo wrote that migrants returning from Katanga and the Transvaal settled down quite well to Christian life.[99] To accuse the migrants, as many missionaries did, of base motives, of an inordinate love of money, the desire for novelty and the chance to escape mission authority, was unfair. Labour migration was becoming an inevitable fact of life. In the end, as Bishop Lechaptois wisely commented, "the only adequate response to labour migration is to give (catechumens) a long and serious preparation for baptism," so that they would be protected against the slings and arrows of modern and urban life.[100]

Negative Cultural Factors—Cannibalism

Among cultural practices which are clearly opposed to Christian morality is the so-called last taboo, cannibalism. Allegations of cannibalism were rife in the Congo during this period, and they were sometimes made by Missionaries of Africa. A question that must be asked is: Were they true? Since Bishop Roelens, with his jaundiced view of African culture, was one of those who made these allegations, the question is an important one. It is well-known that in many cultures, accusations of cannibalism are an ideological and rhetorical device to establish moral superiority over other groups or individuals. It has even been suggested that cannibalism has virtually no factual existence, and that it is simply an exaggeration beloved of explorers, colonials and tourists from Europe.[101] Traditionally, cannibalism is a feature of the social nightmare associated with witchcraft beliefs, and rumours of cannibalism abounded in Africa during this period. It was not only Europeans who accused Africans of being cannibals, but there was a popular belief among Africans that Europeans were blood-sucking vampires, and there were countless accusations of cannibalism by Africans against each other. The Missionaries of Africa found that the people they encountered had a horror of cannibalism, whether or not this fear was founded in fact. It was, of course, a horror which the missionaries shared.

Cannibalism was mostly associated with the peoples loosely known as Manyema, who lived between the Congo basin and Lakes Kivu and (northern) Tanganyika. More specifically, this practice was identified with the Kazanze in the northern part of Bishop Roelens' Vicariate of Upper Congo. In his annual report of 1909, Roelens devoted a section to the Kazanze and their cannibalistic practices. According to him, they consumed their enemies, human sacrificial victims and the familial dead, and he told the story of a young woman who fell into the hands of the Kazanze and was eaten by them in December 1908.[102] Four years later, Roelens' auxiliary, Bishop Auguste Huys, rejoiced that "the cannibal peoples of the northwest are now coming to us."[103] There seems little doubt that Lieutenant Vrithoff's body provided a cannibalistic feast in 1892, because the missionaries at Mpala received his remains—three toes and the scalp—in a cooking pot, on April 11th, although no one claimed to have witnessed the event itself.[104] Other incidents, for which there were eyewitnesses, occurred in 1901 and 1904, near Lukulu mission in Urua, further south; these were reported by Pierre Colle (1872–1961).

In December 1900, missionaries at the newly founded mission of Lukulu succeeded in obtaining a cease-fire during a local conflict. After peace negotiations and in spite of desperate protests, they were obliged to watch helplessly the murder of an old woman. Later in the day, they stumbled by accident on the cannibalistic feast that followed this murder.[105] In April 1904, Colle reported that a woman and her young son had died after a poison ordeal at Kihanga village in Urua, and that their brains had subsequently been eaten.[106] In May 1904, Colle personally confronted Kazanze who he believed were about to kill and eat a young man called Lisutu. Colle punched one of the aggressors in the face, liberated the intended victim and threatened the rest with his gun.[107] It would seem from these accounts that cannibalism was taken for granted in Urua.

Actual or probable incidents of cannibalism reported by the White Fathers in Upper Congo were few and far between. Fear of cannibalism, however, was a notable social fact in the area, and one in which the missionaries participated, and to which they perhaps contributed.

Negative Cultural Factors—Ritual Murder

The most common form of ritual murder encountered by the White Fathers in 1892–1914 consisted of deaths from the poison ordeal. Many of the traditional judicial procedures in equatorial Africa caused bodily harm to the suspects who were made to undergo them, but none were as lethal as the poison oracle. This usually consisted of forcing those accused of witchcraft or other secret crimes to drink water containing splinters of *mwavi* (*erythrophloeum guineenis*). These splinters contained a vegetable poison, in a quantity uncertain and unknown to those who administered the ordeal. Either the poison killed the suspect more or less immediately, or it was vomited. If the latter, the suspect was declared innocent. The poison ordeal was a social fact, accepted by all—save those who were made to undergo it—and was part of the social paranoia that prompted witchcraft accusation. Colonial administrations waged an implacable war against it, as did the White Fathers. Chiefs and others responsible for it were denounced as murderers, but it was only destined to disappear when people felt more secure and witchcraft theory was abandoned. That was a long-term project to which the missionaries dedicated their energies.

Other forms of ritual murder included the live burial of human beings, usually women, slaves or children, with the corpse of a deceased king or chief. This was because of the alleged immortality of the deceased, of which the living things buried with him were a symbol. As in the case of cannibalism, it was not always possible to distinguish fact from rumour. Such burials were usually secret and there were no available witnesses. In many places today, chiefs and members of chiefly families are buried with live chickens, and evergreen trees are planted in their graves.[108] Presumably such contemporary practices are vestiges of a custom that may once have included the burial of live human beings, but when the substitution took place is not known. In any case, the Missionaries of Africa could do little about such a custom, of which they strongly disapproved.

They were more successful, it seems, in their opposition to infanticide. Again and again the White Fathers deplored the superstitious killing of babies born by breech delivery and those whose top teeth grew first. Occasionally also one or both twins were killed at birth. This again provoked condemnation by the missionaries, who sought through education and the teaching of Christian morality to end such practices.

Negative Cultural Factors—Secret Societies

Secret societies involved many practices of which the White Fathers disapproved, and in some places virtually the entire adult population belonged to them. "They promote the power of the devil," wrote a diarist in the Congo in 1904.[109] Some, like the Ukala dance society (Galula Mission, Tanganyika), had the political purpose of inculcating loyalty to the chief and his dynasty through a mixture of fear and fascination. It was suspected by many, with good reason, of being involved in political murders.[110] The Yeye snake charmers' society was also far from innocent, since it extorted money and deployed powerful poisons, which people in Nyanza South believed were responsible for the death of a chief's wife in Mwanza.[111] The Swezi secret society had a sinister reputation in Unyanyembe and Nyanza South, involving not only spirit-mediumship, but nudity and ritual sexual intercourse with several individuals as part of the initiation process.[112] There were numerous spirit-mediumship societies in Upper Congo, and some of these spread into German East Africa and Northern Rhodesia. The White Fathers were not only concerned about their anti-Christian religious character, but also about their effect on the mental health of their members.[113] A statuette of the tutelary of one of these societies was recovered by Joseph Vandermeiren (1873–1936) at Lukulu (Upper Congo) in 1906 and judged to be "very immoral."[114] Christian participation in such societies was punished by excommunication, and in at least one instance the local chief was persuaded to round up and fine the members.[115]

In French Sudan there were powerful secret societies or brotherhoods among the Bambara. They were a kind of spiritual family that imposed circumcision on their initiants. The most important was the Komo, which practised both religious and magical rituals, led by the Komo-Tigi or "high priest."[116] There was also the less important Kore brotherhood, which existed to honour the dead. The Missionaries of Africa believed that membership in these brotherhoods was incompatible with baptism. Two of the mission's best catechists attended a Komo session at Banankuru in 1906, and seven Christians were discovered in a Komo sanctuary there two years later.[117] Among the Mossi, circumcision was an individual or family practice, and was not linked to the membership of brotherhoods as it was among the Bambara. Consequently, it presented less of a problem to the missionaries.

Although they were anxious about the morality of female nubility rites, the White Fathers in equatorial Africa did not have to confront organized male circumcision in their vicariates. In French Sudan however, Bambara circumcision was a major challenge. The missionaries were worried about its pagan character, and also about its possible links to Islam. "The air is saturated with circumcision," wrote a missionary at Banankuru in 1907. At Patyana, where boys defected in large numbers when circumcision took place, attempts were made to attract men who were already circumcised to the baptism classes.[118] At Kita in the same year, the missionaries struck a compromise with the brotherhoods. Although forced to agree to the circumcision of their catechumens, they wrung a concession from the elders, that the Christian initiates should merely watch the sacrifices and not be obliged to participate in them.[119] At Banankuru the following year, the catechumens were asked to choose between baptism and circumcision. After mature reflection, all of them chose circumcision.[120] At Dinguira a fourteen-year-old child only escaped being circumcised by losing consciousness when his parents took him from the mission by force. He was carried back to the mission, where he recovered.[121] At Banankuru, again in 1908, death threats were issued against youths who did not comply with the order to attend the Komo celebrations in the bush.[122] Faced with such pressures, Bishop

Hippolyte Bazin, who had at first obtained Vatican support for his opposition to circumcision, was obliged to abandon his intransigence. This he did without further reference to Rome.[123] Henceforward, with appropriate safeguards for faith and morality, the White Fathers made no further objection to circumcision. Africa had won.

The Missionaries of Africa and Development

The Dream of a Rural Idyll

In 1906, a White Father at Rubya (Nyanza South) wrote a short essay in which he described his ideals for the development of the area west of Lake Victoria in Nyanza.[124] It is worth quoting in full, since it corresponds with an idea widely shared among the Missionaries of Africa at that time.[125]

"(Among) the people on the west coast of Nyanza, the men hardly work at all. Apart from (looking after) the banana plantation and hut-building, all the work is left to the women. This cannot work today. Clothes must be bought, taxes paid. Idleness brings moral dangers. What will take the place of this system? A black proletariat without property, family or culture in the service of a few unbelieving European colonials or Indian merchants? This seems the most likely outcome in the present circumstances. But what will happen to Christianity? It seems to me that we must leave no stone unturned to prevent this disaster, since we have so few means at our disposal. The African Christian must not become merely the colonist's employee or the agent of the Indian merchant. He must be his own man, one who has some ascendancy over his compatriots and some independence with regard to the colonials.[126] He must be the owner of his own land and later on the owner of an enterprise, workshop and house. We want to form a Christian society, but one that is African, one which finds all its constitutive elements among Africans. Do we not wish to form priests and the elite of a Christian society? We must begin at the beginning. Men must become cultivators, not women, but men. The cultivator must become a proprietor and breeder. The foundation of any well-regulated society is private property—not the kind of property we see today, but the ownership of parcels of land, loved, maintained, improved. The foundation of property understood in this sense is work—work on one's own behalf. This will take a long time to realize. I imagine we all agree on this point.

Have our Christians reached this point? Are they better workers than the pagans? I am not speaking of men with a trade, such as that of mason, carpenter, brick-maker etc. Those are more numerous among Christians than among pagans. But they will never be more than a tiny minority. I have in mind, above all, work in the fields. Do Christians cultivate the paternal plot with greater care? Do they dream of improving it? Do they aim to clear more land around them and so increase their patrimony? For the people of western Nyanza and others that I have seen with my own eyes I answer, without fear of contradiction, No. Christians can be found everywhere on the roads, at the markets and in the towns. Visit a village where there are plenty of Christians and ask where so and so is. They will tell you: He is looking for money. He is in business. What is the result? Ignorance of religion and often marital infidelity. For those who know the social situation of this country, there is no need to insist on this point . . . For me, cultivating the land is the most useful kind of work for the African. Of course, he will not make millions out of it. But what does he need with money? Money does not make anyone happy, the African even less than the European, because he knows less how to use it. Do we not see Africans, wearing a heavy black overcoat and carrying an open umbrella in the finest weather? Do we not find people accompanied by a boy, carrying their shoes because their feet are not used to them?"

There is a passionate sincerity about these words, a genuine desire for the betterment of Africans, especially those who become Christians. But there is also evidence of prejudice, naïveté and paternalism. The writer really believed that cultivation would provide the African with all his wants. What did he need with money? Why should he look for work outside the village? Although it was not an ideal that was in harmony with the long-term socio-economic trends of German East Africa, it received some official support at the time. Except for sisal, German plans for the development of plantations were largely a failure. Bernhard Dernburg, the German colonial secretary, visited the country in the wake of the Maji-Maji Rebellion, and introduced reforms that boosted African agriculture, although he was also obliged to appease the German settlers. The ideals of the Rulbya missionary broadly described the policies of the German governors Freiherr Albrecht von Rechenberg and his successor Heinrich Schnee.[127] It was only in certain of their village settlements that the White Fathers were able to accomplish the beautiful ideal of private enterprise farming, which was ultimately lacking in realism.

The Christian villages founded by Cardinal Lavigerie in the Chélif Valley in Algeria, were failures from the point of view of evangelization, but from the point of view of socio-economic development, they were longer-lived and more successful than other Christian villages started by the White Fathers. Moreover, if Lavigerie had not been opposed by a hostile colonial administration, these villages might have been even more successful. Between 1869 and 1878, Lavigerie acquired large panels of land in the area in order to found the two villages of St. Cyprian and Ste. Monique des Attafs. These were to be supervised by the White Fathers and the White Sisters (MSOLA), who looked after the education and social relationships of the boys and girls.[128] Marriages began taking place in the early 1870s.

A body was set up for the material administration of the villages—the Civil Society of Agricultural Orphanages of Algeria (CSAOA). Boarding schools and a hospital were started and houses were built for the settlers, as well as presbyteries and convents for the fathers and sisters. The two villages could accommodate sixty households between them. To avoid placing the villages under the colonial administration, the Arab Christian settlers were given French nationality. The settler paid no rent and the produce from his fields was his own. House, land, furniture and tools belonged to the CSAOA. After twenty-five years, all these became the settler's own property, on condition that he had not been negligent, violent or conjugally unfaithful.

In fact, the settlers needed considerable supervision. As orphans, they had had no experience of family life, and there was extensive unrest in the villages, including several murders. In February 1880, the parish priest of Ste. Monique, Louis Dioré (1850–1880), was murdered by native Muslims, probably with the collusion of Christian settlers. The Missionaries of Africa were clearly unable to handle the situation. Between 1875 and 1892, the parish priest of Ste. Monique was changed fifteen times; and between 1872 and 1892, the parish priest of St. Cyprien was changed eleven times. Nor was the farming in the villages a complete success. The plots were insufficient to sustain large families, and the region was poor and unsuited to cultivation. There were frequent droughts, and continual food relief and other assistance had to be given. However, the Christian practice of the settlers was good, and there were only three apostates. Fourteen were ejected for misbehaviour, but no one ran away. Instead they stayed and adopted the lifestyle of the surrounding Europeans, unfortunately including their vices, and intermarried with them.

Full land-ownership was granted to settlers in 1896, 1904 and 1905. Eventually fifty-eight settlers in the two villages became owners of the property they occupied and farmed. To avoid the consequences of anti-clerical legislation and to ward off the danger of litigation by former settlers, the CSAOA was dissolved in 1906, and the settlers then began selling off their plots, as they were entitled to do. Although the population of the two villages reached a maximum of 380 people in 1909, twelve years later this figure had sunk to 160. In most cases, these Arab Christians prospered and became useful citizens, merging with the French population of Algeria. As naturalized French citizens, they departed to France after the war of independence in the 1960s. The experiment raised many questions in the domain of development. If the villages could not sustain a small number of settlers, one might ask how the whole population of Algeria could be fed, if its numbers and standard of living improved? Much more investment was needed, including measures such as the creation of water reservoirs and the diversification of crops.

Similar in some ways to the Attafs was the Christian village that grew up at the agricultural training school and model farm at Thibar in Tunisia, already mentioned in Chapter Four in connection with the training of missionary brothers.[129] In 1893 the Assistant General, Paul Voillard (1860–1946), created the Société Civile Des Oliviers de Menzel. This body acquired a domain of more than fifteen thousand hectares at Thibar, where an orphanage, Christian village and parish were set up. Missionaries of

Africa staffed these institutions and White Sisters (MSOLA) looked after the "marriage postulants." Missionary brothers made a kind of second novitiate there, and lay *stagiaires* came for agricultural or other training. The orphanage was a costly enterprise, and the village, which was an outgrowth of all these activities, practised what was described by a visitor as "a precarious form of assimilation."[130] Nevertheless, the village, which was largely inhabited by employees of the model farm, enjoyed an existence that lasted well beyond the period covered by this book.

The Christian villages set up by the White Fathers elsewhere in Africa were, on the whole, less successful as development projects than the villages of the Attafs. In Kabylia, the Christian quarters near the mission stations were created to provide a social life for adult Christians. About fifteen were baptized annually throughout Kabylia from 1911 to the early 1920s, but the number dwindled and disappeared by 1923.[131] It was difficult to find wives for the neophytes, and they were often completely dependent on the mission. Most Arab Christians became professionals and the missionaries worked for their assimilation within the French population. Their ultimate destiny was virtually the same as that of the villagers of the Attafs.

There was already a discussion in Chapter Three about the freed slave villages of equatorial Africa and the liberty villages of French Sudan. In some cases, notably at Karema (Tanganyika), there was a scheme of eventual ownership by the villagers. However, there was no immigrant settler community for them to join, and the villages were everywhere regarded as fundamentally unstable. They clearly had no future on their own terms. Villagers drifted away, or merged with the local populations, as Christianity spread among them. The goal of creating communities of Christian peasant entrepreneurs remained a dream, the realization of which would have required heavy investment and the employment of a large supervisory staff. The White Fathers found that their efforts were best directed to improving subsistence agriculture within the tribal system.

Socio-Economic Development

Pre-colonial Africans lived on cultivated crops, such as sorghum, beans, millet and various species of native grain. Plantains had been introduced in certain regions before the end of the first millennium, and mangoes also at an early date. This diet was supplemented by fruit, greens and game from the forest. They also caught fish, and kept goats, chickens and cows. The latter were raised by certain peoples in a semi-religious cattle-complex, resulting in severe problems of overstocking and over-grazing. The only cultivated native fruit tree was the palm, in its different varieties. The Arabs introduced rice, sugar cane, onions, cucumbers and lemons, as well as pigeons. However, most current staples in Africa were introduced by the Portuguese from the sixteenth century onwards: maize, sweet potatoes and cassava, together with tomatoes, pimento, pineapples and tobacco. The Portuguese also introduced ducks and domesticated pigs.[132] These crops and livestock spread from hand to hand.

Crop yields in traditional Africa were poor and animal husbandry deficient, chiefly due to ignorance of animal disease. Fifty percent of all calves died, and milk yields were extremely low. Wood ash was virtually the only known fertilizer, and manuring was exceptional. Slash-and-burn cultivation could prove wasteful in the case of a growing population exploiting a limited area, because, as the forest disappeared, so did the ash fertilizer. The Missionaries of Africa set out to improve traditional agriculture in several ways. First, they facilitated the spread of new crops and trees, not only those introduced by the Portuguese, but also crops they brought themselves. These included especially the common, or white potato, and other European vegetables, such as lettuce, cabbage, turnips, carrots and gherkins. In western Uganda, for example, they were the first to bring the paw-paw, mango, orange and lemon trees, as well as the Bourbon variety of Arabica coffee from Tanzania. At Baudouinville (Upper Congo), they introduced Spanish oranges, Cape gooseberries, cherries, Brazil nuts and seven types of date. They also introduced rabbits and sheep.

Second, the White Fathers introduced new techniques, of which the most important was the plough. One plough could do the work of eighty African hoes, and it increased cultivation by a factor of ten times. Ploughs, however, had to be drawn by ox teams, and that meant an investment in raising livestock. Ox ploughs were introduced at Baudouinville (Upper Congo) in 1900, at Kashozi (Nyanza South) in 1906 and at Ndala (Unyanyembe) in 1909.[133] The missionaries also strove to introduce new methods of soil conservation and fertilization, as well as new methods of rat-proof storage. Mathurin Guillemé (1859–1942) was told by fishermen in 1908 that there were no fish in Lake Nyasa (Malawi). He disproved this at once by producing and using a net instead of a line. Henceforward, young people were employed at Ngumbo, making fishnets from vegetable fibre.[134]

Up to 1918, it must be said that the missionaries acted almost alone in this work of agricultural innovation; the colonial governments did virtually nothing. It was not surprising, therefore, that at the first Ugandan Agricultural and Industrial Show, held at Kampala in 1909, the White Fathers carried away the lion's share of the prizes and earned fulsome praise from the governor, Sir Hesketh Bell.[135] For much of the period, the colonial administrations had their hands full with the pacification of their newly acquired territories, including the ending of the insecurity caused by inter-tribal warfare and slave-raiding. Governments urged the missionaries to encourage people to grow cash crops, and the White Fathers co-operated in this, as we saw in Chapter Four. The crops in question were mainly rice, cotton, coffee and rubber. In 1909, Célestin Hauttecoeur (1852–1940) was sent from Kisubi (Uganda) to the Spiritans' coffee plantation at St. Austin's, Nairobi (British East Africa) to study coffee-growing and processing. At Kisubi, there were ambitious—but in the event unfulfilled—plans to supply

North Africa, the mother house, Kabylia, Carthage and Thibar with coffee.[136]

The early years of the twentieth century were the years of the red Rubber "Terror" in the Congo. The nearest the Missionaries of Africa came to experiencing the terror itself was at Lwisi in northern Urua (Upper Congo), shortly before the closure of this mission in 1905. In the previous year, people had been selling wild rubber to smugglers from Goma on Lake Kivu. So five soldiers were sent by the administration to collect all the rubber in the area.[137] There is no record of atrocity on this occasion. Across Lake Tanganyika at Zimba, the missionaries reported in the same year that Afro-Arabs (*wangwana*) were searching for rubber in every village.[138] From 1905 until 1911, the White Fathers were busy planting rubber trees and growing rubber creepers throughout their vicariates in Uganda, German East Africa and Congo. The White Sisters (MSOLA) had a first harvest of rubber from their trees in 1909 at Ushirombo (Unyanyembe). By 1900, all the techniques for growing and tapping latex rubber trees (*hevea braziliensis, ficus elasticus*) were known. It took five years from planting before the tree could be successfully tapped for latex, and Bishop Gerboin in 1911 complained that this was too long.[139] The bishop, however, was already too late. By 1910, the huge cultivated rubber plantations of Southeast Asia and South America had matured, and had started to become the world's chief suppliers. Africa was out of the running, and the short-lived African rubber boom was over.

In the previous chapter, the development of the White Fathers' mission stations and some of their activities were discussed. Deogratias Byabazaire has compared these stations to the ancient Benedictine abbeys of Europe.[140] They were great agricultural, industrial, educational and medical centres. Ploughs were forged there. Looms produced textiles. Furniture was produced in the carpentry shop. Printing, milling, rope-making, basket-weaving, embroidery and tailoring all took place. The church pioneered all of these in the African interior. From the mission stations came task forces to build roads and bridges. In 1905, a bridge was built over the Lufuko river at Lusaka (Upper Congo), but it needed rebuilding four years later.[141] In 1907, the missionaries at Galula (Tanganyika) were busy rebuilding a bridge over the Songwe river, for which they received financial assistance from the German administration.[142] At Likuni (Nyasa), the White Fathers built two bridges in 1909, and in the previous year there was a fever of road-making at Kate (Tanganyika).[143] Apprentices were trained at the big mission stations. For example, at Rushoroza in southwestern Uganda, ten boys were trained every year during this period. Eventually, rural trade schools were started.

The Changing Status of Women

Before World War I, an ex-slave in German East Africa was quoted as saying: "The chief has many wives, perhaps a hundred, perhaps two hundred. They are like slaves; they live in fear."[144] On the question of the status of women in this context, Marcia Wright has written: "The practical distinction between the rights of slaves and free women was comparatively small."[145] The White Fathers in those pre-war years needed no convincing of this. Although they may sometimes have misread the cultural differences between Europe and Africa where the treatment of women was concerned, their judgement that women were extensively victimized in traditional societies has been supported by modern African women writers and theologians.[146] A missionary was horrified at Ouarzen in Kabylia, when a catechist remarked in 1900: "Women are like beasts of burden. Only a stick will keep them on the right path."[147] Similarly at Galula (Tanganyika) in 1908, the veteran missionary Théophile Dromaux (1849–1909) exploded over a case of forced marriage, in which a young woman was flogged by her brother, and her catechumen's crucifix sent back to the mission. "Women are not allowed heart or conscience," Dromaux wrote; "I am happy to see such tyranny destroyed by European domination."[148] European colonial administrations, however, did not always see eye to eye with the White Fathers in their campaign against forced marriages. This was the case in the Mossi Kingdom of French Sudan, where the refuge given by missionaries to women fleeing parental control of their marriages was a frequent source of conflict with colonial officials.[149]

Everywhere, the White Fathers resisted the forced marriage of female catechumens and welcomed girls who sought refuge at the mission or in the catechumenate. Too often, alas, they were obliged to report violence against women. At Nsasa (Rwanda), a Christian beat his wife to death in 1908, and at Patyana (French Sudan), a young woman was beaten and chained by her parents, before she could escape to the mission.[150] At Kagondo (Nyanza South), sorcery was practised against unmarried girls, widows and divorcees, and many came to the mission for protection.[151] Everywhere in the missions of the White Fathers at this period, the struggle took place. Bishop Joseph Sweens (1858–1950) of Nyanza South saw it as a new phase in the ransoming of "female slaves."[152]

Although it was a battle that the elders and chiefs could not ultimately win, they fought hard, knowing—as they said in French Sudan—that "if you want billy goats, you must get hold of the ewes." The White Fathers, like their founder Lavigerie, knew the truth underlying this maxim: the key to the conversion of an African people was the Christian education of its women. The missionaries felt helpless until the arrival of Sisters. "In the absence of sisters, I am mother as well as father," wrote a missionary at Kirando (Tanganyika) in 1904; "We have started to evangelize the women," wrote another at Patyana (French Sudan), "but we await the sisters."[153] Everywhere, the Missionaries of Africa awaited the coming of the sisters in order to confront more effectively the abuse of women via infant marriage, polygamy and forced marriage. And everywhere women were claiming the freedom to marry a husband of their choice.

By the turn of the century, the White Sisters (MSOLA) were beginning to arrive in both equatorial Africa and the French Sudan. In fact, between 1892 and 1914, the White Sisters made a total of sixty foundations in Europe, Canada and the African continent.[154] At once, they took over the education of female orphans and catechumens, as well as the protection of those who wanted greater control over their own lives. All over Francophone West Africa, religious sisters arranged boarding facilities for young, unmarried women, where they could educate and protect those who wanted to become Christians. These institutions, as we saw in Chapter Three, were known as *sixa*, a corruption of the English word "sister."[155] The missionaries realized that protecting women was as important, if not more important, than safe-guarding their freedom. By 1914, the chiefs had lost much of their coercive power and they no longer exercised control over groups of women, as they had done in the past. The advancement and empowerment of women was a genuine development from within African society, one to which the White Fathers, aided invaluably by the White Sisters, responded.

"Cultural Marriages"

Re-inventing the Missionaries

In several well-known instances, White Fathers were, so to speak, cultur-ally "adopted" by Africa. To mix the metaphor, a "marriage" took place between African categories and the missionaries' own self-understanding. Augustin Hacquard was strongly attracted to the Mossi people, and founded the first mission stations in that kingdom. Had he lived, his attachment might have generated a response like that of the Bemba to Joseph Dupont, and he might possibly have become the "Moto Moto" of the Mossi. Subsequent Mossi hagiography tended to reinvent the first missionaries according to their own categories, principally as rainmakers, chiefs and offerers of effective sacrifices.[156]

Yacouba Dupuis, as we have seen, carried his attachment to the city and people of Timbuktu to the extreme of leaving the Society altogether. His cul-tural "marriage" to the Songhay of Timbuktu was accompanied by the more literal marriage to his Muslim wife, Fatima. Yacouba, who was described in the 1930s as "a benevolent patriarchal bull, disguised as Santa Claus," was a scholar in the traditions of the ancient city of scholars.[157] Although he did not himself become a Muslim, he was considered an outstanding Islamic scholar and linguist. Little or nothing remained of Timbuktu's glory and of its famed Sankore University after the destruction of the Songhay Empire in 1591, but Abderrahman es Saadi had bequeathed his legendary medieval history, the Tarikh es Sudan, to the desolate city in 1655, and it had been discovered there by the German explorer, Heinrich Barth, two hun-dred years later in 1850. Yacouba gained access to this famed manuscript, and he delighted the people of Timbuktu when he obtained permission from the French to found a *medersa*, or native university faculty, and become its president. It was a poor, latter-day substitute for Sankore University, but it earned Yacouba the people's lasting gratitude. Living the social life of a citizen of the historic city, and immersed in its languages and culture, there are some who say that Yacouba Dupuis was the "best missionary" the White Fathers produced in the Sahel area of French Sudan.

In the previous discussion of the concept of the Christian kingdom, the influence of Ganda monarchical traditions on the shape taken by the early Catholic Church in Buddu was described, as were Bishop Henri Streicher's regal innuendos. These developments were perhaps premature idiosyncrasies, but there was a more profound and more lasting "marriage" between the French culture of the missionaries and that of the people of Buganda. This exchange was facilitated by the far-reaching cultural shift that was in the offing when the missionaries first arrived in 1879; the newcomers were welcomed as tactful agents of change. Evangelization took place within this ongoing process, and produced a Christian culture that people sensed to be authentic.

This was demonstrated years later when non-French White Fathers came to Uganda in greater numbers.[158] The new arrivals were Canadian, Dutch and British, and were teachers rather than pastors. They spoke English and identified with the young elite whom they were educating in the schools and seminaries. The French missionaries already in Uganda, by contrast, were almost universally non-English-speaking, and they steered clear of the English-speaking urban centres, identifying rather with the culture of the villages and rural dwellers. In 1946, the British Education Secretary, H.R. Cullen, wrote to the Mill Hill Bishop, Vincent Billington, saying that the British Government wanted English-speaking missionaries in Uganda— Commonwealth citizens or foreigners that had experienced the British "way of life."[159] Bishop Joseph Kiwanuka of Masaka and the apostolic delegate, Archbishop David Mathew, attended the 1947 General Chapter of the White Fathers, which discussed this issue. Bishop Kiwanuka made an impassioned defence of the French missionaries. They had been in the country for decades. They were, he said, more appreciated by the Ganda, and they understood Ganda culture better. The upshot of the discussion was that French White Fathers were allowed to remain in Uganda, and that a "British Way of Life" course was opened at Claughton Hall in Lancashire. Needless to say, this had no impact on the long-standing and successful "cultural marriage" of French and Ganda.

The cultural marriage that was most successful and outstanding was that of Joseph Dupont, the celebrated Bwana Moto Moto, with the Bemba of Northern Rhodesia. There have already been brief treatments of him in earlier chapters, which need not be repeated here. What is important in this context is to understand the reason for the mutual attraction. Dupont was emotionally drawn to the Bemba, partly because of their military reputation and prowess, which appealed to his own military character and experience. He clearly enjoyed their company and was impressed by their religiosity.[160] He sincerely believed that the opening up of the Bemba to the

Gospel was, as he put it, "an extraordinary fruit of God's grace."[161] Certainly, as a child of his times, he was not immune to European prejudice and sense of superiority. Nevertheless, he achieved a high degree of psychological approximation to the Bemba, and his love and compassion for them were genuine. He appreciated their social institutions and their methods of upbringing. He did not harp on their faults or doom them to an eternal state of socio-cultural inferiority. It is difficult to agree with a verdict that sees Dupont as simply a kinder version of Roelens.[162]

For their part, the Bemba were genuinely attracted to Dupont. He was an impressive figure, as photographs of him testify. His first act, the healing of a woman with an ulcer at Makasa's in 1895, made a deep impression on them. At the moment of Dupont's appearance, there was a widespread messianic expectation among the Bemba that centred on the traditional figure of Luchele Nganga, the "Auroral Healer." Dupont accepted their identification of him as the son of Luchele Nganga. His previous experience of the abortive mission at Kwamouth in the Congo prompted his claim to hail from the original Luba-Lunda homeland near Kasai. Consciously, he fulfilled the Bemba legends, and was looked upon as a more powerful healer-priest than other Bemba healers and mediums. Above all, he was the deliverer. He certainly claimed to be Mwamba's successor as chief of Ituna, and he may himself have understood his role as a providential one of deliverance. The mission station that he founded, as bishop and chief, was called Chilubula, meaning "deliverance." A praise hymn, sung by Bemba women up to the present day, modelled partly on Bemba initiation songs and partly on the *Magnificat*, celebrates him as *mulubushi wesu*, "our redeemer." The hymn describes him as the ideal man, one who causes life and nurtures it, one who is strong and hurls down the "mighty lions," that is to say, the oppressive chiefs. But he also heals the people's wounds and is the saviour, the redeemer from slavery.

"Hymn to Mgr. Dupont, our redeemer:
He gives life to our children and nurtures them with food,
He hurls down the lions and heals our ailments.
He is strong, yet so kind, and the Mother of Moto Moto
How great a queen she is!"[163]

The song continues, in African fashion, to praise Dupont's mother, as the source of his goodness. As an example of a cultural "marriage," the legendary Moto Moto is hard to beat.

Rain

Rain is a constant and major preoccupation in Africa. Its uncertainty and apparent capriciousness is proverbial. In many regions, rainfall is always insufficient to produce a good harvest, and the outright failure of the rains means drought and famine. Rainmaking, magical or religious, was a traditional activity that fell under the control of the king or chief. Either he was himself a rainmaker, or he employed specialists who were punished as scape-goats when their techniques failed. In 1907 six of the greatest rainmakers of Rwanda were executed at Marangara, and at Save the following year, another failed rainmaker was killed.[164] Missionary foreigners were also sometimes blamed for the failure of the rain. At Urwira (Tanganyika) in 1907, it was said that the missionaries interrupted the all-important ritual. In the same year, people at Banankuru (French Sudan) blamed the lack of rain on the White Fathers for having given burial to a leper. In Burundi, the following year, the missionaries successfully prevented the execution of a woman accused of "killing the rain."[165]

More frequently, however, the Missionaries of Africa were believed to be able to bring the rain, and their help was enlisted by local chiefs and their people. The most celebrated case of missionary rainmaking occurred in the Gold Coast (Ghana) between the two world wars, when successful prayers for rain were followed by mass conversions among the Dagaaba in 1932, the rainmaker in this instance being Remigius McCoy (1897–1993).[166] However, throughout our period, 1892–1914, there were countless less well-known instances of missionary rainmaking. Chiefs who were desperate fre-quently asked for prayers for rain, and many times the prayers were answered. Sometimes missionary success put the local rainmakers to shame. At Galula (Tanganyika) in 1904, the efforts of the local rainmaker on one particular day were in vain. The following day, children prayed for rain before the cemetery crucifix. Rain fell and the harvest was saved.[167] In 1907, a Mass was celebrated for rain at Msalala (Unyanyembe), and clouds appeared in the afternoon, followed by a heavy downpour.[168] At Mpimbwe (Tanganyika) in 1908, there was a successful novena for rain.[169] There is no doubt that the African reinvention of missionaries as rainmakers was uni-versal, and that it played an important part in the White Fathers' success-ful evangelization.

Ethnography and Science

White Father Ethnographers

Cardinal Lavigerie wanted his missionaries to be primarily apostles, rather than men of science or mere explorers. They were not to be—in Lavigerie's colourful phrase—"Robinson Crusoes."[170] However, he recognized that he was sending his men into the interior of the African continent, virtually unknown to the scientific community of Europe. In the service of science and colonialism, geographers, ethnographers and countless other specialists were busy opening up this unknown territory and he wanted the Missionaries of Africa to contribute to this process. "All [such] services ren-dered to science," he wrote, "can be considered as an effective response to the odious attacks directed against the Church by her enemies."[171] He asked that the missionaries devote a minimum of fifteen to twenty minutes a day to keeping a journal which would be envisaged as a contribution to science.[172] He desired that legends, historical narratives and sacred myths be recorded, because these could confirm the truths of Holy Scripture and Christian teaching about the unity of the human race. Scientific collections and observations, made with the help of instructions and instruments supplied by learned societies in Paris, should be sent in regularly.[173]

One of the finest examples of the implementation of Lavigerie's instructions is provided by a Dutch White Father, Herman Melssen (1883–1963). Melssen took his missionary oath in 1906 and was posted to Tanganyika Vicariate, where he eventually helped to establish the mission of Makete/ Kisa in the Southern Highlands in the 1920s. For more than twenty years, ending with his death, Melssen was the mission diarist. The diary reported the daily events at the mission, but this record was constantly interrupted by notes and essays on scientific subjects: archaeology, etymology, ethnography, botany, zoology.[174] It is also clear from these digressions that the diary accompanied Melssen when he travelled to other parts of the colony. For example, during a train journey to Dar es Salaam, he recorded his speculations on the origin of the place names along the route.[175]

The period 1892–1914 witnessed the birth of missionary ethnography in the Catholic Church. Its leading light and one of the foremost authorities of the time on linguistics, ethnology and the history of religion was Wilhelm Schmidt (1868–1954) of the Divine Word Missionaries. In 1906 Schmidt founded the famous journal *Anthropos* at Moedling near Vienna, Austria. This journal became the focus for the Anthropos Institute, which he directed from 1932 to 1950. Schmidt's monumental twelve-volume work on *The Origin of the Idea of God* began to appear in the journal in 1912. White Fathers were encouraged by Schmidt's example to enter the field of ethnography, and several published their findings in the pages of *Anthropos* during these years. Before Schmidt's *Idea of God* began to appear, another luminary had started to publish articles on "Primitive Religion" and "The Scientific Role of the Missionary" in the first issue of *Anthropos*.[176] This was the Spiritan, Alexandre Leroy. After serving on the island of Réunion, he came to Bagamoyo on the East African coast in 1881 and carried out wide-ranging journeys to acquire ethnographic information. Effectively expelled by the Germans, he went to Paris where he became the first professor of the history of religions at the Institut Catholique and was then appointed vicar apostolic of the Vicariate of the Two Guineas, a territory stretching from Senegal to the Cape of Good Hope. He thus acquired an unrivalled knowledge of Africa and its peoples. In 1896 he was elected Superior General of the Spiritans.

In 1909 Leroy published an important work on primitive religion, which concentrated on the Bantu-speaking areas of Africa.[177] This book presented a totally different picture of traditional religion from that of the explorers and scholars, and made unfashionable comparisons with so-called "higher" religions. It refuted the new European "religion" of evolutionism and its theories of primitive promiscuity and polytheism. Leroy's work was solidly based on oral traditions, languages and observed ritual practices, and he proved conclusively that Africans were monotheists. Only Catholic Christianity, he believed, could answer the questions raised by these religions. Soon after its appearance, Léon Livinhac, Superior General of the White Fathers, wrote to the author, congratulating him on behalf of the Society, and applauding the assault on evolutionism.[178] Already, Livinhac's missionaries were lending published support to Leroy's theses.

The earliest White Father in the field of ethnology was Auguste Achte (1861–1905), who published a dozen or more articles in mission periodicals between 1894 and 1905, the year of his death. Achte's most notable work was his unpublished *History of the Baganda Kings*, finished in January 1900.[179] The account begins with the legendary foundation of the Ganda Kingdom and finishes with the events Achte himself had witnessed in Uganda. Another unpublished work was also produced in 1900. This was a monograph by Auguste "Yacouba" Dupuis (1865–1945) on the physical and human geography of Timbuktu, including a complete ethnography and history of its discovery and occupation by the French.[180] Jean- (or Jan-) Martin-Michel Van der Burgt (1863–1923) was a Dutch White Father and one of the first two missionaries in Burundi after the Rumonge disaster of 1881, who became a prolific writer in the early years of the twentieth century. His *French-Kirundi Dictionary* was sent in manuscript to the Berlin Museum in 1899, along with 348 ethnographic objects packed in three boxes. The ethnographic section of this work was published in 1903 at s'Hertogenbosch in the Netherlands, and the full *Dictionary and Grammar* followed in 1904.[181]

The ethnography reveals Van der Burgt as an eccentric polymath of the first order. Its bibliography counts 491 items, and, after a lengthy introduction of 113 pages, is followed by an ethnographic dictionary of 196 articles, together with 250 printed engravings and figures, and 10 maps. The introduction, which is of extraordinary breadth and erudition, deals with racial classification; the Hamitic theory; African prehistory; ancient Egypt; the Phoenicians, Sabeans, Greeks and Romans in Africa; the Arab writers; the ancient kingdoms of Zimbabwe and Monomotapa; the Oromo-Galla peoples; domestic animals and Negro statistics. The rest of the book is a kind of alphabetical "notes and queries" on the ethnography of Burundi. There are articles on religious beliefs, traditional religious hymns, healers, medicines, rainmaking, myths and oral literature, as well as lists of kings, engravings of 100 hair styles with their names, 14 engravings of tattoos and 138 engravings of buildings, artefacts, utensils and dress.

The theoretical research for the book was conducted in the State Ethnographical Museum of Leiden. After this *tour de force*, it is perhaps not surprising that Van der Burgt received a distinction from the German government. The author, however, did not rest on his laurels. A stream of published articles continued to pour out from his pen, including in 1921, two years before his death, a history of the mission in Central Africa, composed in Dutch.[182] There was considerable controversy among Van der Burgt's confreres over alleged inaccuracies in his publications. The General Council of the Society was also alarmed in 1913 at his publishing articles in German East African and European journals without the authorization of his superiors, and he was cautioned about this.[183] His enthusiasm as an ethnographer appears to have been undaunted.

Bishop Adolphe Lechaptois (1852–1917) of the Tanganyika Vicariate produced a unique ethnography of the Fipa and Bende peoples of his vicariate in 1913, the fruit of twenty years' experience. *On the Shores of Tanganyika* is a sympathetic and positive account of their history, politics, family life, oral traditions, arts, scientific knowledge and industries. It even includes musical scores.[184] The book deservedly won the prize and silver medal of the Paris Geographical Society.

Eugène Mangin (1877–1922) was the brother of World War I General Charles Mangin, known as *mangeur d'hommes*, "the eater of men." Eugène was the ethnographer of the Mossi. Having contributed four important articles on the Mossi to *Anthropos* between 1914 and 1916, these were published by the journal as an offprint book, and later republished by the Missionaries of Africa at Algiers in 1960.[185] The work is a competent ethnography of the Mossi and their royal traditions, with an emphasis on their religious beliefs and rituals.

Bishop Julien Gorju (1868–1942) became first vicar apostolic of Burundi in 1922. Prior to that, he had been at Bukalasa Seminary in Uganda, where he founded the newspaper *Munno*, and directed the printing press. He was also the ecclesiastical notary for the cause of the Uganda Martyrs. Over the years he published an impressive list of articles and small books, especially in the Belgian *Grands Lacs* series. His major work, for which he received a prize from the French Academy, was an ethnographic survey of the peoples in the Uganda (Nyanza North) Vicariate, *Between Lakes Victoria, Albert and Edward*, which appeared in 1920, but which was based on a quarter century of linguistic and cultural studies.[186] The book, which had first appeared as a series of separate articles, was put together at Bukalasa in 1919. The peoples described are the Ganda, Hima, Nyoro and Nkole of Uganda; the Kiziba of Tanganyika Territory (formerly German East Africa); and the Tutsi, Hutu and Twa of Rwanda and Burundi. After moving to Burundi, Gorju described his first journey there in another substantial work, which also included much ethnographic information.[187]

Félix Dufays (1877–1954) was a Luxemburger who went to Rwanda in 1903 and was appointed to found the mission station of Mulera. His published works appeared after the First World War, but were based on earlier research and experience. His history, *Pages from an African Epic—Troubled Times 1928*, tells the story of the difficult beginnings of Mulera from 1903 up to the murder of Loupias in 1910, and his 1939 work, *Au Kinyaga les enchaînés*, consists of ethnographic notes collected over twenty-six years and circulated among confreres in 1913.[188] He also wrote a morality novel in Swahili after World War I, which had two editions in French.

Two other Missionary of Africa ethnographers came to German East Africa during the period 1892–1914. They were Jean-Marie Robert (1879–1966), who arrived in the country in 1906, and the Swiss White Father, Fridolin Bösch (1881–1968), who came in 1909.[189] Robert began publishing his material on the Fipa (Tanganyika) in the 1930s, while Bösch, who began his study of the Nyamwezi in 1912—shortly after the arrival of Bishop Henri Léonard, from whom he received encouragement—started to publish his findings in the 1920s.[190] Altogether, the ethnographic output of the Missionaries of Africa during the years 1892–1914 constitutes a proud record.

Other Sciences

Missionaries were responsible for most of the ethnographic studies carried out at this time, although the human sciences were in their infancy and the writers had no specific training for the task. The White Fathers, like other missionaries, had a vested interest in the study of human societies, but the colonial authorities, with the effective exploitation of natural resources in mind, put more emphasis on the physical sciences than on the human. This was especially the case in German East Africa, where there was a flurry of scientific activity originating with the colonial authorities. The White Fathers, however, also made contributions in these areas.

Some Missionaries of Africa contributed to the history of exploration and geographical discovery, either by joining the expeditions of explorers, or by themselves recording journeys through regions hitherto unobserved by Europeans. One of these was the first German priest of the Society, Auguste Wilhelm Schynse (1857–1891) from Trier, who made his missionary oath in 1883 and who was sent with Joseph Dupont and Armand Merlon to start the ill-fated mission of Bungana at Kwamouth in the Congo in 1885. Schynse wrote an account in German of his two years at Kwamouth, which was published in 1889.[191] In September 1889, H.M. Stanley's Emin Pasha Relief Expedition passed in the neighbourhood of Bukumbi Mission (Nyanza South), and was supplied by the missionaries with linen, shoes and donkeys.[192] On September 24th, Schynse accompanied Ludovic Girault (1853–1941), the provicar of Unyanyembe, who was suffering from river blindness, to see Stanley's doctor, and it was decided that Girault should go to Europe for treatment. On October 4th, Schynse and Girault left Bukumbi with twenty porters and four soldiers to join Stanley and Emin on their way to the coast. Schynse returned the following year in the company of Emin, together with Auguste Achte on his way back to Uganda from the General Chapter and home-leave. They reached Bukumbi on September 8th 1890, and three weeks later Emin himself visited the mission.[193] Schynse wrote an account of the journey with Stanley and Emin which was published in French, German and Italian.[194] It offers a number of insights into the character and habits of both the explorers.[195] Schynse died a year later, at the early age of thirty-four.

Augustin Hacquard, who joined the Hourst Hydrographic Expedition for mapping the River Niger in 1896, gave a presentation to the Algiers Geographical Society about the expedition in the following year.[196] His caravan to French Sudan in 1895 created considerable interest and expectation among the scientific community in Paris, which was anxious for geographical, ethnographic and linguistic information; Hacquard had already, in fact, addressed the Paris Geographical Society in 1894.[197] He published a great many articles in geographical and missionary periodicals about the Hourst expedition, and about his other travels in the Sahara and French Sudan, notably in *Missions Catholiques*. One of his most important articles described his two visits to the Mossi Kingdom.[198]

In German East Africa, Théophile Dromaux (1849–1909) pioneered a new route from Ugogo to Lake Tanganyika in 1897. The journey took him through hitherto undescribed regions of Ukimbu and Ukonongo. His account in the *The Geographical Journal* is a physical and human geography of the areas through which he passed. Paul Langhaus edited the account and provided a map in *Petermann's Mitteilungen*.[199]

Virtually all the missions in German East Africa became meteorological stations after 1908, when pluviometers were distributed by the administration for measuring rainfall.

The greatest White Father scientist of this period was undoubtedly the archaeologist Alfred-Louis Delattre (1850–1932). Delattre, who easily bore comparison with the best archaeologists of the day, spent a lifetime excavating Punic, Roman and early Christian remains on Byrsa Hill at Carthage in Tunisia. His bibliography contains 250 numbered publications, plus another 25 major papers. Delattre sent exhibits for display to museums all over the world. Although his methods are judged today to have impoverished the excavation site, he cannot be ignored by any scholar for whom the excavations at Carthage are relevant. In 1879 Delattre founded the Museum of St. Louis, which was renamed the Lavigerie Museum after the death of Cardinal Lavigerie. Carthage Cathedral was built in 1890, incidentally preventing excavation of the site it occupied, and Delattre became its arch-priest. In 1964 the Lavigerie Museum was renamed the National Museum of Carthage. The cathedral was subsequently secularized and acquired by the museum.[200]

Delattre was the cornerstone of a team assembled by Lavigerie to study the history and archaeology of the early North African church. Bishop Anatole Toulotte was an important member of this team. Although he wrote an account of his journey through French Sudan in 1896–1897, as well as a linguistic study of Arabic usage there, most of his dozen or so works were about the archaeology, geography, history and cults of Christian North Africa, and many were unpublished.[201] Joseph Mesnage (1859–1922), who was Toulotte's literary heir and interpreter, produced an impressive list of writings on Christian North Africa. Probably the two most important were his account of the ancient bishoprics and the ruins associated with them, based on Toulotte's unpublished material, and his account of the decline and extinction of Christianity in Roman Africa.[202] His work also helped in the revision of the so-called Kabyle Christian myth. André Vellard (1865–1906), who was one of the two White Fathers drowned in the *wadi* Biskra in the Sahara, wrote a guide to ancient and modern Carthage. It contains, among other things, a description of the major Punic and Roman archaeological sites.[203] Vellard was also the author of several unpublished manuscripts about the history and geography, physical and human, of the Sahara. His most substantial work, however, was the manuscript journal of the journey he made with Charles Guérin to the western Sahara in 1903, and their stay with Charles de Foucauld at Beni Abbés.[204]

During the years 1892–1914, White Fathers in equatorial Africa, and particularly in the German colony, played host to endless travellers. Colonialism seems to have let loose a rabble of drifters of one kind or another. They were a mixture of eccentric globetrotters, hunters and commercial speculators. The following is a small sample. An Englishman on a bicycle made an unexpected appearance at Bukumbi (Nyanza South) in 1902. An Australian merchant named Carey arrived at Muyaga (Burundi) in 1904. A Dutch duke called at Chilubi (Nyasa) in 1907. An Englishman walking from the Cape with only two mess tins as luggage sought shelter at Utinta (Tanganyika) in 1907. A British vice-consul, walking across Africa from west to east, turned up at Urwira (Tanganyika) in 1908, and a French hairdresser, walking from the Cape to Cairo later in the same year, offered the Urwira missionaries a free haircut to pay for his stay. The offer was declined. A lone backpacker, with long hair and beard and dirty attire came to Kirando (Tanganyika) in 1907, and a German with 750 cows, 36 donkeys and 8 ostriches, appeared at Mkulwe (Tanganyika) in 1908.[205] Among this stream of eccentrics, were some genuine scientists.

The missionaries at Mpala had already begun collecting insects and shells, when they were visited by Edouard Foa, the French explorer, hunter and geographer, in 1898. Foa, who was sponsored by the French Ministry of Public Instruction and the French Museum of Natural History, was delighted with the giant beetle and butterfly specimens the fathers gave him, but he was mortified to learn that the shells he had himself collected were already known to the White Fathers and had been classified, at their request, in an authoritative work on the molluscs of Lake Tanganyika by the French naturalist Jules-René Bourgignat in 1888.[206] An Italian museum director came to Bukalasa (Nyanza North) in 1907, looking for earwigs; there were further visits by entomologists from France, as well as scientists from British and Dutch museums, to Busubizi (Nyanza North) and Lusaka (Upper Congo), collecting butterflies and other insects.[207] Bruno Schmitz (1872–1905) created a private mineralogical museum at Mpala and Baudouinville.[208] Bishop Dupont collected snakes at Chilubula (Nyasa), and sent the venom to the

Pasteur Institute at Lille.[209] Two professors from Vienna University passed through Msalala (Unyanyembe) in 1909, with half a dozen specimens of birds, fish, and rhinoceros jaws.[210]

At Wargla in the Sahara, Edmond Huguenot (1850–1933) created a museum of archaeological artefacts for which he was made an officer of the French Academy in 1907, with *palmes archéologiques*, for services to pre-history.[211] Visiting gold prospectors and geologists abounded in equatorial Africa, French Sudan and the Sahara. A geologist from the French Museum of Natural History, Professor V. Gauthier, visited Timbuktu in 1906, bringing greetings from Charles de Foucauld. News followed soon afterwards of the death of Stanislas Comte (1865–1906), André Vellard's ill-fated companion at the *wadi* Biskra. Comte was himself a geologist who had made a study of the Saharan silex (fused quartz-stone).[212] Not all the famous scientists who visited the missions, however, were as friendly as Gauthier. Leo Viktor Frobenius, the German ethnographer and traveller, repaid the hospitality he received at Wagadugu (French Sudan) by publishing an unfavourable report on the mission, in order, so he later explained, to curry favour with the Kaiser.[213]

On the other side of the continent the scientific visitations reached a climax with the successive arrival of two royal dukes and a royal duchess. The first of these was the Duke of Abruzzi. Luigi Amedeo, Giuseppe Maria Ferdinando, Duke of Abruzzi (1873–1933), was a mountaineer and explorer, the son of King Amedeus of Spain, born in the year of his father's abdication. Although a Spaniard, he was of Italian descent and held an Italian title. The duke's main objective in 1906 was to climb the Ruwenzori Mountains, already conquered ten years previously by Auguste Achte and Bishop Antonin Guillermain. He called at Butiti Mission (Nyanza North) both before and after the ascent. A group of scientists accompanied the duke, whose secondary objective was to collect African lizards. A Ruwenzori chameleon was badly needed to complete the collection, but a search by the fathers and people of the mission was fruitless. In January 1907, after his return to Europe, the duke gave a lecture in Rome about his expedition, and this included a eulogy of the Missionaries of Africa that was gratefully acknowledged.[214]

The visit of the Duke of Mecklenburg-Strelitz at the end of 1907 was on an altogether grander scale. His Royal Highness Prince Adolf Friedrich VI, Grand Duke of Mecklenburg-Strelitz (1882–1918), was the scion of a minor royal house in western Pomerania, connected to the German imperial dynasty and the British royal family, and the autonomous ruler of his ducal enclave. Adolf Friedrich was, in fact, the last grand duke. His *safari* counted no fewer than eight hundred men. In the weeks before the great man's arrival, steamer after steamer crossed Lake Victoria from Uganda to Bukoba bringing supplies, while German officers were everywhere negotiating with the chiefs for porters. The missionaries at Kagondo were also asked to supply a list of names.[215] The duke, a Catholic, was welcomed to

Bukoba by the Rubya seminary band, and then accepted an invitation to dine at Kashozi Mission (Nyanza South).[216] He then moved into Rwanda, where the missionaries at Nyundo were asked to find him a horned chameleon. Children from the mission school were dispatched in all directions, having been promised a hundred beads for each specimen. They returned with five.[217]

The duke was mainly interested in hunting elephants, buffaloes and gorillas (the latter believed at that time to be ferocious carnivores, and not the gentle herbivores that we know them to be today). Paul Barthélemy (1871–1937) was recruited as guide and went to meet him in the forest. The Twa Pygmy trackers were uncooperative without the missionary's presence. The duke had a narrow escape from a wounded elephant, but managed to kill one and a gorilla, while Barthélemy shot two gorillas. Another of the duke's ambitions was to climb Mount Nyiragongo, the highest of the eight volcanoes of the Virunga Chain.[218] This volcano, at 3,465 metres high, had already been described by Félix Dufays, who had climbed it in 1905 with Anselm (Nicolas) Illerich (1863–1942), a German missionary brother.[219] A few months prior to the duke's visit, in May of 1907, this volcano had presented a threatening aspect with columns of smoke, an incandescent cover over the crater, and high flames.[220] (Nyiragongo was also the volcano that erupted in January 2002, destroying much of the town of Goma.) Its usually more active neighbour, Nyamuragira, actually erupted during the duke's visit.[221] Nothing daunted, however, the intrepid duke ascended the volcano to view the crater. He also climbed Mikeno volcano, which Barthélemy had scaled in 1902, but did not reach the summit, even with the best guide the missionaries could provide. Before leaving Rwanda, the duke sent a portrait of himself to Barthélemy.[222] After World War I, the Grand Duchy of Mecklenburg was absorbed into the German Republic, and sadly Adolf Friedrich VI committed suicide by shooting himself at the early age of thirty-six.

The Duke of Mecklenburg had travelled with a scientific commission headed by a Dr. Czekanowski, who remained in Africa after the duke's departure. Czekanowski, a Polish-born Russian, was a professor at the Berlin Museum, and had a major interest in craniometry.[223] The diarist of Nyundo (Rwanda) wrote in 1908: "Mr. Czekanowski collects practically everything, but he holds the record for human skulls. From Bukoba up to here, he has accumulated more than a thousand pieces; it is, he says, the best collection in the world."[224] It was not difficult to collect skulls in the Africa of those days, since burial was not yet a universal practice, and the dead were frequently laid in the open to be disposed of by scavenger animals and birds. Craniometry, or the measurement of cranial features in order to classify people according to fixed racial criteria, criminal temperament or intelligence, was a fallacious pseudo-science that was beloved of colonial apologists, and enjoyed a lengthy and sinister history. It was used to justify the racist policies of Europeans in Africa and of the British towards the Irish, as well as theories of male superiority over women. There were several rival versions of the theory. From the late nineteenth century up to the time of the Nazi Third Reich, craniometry was used to demonstrate the "pure" Aryan descent of modern Germans, while French theorists during the First World War used it to prove that the Prussians were not Aryans at all.[225]

Although based on bad science, craniometry was respectable, and the White Fathers were tempted by it during and after the Duke of Mecklenburg's visit. At the end of 1907, missionaries in Burundi discovered a complete human skeleton on their property. "It would be a pretty specimen to send to an anthropological museum in Berlin," wrote the diarist of Marianseen. However, fearing "the commentaries of the people who would take us for magicians," decency and common sense prevailed.[226] Anyone collecting or handling human bones was regarded in Africa as a witch or sorcerer. Later in the same year, more human skulls and bones were found in the mission wheat field. This time the missionaries could leave the responsibility to Dr. Czekanowski; they remarked that "The anthropologists of Leiden and Berlin will be very happy."[227] On November 10th 1907, Dr. Czekanowski appeared at Kabgayi (Rwanda) and asked the White Fathers to forward fifty boxes to Bukoba for him. The missionaries learned that the boxes were full of human skulls, but they "willingly [accepted] to render this service for him."[228] One wonders what would have happened if the boxes had been rifled en route, as frequently happened to luggage in Africa.

The Duchess of Aosta, who appeared in Uganda in early 1908, was also of royal descent. She was, in her own right, Princess Hélène of France: she was the daughter of Philippe of Orleans, the Count of Paris, and had married Emmanuel Philibert, Duke of Aosta. Her mother was Marie-Isabel, Infanta of Spain, and her husband was another son of ex-King Amedeus, and full brother of the Duke of Abruzzi, the mountaineer. The former king also held the title of Duke of Aosta. It is more than likely that her brother-in-law encouraged the duchess to follow in his footsteps by visiting Uganda. Her journey was humanitarian rather than scientific, and she desired to see the good work the White Fathers were doing for the victims of sleeping sickness. The duchess visited Rubaga and Entebbe Missions, making generous donations to the Missionaries of Africa and to the sleeping-sickness appeal. She then returned to Europe.

This exploration of the White Fathers' interactions with the motley exponents of colonial science reveals the extent to which the missionaries were already independently committed to a variety of scientific projects of their own.

The White Fathers and Anti-Modernism

Adrian Hastings has characterized the theology and spirituality of the White Fathers and other missionaries in Africa during this period as being "narrowly neo-scholastic, papalist and Marian . . . but tolerant of native culture."[229] The judgement may be true as it stands, but it begs the question about the possible theological relevance of this cultural tolerance. It is certainly true that the Missionaries of Africa imbibed neo-scholastic theology during their formation. They could not have done otherwise, since this type of formation was universal for priests and religious at the time. During the period we are studying, the anti-modernist campaign was launched by St. Pius X and Cardinal Merry del Val. This campaign was classicist, integralist and intellectualist. The anti-modernist encyclical *Pascendi* was received with rapture by White Fathers everywhere in 1908. It was read in the refectory of the scholasticate at Carthage. It was acclaimed in Canada as "learned, opportune and magisterial." In Burundi, a White Father diarist wrote: "From the coast we receive the marvellous encyclical *Pascendi* of September 8th 1907. *Deo Gratias*. These are words that will console and reassure Catholic consciences."[230] The enthusiastic superlatives, however, were more indicative of an ardent loyalty to the Holy See, than of an awareness of the theological issues themselves and their relevance for missionary work in Africa.

In fact, many of the anti-modernist propositions were already being undermined by the missionary experience of ethnic cultures. For example, the Holy See issued a decree on the absolute authority of decisions taken by the Vatican Biblical Commission. One of this commission's first decisions, taken in 1909, concerned the true, historical character of the first chapter of Genesis. It is clear that missionary disciples of Wilhelm Schmidt and Alexandre Leroy, who were researching ethnic traditions and the history of religions, and discussing human origins, ethics, racial classification and the idea of God, ran the risk of contradicting the assumptions of anti-modernism. That there was no overt conflict was due, on the one hand, to official ignorance of ethnography in Rome, and, on the other hand, to a lack of serious interest in theology on the part of missionaries.[231] Missionaries could not fail to notice that human beings did not know God by pure reason alone, or that the external proofs of revelation were not, as the text of the anti-modernist oath claimed, "well adapted to the understanding of all eras and all men." Their writings were evidence of a growing conviction that nature was already graced. By the end of our period, the White Fathers were beginning to lessen, if not to drop, their disparagement of African religious cultures. They did this at the behest of a new generation of vicars apostolic, represented by such figures as Henri Léonard and Julien Gorju, and under the inspiration of Wilhelm Schmidt's ideas.[232]

Mariano Cardinal Rampolla del Tindaro (1843–1913) had been Pope Leo XIII's Secretary of State, and was for a short time Secretary of the Holy Office under St. Pius X. As a friend of Lavigerie, he became Cardinal Protector of the Missionaries of Africa after Lavigerie's death in 1892. Although he agreed with Bishop Bonomelli of Cremona that the repressive anti-modernist measures of St. Pius X would lead to an intellectual crisis in the church and endanger true scholarship, he was unable to intervene, especially after his removal from the Holy Office in 1909. Giacomo Della Chiesa, Rampolla's former secretary and confidant, was purged from the Secretariat of State because he had remained on friendly terms with Rampolla. He was made Archbishop of Bologna in 1907, but was denied a cardinal's hat until 1914, in which year he was, of course, elected to the papacy, as Pope Benedict XV. The young Angelo Giuseppe Roncalli, the future Pope John XXIII, was also under suspicion because of his friendship with Rampolla's ally, Geremia Bonomelli, Bishop of Cremona.[233]

Benedict XV's first act as pope was to call a halt to the anti-modernist campaign. This he did in his first encyclical, *Ad Beatissimi*. It was in his encyclical *Maximum Illud*, the first mission encyclical in the history of the papacy, however, that the relevance of language and culture to the church's mission was first acknowledged. In 1920 Pope Benedict XV beatified the twenty-two Uganda Martyrs, the climax of the long process that had been begun by Cardinal Lavigerie himself. It is possible that he had been prepared for this action by the example of the White Fathers and the influence of their Cardinal Protector, whose personal secretary he had been for so long. It was a modest first step towards a more profound encounter between the Catholic Church and Africa.

In the years 1892–1914, the Missionaries of Africa, in spite of many handicaps deriving from a biased European mentality and from the inequities and impositions of the colonial situation, did—with few exceptions—develop a genuine love and understanding of the African people among whom they worked. They also contributed much to the world's knowledge of Africa and to the Africans' own understanding of themselves. Moreover, they helped to lay the foundations of a new form of Catholic Christianity. If this church was an "invention"—and it could not be otherwise—it was certainly one which Africans themselves helped to shape. The next chapter discusses the role of the Missionaries of Africa in education during this period and the first steps taken, through seminary education in particular, to form an African leadership for this church.

CHAPTER SIX

Education and Denomination

Religious Purpose and Importance of Schools

"We do not want to create scholars," wrote a Missionary of Africa at Buhonga (Unyanyembe) in 1906, "but educated people, formed for Christianity, for a serious life and for reflection."[1] That is a fair summary of the White Fathers' objectives in education during this period. The writer went on to describe how his pupils were discarding pagan beliefs, becoming more confident, and carrying Christian ideas back to their families with happy results. Education was a necessary component of evangelization. It was religious, not secular, education. Although catechetical instruction was basically oral, it relied on written aids in the form of small books: catechisms, prayer books, Bible stories and the like. The ability to read was a requirement for baptism. After baptism, this skill was enhanced by writing, numeracy and other subjects that strengthened the Christians' religious commitment and moral life. The Missionaries of Africa considered further schooling to be a guarantee of perseverance.

Several consequences followed from this approach to education. It meant that the lynchpin of evangelization in the White Father vicariates was the catechist and his village school. The establishment of Christianity in these regions of Africa was overwhelmingly the work of the rural catechist. Since rural schools spread Christianity, it followed that the denomination with the most schools would have the biggest number of Christians. "Every place in which there is a school becomes Christian," wrote Bishop Victor Roelens in 1905.[2] If other Christian denominations were present in the same area, it meant that there was a race to set up schools in as many villages as possible. Sadly, this led to unseemly behaviour, including acts of discrimination and even violence. It is difficult for modern readers to comprehend intolerance of this kind, accustomed as they are to the achievements of the ecumenical movement. In the period 1892–1914, however, mutual intolerance of one kind or another was characteristic of all Christian denominations.

The Edinburgh Conference of 1910 is usually accepted as the first major step towards Christian unity. It was an ecumenical missionary conference that brought together representatives of various Reformation churches, but there was never any thought of inviting Roman Catholics to participate. However, in spite of its predominantly Protestant character, the conference was attended by churchmen who belonged to the Catholic tradition of Anglicanism. Moreover, despite the overriding missionary goal of Protestant expansion, which was the theme of the conference, recognition was given to the Roman Catholic Church through the exclusion of Latin America as a Protestant mission field.[3]

Catholic authorities at that time would not have been at all receptive to overtures from the Edinburgh Conference, had there been any. Ecumenism was then regarded by Catholics as a fruit of indifferentism and a denial of Catholic teaching about the church's nature and the universal jurisdiction of the Pope. Nearly two decades later, Pius XI, "the pope of the Missions," issued his encyclical *Mortalium Animos* of 1928, strongly condemning ecumenism. It was, he declared, based on a false premise of equality among churches, and a dangerous form of modernism. Catholics were forbidden to participate in assemblies like that in Edinburgh. The only road to unity was a return to the bosom of Rome.[4] The pope, however, did advocate love and kindness as the right attitude for Catholics and other Christians to have towards one another. Unfortunately, this was not always realized in practice. Ignorance and prejudice dominated these relationships, and there were practically no opportunities for dialogue or joint action of any kind. Moreover, relations were soured by political considerations, since British and German Protestant denominations usually identified with the colonial administration in British and German Africa. It was only in Upper Congo and French Sudan that there was a Catholic monopoly with virtually no denominational rivalry.

A subordinate goal of mission education was to provide secular schooling for the professionals needed by the colonial administration. All the churches started "schools for the sons of chiefs." Education was almost entirely in the hands of missionaries, and it was only in German East Africa and French Sudan that there was any serious competition from government schools. Colonial regimes could offer little in the field of education at this time. The German system was shortly to be swept away as a result of the First World War, and the secularized "lay" schools of French Sudan proved to be a failure. Thus, Catholic and Protestant missionaries enjoyed a virtual monopoly on education. In British territories, Protestant schools offering secular education were notably more successful than Catholic schools of this kind. Catholics had fewer resources, and their missionaries could not, for the most part, speak English. There was more truth than one might care to admit in the jibe that British colonies had a Protestant elite and a Catholic peasantry.[5]

The most serious Catholic contribution towards post-primary education was that of the seminaries. The importance which the Missionaries of Africa gave to the formation of an African clergy contrasts with the ambiguous legacy of an under-educated Protestant clergy. The Catholic seminary tradition in Africa has its origin in the White Fathers' own seminaries and scholasticates in North Africa and Europe, but especially in the experience of St. Anne's Jerusalem, which was the first "diocesan" seminary founded by the White Fathers, and a prototype for all that followed in the African continent. Seminary education was often criticized because of its length and because of its enormous percentage of dropouts. However, these "dropouts" helped to bring into existence a highly educated Catholic laity, which was of great importance in the work of evangelization. The system's drawback was that the African church it helped to create was a clericalized one.

To seminary formation must be added the training of religious, especially African sisters. During our period of 1892–1914, there were several successful projects for creating African sisterhoods in the White Father vicariates. These would have been impossible without the work of the MSOLA (White Sisters), who established their own communities at the turn of the century in all the regions in which the White Fathers worked. Besides making an important contribution to primary education, the African sisters helped generally in raising the social standing of women.

From Orphanage to Mission School

The Decline of Orphanages

The tradition of running orphanages went back to the beginnings of the Society in North Africa. The orphanage, as we saw in Chapter Three, provided a Christian environment in which to educate the victims of both the slave trade and the violence that accompanied it.[6] However, these orphanages tended to become Christian "ghettoes," which contradicted the missionary ideal of permeating the traditional structures of African society. A small orphanage had been started in Uganda in the 1880s. This moved south across Lake Victoria to Bukumbi in 1882, and thence to Kipalapala, near Tabora, where there were sixty-five pupils at the end of 1885, and ninety-five two years later. The regime was monastic, with a syllabus that focused on preparation for baptism. It was in fact a residential school-catechumenate. Pupils were woken in the morning with the cry of *Benedicamus Domino*, and meals were prefaced by the Latin grace *Benedicite*.[7] There was constant surveillance, and a father slept in the dormitory with the orphans. In 1885, the missionaries returned with some of these orphans to Uganda, and Kipalapala was closed in 1889 under the threats of the local Nyamwezi ruler, Isike Mwana Kiyungi. A new installation was made at Bukumbi, with a fortified village for the married orphans. This was combined with the beginning of evangelization in the neighbourhood. Shortly after this, Bishop Jean-Joseph Hirth abolished all the orphanages in Uganda in 1894. The White Fathers had no developed educational theory, and it was not until 1906 that a General Chapter of the Society introduced pedagogy as a subject in the scholasticate syllabus. Hirth, however, with his lengthy seminary experience in Jerusalem, had relatively advanced ideas about education. Orphans were to be cared for in families, rather than institutionalized, and instead of orphanages, schools were to be begun at every mission station. When Hirth left Uganda for Nyanza South in 1894, there were five mission schools in the vicariate and more than seven hundred pupils. In Nyanza South, he found orphanages still in place at Bukumbi and Kashozi, but he started small schools there, which eventually replaced the orphanages. There were to be no more orphanages in his vicariate.

In Unyanyembe, François Gerboin founded the mission station at Ushirombo in 1891. Although he started orphanages for boys and girls there, they had few residents. A school was started at the mission, which operated well and eventually superseded the orphanages. Around Lake Tanganyika it was a different story. In 1892 Kibanga, Mpala and Karema were still confronted by a seemingly endless war. Each of these missions stations was composed of one or more orphanages, supplying settlers to the Christian villages that surrounded a "medieval fortress" at its centre. Bishop Victor Roelens repeated the formula when Kibanga was closed and a fresh start was made at Baudouinville in 1893. These were agricultural settlements in which the children received little in the way of formal education, but did a great deal of cultivation. With the ending of the Arab war, the orphanages gradually disappeared and schools took their place.

In 1895 Bishop Joseph Dupont established the boarding school at Kayambi, which he called his "college." The school had a floating population of pupils, and functioned in fact like an orphanage. A missionary remarked in 1899 that out of the seven hundred boarders at the college, scarcely two or three were competent to teach catechism.[8] Dupont went to Europe in 1899 and the college was closed the following year. After that, the vicariate established a school system similar to that of the other vicariates.

In French Sudan, mission schools existed side by side with orphanages. After the application of the French anti-clerical laws, and the withdrawal of government subsidies, mission schools faced an uncertain future, and some had to be closed. However, orphanages tended to have a longer life here than in other missions of the White Fathers. This was because they still received some official support, as well as new candidates from the administration. Bishop Alexis Lemaître, on taking over the vicariate in 1911, launched an onslaught against the surviving orphanages and commenced a campaign for their replacement everywhere by schools.

Mission Schools

The thirteenth General Chapter of the Society in 1906 gave considerable thought to the subject of education and the increasing number of schools. It even reversed Lavigerie's edict that Africans should not be taught European languages. In the new situation created by colonialism, colonial administrations were requesting that the official language of the country be taught in schools, and that schools be set up to train young people for administrative posts. In the scholasticate, future missionaries were to be taught education theory and the skills of teaching and public speaking.[9] The primary schools that came to be established in mission stations were supervised by the missionaries who were also the teachers. Bishop Henri Streicher of Nyanza North made sure that there was a school at every mission centre. With the birth of a second generation of Catholics, provision had to be made for baptized children and the children of Catholic parents. By 1906, Streicher had fifty-two schools, with 3,415 schoolboys and 2,965 schoolgirls. At Bukumi (Nyanza North), for example, in 1905, in a school of 184 pupils, more than a hundred could read well, and ten were studying music, church history, arithmetic and geography.[10]

In German East Africa, Bishop Hirth was forced to introduce German teaching in his mission schools in Nyanza South. Where there was no German White Father, German speakers from Alsace and Holland helped out. In 1902, Hirth could report to Dar es Salaam that German was being taught at every mission school in his vicariate.[11] At Ushirombo (Unyanyembe) in 1905, Gerboin stated that, besides basic literacy and Swahili, German and Latin were being taught. The pupils ranged from toddlers to twenty-year-olds, and half of them were already married. Princes and princesses sat alongside former slaves in the schoolroom. At Ndala (Unyanyembe), the orphanage had only eleven boys in 1909 and it was converted into a boys' boarding school.[12] Unyanyembe had only seven mission stations in 1905, but they all had schools. However, there was still a confusion between school and catechumenate. A similar situation was seen in Tanganyika Vicariate.

In Upper Congo, Victor Roelens' aims in starting schools at the mission stations were to open the minds of the pupils, to teach them religion and to carry out a moral surveillance. Schools were a form of protection against what he regarded as the negative influences of traditional African life. There was always the further objective of training catechists and perhaps candidates for the priesthood. Just as catechist training centres grew out of the elementary mission schools, so junior seminaries were to emerge from the catechist training centres. At Mpala (Upper Congo) in 1900, sixty out of a hundred pupils in the catechism class were literate and went on to study arithmetic. Forty were chosen for Bible study, and five of "the most intelligent and most virtuous" began Latin grammar and syntax.[13] In 1912 Auguste Huys wrote that the schools in Upper Congo were directing a current of people towards the Christian religion, and that with football, sports and French, together with the example of the missionary brothers at work, the pupils were receiving a useful character-training.[14]

In the Nyasa Vicariate, out of 150 schoolgirls at Chilubula in 1904, 30 knew how to read and write, and they were also learning English. At Kayambi in the same year, there were three grades. In the first, the pupils learned the alphabet. In the second, they began reading in Bemba and started some writing, in addition to receiving lessons in arithmetic and geography. In the third grade, they started English.[15] At Mua (Nyasa) in 1907, classes started in the open air with 164 students.[16] At Wagadugu (French Sudan), the "private" mission school had fifty pupils in 1906. At Navrongo (Gold Coast in 1908), the pupils were thought to be too old: the local British representative, Captain Fleury, advised the fathers to dismiss the ten dullest, and offered to find ten younger, brighter replacements. The result was a student strike, and all twenty had to be retained.[17]

Village Schools

As the outreach of mission stations grew, and resident catechists were placed in the surrounding villages, rural schools were started. Inevitably, they were of an inferior quality to the mission schools at the central stations, but they were vitally important for the growth of Christianity, and there was a veritable explosion in the numbers of schools and pupils. The schools were helped by two major factors: the desire for literacy and the support of the colonial administrations. By 1906, Streicher had 433 village schools, attended by a total of 6,885 pupils of both sexes.[18] In 1913, Lechaptois counted 11,500 schoolchildren in Tanganyika Vicariate.[19] In the villages of the plain at Mua (Nyasa), there were more than 3,000 pupils in 1909.[20]

The value of literacy was quickly perceived by local chiefs and many of their subjects. This was the kind of education they wanted, rather than endless catechism classes. The missionaries, however, did not offer one without the other. At Kashozi (Nyanza South), the missionaries reported "a frenzy for reading and writing" among the chiefs, and no fewer than six of them attended school. In Burundi, Chief Makwaruzo evinced "an insatiable desire to learn how to read and write," and in Upper Congo Huys reported "a real ardour to learn reading and writing among the people of Manyema, including the adults."[21]

The Germans permitted the White Fathers to open four schools in Mwanza (Nyanza South), made attendance obligatory in Ukerewe, and requested a school in every village on Kome Island.[22] At Kashozi and Usuwi, pressure coming from both government and mission allowed for the creation of twenty-seven schools.[23] In Bangweolo (Northern Rhodesia), the British administration was favourable towards the village schools, and only regretted that there were not more teachers trained in secular subjects.[24] In Tanganyika Vicariate, Congo and the Gold Coast, government officers gave inducements to chiefs and parents to encourage or even oblige them to send children to school.[25] At the end of our period, in 1913, Streicher counted 764 schools in Nyanza North, with more than fourteen thousand schoolboys and nine thousand five hundred girls. The forty schools of Upper Congo were attended by six thousand boys and three thousand girls. Bangweolo counted 505 schools with ten thousand boys and a thousand girls, while Nyasa had 386 schools attended by nearly twenty thousand boys and girls. Rwanda and Burundi, between them, had 77 schools, with five thousand boys and two thousand girls, and Tanganyika Vicariate had more than eleven thousand schoolchildren. French Sudan, a late starter in difficult circumstances, had only eight schools, with 132 boys and 60 girls, but even Kabylia in Muslim Algeria had fourteen schools with 630 boys and 301 girls.[26] The statistics were impressive, but Joseph Malet (1872–1950) uttered a word of caution during a visitation to German East Africa. The registration figures did not always reflect actual attendance. The statistics, he feared, might be "a vast smokescreen."[27]

Problems of Attendance

Although Victor Roelens' jaundiced view of children's upbringing in traditional Africa was wide of the mark, it remained a fact that the formal education introduced by the Missionaries of Africa ran completely counter to the people's socio-cultural traditions. Africans were slow to appreciate its value in rural areas where cultivation and food production were at a premium, and the "frenzy" for literacy did not occur overnight. On the contrary, the regularity and discipline of the school regime was felt at first to be alien. Punctuality was a problem, and commanding the pupil's attention for hours on end was an uphill task for the teachers.

"We are working on a rough block of stone," wrote a missionary at Mugera (Burundi) in 1904.[28] At Navrongo (Gold Coast), a White Father confessed in 1908 that it was "almost impossible to retain [the pupils'] attention for four hours at a stretch."[29] At Kupela (French Sudan), another missionary complained that the children returned to school after the holidays "doubly mischievous" and having forgotten all they learnt in the previous term. "We have to begin the alphabet all over again."[30] At Kayambi in 1907, there were few children in school and there seemed to be no taste among the pupils for reading and writing.[31] But it was in French Sudan, where some anti-clerical colonial officers told chiefs that there was no obligation to send children to mission schools, that problems of attendance were the most intractable. At Kupela in 1907, nobody seemed interested in the school anymore, and Hippolyte Bazin reported two years later that the people in his vicariate were still not convinced of the usefulness of education. In this context, either the administration forbade the missionaries to open schools, or when they did give permission, it proved impossible to recruit pupils.[32]

The White Fathers resorted to crude "carrot-and-stick" methods, and they had no qualms about enlisting the help of colonial officials when it was forthcoming. In 1903, the Germans in Ukerewe (Nyanza South) imposed sanctions, presumably at the missionaries' request, on parents who would not send their children to school.[33] In the Tanganyika Vicariate, German officers pressured chiefs and parents to send their children to the mission schools.[34] In French Sudan, at least one White Father imitated the Mossi authorities' use of physical force. Not only did he beat recalcitrant villagers, but—on one famous occasion—slapped the *naba* (chief) himself. This "reign of terror," however, proved counterproductive, because those who were forced into school abandoned it soon afterwards.[35] At Mkulwe (Tanganyika), the German administration announced tax-reduction and even, in some cases, complete tax-exemption, for those who sent their children to school.[36] By 1906, the Missionaries of Africa at Mkulwe had themselves resorted to gifts. However, as one of them wrote, "We cannot afford to give out cloth all the time." Instead, they distributed zinc tokens for attendance, which could be exchanged for two pieces of cloth after a year.[37] At Nya Gesi (Upper Congo), the Belgian commandant distributed prizes of cloth for regular attendance in 1907. Those who received the cloth were overjoyed. Those who did not had to be content with the regulation loincloth as their only clothing.[38] At Kate (Tanganyika), the missionaries resorted to a point system for punctuality in 1908. The points could be redeemed for various rewards, especially cloth.[39]

Competition

Competition with Protestants

Competition with Protestants was keenest in Uganda, Northern Rhodesia, Nyasaland and south central German East Africa: these were places where there had been a history of tension and controversy or where the denominations were disputing territory. In Uganda, educational rivalry was part of the wider ongoing controversy between Catholics and Anglicans, which went back to the origins of Christianity in that country. At Villa Maria, Protestants were said to be giving away cloth to attract pupils and adherents. "We redouble our visits to counteract them," wrote the White Father diarist.[40] The Missionaries of Africa at Rubaga reported that the Protestants were forcing children into their school, and at Butiti they were building a mission and school a mere five hundred metres from the Catholic station.[41] Protestant teachers were better trained and more presentable than their Catholic counterparts, and Henri Streicher was conscious of lagging behind them, where education was concerned. Our schools, he wrote, are "caricatures of the Protestant schools."[42]

In Nyasaland and Northern Rhodesia, several Protestant denominations were well established long before the advent of the White Fathers, whose arrival they strongly resented. The London Missionary Society (LMS), the Congregationalist society to which the explorer-missionary David Livingstone belonged, had started to evangelize the highlands southwest of Lake Tanganyika in 1887. Mortality among the missionaries, as well as the desire for protection by the British South Africa Company, which had not yet extended its influence to the region, delayed the expansion of the LMS into Bembaland.[43] Bishop Joseph Dupont's thrust into the Bemba heartland in 1898 was a calculated move against the "Protestant threat." "We must cut the ground from under the Protestants' feet," wrote a White Father at

Kayambi in 1899.[44] Difficulties with the LMS were reported from Chilubula in 1906, and Chilubi Mission on Lake Bangweolo was founded in the same year "as a quick move to forestall the Protestants."[45] The latter had more catechists than the Catholics, and had occupied all the villages in the Mambwe area, while the Bemba-speaking areas, which they had not yet occupied, were reached through the spread of publications in the Bemba language.[46]

In 1907, the Missionaries of Africa at Kaliminwa were visited by Judge Beaufort, who had come to the area in connection with the arbitration of the Luapula boundary with Congo. The judge had visited Maison Carée in Algiers and had met Livinhac. Asked if the White Fathers could start schools in the area claimed by the LMS, the judge gave permission on the dual condition that the Protestants were not already there, and that the local chief agreed. This controversial ruling was to be the source of endless trouble.[47] The White Fathers attempted to reach the Lunchinda area before the Protestants could get there, but Protestant presence in the north effectively blocked Catholic expansion, and in 1909 the British administration made the White Fathers give up their northern villages.[48] Protestants arriving after the Catholics pulled down the structures that had been erected and threatened the catechists. Governor Wallace ordered a Catholic withdrawal from all places regularly visited by the LMS, but the Protestants encroached on *bona fide* Catholic areas, and Catholics started to reclaim villages lost to the Protestants. The Kalungwishi area had to be abandoned as being too close to the LMS centre at Mbereshi, but the Catholics were allowed to found a station at Kafula on Lake Mweru, far away from both the Protestants and the administration. The Luapula Valley, however, remained closed to the Catholic Church until 1930.[49]

In Angoniland, the White Fathers found that they were locked in combat with ministers of the Dutch Reformed Church, to whom the mission had been handed over by the United Free Church of Scotland at Livingstonia in 1897.[50] The White Fathers' impression of these Boer missionaries was of "frigid Calvinists," who were "implacable enemies" of the Catholic Church. They were determined to "head them off," as far as possible. Relations between the Boers and the British colonial officers were also far from cordial, and the Nyasaland administration was prepared to back the Catholic missionaries and even to offer them a subsidy.[51] Some Catholic initiatives failed, but, in general, the White Fathers were allowed to stay in Angoniland.

In 1888, the LMS asked the United Brethren, or Moravian Church, from Herrenhut, Germany, to found missions in German East Africa. The Moravians started work at Rungwe in the Southern Highlands in 1891, and five years later agreed to take over the LMS station of Urambo in Unyamwezi, spreading out from there into the Tabora area.[52] Thenceforward, it was the Moravians' ambition to link their two centres in Tabora and the Southern Highlands by means of foundations in southern Unyamwezi and Ukimbu. This meant traversing an area claimed by the Catholic Vicariate of Tanganyika, which already possessed stations at

Mkulwe and Galula in the Rukwa plain.[53] The Moravians complained of "unusually aggressive competition from neighbouring Roman Catholic missions."[54] In fact the Moravians, who as Germans enjoyed a better liaison with the authorities than did the White Fathers, lodged a protest against two Catholic mission projects at Kiwele and Ruiwa in 1901. The Catholic missionaries complied with the German ruling against these plans, and declined thereafter to make any move eastwards, although steps were taken to "block the Protestants" in the northern part of the vicariate.[55] However, the Brethren attempted to enter the Rukwa plain, using methods of which Rudolph Stern, the Moravian superintendent in Kiwele, disapproved, such as distributing cash and dismantling Catholic chapel-schools.[56] A state of "war" developed between the adherents of both missions, and it was the White Fathers' turn to appeal to the German authorities.[57] The case was taken to Dar es Salaam and ultimately to Berlin. Although the Berlin Colonial Office subscribed to the principle of religious freedom, it was decided that the maintenance of order in the colonies took precedence over this principle, and that a line of demarcation should be drawn between Moravians and Catholics. By this time, relations between the missionaries on the ground had so far improved as to allow the Moravian Pastor Adami to accept an invitation to dine with the White Fathers at Galula.[58] Bishop Lechaptois and Moravian Superintendent Theodore Meyer met in 1910, and agreed to observe the line of demarcation for ten years. This arrangement met with the strong disapproval of Cardinal Gotti at *Propaganda Fide* in Rome, whose conviction was that no Catholic missionary bishop should ever surrender the right to evangelize a part of his vicariate. Lechaptois defended himself, however, by saying that he had been constrained by the German administration and that he had believed the cardinal would not disapprove of a temporary agreement of this kind.[59]

Competition with Governments

During this period, no colonial administration had the resources to rival the educational initiatives undertaken by missionaries. The most they could do was to assist the missionaries where possible and thus exert an influence on the teaching of secular subjects. Only in a few instances was it possible to set up government schools, and these cannot be said to have been a success. In 1893 the Congo Free State planned to set up "school colonies" in which children were to receive agricultural and industrial training. The schools were to have a military character, and the graduates would be expected to join the armed forces. The administration sought the help of the Missionaries of Africa in running these institutions, but Roelens was sceptical. He feared that the pupils would simply end up in the corrupt atmosphere of the military camps, and refused to participate in the scheme except on his own terms.[60] In this he received the backing of the Society's General Council, which did not want White Fathers to teach alongside lay military officers.

However, the Council left the decision to the bishop and the local colonial officials.[61] In Upper Congo the project never got off the ground.

In German East Africa, the government started its own school at Tanga in 1892. The missionaries were worried about the German preference for Islam, and even after the administration's attempt to find Muslim teachers for the school failed, the White Fathers still regarded the government as a propagator of Islam. The reality of the situation was that, if they were to expand their school programme, the colonial officials needed the missionaries more than the missionaries needed them. When government schools were started at Mwanza, Shirati and Bukoba in 1901, the White Fathers dubbed them "education without prayer," but the missionaries were nevertheless expected to appoint and control the teachers.[62] The Missionaries of Africa opened a school at Kipalapala in 1901, and its first pupils were employees of the German officers.[63] It did not survive.

One of the attractions of Rwanda as a mission field for the White Fathers had been the absence of any competition from other denominations. In 1907, however, the German East Africa Mission Society of Berlin, known as "Berlin III" or the Bethel Society, made an appearance in Rwanda. It was a group that has been described as "more imperialist than missionary," and was perceived as enjoying the favour of the German administration. With government backing, the group founded mission stations and schools at Nsasa and Marangara, which alarmed the White Fathers.[64] The diarist at Kabgayi agonized over the prospect in 1907: "Our beautiful country is now open to heresy; let us all redouble our efforts, and pray that Jesus and Mary will save Rwanda."[65] Léon Classe (1874–1945) wrote in 1913 that when the Protestant pastors occupied an area in Rwanda, it was virtually impossible for Catholic catechists to penetrate it afterwards.[66] By that time, however, events were moving towards the outbreak of World War I, and with the war came a complete change in the educational scene of what had been German East Africa.

The French were slow to apply anti-clerical legislation in Algeria, but the missionaries there soon experienced harassment and a slump in school attendance as government schools multiplied. Before the axe fell on June 8th 1914, when a government decree closed all the mission schools, the White Fathers had already begun concentrating on extramural and post-school programmes.[67] The only other White Fathers' region in which there was government opposition to mission schools was French Sudan. As in Algeria, the Law of Separation, rather than the Law of Association, was put into effect. Government subsidies were withdrawn from mission schools in 1903. Thereafter, they were private schools, and only continued to operate at the discretion of the governor, who could suppress them if he wished. Schoolchildren sent by the administration were withdrawn and others discouraged from attending. As a result, numbers dropped dramatically, and some schools were closed in order to avoid difficulties with the government.[68] The consequences of these anti-clerical policies were disastrous.

Regional "lay schools" were started by the administration, but lay teachers were hard to find, and the mission schools that would normally have supplied them with French-speaking students, were now being reduced in number or rendered less effective. As a result, educational development was set back twenty years in French Sudan, and the first secondary school in the colony was the Catholic junior seminary of Pabré, outside Wagadugu, which only opened its doors in 1922.[69]

By contrast, Uganda made the most progress towards full-fledged secondary schooling, largely as a result of government backing for missionary initiatives. The White Fathers had been dreaming about "schools for chiefs' sons" since the 1880s, but by 1905, the sole example was the royal elementary school at the Rwandan capital, Nyanza, in German East Africa, where a Ugandan catechist taught Swahili to the king's sons and pages.[70] By this time in Uganda, other missionary societies were already forging ahead. The Catholic Mill Hill Fathers were the first in the field: there Namilyango College was founded in 1901, and boasted forty pupils in 1907, among them two princes of the Buganda royal family.[71] The Anglican Church Missionary Society (CMS) founded three important schools in 1906: Mengo High School, Gayaza Girls' School and King's School Budo. It was high time for the White Fathers to overcome their prejudice against teaching European languages and offering secular education, and to start an "English school" of their own.

The impetus, when it came, was provided by the General Council of the Society, which invited Henri Streicher to create a boys' secondary school at Rubaga, at which English would be taught. The pupils would be aged twelve to eighteen and earmarked for public employment.[72] This request followed the discussion about training young people for administrative posts which took place at the 1906 General Chapter.[73] Already in 1906 a British White Father, Arthur Prentice (1872–1964), was teaching English together with arithmetic, history and geography, to fifteen "intelligent youngsters" at Rubaga.[74] Funds were sent to realize the General Council's plan at Rubaga, but more land was needed, and this was eventually donated by the Catholic regent, Stanislaus Mugwanya. Modeste Raux (1870–1965) was appointed director of the proposed school, and visited Catholic schools in Britain to learn the British system.[75] From this experience, Raux, who controlled the funding, built up unrealistic dreams for a "college," and immediately fell foul of Streicher. He also lost the confidence of the General Council, who were impatient for teaching to start at Rubaga. Raux became discouraged and was shortly afterwards dismissed. In his place, Célestin Dupupet (1876–1949), the first French White Father in Uganda who was fluent in English, was appointed director of what became known as St. Mary's School, Rubaga.[76] Prentice wrote to Livinhac in 1908 that the first twelve students were graduating from the Aglican King's School at Budo, and that six had been promised employment in government offices. It would take St. Mary's another three or four years to compete with this.[77] As a fee-paying school, the problem was how to attract the gifted poor. Streicher feared a government subsidy, but one was eventually requested and granted. In 1910, Streicher could boast of St. Mary's impressive teaching staff and 138 pupils. "Budo," he crowed, "no longer has the monopoly."[78]

By 1913, it was clear that there was not enough room at Rubaga for the expanding school, and Dupupet requested that it be moved to a more favourable location. The General Council discussed the request in June 1913 and again in January 1914.[79] The plan to move St. Mary's to a site near Entebbe, next to the junior seminary at Kisubi, was approved. In a lengthy discussion, the General Council urged that it should become a real "High School." Several vicars apostolic had dreamed of inviting an order of teaching brothers to staff their schools, and this was now suggested for St. Mary's. Streicher agonized over the question, being unwilling to relinquish his control. Eventually, however, he approached the Brothers of Christian Instruction of Ploermel, but it was only in 1926 that Canadian members of this teaching order were able to go to St. Mary's. It has since become one of the most prestigious schools in Uganda. According to Roland Oliver, it is Buganda's "Downside," matching up to Budo as Buganda's "Eton."[80]

Seminaries

Missionary Formation

Training an indigenous clergy had been advocated by *Propaganda Fide* almost since its inception in the seventeenth century, and there were many instructions on the subject in its *Collectanea*. However, it was only in Pope Benedict XV's 1919 missionary encyclical, *Maximum Illud*, that an explicit call was made by a pope for the training of an indigenous clergy. The training, he said, was to be as full and as adequate in extent of studies and length of years, as was given to priests in Europe. This was necessary if the indigenous priests were to take eventual responsibility for running their own church. In contemplating the possibility of starting seminaries in sub-Saharan Africa, the White Fathers had, in the first place, their own experience of missionary formation as reference.

Cardinal Lavigerie was a man in a hurry, and the theological training of the early Missionaries of Africa was often somewhat superficial. In any case, a fair proportion of these missionaries came to the Society from seminaries in France, and had completed all or most of their theological studies already. The White Fathers novitiate was housed at Maison Carée in Algiers, and novices went on to study theology in the same place. In 1879, however, building had started on Byrsa Hill at Carthage, and the theology scholasticate moved there in 1882, incorporating the Carthage diocesan seminary. This remained the Society's chief centre of theology studies for more than fifty years. Candidates who had not yet studied philosophy before coming to the novitiate did so at the house beside the Basilica of Our Lady of Africa in Algiers. This philosophy seminary eventually moved to France and finally settled at Binson Priory near Paris in 1895. As numbers increased, pressure had to be taken off Carthage, and a first year of theology was opened at Binson. This became the pattern for other "feeder seminaries" at Antwerp (later Bouchout) for Belgian candidates, at Trier in Germany and Boxtel in the Netherlands. When a house was opened in Quebec in 1901, the Canadian postulants studied philosophy at the University of Laval, before travelling to the novitiate at Algiers.

By 1909–1910, Binson had more than thirty seminarians, Trier thirteen, Boxtel six and Bouchout and Quebec each had nine. Carthage usually had a total enrolment of more than a hundred seminarians, and every year celebrated the ordination of some thirty to forty priests. With all of these formation houses, there was ample opportunity for White Fathers to learn the skills of seminary teaching and administration. The Vatican decreed in 1899 that Thomistic philosophy should be taught to all seminarians, and the theology syllabus laid down by the General Council was the simplest possible: dogmatic theology in the first year, moral theology in the second and sacramental theology in the final year.[81]

The Missionaries of Africa also started junior seminaries or apostolic schools, as they came to be called. An Arab Junior Seminary had been started by Lavigerie in the buildings of the diocesan junior seminary of Algiers. Pupils at this school received a liberal education, but those who were attracted to the priesthood made a "junior novitiate," before entering the novitiate proper. Among those who entered the novitiate, two were eventually ordained priests. The Arab Junior Seminary was moved to France, to a district called Saint-Laurent-d'Olt, in 1874. Three years later French boys wishing to become missionary priests were admitted to the school, and the number of Arabs dwindled. In the course of time, apostolic schools were started in other countries, including Bishop's Waltham in Britain in 1912. This was an outgrowth of Saint-Laurent-d'Olt, which, under the prevailing anti-clerical legislation, could not start a "sixth form" college or high school in France.[82] Meanwhile, back in Algiers, the apostolic school continued at St. Eugène. A number of missionaries in sub-Saharan Africa did have experience of teaching in the apostolic schools, particularly at St. Eugéne. Here the six Ugandans who became the first sub-Saharan Missionaries of Africa began their preparation for joining the postulancy and novitiate of the Brothers at Maison Carée. They were: Fortunat Kwatoti, Léon Lwanga, Tobie Kizza, Paolo Kiwanuka, Barnabé Walabieki and Caroli Nampagi. In spite of this spectacular "first," the General Council of the Society came to the conclusion in 1899 that the "experience of African Brothers had not been good," and the application of another Ugandan was refused.[83]

St. Anne's Jerusalem

The most important precedent, however, for starting seminaries in sub-Saharan Africa was the foundation of St. Anne's Jerusalem.[84] After the Crimean War, the French ambassador at Constantinople asked the Turkish government, on behalf of the Latin patriarch of Jerusalem, for the gift of the ancient crusader church of St. Anne and its adjoining land. Because of French services in the war, the sultan of Turkey acquiesced. The French government wished to entrust the sanctuary to a French religious order, and in 1877 it was finally offered to Lavigerie and the Missionaries of Africa. A majority of the General Council accepted the offer, on condition that an apostolic school for the African mission be established there. The only dissenting voice was that of Livinhac. After a meeting with Lavigerie himself, the same majority of the General Council voted in favour of the project, without any condition. Livinhac, however, again cast a negative vote. Lavigerie visited St. Anne's in June 1878. In September, Anatole Toulotte and three other missionaries took possession of the property. Without further consultation with the General Council, Lavigerie obtained the agreement of the Greek-Melkite patriarch and the French government to open an apostolic school for Arabic-speaking boys of the Greek-Melkite rite. This junior seminary opened its doors at St. Anne's in 1882.

Lavigerie felt very strongly about the need to promote the Catholic oriental rites and prevent their Latinization. So strongly did he feel, in fact, that he was ready in 1872 to accept appointment as Latin patriarch of Jerusalem himself, should the post be offered to him.[85] His vision of a seminary for indigenous priests of the Greek-Melkite rite in the Near East elicited from him principles of cultural adaptation that are a classic statement of his missiology. He sketched out these ideas in a letter to the Cardinal Prefect of *Propaganda Fide* in 1881, and in the following year issued his detailed instructions for the school.[86] The Missionaries of Africa were there to instil the priestly and apostolic virtues and the requisite knowledge for future ministry into their pupils from Palestine, Syria and Lebanon. They were to "accept and respect everything in the Oriental way of life, except vice and error." They should speak Arabic at all times and become in spirit Orientals themselves.

To a greater or lesser extent the White Fathers appointed to St. Anne's entered into this perspective. Jean-Joseph Hirth, who was director of the junior seminary there from 1882 to 1886, took this advice especially to heart.[87] In 1921, the year before his retirement as vicar apostolic of Kivu, Hirth wrote to St. Anne's to say that he was still "keenly interested" in the Jerusalem seminaries. Julien Gorju, his successor as bishop in Burundi, also spent a year at St. Anne's.[88] Joseph Mercui, who arrived at St. Anne's at the same time as Hirth and served with him in Uganda, authorized the first excavation of the Probatic Pool of Bethesda, which is situated on the grounds.[89] The major seminary was built in 1887 and opened in the following year. Three future bishops were professors there: Henri Streicher from 1887 to 1889, John Forbes from 1888 to 1893 and Victor Roelens, professor of dogma from 1889 to 1891.[90] Forbes composed a Greek grammar while in the seminary. According to the discipline of the oriental churches, the major seminarians were permitted to marry before receiving major orders, and Lavigerie, taking a hint from this oriental custom, even proposed to Pope Leo XIII that major seminarians in sub-Saharan Africa should be allowed to marry. The pope did not agree.[91]

Hirth and the Seminaries in Uganda

In 1886 Hirth was named director of the Junior Seminary of St. Eugène in Algiers, where he had been preceded by the future bishop, Adolphe Lechaptois, and was followed by yet another future bishop, Augustin Hacquard. The following year, however, Hirth received his appointment to Uganda and reached Bukumbi on the southern shore of Lake Victoria in October. Livinhac, who at that time was still vicar apostolic of Nyanza, appointed him superior and asked him to start a catechists' school and junior seminary there. The survivors of the Kipalapala orphanage were now at Bukumbi, including some forty Ugandan boys. In spite of his initial misgivings about the Jerusalem project, Livinhac now realized its relevance for the work at Bukumbi. He wrote to the Association for the Propagation of the Faith at Lyons in 1888, "We have chosen the most pious and the most intelligent of our ransomed slaves. Father Hirth has taken charge of this junior seminary of piccaninnies [*négrillons*], having been prepared for it by several years experience at the Greek junior seminary of St. Anne's, Jerusalem. Under his direction there have been several months of rapid progress, which promise happy results for the future."[92] The project, however, was not a lasting one.

News reached Livinhac in early 1890 that he had been appointed Superior General of the Society, and that Hirth was to be his successor as vicar apostolic in Uganda. Livinhac consecrated Hirth at Bukumbi in May, and the new bishop went to Uganda with Achte to begin a difficult takeover of the vicariate in the circumstances that led to the outbreak of hostilities in January 1892. Meanwhile, the two West African doctor-catechists, Michael Abdou and Francis Gogé, reached Rubaga in February 1891 and were appointed to teach in the catechumenate there, pending the organization of a new junior seminary. The seminary opened in June, with Abdou and Gogé as the sole teachers.[93] The tragic events of January 1892 overtook the project, and in the battle of Mengo, Gogé was shot dead defending Rubaga Mission.

Later in 1892, the seminary reopened at Villa Maria in Buddu, with Abdou still teaching, and Achte, an old Jerusalem hand, scouting for students. In 1893, Hirth put yet another Jerusalem veteran, Henri Streicher, in charge of his seminary; but as a result of a flu epidemic, Streicher moved the seminary back to Rubaga with Jean Marcou (1867–1940) in charge. After Hirth's departure to Nyanza South in 1894, the new vicar apostolic, Antonin Guillermain, moved the seminary to Kisubi on Lake Victoria in 1895. Streicher became vicar apostolic in 1897 and invited thirty-three of his seminarians to the ceremony of his consecration at Bukumbi. In his address, the new bishop declared that training African priests was to be his priority. In fact, in a later pastoral letter he wrote: "To get one indigenous priest is for me more important than to convert ten thousand people."[94] The seminary at Kisubi had to be disbanded for a year in 1899 because of food shortages, and in 1900 it was forced to quit the lakeshore altogether because of sleeping sickness. It reopened in 1902 at Bukalasa near Villa Maria. The syllabus consisted of religious education, catechetics, church history, liturgy for Mass servers, religious music, geography, Luganda grammar, Swahili, English and Latin, with harmonium for a chosen few. A strong emphasis was placed on Latin, which was taught through Luganda. There was a dearth of textbooks, but the seminary operated a small printing press and could produce its own.[95] A rigorous selection of students took place. Between 1893 and 1903, only 41 out of 487 entrants persevered, and only one, Basilio Lumu, was eventually ordained priest.

Meanwhile, Streicher opened a major seminary with ten students in the vacant buildings at Kisubi in 1903, but in the following year it was moved to Bikira Mission. A missionary at Bikira left a somewhat patronizing impression of these first major seminarians, dated February 10th 1904:

> We do not find in them the delicacy of feeling, strength of abnegation, simplicity composed of candour and frankness, the elevation of ideas or the true priestly dignity that makes a seminarian charming and attractive in Europe. But a transformation is at work, and there is good will, fidelity to work, sacrifice, solid piety and attraction for the things of God. Their dispositions of heart and soul offer nothing but consolation.[96]

Then an outbreak of bubonic plague forced the seminary to move once more, this time to join the juniors at Bukalasa. From 1905 to 1911, this first major seminary remained at Bukalasa, until it could move into a newly constructed building at nearby Katigondo.

Theology and the other ecclesiastical sciences were taught in Latin, and manuals were provided for every subject in this language. Both Bukalasa and Katigondo seminaries were situated in the neighbourhood of Villa Maria where Streicher resided, which was a little too close for comfort. His interventions in seminary discipline were notorious. Streicher abolished the teaching of English and Swahili at Bukalasa, because he feared his future priests might be lured away to secular employment. He also refused to allow them to learn French until after ordination. This raised a problem for the seminarians during the pastoral experience they were given in 1908. The students on probation were obliged to eat by themselves and make their spiritual reading on their own, because they did not understand French. Michele Franco (1874–1955) was the only Italian White Father at the time, but he held a doctorate in dogmatic theology. On his appointment as rector of the major seminary, he secured the support of Livinhac in Algiers for the re-introduction of English, and Arthur Prentice was appointed to teach it.[97] After the move to Katigondo, science and carpentry were added to the syllabus.

Although the Latin results were at first feeble, the majority of students became proficient and their versification and recitations in honour of visitors never failed to impress. Joseph Sallam (1878–1947), an Arab Missionary of Africa, joined Katigondo to teach Latin, and his ordination to the priesthood there in May 1907 gave much-needed encouragement to the Ugandans in their twenty-year odyssey to the altar. In 1907, the first three Ugandans began their theology studies. Two were ordained deacon in 1912 and the same two, Basilio Lumu and Victoro Womeraka, were ordained priest on June 29th 1913—the first black priests of modern times from the African interior. More candidates were in the pipeline, and by 1920 Uganda had produced ten indigenous priests.

Of the hundreds who left the seminary during the twenty years prior to these first ordinations, some left the church, but most became fervent and active Catholics. Many became teachers or catechists. As Arthur Prentice reported to Livinhac, the rise of both a highly educated Ugandan Catholic clergy and of an elite that was well-formed in the teachings of Catholicism presented a challenge to the Anglicans.[98] The latter had begun by ordaining chiefs as deacons, not because of their theological qualifications, but because they were already community leaders. For example, in 1893, seven chiefs had been ordained after an intensive five-month course in the vernacular.[99] The decision to ordain men of lower educational standards proved disastrous. Ordained chiefs were politically, rather than pastorally, important, and when the policy was abandoned, no specific programme of ordination for ministry was adopted. In 1913 the Namirembe Bible School moved from Kampala to Mukono and became a Bible College. This eventually became a theological college for equipping students for ministry.

Victoro Mukasa Womeraka

As we have seen, Victoro Mukasa Womeraka and Basilio Lumu were ordained by Bishop Henri Streicher on June 29th 1913. Lumu was Womeraka's senior by seven years, and had been one of the boys in the first school at Bukumbi. He was a lifelong invalid, and predeceased his fellow priest by thirty-six years in 1943. Womeraka was born on May 5th 1882 at Bubwe-Bugajju in the Catholic parish of Matale. His father was Petro Lugi and his mother, Anne Ndisala. He belonged to the Ganda monkey clan (*nkima*). His mother died when he was four years old, and he was brought up in the family of his uncle, Cyril Mbuga of Kyato in Kalungu parish. He joined the catechumenate at Villa Maria in 1893 and was baptized the following year. After his baptism he remained at Villa Maria, serving its parish priest, Henri Streicher, looking after the village chapel at Kyawangabi, and acting as herdsman of the goats belonging to the parish. In 1897, he accompanied Streicher to Bukumbi on the southern shore of Lake Victoria to assist at his episcopal consecration. Struck by the new bishop's homily on the importance of training an indigenous clergy, Womeraka joined the junior seminary at Kisubi in September of the same year. He then underwent sixteen years of rigorous training at Kisubi, Bikira, Bukalasa and Katigondo seminaries, following in Latin all the courses of philosophy and theology that were customary for a candidate for the Catholic priesthood of whatever nationality. Womeraka and Lumu undertook two years of probation from 1908 to 1910 at Nandere and Villa Maria. On Christmas Eve 1911, they were ordained subdeacon, and at Christmas 1912, deacon.

Their ordination to the priesthood at Villa Maria in 1913 drew the largest crowd—estimated at fifteen thousand—ever seen in the Ganda Kingdom up to that date. Many Christians, including white missionaries, were sceptical that an African could succeed in becoming a Catholic priest, and thought that the work of the major seminary was a waste of time. There was amazement among the people when they beheld the bishop and the missionaries kneeling for the new priests' blessing. The Anglican church historian, Louise Pirouet, wrote: "This ordination was an event of immense significance for the Catholic Church in Uganda and elsewhere in Africa."[100] Henceforward, the success of the major seminary and the future of the Catholic Church in Uganda were assured beyond any question.

Womeraka served on the teaching staff of the junior seminary and in a number of parishes of Masaka Diocese, celebrating his silver jubilee in 1938, his golden jubilee in 1963 and his diamond jubilee in 1973. He also played a part in alleviating the tensions between missionaries and diocesan priests that preceded the creation of the autonomous diocese of Masaka. Womeraka received papal honours, being named a domestic prelate or "monsignor," and finally a protonotary apostolic, with the privilege of wearing a bishop's insignia. It was in these vestments that he attended the dedication of the Uganda Martyrs Shrine at Namugongo by Cardinal Sergio Pignedoli on June 3rd 1975, and received the plaudits of the huge crowd of worshippers that had gathered for the event.[101] He died four years later in 1979, at the age of 97.

Hirth and the Seminaries in German East Africa

John Joseph Hirth returned to Bukumbi as vicar apostolic of Nyanza South, after home leave, at the end of 1895. One of the first things this "Father of the Seminaries" did was to gather around him a group of eleven boys who could form the nucleus of a new junior seminary.[102] The boys came from the new mission stations the bishop was founding in Bukoba, Ukerewe and Kome Island. Four of them eventually became the first priests of what is now Tanzania. The junior seminary was formally constituted at Bukumbi in 1903. It moved first to Kagondo near Bukoba in 1904, and then to Rubya, next to the bishop's residence. Like Streicher at Villa Maria, Hirth kept his seminary under close surveillance, constantly interfering in disciplinary matters, to the chagrin of the seminary staff. The latter thought he was far too indulgent.[103] Hirth composed the rule for the seminary, based on the premise that the students were there of their own free will and the germ of their vocation needed to be guarded and tended. The children were expected to contribute to their own moral education in an adult manner.[104] No students were expelled or sent away, but not all became priests. Those who did not make it to the priesthood could become teacher-catechists.

Latin was the principal subject for study, and besides history, reading, writing and arithmetic, Gregorian chant and German were also taught. Cornelius Smoor (1872–1953) thought that teaching German at Rubya was as easy as teaching French at Jerusalem. Nobody left the seminary for secular employment because of being taught German, and there were fewer tensions at Rubya than at Katigondo. Hirth became increasingly oriented towards Rwanda, and he brought to his seminary at Rubya a growing number of Rwandans, who proved to be the best students. The major seminary started in 1909, after students had completed six grades in the junior section. In 1911, Hirth had a total of 85 students at Rubya. Then in 1912 Hirth was named vicar apostolic of Kivu (Rwanda and Burundi), and immediately started junior and senior seminary streams at Kabgayi (Rwanda), bringing his Rwandan students there from Rubya, as well as Burundi students from Gerboin's seminary at Ushirombo. Once again, he took up residence beside the seminary.

In 1917, ordinations took place at both Rubya and Kabgayi. In August, Willibald Mpapi and Oscar Kyakorwa from Bukoba and two other deacons from Kome were ordained priest by Bishop Joseph Sweens at Rubya. In September, Hirth ordained Balthasar Gafuka, Donat Leberaho and Joseph Bugondo at Kabgayi. By 1929, Uganda had thirty-one African diocesan priests; Nyanza South had twelve; Rwanda had eight and Burundi two. Monsignor Willibald Mpapi continued to be pastorally active until the late 1970s.

François Gerboin was not able to start a seminary at Ushirombo until 1908. The building of St. Charles's Seminary was begun during that year, and the seminary was opened in November. The usual formula was followed: the seminary trained catechists alongside a few seminary hopefuls. When Henri Léonard took over the Vicariate of Unyanyembe in 1912, he made it clear that he had an immediate need for catechists, and could not wait for the final products of a lengthy seminary formation.[105]

In Tanganyika Vicariate, seminary development was more advanced. At Karema, a Latin stream was started alongside the catechist training programme, and in 1911 the first two seminarians were ready to start philosophy at Utinta on the shores of Lake Tanganyika, which Adolphe Lechaptois thought was a suitably quiet place for a major seminary. Lechaptois also declared that training a local clergy was a first priority of the vicariate. In 1913 the two seminarians were ready to receive the tonsure and begin theology. The First World War delayed their formation, but after a stay of several years in Upper Congo, the two—one of whom was Joseph, son of Dr. Adrian Atiman—returned to receive priestly ordination in 1923. By this time, their former teacher, Joseph Birraux (1883–1947), was Lechaptois' successor and the ordaining bishop.

Seminaries in Upper Congo and Stefano Kaoze

The Latin stream which was begun at the catechists' training centre at Mpala (Upper Congo) in 1899 ended five years later with a final examination in which the students construed passages from Cicero. They had also been allowed to learn French as a medium for science subjects and philosophy in the major seminary.[106] A similar regime was followed at Lusaka Mission, to which the junior seminary moved in 1905, with Cicero and other classical authors being studied. The students instructed the catechumens, and were allowed to go home for the school holidays.[107] The major seminary opened at Baudouinville in the same year, but by 1907 there was only one student there, studying philosophy. This was Stefano Kaoze, who, in his spare time, was catechizing the soldiers of the Fontana expedition, at their request.[108] A second seminarian joined him in the following year and by 1912 the number had risen to three.[109]

Stefano Kaoze, a member of the Tabwa tribe, was born about 1884 at a village in the neighbourhood of Katenga, in the Marungu plain.[110] His parents were Kyezi and Kapazya, and he was descended from a matrilineal dynasty of chiefs. In 1893, two Missionaries of Africa and twelve followers arrived at Mwembezi, to which village Stefano Kaoze had moved with his mother. Kaoze, at the age of nine, was attracted by the mystery of letters and numbers, and was noticed by Bishop Roelens, who invited him to attend school. After some initial opposition from his family, Kaoze continued his schooling, attending the catechists' training centre and junior seminary of Mpala. When the rector, Gustave De Beerst (1865–1896), died, Auguste Huys (1871–1938), the future auxiliary bishop, took charge of the mission and catechists' school, which then had fifty pupils. Although he was not yet baptized, Kaoze asked to join the Latin course when it started, in order to prepare for the priesthood. Baptized on August 15th 1900, Kaoze showed himself to be pious and hardworking. Huys spoke to the pupils about the legitimate aspirations of Africans towards the priesthood, and Kaoze pondered his vocation, accepting the renunciation of marriage. In 1905, because of the epidemic of sleeping sickness, the seminary was moved to Kirungu and remained there until 1925.

Julio Mulongo, Kaoze's only fellow seminarian, left in 1909, but Kaoze was joined almost immediately by two more: Joseph Faraghit (the son of the doctor-catechist, Charles Faraghit) and Felix Makolovera. Because Kaoze had been the only candidate for so long, those who came to the seminary after him were known as "Ba-Kaoze." Kaoze lived and ate with the missionaries, studying Aristotle with Auguste Huys and Albert Smulders (1880–1957), and showing a remarkable understanding of philosophical problems. He was also interested in medicine and music, learning the harmonium at this time. Kaoze and Faraghit crossed Lake Tanganyika for a short stay at Utinta seminary, and found Bishop Lechaptois "full of peace and sweetness." Back at Baudouinville in 1909, Kaoze received minor orders during the silver jubilee celebrations of Victor Roelens, and was put in charge of the dispensary. There, he made use of traditional remedies when the western medicines ran out.

In 1910, Kaoze finished dogmatic theology and embarked on moral theology. The building of a permanent seminary was started at Baudouinville in the following year and Huys was made auxiliary bishop. In 1913, six more major seminarians were admitted. Kaoze accompanied Roelens on his tour of the Kivu district in 1914, but remained there for a two-year probationary period when war was declared. During this time he taught religious education, literacy, arithmetic, music and harmonium at the first teacher-training college in Kivu (Thielt-S. Pierre). After the virtual capitulation of German East Africa in 1916, Kaoze returned to Baudouinville and was ordained to the subdiaconate and diaconate by Roelens in February 1917.

By this time, Kaoze was already well-known in the Congo. This was because of two articles he had written in French on Bantu psychology, published by the Jesuits in *Revue Congolaise* in 1910–1911. Kaoze had been captivated by Thomistic philosophy, and set about making a synthesis with African tradition. His articles were a clear reaction against the kind of European ethnocentrism espoused by Roelens, and against the western dismissal of African religion. A review of pastoral theology completed Kaoze's twenty years of formation, and he was at last ready for priestly ordination. This was conferred by Roelens, assisted by Huys, on July 21st 1917 at Baudouinville, in the presence of Bishop Lechaptois of Tanganyika; Bishop Henri Léonard of Unyanyembe; Auguste Van Waesberghe (1870–1934), the White Father regional superior; twenty-five other priests and the outgoing commissioner general of the Congo Free State, Justin Malfeyt (1862–1924). An immense crowd of more than ten thousand people came to the celebration, which ended with dances and a gymnastic display. Joseph Faraghit and Felix Makolovera were ordained priests in 1921 and 1922 respectively, and more followed in every subsequent year. In 1951, the year of Kaoze's death, there were twenty-six African diocesan priests in Upper Congo.

After his ordination, Kaoze accompanied Roelens to Kisantu, in order to attend a meeting of the major religious superiors of the Congo, and then went with him in 1920 to Europe for the beatification of the Uganda Martyrs in Rome. During the ceremony, Benedict XV stopped the papal procession in order to give Kaoze a special blessing. In Belgium the new priest toured seminaries and colleges, and was introduced to Cardinal Mercier and King Albert I. He also took part in the National Colonial Congress in

December, where his eyes were opened for the first time to the socio-economic and political realities of colonialism. There were numerous other engagements in Belgium and the Netherlands.

Back in Upper Congo, he started to study his own people more profoundly and taught until 1928 in the junior seminary. Most of his work remains unpublished. Kaoze was both seminary professor and parish priest at Lusaka (Upper Congo) in 1924. In 1927 he delivered the panegyric at the funeral of Leopold Joubert, hailing him as "the true king of our country, the father of Africans and a saint." For ten years (1933–1943), he was in charge of the new parish at Kala, which was entrusted to the African clergy. It was during this time that his old teacher, friend and supporter, Bishop Huys, died at Albertville (Kalémié) in 1938. Then in 1943, during the Second World War, Kaoze returned to Lusaka again, as parish priest until 1950.

While at Kala, he was visited by the governor-general of the Congo, Pierre Ryckmans (1891–1959), and received a decoration from King Leopold III. Roelens, who had resigned in 1941, attended Kaoze's silver jubilee in 1942, and died five years later. However, he lived to see Kaoze's appointment to the Congolese Council of Government, and his membership in the government's "Commission for the Protection of Natives." Between 1946 and 1948, Kaoze made frequent journeys to Leopoldville (Kinshasa) and Elizabethville (Lubumbashi) to attend the sessions of the Council and Commission. In 1950, he became seriously ill and went to Albertville (Kalémié) for treatment. In 1951, it was clear that he was dying, and he was admitted to the European hospital, where he breathed his last on March 25th, Easter Day. He died in a European environment, in virtual isolation from his own family and former parishioners. Although there was no formal African mourning ritual, the Christians of Albertville made a spontaneous gesture. They came out of Mass, leaving the European priest at the altar, in order to receive Kaoze's coffin into the church. Stefano Kaoze was a scholar and a conscientious pastor, and his letters reveal him as a man of genuine holiness.

The White Fathers and an African Clergy—Rendering an Account

To have formed the first African Catholic priests in Uganda, German East Africa (Tanzania) and Congo before or during the First World War was a notable achievement of the White Fathers. There were other, though later, "firsts." In 1921, Utinta on Lake Tanganyika became a regional seminary. There was no major seminary in Bangweolo (Northern Rhodesia) or Nyasa (Malawi) Vicariates, and Utinta was designed to cater to them as well as to the vicariates in Tanganyika Territory (former German East Africa). However, in 1921 the seminary only had candidates from Unyanyembe and Tanganyika Vicariates, and none from Central Africa.[111] Part of the problem was Utinta's inaccessibility, and so it was decided in 1923 to transfer the seminary to the ancient White Father site of Kipalapala, south of Tabora town. St. Paul's Senior Seminary, Kipalapala, opened its doors in 1925, and students from Malawi and Northern Rhodesia were eventually able to join it. The first African priest from Nyasaland (Malawi) was the future bishop Cornelius Chitsulo, ordained in 1937, and the first from Northern Rhodesia (Zambia) was John Lyamibaba, ordained in 1946.

Ten years previously, the first African priest of French Sudan had been ordained. This was Prosper Kamara (1902–1961). Kamara was born at Dinguira and began secondary school at Bamako (Mali).[112] At the age of seventeen, he entered the junior seminary which had opened at Kati in 1924. Prior to that, groups of students interested in the priesthood had been brought together for formation in successive missions: at Segu, then Minankofu, then Kita and again at Segu. Kamara was the only survivor of these early experiments. In 1929, he was sent to the White Fathers' philosophy seminary at Kerlois in Brittany. While there he decided to become a Missionary of Africa. After novitiate at Maison Carée (Algiers), he studied theology at Carthage, took his oath there in 1935 and was ordained the following year. He worked in different parishes in Mali until his death at Segu in 1961, at the age of fifty-nine.

The precocity of producing an indigenous clergy so early on in its history gave the Catholic Church in equatorial Africa an enormous lead, but it also had an unfortunate consequence. This was that the Missionaries of Africa in these countries, especially Uganda and Congo, did not welcome the African priests as wholeheartedly as they should have done. There is no doubt that bishops such as Streicher, Hirth, Huys and Lechaptois were entirely sincere in their desire to form an African diocesan clergy as quickly as possible. Not only were they aware of the church's official desire for an indigenous priesthood, but their experience in the seminaries of Jerusalem and North Africa had strengthened their convictions on this point. However, these bishops did not carry their fellow missionaries with them. The General Chapter of 1912 strongly endorsed the ordination of native priests, but left it to the vicars apostolic, with their clergy, to see what shape their relationships with native priests should take.[113] Streicher wrote the White Fathers in Uganda about the approaching ordinations of Lumu and Womeraka, but gave no specific instructions.[114] Arthur Prentice, to his credit, took the newly ordained priests on a tour of the mission stations to introduce them to the missionaries.[115] Yet Streicher's ban on learning French in the seminaries, possibly in deference to the sensibilities of his confreres, made communication with the other priests of the diocese impossible, other than in the vernacular or Latin. The newly ordained spoke English, but not French. The White Fathers spoke French, and for the most part knew no English. Pastoral experience during the years of formation had also been bedevilled by the language barrier, which—as we have seen—was made an excuse for separate eating arrangements and separate spiritual exercises. The lengthy formation of the new priests had been conducted largely in isolation from their families and from their future colleagues in the priesthood. Moreover, for the first few years after ordination, they were refused pastoral faculties and were kept as teachers in the junior seminary. It is clear that much more thought should have been given to their initiation to pastoral work as ordained priests, and to the preparation of the missionaries to receive them, if not to the missionaries' indirect participation in the candidates' formation itself.

In Upper Congo, the situation was aggravated by the bishop's own personal animus. Roelens' attitude towards the seminary was ambiguous. On the one hand, he accepted the theory that indigenous priests must be formed and eventually take over the running of their church. His own experience at Jerusalem was a practical confirmation of this point of view. On the other hand, his psychological understanding of Africans ran completely counter to that policy. Roelens accepted praise for having ordained the first Congolese priest and he showed him off with pride during the 1920 European tour, but the fact remained that Stefano Kaoze was a living contradiction of the bishop's own perception of Africans, their abilities and their culture. So far from being bereft of intelligence or logic, Kaoze was a scholar, profoundly attracted by the logic of Thomism. So far from having no culture worth mentioning, Kaoze set himself to rehabilitate African tradition in the eyes of his fellow students and the missionaries. He sought to integrate it in the scheme of knowledge he had learned at the seminary. Moreover, he reacted to the reigning tendencies of Europeanization, in particular by using the original African place names rather than the new European ones, such as "Kalimye" (Kalémié) instead of Albertville.[116] Roelens, who had a love-hate relationship with the Congo Free State, must also have found the recognition which Kaoze received from the Congolese administration particularly galling.

If Kaoze had been at the mercy of Roelens alone, he might never have achieved the goal of priesthood. As it was, he received the support and encouragement of his old teacher, Auguste Huys, now Roelens' coadjutor. Huys had been appointed immediately after his ordination in 1895 to teach theology at the major seminary of Binson, and from there went to the junior seminary of Malines. It was at Malines that he first met Roelens. On arrival in Upper Congo, Huys was straightaway appointed to teach Latin at Mpala, and while there produced a Latin-Swahili Grammar. Huys, therefore, had some experience of seminaries, and this helps to explain his interest in their development in Africa. Missionaries in the vicariate, however, were opposed to the major seminary project, jealous of the progress being made by the African seminarians and critical of Huys' close association with them. Roelens shared this view and expressed it in a letter to Livinhac in December 1912:

> The affection which Mgr. Huys has for his seminarians, and especially the eldest [Kaoze], prevents him from seeing clearly their faults. It makes him listen to them too much, surround them with attentions

and turn them into spoiled children, according to my confreres. The seminarists can do nothing wrong. If anyone speaks in their disfavour, it is not well seen. If there is a problem with a missionary, it is the latter who is at fault, and the seminarians are excused. All the confreres of Baudouinville believe that the seminary is destined to fail, due to an excess of kindness.[117]

The seminary did not fail, and Huys wrote to Livinhac at the beginning of 1914: "It seems to me that certain missionaries do not love the Africans as they should."[118] Roelens, returning to his vicariate in January 1914 after a lengthy stay in Europe, personally took over the direction of the seminary, temporarily displacing Huys. "I prefer not to have seminarians, if I cannot have good ones," he wrote to Livinhac, claiming that it was "better [to have] no African priests than bad priests."[119] He then took Kaoze with him on the lengthy tour of Kivu, from which the young man emerged to be ordained three years later. Roelens, according to Kaoze's biographer, quoting the comment of another observer, was "a pitiless Christian, who went ahead blindly, sometimes colliding with others inadvertently."[120]

In his instructions to the missionaries of Upper Congo, Roelens laid down rules for their relationships with the African diocesan priests. Seminaries were not to be hothouses, and the students were to have two years of probation before receiving major orders (as had been the case with Kaoze). African priests were to take precedence after all missionary priests, even the youngest, but above lay brothers. They were never to exercise authority over any missionary priest or brother.[121] In contrast with these harsh regulations, the Congolese government issued Kaoze with a first-class ticket to travel on the boat to Leopoldville in 1946. When the captain made him join the Asian class, Kaoze complained and the European captain was disciplined.[122] This must have been gall and wormwood to Roelens in his last year of life.

When Kaoze died in 1951, bizarre rumours began to circulate, which seem to express an African reaction to the discriminatory treatment he had received at the hands of his bishop and fellow priests. It was said that Kaoze had appeared to the sacristan of Kirungu after his death and told him there were only white people in heaven. Others attributed the tale to the sacristan of Kalémié. Both sacristans denied the story. Another rumour was that the Europeans had surrounded his grave with chains, so that his body and soul would be imprisoned forever. The rumours, which are believed to have come from a mentally unstable priest at Kisangani, reflect the racial polarization of the colonial period. God did not want black priests, that is why he made Kaoze suffer![123]

Why, in the final analysis, did the White Fathers of Upper Congo, Uganda and elsewhere nourish such misgivings about the prospect of an African diocesan clergy? Were they afraid of them, as Heremans suggests?[124] That is difficult to believe. There was no timetable for Africanization in the early twentieth century, and the threat was not to materialize for a quarter of a century, at the earliest. In any case, the first expedient was to create parishes, and even dioceses, for the African clergy on their own.[125] The reason must lie elsewhere. The education that the first African clergy received was so lengthy and of such an exceptionally high level, that they stood far above their fellow Africans. They were even more highly versed in theology and Latin than many missionaries. In Uganda they could speak English, which most missionaries did not understand. Above all, African priests were able to give a rational account of their own culture and tradition, which refuted missionary superficiality and scepticism.

In spite of their lengthy isolation in the seminary, they were more articulate interpreters of African thought and behaviour than the catechists who had preceded them. After the appearance of an African clergy, missionaries could no longer enjoy the monopoly of this interpretation. Some missionaries argued that the ordination of an African clergy was offensive to the colonial regime. Certainly, Kaoze's research was contested on occasion by the administration, but its readiness to consult him and to make him a member of the Government Council, which was almost entirely composed of whites at that time, shows that they did not bear any extensive resentment. The ordination of the first African priests was a moment of truth for the mission, a litmus test of missionary faith and authenticity. The White Fathers did not ultimately fail that test. Indeed, they were its authors. But they faltered momentarily on observing the outcome of their experiment.

The First African Religious

Uganda and Maria Machtilda Munaku

In an earlier chapter, there was an account of the women catechists in Uganda, and of how a religious congregation, the highly successful Bannabikira, sprang from their ranks in the first decade of the twentieth century. The White Sisters (MSOLA), who had been established in all the White Father vicariates by the turn of the century, nurtured the Bannabikira and other religious congregations. The fact remains, however, that Christians in Uganda discovered and developed the religious vocation for themselves even before the missionary sisters arrived. The one whose name is most associated with this spontaneous movement was Maria Machtilda Munaku, whose story has already been told in an earlier chapter.[126] Maria Machtilda Munaku (1858–1934) was not only a confessor of the faith, but the first Ugandan woman to take a vow of virginity. Soon other women, including Elisa and Nantinda, joined her in her catechetical work, in running an orphanage for girls and in forming an association of unmarried women to be cooks and matrons of the seminary.

White Sisters (MSOLA) had arrived at Rubaga (Nyanza North) in 1899, and established themselves at Villa Maria in 1902.[127] The White Sister, Mother Mechtilde, known as "Mameya" (ma mère), was the first director of the religious novitiate of the Bannabikira, which opened at Villa Maria (Nyanza North) in November 1908. More than a year previously, a novitiate for religious sisters had opened in Karema (Tanganyika). It is to this vicariate and its bishop, Adolphe Lechaptois, that belongs the honour of founding the first indigenous congregation of religious in equatorial Africa.

The Sisters of St. Peter Claver and Sister Adolphina Unda

In 1906 three pious African young women approached Bishop Adolphe Lechaptois, the vicar apostolic of Tanganyika, and asked if they could embrace the religious life.[128] The White Sisters (MSOLA) had been established at Karema since 1894, and at Kirando since 1902, and it was their example that had awakened these African vocations. The bishop accepted the request, and on May 1st 1907 a novitiate opened at Karema with seven postulants. Sister Saint-Philippe MSOLA was novice mistress, and the new congregation was known as the Society of St. Peter Claver. After three days of prayer the seven young women received the habit, one of them being Sister Adolphina-Maria Unda, who is reckoned to be the first African religious sister in the White Fathers' missions.

Adolphina was born about 1882, and was therefore a young woman of twenty-six when she entered the religious life. She was the daughter of Kapufi I, king of Ufipa, and sister of Kilatu (Kapufi II). In childhood she had been given in marriage to King Kapele, Kilatu's predecessor, but in 1903 obtained permission to withdraw from the polygamous marriage and resign her title as queen, going to live with the White Sisters at Karema. There she made her catechumenate and was baptized, in time to enter the novitiate in 1907. As a Hima princess, Adolphina gave evidence of an unusual dignity and intelligence. She was instrumental in bringing her brother, King Kilatu, to the faith, as well as a niece called Nti or Kataï, aged about fourteen, who was the heiress of the king of Lyangalile. Kilatu sent his wife, together with Adolphina's sister and her husband, to be instructed at Karema shortly after Adolphina and her companions entered the convent there.[129]

On February 17th 1908, a party of fourteen men, sent by the king of Ufipa, came to accompany Adolphina back to her brother's palace. The king was about to travel to the coast for medical treatment and wanted Adolphina to be regent in his absence. Adolphina left with the party on February 19th, but in less than a month returned, having refused to accept this charge. On May 3rd 1908, six of the novices, including Adolphina, made their first profession. They took vows of obedience and chastity, but not poverty, as Lechaptois believed such a vow unnecessary in Africa. One of the junior seminarians at Karema exclaimed: "What a blessing today for the Church of Tanganyika! God has deigned to receive its first fruits. It is certain that these religious will be for our country an abundant source of heavenly favours!"[130] Meanwhile, three more novices received the habit.

Immediately after her first profession, Sister Adolphina went to Zimba, as superior of a small community of her fellow professed, to run a boarding school for girls and a dispensary, and to give catechism classes for small children at the mission. In 1911 she came back to Karema as assistant novice mistress. In the same year, the name of the congregation was changed to Sisters of Our Lady of Africa, and two years later to Sisters of Mary Queen of Africa. Bishop Lechaptois could congratulate himself in 1913 on "his successful project for indigenous sisters."[131] It was an example followed in the same year by Henri Léonard in Unyanyembe, with a first intake of nine professed African sisters.[132] The Tanganyika congregation was officially approved as a diocesan institute in 1949.[133] From these small beginnings in German East Africa, and the larger numbers of Bannabikira in Uganda, the religious life was born in equatorial Africa in the years before the First World War. These African women became precious auxiliaries of the missionary sisters, soon overtaking them in numbers.

Christian Unity and Disunity

The Yearning for a New Christendom

It is frequently said that the ecumenical movement was born in the context of mission, and that it was no accident that the first moves towards Christian unity took place at international missionary conferences such as Edinburgh 1910. Missionaries of nearly all denominations hailed from places in which their religious confession went unchallenged. In many cases the churches they represented enjoyed a virtual monopoly in their own homeland. If their churches were not officially established, as some indeed were, they benefited from the patronage and favour of local or national government. Indeed, in spite of the spread of liberal ideas throughout the nineteenth century, the concept of Christendom—the conviction that church and state should ideally be one—died hard. Moreover, Christian tenets and values entered into the missionaries' expectations of colonialism, even when the missionaries themselves were explicitly disavowed by representatives of colonial governments, as was the case with French anti-clericals and Belgian freemasons. Colonial expansion was linked in the popular mind with the spread of Christianity—specifically the spread of a particular Christian denomination—and there were missionary icons, such as Livingstone and Lavigerie, to prove the point.

In the field, however, missionaries found themselves uncomfortably close to their counterparts of other denominations, sharing the same cultural experiences and disputing the same terrain. In this situation, their cherished prejudices and stereotypes were challenged by reality, and proved difficult to substantiate or to maintain. Moreover, even when missionaries and colonials were compatriots, the latter were bound by the provisions of the Berlin Act of 1885 to some measure of religious freedom and equality. Particular denominations often laid claim to special treatment, or asserted the rights of prior occupation against other denominations whom they dubbed "intruders." Colonial administrations, however, could only hold them apart as a temporary measure, and in the long run the denominations had to learn to live with one another. Slowly the realization dawned that the Christendom concept was dead, and that Christians were now living in a plural society.

The White Fathers in Upper Congo were in the exceptional situation of having virtually no competition from other denominations during this period. In fact, Auguste Huys was able to write in 1913: "Up till now there is only one Protestant mission in the whole vicariate apostolic, thanks be to God!"[134] On May 16th 1906, Leopold II signed a convention with the Vatican, which gave Catholic missionaries in the Congo many privileges and advantages, and which bound them more closely to the Congolese state. This was, as Hastings has remarked, an old model of church-state relationship, still anachronistically favoured by Rome.[135] Although the Missionaries of Africa belonged to an international society and were subject to the control of an international Vatican congregation, *Propaganda Fide*, this agreement imposed constraints on their freedom of action and tied them to a colonial state, in return for mainly territorial concessions.[136] It was an association which did not augur well for the future.

In French Sudan, the White Fathers also enjoyed a clear field of action, and in the early years of the mission were closely associated with, and financially assisted by, the colonial administration. All this changed, however, when anti-clerical legislation began to be applied to the French colonies. Although the White Fathers were allowed to stay on, they lost their subsidies and their standing with the government. Moreover, they possessed no juridical existence, and throughout the colonial era were obliged to create various "lay" cover organizations, under which they could operate.[137] However, this relative alienation from the colonial regime placed them at an advantage when the time came for political independence.

In the British and German territories, the White Fathers felt that Protestants were favoured. In Uganda, relations were regulated by the Agreement of 1900, which, although it made a basically unfair allocation of political offices between Anglicans and Catholics, nevertheless subscribed to freedom of religion. Catholics outnumbered Anglicans and were able to field large numbers of catechists and clergy to proselytize in chiefdoms other than their own. This they did successfully in spite of much illicit obstruction and abuse of office by individual Protestant kings and chiefs. Although their church was not an established one in Uganda, Anglicans were more at home with monarchies and identified strongly with their royal converts. As Louise Pirouet has pointed out, chiefdoms and monarchies became increasingly unpopular as instruments of colonialism, and after political independence, the Church Missionary Society was left with "the debris of these traditional institutions."[138] Catholics in Uganda had also yearned for a Christian kingdom at the beginning, but "a happy accident" deprived them of this disadvantage.

Protestants had long been at work in Nyasaland and Northern Rhodesia, but the White Fathers began by occupying the largely "vacant" Bemba area, and the administration could not effectively prevent them from entering "unoccupied" neighbouring territories which had been earmarked for Protestant expansion. Hence the acrimonious rivalry that developed in these colonies. Almost from the beginning, the Missionaries of Africa found themselves, whether they acknowledged it or not, living in a plural situation.

In German East Africa, denominational confrontation was at a minimum in the areas covered by most of the White Father vicariates. Moreover, the unrewarding efforts to Christianize petty African monarchies were not as contentious as in Uganda. In the struggle between the Moravian Brethren and the Missionaries of Africa in the Rukwa plain of Tanganyika Vicariate, the Germans strove even-handedly to contain the rivals within separate spheres of action. This certainly took the heat out of the situation, and the arrangement lasted for a decade. In Rwanda, however, the German authorities gave their blessing to the incursion of the Berlin III missionaries, when they challenged the White Fathers' monopoly in the kingdom.

At the beginning of our period, Protestant missionaries were mostly unmarried. By 1914, however, to take the example of Uganda, there were twenty-four married Church Missionary Society ministers to fourteen unmarried.[139] Raising a family in Africa certainly made it more difficult for European missionaries to identify with the people they were evangelizing. Their standard of living was necessarily higher. Tours of duty were short and home leaves frequent. The celibate White Fathers had no such disadvantages. Moreover, as Adrian Hastings points out, they dressed differently and did not fuse with other white groups.[140] However, the very fact that they identified so completely with the country of their adoption gave them, in Oliver's words, "something of the spirit of the colonist."[141] In Uganda, the CMS ministered to the British colonial officials and their families, and this led to a measure of racial discrimination in worship. At the colonial capital of Entebbe, there were separate Anglican chapels for whites and blacks. "Is there a special God for the British and another for the Ganda?" asked a White Father in 1903.[142] All in all, it must be said that the colonial experience was ambiguous with regard to Christian unity. It is ironic that Catholics and Protestants were eventually made to co-operate with one another by independent African governments, and that their first joint ventures concerned the creation of common religious education syllabuses.

Stereotypes and Prejudices

Protestant missionaries of different denominations were more tolerant of each other than they were of Catholics, and also more tolerant than Catholics were of them. The ecumenical movement began after all as a Protestant enterprise. Nevertheless, the tensions that developed between Protestants and Catholics were not disastrous. On the contrary, as Hastings has pointed out, they created a genuine intellectual challenge and made Christianity more appealing.[143] Young Christians in Uganda, if they were Catholics, knew all about the six wives of King Henry VIII or, if they were Anglicans, about Catholic devotion to Mary. Catholics were even blamed for the execution of Louis XVI and for the Franco-Prussian War.[144] At Galula (Tanganyika), where the Moravians concentrated their attacks on Catholic Marian practice, devotion to the Blessed Virgin escalated, and the "persecuted" Catholics tried to emulate her virtues of kindness and compassion.[145]

The name "Protestant" derives from "protest," and there was inevitably an element of protest against Catholicism in the teaching of the Protestant missionaries. Unfortunately, this protest was sometimes inspired by ignorance and prejudice, rather than theological principle, although it was also accompanied by acts of kindness from Protestant ministers towards Catholic missionaries. Among British and Irish Evangelicals, the protest could amount to a palpable hatred of Catholic teaching, fuelled by the violence that characterized the Reformation in Britain and by three centuries of subsequent anti-Catholic propaganda. The vehemence of such attacks was a shock to the White Fathers, who had never experienced anything like this before. However, attacks on the pope, on Eucharistic doctrine and on devotion to the Blessed Virgin had little or no effect on African Catholics. They had no reason to reject the leader of their church, who had sent them missionaries and espoused the cause of their martyrs. The new practice of frequent communion, introduced by Saint Pius X, had everywhere generated a deep faith in the real presence of Christ in the Eucharist; and devotion to the Blessed Virgin was immensely popular, since it corresponded to the traditional veneration paid to a mother in Africa.[146]

Protestants also regularly attacked the Catholic custom of wearing religious medals. They denounced the medals as "charms," and frequently confiscated them.[147] Stolen medals were even sometimes attached to the necks of dogs. For Catholics, the medal was a sign of commitment as a catechumen, and was intended to replace the charm. Perhaps the missionaries were naïve about this, but they were also aware of the dangers of syncretism, and avoided multiplying medals. The only other widespread Catholic emblem was the Carmelite scapular, which also roused the Protestants' ire. In 1906, more than five thousand received the scapular at Rubaga (Nyanza North).[148] A medal or a scapular was a guarantee of the wearer's faithfulness to Christian morality. It also had the practical effect of exempting the wearer from being conscripted to help build Protestant churches or schools.[149]

The Missionaries of Africa did not make a practice of attacking Protestant doctrines in their regular preaching. However in teaching church history, they interpreted the Reformation and Protestantism as a revolt against the Catholic Church. More importantly, they had an almost paranoid fear of heresy, which they described in terms similar to a viral infection or disease that could contaminate hearts and minds, and undermine Catholic values. In 1908, Bishop Streicher described the ongoing "struggle with the Anglican heresy" in Uganda, and Henri Léonard wrote in the following year from German East Africa that "the invasion of heresy is a great danger."[150] In Uganda, Julien Gorju wrote in 1913 that heresy was ruining the sense of authority, by promoting private judgement in matters of religion.[151]

Catholic missionaries did not have a high opinion of Protestant worship. They were scandalized by the unseemly baptism by immersion of scantily clad women in a river near Virika in 1897.[152] They also imagined that Protestants were jealous of Catholic ritual, and accused them of imitating the *angelus* by reciting a prayer three times a day "to give more colour to their cold religion," a remark that probably says more about the Catholic superiority complex than about Protestant lack of imagination.[153]

The White Fathers seldom had to deal with adverse propaganda about them by Protestants in Europe. One occasion was when the Berlin III Pastor Riccius from Rwanda, delivered a strong verbal attack on the Catholic missions there to an audience in Germany. The White Fathers at Trier complained about the conference, and received an apology. The speaker, however, excused himself by saying that he had not mentioned the White Fathers by name. The latter felt that the reply was unsatisfactory, since the Missionaries of Africa were the sole Catholic society in Rwanda, but the matter was not taken any further.[154] The White Fathers had yet to encounter the Pilkington phenomenon.

George Lawrence Pilkington

George Pilkington was a respected yet eccentric figure, exhibiting some of the finest qualities of a Protestant missionary, but also—in the eyes of his White Father contemporaries—some of the most questionable.[155] He is revered by thousands of African Christians as the founder of the East African Revival. Pilkington was an ardent lay evangelist and linguist, influenced by the English holiness movement launched at Keswick in 1875. He came to Uganda in 1890, and after three years of missionary work with the CMS was so discouraged that he toyed with the idea of leaving the field altogether. In 1893, he withdrew to Kome Island in Lake Victoria to be alone with God and returned to Kampala on December 7th having undergone a spiritual experience. People noticed a wonderful change in him, which was attributed to the power of the Holy Spirit. He himself said that God had commanded him to be filled with the Spirit. In the days that followed this baptism in the Spirit, he immediately organized special services attended by hundreds, during which public confessions were made by people high and low. A storm of evangelism took place in 1894, with evangelists going as far as Congo and Sudan, and accompanied by the rapid building of meeting houses called "synagogues." Soon Pilkington was addressing a congregation of twenty thousand people in Kampala every Sunday. He claimed to have evangelized a hundred thousand, to have baptized seventeen thousand, to have commissioned two hundred African evangelists and to have built more than four hundred churches.[156] The White Fathers in 1894 believed he was the richest man in Uganda because he had received two hundred and fifty head of cattle, many of which were thought by Catholics to be booty taken from them in the recent religious wars.[157]

Pilkington was also well-known to Catholics for what the White Fathers called his "papophobia" or rage against the pope. On May 23rd 1894, five months after his return from Kome, Pilkington appeared on Rubaga hill in a hysterical condition, giving vent, as the White Fathers put it, to an "access of papophobic fury" in front of the Catholic mission, screaming abuse against the pope. "He vomited against us all the usual insults," wrote the diarist. "Since this gentleman received the Holy Spirit, he has become completely mad." The missionary noted that he attracted a crowd of Ganda Catholics who ridiculed his fanatical frenzy, and attributed it, not to the Holy Spirit, but to the devil.[158]

During 1896, Pilkington was in England finishing and printing a complete Bible in the Ganda language, as well as other works. He had assembled a team of translators in Uganda, both European and African. For five years these had hammered out a text, putting together and completing the various Biblical books and extracts already translated, and using Bishop Edward Steere's Swahili Bible as a model and a "bridge." For half a century this Bible was recognized as being of incomparable standard.[159] Even the Missionaries of Africa recognized this Biblical *tour de force* of their detractor.[160] Pilkington's return to Uganda in 1897 was spectacular. He appeared "in rags and on a bicycle," having bicycled most of the way to Kampala from the coast. From Kibwezi in Ukambani (Kenya), it had taken him twenty-three days to the Ugandan capital.[161]

With the premium placed by missionaries of all denominations on literacy, it was necessary to produce reading material. Pilkington, with his Bible-based evangelism, was dedicated to its production. "What we want are books," he wrote, "not thousands, but millions of books."[162] In Pilkington's hands, however, publishing became a polemical weapon. His vernacular works included the tract *He Who Searches Finds*, which contained a string of attacks on "the religion of Rubaga." The Missionaries of Africa were also saddened by his vernacular version of John Bunyan's *Pilgrim's Progress*, with interpolations against the pope as "the butcher of humanity" and an illustration of the pope seated on a heap of corpses and skulls.[163]

To what extent such diatribes left their mark is open to question. What is beyond doubt is Pilkington's legacy of the East African Revival. Although its first phase was short-lived, it became a recurring phenomenon within Anglicanism, Lutheranism and in many African instituted churches, catering to needs which in the Catholic Church were supplied by the sacraments, sacramentals, devotions and pious associations.[164] In spite of their mutual antagonism, Pilkington and the White Fathers were in some ways complementary. Moreover, despite his horror of "the religion of Rubaga," Pilkington was generous in praise of the White Fathers' French-Luganda Grammar and thought it better than the English one composed by the CMS.[165] Pilkington died as spectacularly as he had lived, being fatally wounded by Nubian mutineers in the assault on Luba's Fort, Busoga, on October 23rd 1897.[166]

Towards Christian Unity

The Anglican missionary O'Flaherty wrote from Uganda in 1881 about his friendship with Léon Livinhac.[167] They went for frequent walks together, during which the Anglican laid before the Catholic missionary the fundamental teachings of a Bible-based Christianity. Livinhac and his confreres were apparently surprised to learn about this doctrine of "pure Protestantism," which was entirely new to them. Although the evidence is sparse, Catholic and Protestant missionaries did begin to learn from one another in these early years.

Livinhac, in particular, was impressed by Protestant achievements in Bible translation and by their linguistic contributions. Having himself authored a French-Luganda dictionary, he kept a close watch on linguistic developments in Uganda. Writing from Algiers in 1909 (possibly to Henri Le Veux [1879–1965]), he urged that a Luganda-English, English-Luganda dictionary be created, since Uganda was a British colony. Missionaries who could not speak English would have to use the existing Latin-Luganda dictionary, and either a Luganda-Latin dictionary should be made, or the Latin word added to entries in a Luganda-English volume. Earlier he had spoken to Simon Moullec (1861–1924) about the need for Henri Streicher to set up a committee to correct the grammar and spelling of existing texts. Livinhac urged that there should be a unified form of Luganda spelling, and that not only the Mill Hill Missionaries should be consulted about this, but also the Anglicans.[168]

Two years earlier in 1907, the Anglican Archdeacon Walker, who had been a friend of Auguste Achte, visited Livinhac in Algiers. Having no other language in common, they conversed in Luganda.[169] In Africa itself, there were frequent visits of Protestant missionaries to Catholic mission stations. In spite of their polemics with the Berlin III missionaries, the White Fathers at Nsasa (Rwanda) were embarrassed, but impressed, in 1908 by the asceticism of two Protestant missionary visitors who slept without bed or blanket.[170] In the same year an Anglican missionary couple camped in the forecourt of Chilonga Catholic Mission (Northern Rhodesia). During the night their tent was blown down and the White Fathers invited them to doss down in their dining room.[171]

Very rarely is there any hint of sharing at a deeper level between Catholics and Protestants. One such exceptional moment was the visit of the Lutheran pastor Johanssen to the White Fathers at Save (Rwanda) in 1908. The Catholic missionaries had already been in the area for seven years, and the newly arrived Johanssen told them he rejoiced "that the leaven of Christ

was already at work in Rwanda."[172] Without doubt, the mutual appreciation of Catholics and Protestants did grow, and the dialogue of life did take
place, but the plant was a young and tender shoot that had to withstand
many storms before it could become a fully grown tree. In 1892–1914, inter-
church rivalry and competition was the order of the day.

The First World War changed many things, not least the missionary map
of Africa, and various ecumenical initiatives took place on the Protestant
side during the war years. The Kikuyu Conference of 1913 was a major
landmark shortly before war broke out. This was a meeting of Europeans
belonging to Protestant missionary societies. Neither Catholics nor Africans
were invited, and there was a rift between episcopal and non-episcopal societies at the conference that led to the secession of three denominations.[173]
Following the conference, the Alliance of Protestant Churches in Kenya was
created in 1918, but it was not until the time of the Second Vatican Council
(1962–1965) that Catholic participation in formal dialogue and inter-church
projects helped to launch a genuine and vigorous dialogue between the
majority of Christian denominations.

EPILOGUE

Roots and Seeds

On June 28th 1914, the Austrian Archduke Franz Ferdinand and his wife were assassinated at Sarajevo, and there was a month of posturing and mobilization by the great powers before hostilities began. Germany declared war against France on August 3rd, and forced its way through Belgium. This prompted Britain to declare war on Germany on August 4th. The following day, Léon Livinhac penned his first circular on the war to his fellow Missionaries of Africa. Habitually pessimistic by nature, Livinhac was filled with foreboding about what the war would do to the Society and its resources. He urged the White Fathers to pray for peace and to avoid all journeys until the war was over.[1] On August 20th, *Petit Echo*, the internal bulletin of the Society, announced news of the general mobilization. All the White Father communities of Europe and North Africa were immediately affected, including eight newly ordained priests, ten novice clerics and one novice brother.[2] In fact, nearly half of the membership of the Society, including both priests and brothers, was eventually conscripted.[3] It was then announced that there would be no more issues of *Petit Echo* until further notice.[4]

Livinhac's gloomy prognostications were this time fulfilled. Sixty Missionaries of Africa died on the field of battle, as a result of wounds sustained in battle or of diseases and conditions contracted on active service, in internment or under enemy occupation.[5] Houses were closed, mission stations pillaged, communities dispersed, missionaries interned or repatriated as aliens. Mission appointments shrank and came to a virtual standstill, as did the growth of the Society itself.[6] But it survived.

The Society of Missionaries of Africa survived because it had put down roots in the two preceding decades. By 1914, it had reached maturity. Numerically, it had grown from 234 members in 1892 to nearly 900 in 1914. It had doubled the number of its houses in Europe, the Near East and the Americas. Its mission stations in Africa had nearly quadrupled.[7] Juridically, the Society had also come of age. Its constitutions had been officially approved and a new directory issued. It was responsible for nine African ecclesiastical circumscriptions, and the foundations of the Catholic Church had been laid in fifteen future countries of Africa.[8] The Society had put down roots, in spite of the brutality and violence which accompanied the aftermath of the slave trade and the imposition of colonial rule.

The Society had also sown the seeds of Africanization. In 1914 the Missionaries of Africa could count two hundred thousand baptized Catholics in its vicariates (two-thirds of them in Uganda), and an equal number of catechumens. Already the first African priests had been ordained in Uganda, and more were soon to follow in German East Africa and Congo. An educated Catholic elite was in the process of being formed, largely as a result of the seminary system. These seeds would bear fruit fifty years later and ensure a smooth transition of the church from missionary to indigenous hands. The establishment of catechumenates through a network of village chapel-schools brought about an influence on African society that was more lasting and more comprehensive than any nationalist, let alone colonial, ideology. It eventually turned the Catholic Church into a credible alternative authority, more resilient and more enduring than colonialism and its politically independent successor governments. Through the "cumulative influence of the dialogue of life," the faith conviction of African Christians grew, and a positive relationship developed between the White Fathers and Islam.[9]

Not only did the Missionaries of Africa survive the trauma of the European battlefields, they survived into a new colonial era. The First World War redrew the colonial map of Africa. German Africa disappeared, and the White Fathers had now only to deal with the Allied powers. With these, their relations underwent a sea-change. The so-called *union sacrée*, or patriotic integration of France in the face of the common enemy, virtually spelt the end of anti-clericalism. French missionaries were recognized as courageous allies by erstwhile anti-Catholic British colonials. Even the Belgians recognized the French as fellow sufferers in the same cause. The problem of what to do with the German missionaries after the armistice would of course exercise the minds of White Father superiors, as well as those of other missionary societies. When the post-war chaos subsided, colonial regimes emerged institutionally and materially stronger than they had been before the war, but their belligerence had caused them to forfeit moral credibility in the eyes of Africans, for whom the outbreak of World War I had been a shock. It would be important for Catholic missionaries to distance themselves from colonial regimes as the latter gathered strength and provoked a growing confrontation with emerging nationalist movements. By the same token, missionaries, who increasingly became partners of the colonial state where education was concerned, had to draw discreetly nearer to the emerging nationalist leaders, many of whom were Catholics.

The twenty-two years examined in this book, from 1892 to 1914, had seen a very different relationship between the White Fathers and Colonialists. As Roland Oliver pointed out, the missionary movement was relatively more powerful than colonialism in the early years of contact.[10] The White Fathers were already present in the African interior, fending for themselves and frequently obliged to exercise civil power, before the colonial armies reached their doorstep. For the first half of the twenty-two years covered by this book, the colonial powers were still basically asserting their presence. In German East Africa, the climax was the Maji-Maji Rebellion and its aftermath (1905–1908). In Congo, the mutiny of the *Force Publique* dragged on for a similar length of time, to 1908. In Uganda, the Mwanga War carried violent upheavals to the end of the century, while in French Sudan the year 1908 saw the Mossi Revolt. When the violence subsided, the Missionaries of Africa had the men and the resources to carry out programmes of education and development, to which no colonial administration could yet aspire.

The men who led the White Fathers were soaring figures with strong personalities. For the most part, they distanced themselves from the colonial administration and the social life of settlers, keeping a low profile as far as possible. Where linguistic and ethnographic studies were concerned, the missionaries led the field, and took relatively little interest in the sciences that were invoked to buttress or justify colonialism. They supplied humane alternatives to slavery and were critical of colonial violence and immorality. Even Victor Roelens, whose attitudes were more affected by the colonial outlook than his brother bishops, was a more persistent and petulant critic of colonial authority than they were.

In these twenty-two years, the Missionaries of Africa entered into a dialogue with Africa, its languages, social institutions and traditions. This already gave promise of a church—led almost overwhelmingly by the example of Uganda—that would be enriched by the African tongue, style and genius. It was a missionary experience that already showed signs of making an eventual contribution to Catholic doctrinal development. Joined to the pre-eminent example of Uganda was the figure of Léon Livinhac, that country's first bishop, guiding the Society and addressing its members through four or five circular letters every year. These letters, to which White Fathers looked forward with genuine anticipation, were both informative and inspirational. Above all, they interpreted the spirit of the Society according to its founder, Cardinal Lavigerie, and helped to make his dream a reality.[11] Livinhac would have another eight years of life to carry the White Fathers through the Great War and into the era of post-war reconstruction, but the heroic age, the pioneering epoch of the Catholic missions in Africa, was over.

ABBREVIATIONS

AACC	All-Africa Conference of Churches
AGMAfr.	Archivio Generale di Missionari d'Africa (General Archives of the Missionaries of Africa)
AMECEA	Association of Member Episcopal Conferences in Eastern Africa
BSAC	British South Africa Company
CMS	Church Missionary Society
CSAO	Civil Society of Agricultural Orphanages of Algeria
CT	*Chronique Trimestrielle*
DACB	Dictionary of African Christian Biography
DOA	Deutsch Ost-Afrika (German East Africa)
GLANA	*Grandes Lignes de l'Apostolat au Nord de l'Afrique*
IBEA	Imperial British East Africa
IBLA	*Institut des Belles Lettres Arabes*
IBMR	International Bulletin of Missionary Research
IPEO	*Institut Pontifical d'Études Orientales*
LMS	London Missionary Society
M.Afr.	Missionaries of Africa ("White Fathers")
MHM	Mill Hill Missionaries
MSOLA	Missionary Sisters of Our Lady of Africa ("White Sisters")
MSOLA/CT	MSOLA *Chronique Trimestrielle*
OMSC	Overseas Ministries Study Center
PISAI	*Pontificio Istituto di Studi Arabi é Islamici*
PUG	*Pontificia Universitá Gregoriana*
UMCA	Universities Mission to Central Africa

NOTES

1. The Legacy of Cardinal Lavigerie

[1] Hastings, Adrian, *The Church in Africa 1450–1950*, Oxford, Clarendon Press, 1994, p. 254.

[2] Burlaton, Louis, *Monseigneur Léon Livinhac, Archevêque d'Oxyrhynque, Supérieur-Général de la Société des Missionnaires d'Afrique (Pères Blancs), Fondateur de la Mission de l'Ouganda*, typescript, Carthage, 1932, AGMAfr. B2 Livn 1–4. p. 492.

[3] *Le Patriote de Chambéry*, of November 28th 1892, quoted by Perrier, Joseph, *Wind of Change, Cardinal Lavigerie 1825–1892*, Slough, St. Paul's, 1993, p. 141.

[4] Hastings, *op. cit.*, p. 298.

[5] *Chronique Trimestrielle (CT)*, no. 57, 1893, p. 79.

[6] The transfer took place on July 14th 1964. Lavigerie's remains now rest in the crypt of the Missionaries of Africa Generalate, Via Aurelia. The monument by the sculptor Crauk, which was installed in 1898, was also moved to Via Aurelia.

[7] Ceillier, Jean-Claude, *A Pilgrimage from Chapter to Chapter, The First General Chapters of the Society of Missionaries of Africa 1874–1900*, Missionaries of Africa History Series no. 1, Rome, 2002, pp. 36–39.

[8] *Ibid.*, p. 44.

[9] Lavigerie, Charles, *Instructions aux Missionnaires*, Namur, Grands Lacs, 1950, pp. 99–100.

[10] Cuoq, Joseph, *Lavigerie, Les Pères Blancs et les Musulmans Maghrebins*, Rome, Missionaries of Africa, 1986, pp. 85, 92.

[11] AGMAfr. Armed Brothers B-16-3 (1).

[12] AGMAfr. General Council Minutes, 1897, p. 445.

[13] Joseph-Anatole Toulotte, Jean-Joseph Hirth, Henri Streicher, Victor Roelens and John Forbes.

[14] A catechist school and junior seminary had been started by Livinhac at Bukumbi in 1890. Transferred to Rubaga, it was closed as a result of the 1892 civil war. Streicher refounded it at Villa Maria in Buddu in 1893. It is the ancestor of all the White Fathers' seminaries in sub-Saharan Africa.

[15] Biographical details are from Burlaton, *op. cit.*

[16] Burlaton, *op. cit.*, p. 285.

[17] Livinhac's exhortation to novices, *CT*, no. 79, 1898, pp. 265–266.

[18] Burlaton, *op. cit.*, pp. 62, 68; I am grateful to William Russell M. Afr. for information on Livinhac's spirituality.

[19] Burlaton, *op. cit.*, p. 276.

[20] Ceillier, *op. cit.*, p. 75.

[21] AGMAfr. *Notices Nécrologiques*, vol. 4, pp. 48–52.

[22] Ahern, Patrick, *Maurice and Thérèse: The Story of a Love*, New York, Doubleday, 1998, p. 258, quoting Lavigerie; Lavigerie, *Instructions aux Missionnaires*, p. 41.

[23] Joachim Pascal (1847–1878), Toussaint Deniaud (1847–1881), Joseph Augier (1851–1881).

[24] Waliggo, John Mary, "The Catholic Church in the Buddu Province of Buganda 1879–1925," Cambridge Ph.D. Dissertation, 1976, pp. 44–49; Low, D. A., *Religion and Society in Buganda 1875–1900*, East African Studies, no. 8, EAISR, Kampala no date, p. 7.

[25] Low, *op. cit.*, p. 8; Waliggo, *op. cit.*, pp. 48–60.

[26] Low, *op. cit.*, p. 9.

[27] AGMAfr. General Council Minutes, p. 171, April 22nd 1892; p. 580, March 4th 1901; Livinhac, Léon, *Lettres Circulaires*, Algiers, Maison Carée, 1912, no. 45, January 6th 1902.

[28] *Rapports Annuels*, no. 1, (1905–1906), pp. 71, 94, 148, 196, 206, 258.

[29] AGMAfr. Y15, Beatification *Acta*.

[30] Waliggo, John Mary, *A History of African Priests—Katigondo Major Seminary 1911–1986*, Nairobi, Matianum Press, 1988, pp. 52–53.

[31] *CT*, no. 68, (1895), p. 115.

[32] Renault, François, *Cardinal Lavigerie, Churchman, Prophet and Missionary*, London, Athlone Press, 1994, p. 415.

[33] Livinhac to Lavigerie June 25th 1890, Burlaton, *op. cit.*, p. 475.

[34] Burlaton, *op. cit.*, p. 477.

[35] Burlaton, *op. cit.*, p. 491.

[36] Burlaton, *op. cit.*, p. 498.

[37] Renault, *op. cit.*, p. 415.

[38] Hastings, *op. cit.*, p. 411.

[39] Rowe, John, "Mutesa and the Missionaries: Church and State in Pre-colonial Buganda," in Hansen, Holger Bernt and Twaddle Michael (eds.), *Christian Missionaries and the State in the Third World*, Oxford, James Curry, 2002, p. 57.

[40] Renault, *op. cit.*, p. 268; Goyau, Georges, *Un Grand Missionnaire Le Cardinal Lavigerie*, Paris, Plon, 1925, p. 176.

[41] Goyau, *op. cit.*, p. 195.

[42] Livinhac, Léon, *Lettres Circulaires*, Algiers, Maison Carée, 1912, no. 15, January 1st 1895.

[43] Cf. *Rapports Annuels*, no. 1, (1905–1906), p. 91.

[44] Pirouet, M. Louise, *Black Evangelists—The Spread of Christianity in Uganda 1891–1914*, London, Rex Collings, 1978, p. 11.

[45] Cf. Pakenham, Thomas, *The Scramble for Africa*, London, Weidenfeld and Nicolson, 1991, pp. 527–538, 547–554.

[46] Quoted in Hansen, H.B., "The Colonial State's Policy towards Foreign Missions in Uganda," in Hansen, Holger Bernt and Twaddle, Michael (eds.), *Christian Missionaries and the State in the Third World*, Oxford, James Curry, 2002, p. 161, and fn. 12.

[47] Hastings, *op. cit.*, p. 384.

[48] Cf. Hansen, *op. cit.*, p. 161.

[49] The account in Pakenham, *op. cit.*, pp. 413–433, relies heavily on Lugard's own apologia and is consequently biased in his favour.

[50] Pakenham, *op. cit.*, p. 416 ff. and p. 426; *Macdonald Report*, 7, "Atrocities," p. 64. See footnote 62. The fifty thousand slaves mentioned by Pakenham must surely be an overestimate. The *Macdonald Report* mentions five to six thousand slaves. The Catholics, of course, also enslaved Protestants.

[51] Lavigerie to Manning, April 28th 1891, in Burlaton, *op. cit.*, p. 519; AGMAfr. 3149 (23).

[52] Lavigerie to Manning, July 17th 1891, in Burlaton, *op. cit.*, p. 520; AGMAfr. 3149 (23).

[53] Renault, *op. cit.*, p. 417; *Missions d'Alger*, July 1892, no. 94, pp. 397–400.

[54] AGMAfr. General Council Minutes, p. 171, April 22nd 1892.

[55] *Missions Catholiques*, no. 1199, May 27th 1892, pp. 259–263; no. 1200, June 3rd 1892, pp. 271–273; no. 1205, July 9th 1892, pp. 331–334; no. 1211, August 19th 1892, pp. 413–415; no. 1213, September 2nd 1892, p. 437; no. 1218, October 7th 1892, pp. 497–501; no. 1220, October 21st 1892, pp. 521–522.

[56] *The Tablet*, June 18th 1892, pp. 962–963; June 4th 1892, pp. 897–899; August 27th 1892, pp. 321–323; August 27th 1892, p. 345; October 15th 1892, pp. 618–620.

[57] Hirth to Livinhac, *The Tablet*, October 15th 1892, p. 619.

[58] Mercui, Joseph, *L'Ouganda—La Mission Catholique et les Agents de la Compagnie Anglaise*, Paris, Missions d'Afrique, 1893, p. 24.

[59] *The Tablet*, December 17th 1892, pp. 956–966.

[60] Waliggo, 1976, *op. cit.*, p. 4.

[61] Mercui, *op. cit.*, p. 284.

[62] Typescript copy of *Captain Macdonald's Report of 1892 on the Uganda Disturbances—Original Report and Evidence*, no. 13. In the possession of the White Fathers' St. Augustine's Seminary, Blacklion, Co. Cavan, Ireland, seen by the author in 1956; AGMAfr. copy, P 103/1.

[63] Letter of Kenelm Vaughan, *The Tablet*, September 17th 1892, p. 456; O'Neil, Robert, *Mission to the Upper Nile*, London, Mission Book Service, 1999, p. 15.

[64] Livinhac, *Lettres Circulaires*, no. 15, January 1st 1895.

[65] Portal, Sir Gerald, *The Mission to Uganda of 1893*, London, Edward Arnold, 1894, pp. 225–226.

[66] Henry Fitzalan Howard, Duke of Norfolk, 1847–1917.

[67] AGMAfr. General Council Minutes, p. 282, February 16th 1894.

[68] *Concise Dictionary of National Biography*, Oxford University Press, 1992, p. 2586.

[69] *Thom's Irish Whose Who*, Dublin, Alexander Thom, 1923, p. 221; *Kelly's Handbook to the Titled, Landed and Official Classes*, London, Kelly, 1931, p. 1480; *Debrett's Peerage*, London, Dean and Co., 1894; I am indebted also to Sara Rodger, Assistant Librarian at Arundel Castle for information about Ross, Letter of November 26th 2003.

[70] Studd, H.W., "Biographical Note," August 1926, in Ross-of-Bladensburg, Lieutenant Colonel Sir John, *The Coldstream Guards 1914–1918*, London, Oxford University Press, 1928, vol. 1, pp. vii–ix.

[71] *The Tablet*, February 4th 1893, p. 190; March 11th 1893, p. 365.

[72] AGMAfr. 0838/0839, Ross to Livinhac, December 9th 1893.

[73] AGMAfr. 083042, Ross to Livinhac, January 10th 1894.

[74] Tourigny, Yves, *So Abundant a Harvest—The Catholic Church in Uganda 1879–1979*, London, Darton, Longman and Todd, 1979, p. 56, states that Livinhac was "called to London by Lord Salisbury's government." In fact, Lord Salisbury was no longer in the government. Tourigny also states that the idea of inviting the Mill Hill Fathers to Uganda rose in correspondence between Hirth and Livinhac after the events of 1892 (ibid., p. 20). This is repeated in O'Neil, Robert, *Mission to the Upper Nile—The Story of St. Joseph's Missionary Society of Mill Hill in Uganda*, London, Mission Book Service, 1999. These assertions, which are based on a letter dated September 12th 1895 from Bishop Henry Hanlon to Fr. Henry Brouwer, are to be found in the archives of Jinja Diocese. O'Neil also gives 1892 as the year of Livinhac's meeting with Vaughan, instead of 1894.

[75] This account is based on AGMAfr. General Council Minutes, p. 282, February 16th 1894.

[76] These drafts are in AGMAfr. 083005, 083006, 083008, 083007, 083020. All are undated, but written in London.

[77] AGMAfr. 083046, Ross to Livinhac, February 17th 1894.

[78] AGMAfr. 083051, Ross to Livinhac, March 20th 1894.

[79] AGMAfr. 083053, Ross to Livinhac, April 15th 1894.

[80] AGMAfr. General Council Minutes, p. 470, April 19th 1898.

[81] AGMAfr. General Council Minutes, p. 315, October 15th 1894.

[82] AGMAfr. General Council Minutes, p. 455, November 29th 1897.

[83] Jinja Diocesan Archives, 14, Livinhac to Biermans, April 1917; O'Neil, *op. cit.*, p. 102.

[84] Tourigny, *op. cit.*, p. 72; Tucker, Alfred R., *Eighteen Years in Uganda and East Africa*, London, Edward Arnold, 1911.

[85] *CT* no. 98, (1903), p. 155.

[86] Livinhac, *Lettres Circulaires*, no. 42, January 6th 1901.

[87] AGMAfr. General Council Minutes, p. 604, September 16th 1901.

[88] AGMAfr. 205038–25065, Government note no. 14, February 3rd 1902.

[89] AGMAfr. General Council Minutes, p. 604, September 16th 1901.

[90] Livinhac, *Lettres Circulaires*, no. 45, January 6th 1902.

[91] AGMAfr. 25144–25162, Draft bill for Senate session of December 2nd 1902.

[92] AGMAfr. General Council Minutes, p. 646, December 15th 1902, p. 747, December 29th 1902.

[93] Livinhac, *Lettres Circulaires*, no. 48, January 6th 1903.

[94] *CT*, no. 98, (1903), p. 163, no. 99, 1903, pp. 11, 45.

[95] *CT*, no. 99, (1903), pp. 31, 36; no. 100, (1903), p. 152.

[96] This account relies on: Thuillier, Guy, *La Bureaucratie en France aux XIXe et XXe Siècles*, Paris, Economica, 1987, "Dans les coulisses: Emile Combes et la Princesse Jeanne Bibesco," pp. 141–154, and Gray, Richard, "Christianity," in Roberts, A.D. (ed.), *The Cambridge History of Africa 1907–1940*, vol. 7, Cambridge, Cambridge University Press, 1970, chap. 3, p. 160.

[97] AGMAfr. 25164; Thuillier, *op. cit.*, p. 149.

[98] Thuillier, *ibid.*

[99] Thuillier, *op. cit.*, pp. 153–154.

[100] Livinhac, *Lettres Circulaires*, no. 56, January 6th 1905.

[101] *Petit Echo*, vol. 2, no. 19, July 1914, pp. 109–110.

[102] De Benoist, Joseph-Roger, *Eglise et Pouvoir au Soudan Français*, Paris, Karthala, 1987, p. 181.

[103] *CT*, no. 139, (1907), p. 340.

[104] Cf. Gray, Richard, "The Catholic Church and National States in Western Europe During the Nineteenth and Twentieth Centuries, from a Perspective of Africa," in *Kirchliche Zeitgeschichte*, no. 1, 2001, pp. 148–158.

[105] Address to the 9th Caravan, June 29th 1890, in *Cardinal Lavigerie—Selected Texts*, Rome, Missionaries of Africa, 1980, p. 75.

[106] The statistics given here are from Casier, Jacques, *Développment de la Société*, MS in AGMAfr., 1961.

[107] Gray, 2001, *op. cit.*, p. 152.

[108] AGMAfr. General Council Minutes, p. 316, November 20th 1894, p. 334, February 26th, 1895.

[109] AGMAfr. 113 007, Roelens to Livinhac, November 1st 1893.

[110] Ceillier, 2002, *op. cit.*, pp. 64–65.

[111] *CT*, no. 80, (1898), p. 465.

[112] *CT*, no. 137, (1907), p. 212, no. 154, 1908, p. 781.

[113] *CT*, no. 154, (1908), p. 785.

[114] AGMAfr. General Council Minutes, p. 927, March 13th 1911.

[115] AGMAfr. Chapter Minutes, *Chapitres Généraux 1874–1947*, p. 275.

[116] *CT*, no. 85, (1900), p. 90; no. 99, (1903), p. 69.

[117] *CT*, no. 151, (1908), p. 560.

[118] *Petit Echo*, vol. 2, no. 13, January 1914, p. 8.

[119] Portal, *op. cit.*, pp. 225–226.

[120] Cf. Finn, Peter, *The History of the Priory Bishop's Waltham*, Winchester, Hedera Books, 2002.

[121] Pelletier, Raynald, *Bishop John Forbes (1864–1926), Coadjutor Vicar Apostolic of Uganda, The First Canadian White Father*, Rome, Missionaries of Africa History Series, no. 2, 2003, p. 24.

[122] Pelletier, *op. cit.*, p. 36.

[123] Pelletier, *op. cit.*, p. 39.

[124] AGMAfr. General Council Minutes, p. 317, November 27th 1894, De Benoist, *op. cit.*, pp. 47, 64–66.

[125] Ceillier, *op. cit.*, 2002, pp. 51–53.

[126] Quoted by Vanlande, René, *Chez les Pères Blancs, Tunisie, Kabylie, Sahara*, Paris, J. Peyronnet, 1929, p. 203.

[127] AGMAfr. General Council Minutes, p. 1044, October 1913.

[128] AGMAfr. General Council Minutes, p. 554, September 10th 1900, p. 573, January 14th 1901, p. 577, February 17th 1901, p. 642, November 21st 1902.

[129] *CT*, no. 148, (1908), p. 284.

[130] AGMAfr. General Council Minutes, p. 692, October 7th 1904.

[131] Livinhac, *Lettres Circulaires; Instructions de Monseigneur Livinhac aux Missionnaires d'Afrique (Pères Blancs)*, Algiers, 1938; Ceillier, Jean-Claude, *Lettres d'un Supérieur Général à ses Confrères Missionnaires*, unpublished, 2001.

[132] Ceillier, 2002, *op. cit.*, pp. 44–82, AGMAfr. General Chapter Minutes, *Chapitres Généraux 1874–1947*, pp. 172–242, 250–309.

2. The Missions and the "Colonial Scramble"

[1] *CT*, no. 57, (1892), p. 132.

[2] Cf. Strachan, Hew, *The First World War*, London, Simon and Schuster, 2003, pp. 35–38; Pakenham, Thomas, *The Scramble for Africa*, London, Weidenfeld and Nicolson, 1991, pp. xxiii–xxiv.

[3] Hastings, Adrian, *The Church in Africa 1450–1950*, Oxford, Clarendon Press, 1994, p. 564.

[4] Society of Missionaries of Africa (White Fathers), *Constitutions*, Algiers, Maison Carée, 1908, p. 1, no. 2.

[5] AGMAfr. General Council Minutes, p. 924, March 13th 1911.

[6] *Rapports Annuels*, no. 4, (1908–1909), p. 231; Strachan, *op. cit.*, p. 62.

[7] Cf. De Benoist, Joseph-Roger, *Eglise et Pouvoir au Soudan Français*, Paris, Karthala, 1987, pp. 111–151.

[8] Hochschild, Adam, *King Leopold's Ghost*, London, Pan Books, 2002, pp. 43–46.

[9] Storme, Marcel, *Rapports du Père Planque, de Mgr. Lavigerie et de Mgr. Comboni sur l'Association Internationale Africaine*, Brussels, Académie Royale des Sciences Coloniales, Mémoire, tome x1, facs. 2, 1957.

[10] Society of Missionaries of Africa (White Fathers), *Directory of the Constitutions*, Algiers, Maison Carée, 1914, p. 250.

[11] De Benoist, *op. cit.*, p. 85; *CT*, no. 78, 1898, p. 239.

[12] Stenger, Friedrich, *White Fathers in Colonial Central Africa*, Münster, Hamberg, London, Lit Verlag, 2001, pp. 61–98; *Rapports Annuels*, no. 6, (1910), pp. 130–136.

[13] De Benoist, *op. cit.*, p. 85; *CT*, no. 139, 1907, pp. 361–372.

[14] De Benoist, *op. cit.*, pp. 190–191.

[15] De Benoist, *op. cit.*, p. 104; Waliggo, John Mary, *A History of African Priests—Katigondo Major Seminary 1911–1986*, Nairobi, Matianum Press, 1988, pp. 275 ff.

[16] *CT*, no. 145, (1908), p. 57; *Rapports Annuels*, no. 8, (1912–1913), p. 353.

[17] *CT*, no. 136, (1907), p. 85.

[18] *CT*, no. 87, (1900), p. 398; cf. also *CT*, no. 73, (1897), p. 134; no. 90, (1901), p. 120.

[19] *CT*, no. 109, (1904), p. 62.

[20] *CT*, no. 162, (1909), p. 486.

[21] *CT*, no. 84, (1899), p. 491.

[22] *Directory*, (1914), pp. 29–30.

[23] Croegaert, Luc, *Les Pères Blancs au Rwanda—Jalons et Balises*, unpublished MS, no date, AGMAfr. Casier 341, p. 99.

[24] De Benoist, *op. cit.*, p. 102.

[25] *CT*, no. 112, (1905), p. 12.

[26] De Benoist, *op. cit.*, pp. 74, 132.

[27] De Benoist, *op. cit.*, p. 77.

[28] *CT*, no. 81, (1899), p. 7, no. 160, (1909), p. 242, AGMAfr. General Council Minutes, December 5th 1910, p. 911.

[29] Vanlande, René, *Chez les Pères Blancs—Tunisie, Kabylie, Sahara*, Paris, J. Peyronnet, 1929, p. 17.

[30] *CT*, no. 126, (1906), p. 220.

[31] *CT*, no. 159, (1909), p. 212.

[32] De Benoist, *op. cit.*, p. 108.

[33] AGMAfr. General Council Minutes, p. 270, November 20th 1893.

[34] *CT*, no. 98, (1903), p. 194; no. 146, (1907), p. 139; no. 149, (1908), pp. 354–355.

[35] *CT*, no. 149, 1908, p. 355.

[36] Bell, Hesketh, *Glimpses of a Governor's Life*, London, Sampson Low, no date, p. 194; *CT*, no. 158, (1909), p. 105.

[37] *CT*, no. 155, (1908), p. 846; no. 157, (1909), p. 42.

[38] *CT*, no. 142, (1907), p. 547.

[39] De Benoist, *op. cit.*, p. 78.

[40] *CT*, no. 156, (1908), p. 941.

[41] *CT*, no. 85, (1900), p. 7.

[42] *CT*, no. 101, (1903), Sahara Province Report, pp. 233–240.

[43] Grévoz, Daniel, *Sahara 1830–1881—le mirages Français et la tragédie Flatters*, Paris, l'Harmattan, 1989, pp. 25–195.

[44] Fleming, Fergus, *The Sword and the Cross*, London, Granta Books, 2003, pp. 88–93, 98–107.

[45] *CT*, no. 139, (1907), p. 391; Fleming, *op. cit.*, pp. 227–228.

[46] Pakenham, *op. cit.*, and De Benoist, *op. cit.*, give good accounts of the conquest of French Sudan.

[47] *CT*, no. 81, (1899), p. 18.

[48] *CT*, no. 108, (1904), p. 400; no. 152, 1908, p. 595ff; no. 158, (1909), p. 79; no. 161, (1909), p. 337.

[49] Renault, François, *Tippo Tip—un potentat Arabe en Afrique Centrale au XIXe siècle*, Paris, Société Française d'Histoire d'Outre-Mer, 1987, p. 196.

[50] Renault, 1987, *op. cit.*, pp. 289, 299.

[51] *CT*, no. 75, (1897), pp. 408–409.

[52] *CT*, no. 139, (1907), pp. 360–373.

[53] Hochschild, *op. cit.*, pp. 158–166.

[54] Hochschild, *op. cit.*, quoting Jan Vansina, p. 233; *La Libre Belgique*, April 8th 2004, pp. 1–4, 43, 30, deals with the controversy raised by Peter Bates' BBC documentary *White King, Red Rubber, Black Death*, shown on RTBF. To speak of "genocide" or "holocaust" is a fantasy. People died in the Congo because of an ensemble of brutalities as well as new epidemics.

[55] This account follows that of Iliffe, John, *A Modern History of Tanganyika*, Cambridge, Cambridge University Press, 1979.

[56] Iliffe, *op. cit.*, p. 150.

[57] *CT*, no. 125, (1906), pp. 201–203; no. 128, 1906, p. 368; no. 129, (1906), p. 476; no. 130, (1906), pp. 538–539; no. 133, (1906), p. 664; AGMAfr. *Tabora Mission Diary*, August 24th 1905 to March 27th 1906.

[58] *CT*, no. 78, (1898), p. 219; no. 81, (1899), p. 88; no. 85, (1900), pp. 83–84; no. 86, (1900), pp. 205, 234; no. 90, (1901), p. 111; no. 125, (1906), p. 136; no. 130, (1906), p. 536; no. 134, (1907), p. 41; no. 136, (1907), pp. 87, 92; no. 153, (1908), p. 688; no. 156, 1908, p. 896; no. 159, (1909), pp. 165, 175; no. 162, (1909), p. 453; *Rapports Annuels*, no. 7, (1911–1912), p. 395; AGMAfr. *Tabora Mission Diary*, October 30th 1905; June 11th 1906.

[59] Iliffe, *op. cit.*, pp. 123–125, 163–167.

[60] Bell, *op. cit.*, pp. 98, 112.

[61] *CT*, no. 152, (1908), p. 652.

[62] AGMAfr. *Tabora Mission Diary*, February 17th 1912.

[63] Pirouet, M. Louise, *Black Evangelists—The Spread of Christianity in Uganda 1891–1914*, London, Rex Collings, 1978, p. 91; Nyakatura, J.W., *Anatomy of an African Kingdom: A History of Bunyoro-Kitara*, New York, NOK Publishers, 1973, pp. 153–163.

[64] *CT*, no. 72, (1896), p. 596; Nicq, A., *Vie du Révérend Père Siméon Lourdel*, Paris, 1896.

[65] Ashe, Robert Pickering, *Chronicles of Uganda*, London, Hodder and Stoughton, 1894, pp. 249–251.

[66] *CT*, no. 86, (1900), p. 209.

[67] Bell, *op, cit.*, pp. 209–210.

[68] This account is based on Roberts, Andrew D., *A History of the Bemba–Political Growth and Change in North-Eastern Zambia before 1900*, London, Longman, 1973; Garvey, Brian, *Bembaland Church—Religious and Social Change in South Central Africa 1891–1964*, Leiden, E.J. Brill, 1994; Linden, Ian, with Linden, Jane, *Catholic Peasants and Chewa Resistance in Nyasaland 1889–1939*, University of Califormia Press, Berkeley and Los Angeles, 1974.

[69] Iliffe, John, *Africans, the History of a Continent*, Cambridge, Cambridge University Press, 1995, p. 1.

[70] Roelens, Victor (ed. Antoine N.), *Notre Vieux Congo 1891–1917—Souvenirs du premier evêque du Congo Belge*, Namur, Grands Lacs, 1948, vol. 2., pp. 199–214. Roelens was not alone in passing such judgements.

[71] Iliffe, 1995, *op. cit.*, p. 200.

[72] Leblond, G., *Le Père Auguste Achte des Missionnaires d'Afrique (Pères Blancs)*, Algiers, Maison Carée, 1912, pp. 388–390. Achte took the old caravan route in 1902 because of the Nandi war.

[73] Missionaries of Africa, *Quelques indications pouvant servir pour le Voyage des Missionnaires d'Europe en Ouganda*, Algiers, Maison Carée, 1894 (cited by Burgman, Hans, *The Way the Catholic Church Started in Western Kenya*, London, Mission Book Service, 1990, pp. 8–9); *CT*, no. 149, (1908), Addendum.

[74] *CT*, no. 147, (1908), p. 208.

[75] Burgman, *op. cit.*, p. 10.

[76] Leblond, *op. cit.*, pp. 328–330.

[77] *CT*, no. 98, (1903), p. 235.

[78] *CT*, no. 150, (1908), p. 466.

[79] *CT*, no. 148, (1908), p. 213.

[80] *CT*, no. 80, (1898), p. 477.

[81] *CT*, no. 87, (1900), pp. 386, 389.

[82] *CT*, no. 103, (1902), p. 103; no. 98, (1903), p. 227.

[83] AGMAfr. *Notices Nécrologiques*, vol. 3, pp. 114–119.

[84] Leblond, *op. cit.*, pp. 268–270.

[85] AGMAfr. General Council minutes, November 24th 1902, p. 644; *CT*, no. 101, 1903, p. 264.

[86] *CT*, no. 93, (1902), p. 90.

[87] *CT*, no. 104, (1904), p. 148; no. 144, (1907), pp. 709–711; no. 149, (1908), Addendum; Bell, *op. cit.*, p. 107.

[88] *CT*, no. 146, (1907), pp. 142–148; no. 149, (1908), p. 400.

[89] *CT*, no. 150, (1908), p. 447.

[90] *Petit Echo*, vol. 1, no. 4, March 1913, p. 38.

[91] AGMAfr. General Council Minutes, November 13th 1911, p. 957; December 22nd 1913, p. 1049.

[92] *CT*, no. 141, (1907), p. 523.

[93] *Petit Echo*, vol. 1, no. 10, 1913, pp. 121–122.

[94] Marin, Eugène, *Algérie, Sahara, Soudan, Vie Travaux, Voyages de Mgr. Hacquard des Pères Blancs (1860–1901)*, Paris, Berger-Levrault, 1905, pp. 282–359.

[95] *CT*, no. 102, (1903), p. 13; no. 116, (1905), p. 249.

[96] *CT*, no. 152, (1908), p. 589.

[97] Toulotte to Livinhac, May 11th 1897, AGMAfr. 071150; Toulotte, Anatole (ed. Joseph-Roger de Benoist), *Voyage au Soudan 1 Oct. 1896–14 Mai 1897*, AGMAfr., n.d., pp. 110–138.

[98] *Rapports Annuels*, no. 1, (1905–1906), p. 39; cf. Tiquet, Jean, *Une expérience de petite colonisation indigène en Algérie—les colons Arabes-Chrétiens du Cardinal Lavigerie*, Algiers, Maison Carée, 1936.

[99] Ceillier, Jean-Claude, "Les Missionaires d'Afrique et le Dialogue Interreligieux: Quelques Jalons Historiques," unpublished conference paper at the Colloque de Paris, December 2002, p.4.

[100] AGMAfr. General Council Minutes, May 9th 1910, p. 885.

[101] AGMAfr. General Council Minutes, September 13th 1897, p. 445.

[102] AGMAfr. General Council Minutes, April 2nd 1894, p. 292.

[103] AGMAfr. General Council Minutes, July 17th 1893, p. 249.

[104] *CT*, (1906), Supplement pp. 143–179.

[105] *Ibid.*, p. 167.

[106] Fleming, *op. cit.*, pp. 214–215.

[107] De Benoist, *op. cit.*, pp. 76–77; Hourst in Marin, *op. cit.*, p. v.

[108] De Benoist, *op. cit.*, p. 83.

[109] *CT*, no. 84, (1899), p. 456.

[110] *CT*, no. 102, (1903), p. 15; no. 105, (1904), p. 207.

[111] *CT*, no. 102, (1903), p. 6; no. 143, (1907), p. 616.

[112] Ilboudo, Jean, *Le Christ au Burkina: Les Actes des Premiers Chrétiens*, vol. 1, *Promenade au Mossi*, Ouagadougou, Presses Africaines, 1993, pp. 88–93.

[113] AGMAfr. *Segu Mission Diary*, vol. 1, April 4th–21st 1901, pp. 133–137.

[114] The author visited his grave at Kolongotomo, Mali on 11-02-04, and spoke to Pierre Ky, who knew him personally.

[115] GMAfr. *Notices Nécrologiques*, vol. 3, pp. 49–60; Arnauld, Dominique, *Les Débuts de l'évangélisation en Pays Mossi-Nakomse d'Après les Archives des*

Missionnaires d'Afrique (Pères Blancs), Mémoire pour la Licence, MS, Rome, 1979, pp. 73–74.

[116] AGMAfr. General Council Minutes, March 17th 1913, p. 1011; October 1913, p. 1044.

[117] AGMAfr. *Notices Nécrologiques*, vol. 3, pp. 29–36.

[118] Fleming, *op. cit.*, pp. 25–131.

[119] *CT*, no. 97, (1903), Supplement pp. 9–14.

[120] de Foucauld, Charles, *Lettres et Carnets*, ed. Jean-François Six, Paris, Editions du Seuil, 1966, p. 160.

[121] *Ibid.*, pp. 168, 198; Fleming, *op. cit.*, pp. 180–181, 187–188.

[122] *CT*, no. 137, (1907), p. 183.

[123] De Foucauld, Charles, *Correspondences Sahariennes*, ed. Thiriez, Philippe and Chatelard, Antoine, Paris, Editions du Cerf, 1998.

[124] Guérin to Livinhac, June 3rd 1903, *Correspondences Sahariennes*, p. 188.

[125] Guérin to de Foucauld, June 29th 1903, *Correspondences Sahariennes*, pp. 196–197.

[126] *CT*, no. 101, (1903), p. 261.

[127] *Petit Echo*, (1913), vol. 1, no. 4, p. 35.

[128] de Foucauld, *Lettres et Carnets*, p. 160; Saadia, Ossilia, *Catholiques et Musulman Sunnites, Discours Croisés 1920–1950, Approche Historique de l'Alterité Religieuse*, doctoral thesis, University of Lyon, 2001, pp. 290–295.

[129] Guérin to de Foucauld, October 20th 1903, *Correspondences Sahariennes*, pp. 232–233.

[130] *CT*, no. 148, (1908), p. 279; Fleming, *op. cit.*, p. 214.

[131] Fleming, *op. cit.*, pp. 174–176.

[132] Guérin to de Foucauld, March 3rd 1904, April 21st 1904, *Correspondences Sahariennes*, pp. 252, 336–338.

[133] *CT*, no. 139, (1907), p. 391.

[134] AGMAfr. *General Council Minutes*, February 15th 1909, p. 830.

[135] AGMAfr. *Notices Nécrologiques*, vol. 3, pp. 29–36.

[136] Fleming, *op. cit.*, pp. 278–279.

[137] Leblond, *op. cit.*, p. 216.

[138] This account of Achte's life is based on Leblond, *op. cit.*

[139] Achte, Auguste, *Histoire des rois Baganda*, 1900, MS, longhand, AGMAfr. P157/1.

[140] This account of Streicher's life is based on AGMAfr. *Notices Nécrologiques*, vol. 10, pp. 3–47; Waliggo, *op. cit., passim.*

[141] Bell, *op. cit.*, p. 194.

[142] This account of Kitagana is based on Duval, Armand, *Yohana Kitagana Catéchiste*, Condé-sur-Noireau, Corlet, 2002; and Pirouet, *op. cit.*

[143] Duval, *op. cit.*, p. 105; Pirouet, *op. cit.*, p. 133.

[144] This account of Hirth is based on AGMAfr. *Notices Nécrologiques*, vol. 4, pp. 387–393.

[145] Gorra, Philippe, *Sainte-Anne de Jérusalem, Séminaire Grec Melkite dirigé par les Pères Blancs 1882–1932*, Harissa, Lebanon, Imprimerie de Saint Paul, 1932, pp. 65, 72, 232.

[146] This account of Gerboin is based on AGMAfr. *Notices Nécrologiques*, vol. 3, pp. 114–119; Nolan, Francis Patrick, *Christianity in Unyamwezi 1878–1928*, Cambridge Ph.D. Dissertation, 1977, *passim.*

[147] This account is based on AGMAfr. *Notices Nécrologiques*, vol. 3, pp. 268–282.

[148] Kirando, Zimba, Utinta, Mkulwe and Galula.

[149] Cf. Nolan, *op. cit.*, p. 196; *Rapports Annuels*, no. 8, (1912–1913), pp. 509–511.

[150] Linden and Linden, *op. cit.*, p. 19.

[151] Lechaptois, Adolphe, *Aux Rives du Tanganyika*, Algiers, Missionaries of Africa, 1913.

[152] The diocese centred on Moba eventually became known as Kalémie-Kirungu.

[153] This account is based on AGMAfr. *Notices Nécrologiques*, vol. 8, pp. 211–218; Roelens, *op. cit.*, and Stenger, *op. cit.*

[154] Gorra, *op. cit.*, p. 233.

[155] AGMAfr. General Visitation Report on Upper Congo, 114280.

[156] *CT*, no. 73, (1897), p. 28, Hochschild, *op. cit.*, pp. 134, 244.

[157] Pakenham, *op. cit.*, p. 657.

[158] Roelens, Victor, *Lettre Ouverte à Messieurs les Membres de la Commission Chargée d'Examiner le Rapport sur l'Enquête au Congo—Protestation des Supérieurs des Missions Catholiques du Congo*, Brussels, J. Goemaere, 1905.

[159] *CT*, no. 139, (1907), p. 373.

[160] The complete correspondence can be found in *CT*, no. 139, (1907), pp. 360–373.

[161] Lusaka, Congo, not to be confused with Lusaka, Zambia.

[162] AGMAfr. *Karema Mission Diary*, vol. 2, p. 197, May 12th 1895.

[163] The following account of Dupont's activities is based on: AGMAfr. *Notices Nécrologiques*, vol. 4, pp. 348–353; Garvey, Leloir, L., *Un Evêque Missionnaire—Roi des Brigands*, Brussels, Editions du Rendez-Vous, 1945; Linden and Linden, *op. cit.*; Pineau, Henry, *Evêque-Roi des Brigands—Monseigneur Dupont, Premier Vicaire Apostolique du Nyassa 1850–1930*, Paris, White Fathers, 1937; Stenger, Friedrich, *op. cit.*

[164] AGMAfr., Livinhac 103 085, Lechaptois to Livinhac, June 21st 1893.

[165] Mua, Likuni, Kachebere, and eventually Ntakataka.

[166] Vezeau, Roland, *The Apostolic Vicariate of Nyasa—Origins and First Developments 1889–1935*, Rome, Missionaries of Africa, 1989, pp. 46–57.

[167] AGMAfr. Livinhac to Dupont, 106219, August 19th 1910; Dupont to Livinhac 106220, October 16th 1910; Dupont to Livinhac 106222, December 7th 1910; cf. also General Council Minutes, p. 893, July 11th 1910; p. 896, August 14th 1910.

[168] Fr. Felix Phiri M. Afr. was responsible for the translation of Dupont's remains to Bembaland.

3. Slavery, Missionaries and Civil Power

[1] Livingstone, David, *The Last Journals*, London, John Murray, 1874, vol. 2, p. 182.

[2] Baunard, Mgr., *Le Cardinal Lavigerie*, Paris, 1896, vol. 2, p. 456.

[3] Walvin, James, *Black Ivory*, London, Fontana Press, 1993, p. 322.

[4] Storme, Marcel, *Rapports du Père Planque, de Mgr. Lavigerie et de Mgr. Comboni sur l'Association Internationale Africaine*, Brussels, Académie Royale des Sciences Coloniales, Mémoire, tome x1, fasc. 2, 1957, pp. 86, 108, 111.

[5] Renault, François, *Tippo Tip—un potentat Arabe en Afrique Centrale au XIXe siècle*, Paris, Société Française d'Histoire d'Outre-Mer, 1987, p. 222; Nolan, pp. 141, 144, 260.

[6] The author came across instances of such feuds during fieldwork in East Africa in 1964–1978.

[7] Walvin, *op. cit.*, p. 312.

[8] Renault, 1987, *op. cit.*, pp. 165–168; McLynn, Frank, *Stanley—Sorcerer's Apprentice*, Oxford, Oxford University Press, 1992, p. 154.

[9] Houdebine, T.L. and Boumier, Marcel, *Capitaine Joubert*, Namur, Grands Lacs, no date; AGMAfr. WA 644, *Archives of Captain Joubert* (005199 92 TAN JOU).

[10] Houdebine and Boumier, *op. cit.*, pp. 89–90, 97–103; Renault, François, *Lavigerie, L'Esclavage Africain et l'Europe 1868–1892*, Paris, E. De Boccard, 1971, pp. 378–379.

[11] Renault, 1987, *op. cit.*, pp. 410–415.

[12] *CT*, no. 57, (1892), pp. 126–127, 134. His body parts were found afterwards in a cooking-pot.

[13] Renault, 1987, *op. cit.*, pp. 289, 299.

[14] AGMAfr. *Karema Mission Diary*, vol. 2, pp. 143–167.

[15] *CT*, no. 80, (1898), p. 460.

[16] *CT*, no. 80, (1898), p. 460; no. 82, (1899), p. 194.

[17] *CT*, no. 130, (1906), p. 452.

[18] *CT*, no. 159, (1909), pp. 166–167.

[19] *CT*, no. 93, (1902), p. 125.

[20] *CT*, no. 75, (1897), pp. 408–409.

[21] *CT*, no. 79, (1898), p. 355; no. 93, (1902), p. 125.

[22] *CT*, no. 139, (1907), pp. 360–373.

[23] *CT*, no. 138, (1907), p. 308.

[24] Tiama, Jean-Baptiste, *Les Missionnaires d'Afrique (Pères Blancs) et la lutte anti-esclavagiste au Mali 1895–1905*, Licentiate Dissertation, Rome, P.U.G., 1992, p. 27; Gouraud, General, *Souvenirs d'un Africain au Soudan*, Paris, Pierre Tisné, 1939 (1899), p. 220.

[25] Tiama, *op. cit.*, p. 23.

[26] Mangin, Eugène, *Les Mossi—Essai sur les us et coutûmes du peuple Mossi au Soudan Occidental*, Algiers, Maison Carée, 1960, p. 28.

[27] Tiama, *op. cit.*, pp. 28–29.

[28] *CT*, no. 64, (1894), p. 582; no. 77, (1898), p. 90.

[29] *CT*, no. 68, (1895), p. 170; no. 98, (1903), p. 226.

[30] *CT*, no. 79, (1898), p. 351; no. 86, (1900), p. 223.

[31] *CT*, no. 146, (1907), p. 137.

[32] *CT*, no. 77, (1898), pp. 97–98.

[33] *CT*, no. 136, (1907), p. 92.

[34] *CT*, no. 68, (1895), p. 177; no. 75, (1897), p. 404; no. 78, (1898), p. 223.

[35] *CT*, no. 90, (1901), p. 153; no. 130, (1906), p. 545.

[36] *CT*, no. 139, (1907), p. 463; no. 147, (1908), p. 215.

[37] *CT*, no. 105, (1904), p. 208.

[38] Roelens, Victor, (ed. Antoine, N.), *Notre Vieux Congo 1891–1917—Souvenirs du premier evêque du Congo Belge*, Namur, Grands Lacs, 1948, vol. 1, p. 24.

[39] *CT*, no. 80, (1898), p. 472.

[40] Ki-Zerbo, Joseph, *Alfred Diban—Premier Chrétien de Haute-Volta*, Paris, Cerf, 1983, pp. 15–48; Pichard, Gabriel, *Dii Alfred-Simon Diban—Témoin de Dieu . . . Fondateur d'Eglise*, Bobo-Dioulasso, Savane, 1997, pp. 7–20.

[41] *CT*, no. 57, (1892), pp. 103–104.

[42] *CT*, no. 72, (1896), p. 468; no. 73, (1897), p. 107.

[43] *CT*, no. 118, (1905), p. 338; no. 145, (1908), p. 34.

[44] *CT*, no. 161, (1909), p. 394.

[45] Wright, Marcia, *Strategies of Slaves and Women—Life Stories from East*

/*Central Africa*, London, James Currey, 1993, p. 155. The practical differences between slaves and free women were comparatively small.

⁴⁶ Nolan, Francis Patrick, *Christianity in Unyamwezi 1878–1928*, Cambridge Ph.D. dissertation, 1977, pp. 141–143, 147, 266–267, 320.

⁴⁷ Tiama, *op. cit.*, pp. 30–45.

⁴⁸ *CT*, no. 143, (1907), p. 611.

⁴⁹ Fleming, Fergus, *The Sword and the Cross*, London, Granta Books, 2003, pp. 147–148.

⁵⁰ De Foucauld, Charles, *Correspondences Sahariennes*, ed. Thiriez, Philippe and Chatelard, Antoine, Paris, Editions du Cerf, 1998, pp. 86–87, 114–115, 117.

⁵¹ Lavigerie, Charles, *Instructions aux Missionnaires*, Namur, Grand Lacs, 1950, pp. 130–132.

⁵² *CT*, no. 80, (1898), p. 481; no. 82, (1899), p. 228.

⁵³ *Rapports Annuels*, no. 5, (1909–1910), p. 369.

⁵⁴ *CT*, no. 81, (1899), p. 78; no. 93, (1902), p. 124; no. 128, (1906), p. 375.

⁵⁵ Tiama, *op. cit.*, p. 77.

⁵⁶ *CT*, no. 141, (1907), p. 515.

⁵⁷ Ilboudo, Jean, *Christianisation du Moogo—Pourquoi les Mossi se sont-ils convertis? Le point de vue de l'historien*, Ouagadougou, Centre Spirituel Paam Yoodo, 2000, p. 124.

⁵⁸ Ilboudo, Jean, "La Christianisation du Moogo (1899–1949), la contribution des auxiliaries indigenes," in Ilboudo, Jean (ed.), *Burkina 2000, une église en marche vers son centenaire*, Ouagadougou, Presses Africaines, 1993, p. 106.

⁵⁹ *Ibid*.

⁶⁰ Sondo, Rose-Marie, *Monseigneur Joanny Thévenoud, Père Fondateur des Soeurs de l'Immaculée Conception de Ouagadougou*, Ouagadougou SOGIF, 1998, p.50.

⁶¹ Cf. Renault 1971, vol. 1, pp. 197–208; Matheson, Elizabeth Mary, *African Apostles*, New York, St. Paul's Publications, 1963, pp. 71–86.

⁶² Tiama, *op. cit.*, p. 88.

⁶³ *CT*, no. 147, (1908), p. 203.

⁶⁴ Lavigerie, *Instructions aux Missionnaires*, p. 132.

⁶⁵ Tiama, *op. cit.*, p. 97.

⁶⁶ Lavigerie, *Instructions aux Missionnaires*, pp. 99–100.

⁶⁷ Nolan, *op. cit.*, p. 140.

⁶⁸ *CT*, no. 159, (1909), p. 208.

⁶⁹ *CT*, no. 82, (1899), p. 208.

⁷⁰ *CT*, no. 130, (1906), p. 532.

⁷¹ Heremans, Roger, *L'Education dans les Missions des Pères Blancs en Afrique Centrale 1879–1914*, Brussels, Editions Nauwelaerts, 1983, p. 102; Duval, Armand, *Le Père Siméon Lourdel, Apôtre de l'Ouganda (1853–1890)*, Paris, F-X de Guibert, 2004, p. 146; AGMAfr. *Rubaga Diary*, July–August 1982.

⁷² AGMAfr. *Bukumbi Mission Diary*, February 16th 1888, p. 317.

⁷³ Tiama, *op. cit.*, p. 59.

⁷⁴ *CT*, no. 150, (1908), p. 504.

⁷⁵ Tiama, *op. cit.*, p. 76; *CT*, no. 130, (1906), p. 532.

⁷⁶ Waliggo, John Mary, *A History of African Priests—Katigondo Major Seminary 1911–1986*, Nairobi, Matianum Press, 1988, pp. 12, 90; Rooijackers, Marinus, "History of the White Fathers in Uganda," Working Paper no. 13, *pro manuscripto*, no date.

⁷⁷ Nolan, *op. cit.*, p. 149.

[78] Tiama, *op. cit.*, p. 44.

[79] *CT*, no. 100, (1903), p. 170.

[80] Ilboudo, Jean, *La Christianisation du Moogo—Pourquoi les Mossi se sont-ils convertis? Les Point de Vue de l'Historien*, Ouagadougou, Publications du Centre Spirituel Paam Yoodo, 2000, pp. 125–126.

[81] Ilboudo (2000), p. 126.

[82] *Rapports Annuels*, no. 8, (1912–1913), p. 140.

[83] Roelens, Victor, *Instructions aux Missionnaires Pères Blancs du Haut Congo*, Congo, Baudouinville 1920, Part 3, pp. 3, 14–20.

[84] *CT*, no. 77, (1898), p. 93; no. 81, (1899), p. 82.

[85] *CT*, no. 81, (1899), p. 78.

[86] *CT*, no. 135, (1907), p. 67.

[87] *CT*, no. 146, (1907), p. 137.

[88] *CT*, no. 150, (1908), p. 458.

[89] *CT*, no. 147, (1908), p. 218.

[90] *CT*, no. 99, (1903), p. 27.

[91] Ilboudo (2000), pp. 127–129; De Benoist, Joseph-Roger, *Eglise et Pouvoir au Soudan Français*, Paris, Karthala, 1987, pp. 170–172.

[92] *CT*, no. 102, (1903), p. 10.

[93] *CT*, no. 159, (1909), p. 200.

[94] Lavigerie, *Instructions aux Missionnaires*, p. 69.

[95] Stanley's appeal appeared in *The Daily Telegraph* in August 1877. It was reprinted in H.M. Stanley, *Through the Dark Continent*, London, Sampson Low, 1878. In the 1899 edition (London, George Newnes) it appears in vol. 1, p. 164.

[96] Rowe, John, "Mutesa and the Missionaries: Church and State in Pre-colonial Buganda," in Hansen, Holger Bernt and Twaddle, Michael (eds.), *Christian Missionaries and the State in the Third World*, Oxford, James Curry, 2002, pp. 52–65.

[97] Low, D.A., *Religion and Society in Buganda 1875–1900*, East African Studies, no. 8, EAISR, Kampala no date, pp. 5–6.

[98] Pirouet, M. Louise, *Black Evangelists—The Spread of Christianity in Uganda 1891–1914*, London, Rex Collings, 1978, p. 2; Lavigerie, *Instructions aux Missionnaires*, p. 136.

[99] Lavigerie, *Instructions aux Missionnaires*, p. 73.

[100] Lavigerie, *Instructions aux Missionnaries*, p. 136.

[101] Lavigerie, *Instructions aux Missionnaires*, pp. 112–113.

[102] Waliggo, 1976, *op. cit.*, pp. 44–49; Low, *op. cit.*, p. 7.

[103] Mercui, Joseph, *L'Ouganda—La mission Catholique et les agents de la compagnie Anglaise*, Paris, Procure des Missions d'Afrique, 1893, p. 278.

[104] Cf. Waliggo, John Mary, "The Catholic Church in the Buddu Province of Buganda 1879–1925," Cambridge, Ph.D. Dissertation, 1976, pp. 5, 135–138.

[105] The immediate successor of Hirth in Nyanza North was Antonin Guillermain, who died of blackwater fever in 1897 at the age of thirty-four.

[106] Waliggo, 1976, *op. cit.*, pp. 93–127.

[107] This loose-fitting black garment may also have been the clerical *douillette*, which, being open at the front, resembled the royal *joho*.

[108] Waliggo, 1976, *op. cit.*, pp. 130–131.

[109] Streicher, Henri, *Extraits des Lettres Circulaires 1897–1909*, Bukalasa, White Fathers, 1910, pp. 1–6, 11–13.

[110] *CT*, no. 82, (1899), p. 197; no. 152, 1908, p. 628.

[111] *CT*, no. 64, (1894), p. 115.

[112] Rooijackers, *op. cit.*, p. 5.

[113] *Ibid.*

[114] *CT*, no. 152, (1908), p. 613.

[115] Pirouet, *op. cit.*, pp. 54–55.

[116] Croegaert, Luc, S.J., *Les Pères Blancs au Rwanda*, unpublished typescript, no date, AGMAfr. *casier* 341.

[117] Linden, Ian and Linden, Jane, *Church and Revolution in Rwanda*, Manchester, Manchester University Press, 1977.

[118] Croegaert, *op. cit.*, p. 3.

[119] The picture presented here is based on Croegaert and on numerous references in the diaries and the *Chronique Trimestrielle*.

[120] Croegaert, *op. cit.*, pp. 116–118; AGMAfr. *Rwaza Mission Diary*, vol. 1, 1903–1910, pp. 153–165; *Notices Nécrologiques*, vol. 3, pp. 38–41.

[121] *Rapports Annuels*, no. 7, (1911–1912), pp. 412–414.

[122] *CT*, no. 153, (1908), p. 684.

[123] Gorju, Julien L., *En Zigzags à travers l'Urundi*, Namur, Missionaries of Africa, 1926, pp. 102–117.

[124] Ilboudo, Jean, 2000, *op. cit.*, p. 113.

[125] Ilboudo, Jean, *Le Christ au Burkina Faso—Les Actes des Premiers Chrétiens*, vol. 1, *Promenade au Mossi*, Ouagadougou, Presses Africaines, 1993, p. 96.

[126] Ilboudo, 1993, *op. cit.*, pp. 38–40.

[127] Mangin, Eugène, *op. cit.*, pp. 117–118.

[128] Mangin, *op. cit.*, pp. 29–32.

[129] Ilboudo, 2000, *op. cit.*, pp. 82–91.

[130] Hacquard to his sister, March 17th 1901, in Ilboudo, 1993, *op. cit.*, p. 101.

[131] Letter of August 2nd 1900, cited in Ilboudo, 1993, *op. cit.*, pp. 97–98.

[132] *CT*, no. 123, (1906), pp. 15–19; no. 130, (1906), p. 509.

[133] Austen, Ralph A., *Northwest Tanzania under German and British Rule: Colonial Policy and Tribal Politics 1889–1939*, New Haven, Yale University Press, 1968, p. 57.

[134] *CT*, no. 64, (1894), p. 117.

[135] *CT*, no. 79, (1898), p. 338; no. 80, (1898), p. 464; no. 97, (1903), p. 65.

[136] *CT*, no. 90, (1901), p. 82.

[137] *CT*, no. 78, (1898), p. 200; no. 82, (1899), p. 208.

[138] *CT*, no. 132, (1906), p. 626.

[139] Nolan, *op. cit.*, pp. 115–122, 157–179; *CT*, no. 119, (1905), p. 431; no. 141, (1907), p. 478.

[140] *Rafiki Yetu*, January 1910, quoted by Iliffe, John, *A Modern History of Tanganyika*, Cambridge, Cambridge University Press, 1979, pp. 218–219.

[141] Nolan, *op. cit.*, p. 153.

[142] Shorter, Aylward, *Chiefship in Western Tanzania, A Political History of the Kimbu*, Oxford, Clarendon Press, 1972, p. 298.

[143] Lourdel to his parents, in Duval, Armand, *op. cit.*, p. 56.

[144] Galton, Francis, *The Art of Travel or Shifts and Conveniences Available in Wild Countries*, London, John Murray, 1860, p. 107.

[145] Lavigerie, *Instructions aux Missionnaires*, pp. 90–91.

[146] Lavigerie, *Instructions aux Missionnaires*, p. 38.

[147] *CT*, no. 142 (1907), p. 578.

[148] AGMAfr., *Bukumbi Mission Diary*, 1882–1905, pp. 240–433.

[149] Goodall, Norman, *A History of the London Missionary Society 1895–1945*, Oxford, Oxford University Press, 1954, p. 271.

[150] Lavigerie, *Instructions aux Missionnaires*, pp. 112–114.

[151] Renault, François, *Lavigerie, L'Esclavage Africain et l'Europe 1868–1892*, vol. 1, Paris, E. De Boccard, 1971, pp. 236–251.

[152] Shorter, *op. cit.*, pp. 207, 307.

[153] Stanley, Henry M., *How I Found Livingstone in Central Africa*, London, Sampson Low, 1895, p. 403.

[154] AGMAfr., Jerome to Livinhac, January 14th 1898. Personal Dossier.

[155] AGMAfr., Lavigerie to Charbonnier, November 1st 1881, cited by Renault, 1971, *op. cit.*, pp. 185–195.

[156] Renault, 1971, *op. cit.*, p. 248.

[157] Renault, 1971, *op. cit.*, p. 387.

[158] Houdebine, T.L. and Boumier, Marcel, *Capitaine Joubert*, Namur, Grands Lacs, no date; AGMAfr. WA 644, *Capitaine Joubert Archives, Letters, Journals and Judgements*.

[159] AGMAfr. *Mpala Mission Diary*, vol. 1, pp. 77a–87, Judicial Review March–April 1886.

[160] Renault, 1971, *op. cit.*, pp. 372–375.

[161] Renault, 1971, *op. cit.*, pp. 390–391.

[162] Roelens, Victor (ed. N. Antoine), *Notre Vieux Congo 1891–1917—Souvenirs du premier evêque du Congo Belge*, Namur, Grands Lacs, 2 vols., 1948, vol. 1, pp. 6–7; *Rapports Annuels*, no. 7, (1911–1912), Algiers, White Fathers, 1912, p. 533.

[163] AGMAfr. 113022, Roelens to Livinhac, June 1st 1894.

[164] Roelens and Antoine, *op. cit.*, p. 7.

[165] *CT*, no. 72, (1896), p. 622.

[166] *Rapports Annuels*, no. 6, (1910), p. 130.

[167] *CT*, no. 75, (1897), pp. 408–409.

[168] *CT*, no. 139, (1907), pp. 360–373.

[169] For this account I am indebted to Delathuy, A.M., *Missie en Staat in Oud Congo 1880–1914, Witte Paters, Scheutistenen, Jezïten*, Brussels, EPO, 1988, pp. 13 ff., 44–51, 80–86. Passages kindly translated for me by Joseph Vanrenterghem M. Afr.

[170] Delathuy, *op. cit.*, pp. 5–6.

[171] AGMAfr. 114287, Visitation Report.

[172] AGMAfr. 114281, Visitation Report.

[173] AGMAfr. 114290, Visitation Report.

[174] Roelens, Victor, *Instructions aux Missionnaires Pères Blancs du Haut Congo*, Congo, Baudouinville, 1920, III 4, 26; V 13 (AGMAfr. 011.1–6).

[175] AGMAfr. 148 055, p. 33, art. 9.

[176] AGMAfr. *Karema Mission Diary*, vol. 1, p. 154, January 1st 1892.

[177] AGMAfr. *Karema Mission Diary*, vol. 2, p. 176, November 1st 1893.

[178] AGMAfr. *Karema Mission Diary*, vol. 2, pp. 178–179, November 21st–25th 1893.

[179] *Ibid.*

[180] *CT*, no. 87, (1900), p. 402.

[181] AGMAfr. *Karema Mission Diary*, vol. 2, p. 197, May 12th 1895.

[182] AGMAfr. *Kayambi Mission Diary*, vol. 1, p. 36, November 4th 1898.

[183] Vezeau, Roland, *The Apostolic Vicariate of Nyasa, Origins and First Developments 1889–1935*, Rome, AGMAfr. 1989, p. 44.

[184] Garvey, Brian, *Bembaland Church—Religious and Social Change in South Central Africa 1891–1964*, Leiden, E.J. Brill, 1994, pp. 62–65, 71; AGMAfr. *Chilubula Mission Diary*, January 1904; cf. also June 21st 1908, June 12th 1914.

[185] Garvey, *op. cit.*, 72.

[186] Cf. Arnauld, Dominique, *Les Débuts de l'évangélisation en Pays Mossi-*

Nakomse d'Après les Archives des Missionnaires d'Afrique (Pères Blancs), Mémoire pour la Licence, Rome, 1979, MS, p. 64.

[187] Ceillier, Jean-Claude, *A Pilgrimage from Chapter to Chapter, The First General Chapters of the Society of Missionaries of Africa 1874–1900*, Missionaries of Africa History Series, No. 1, Rome, 2002, p. 29.

[188] AGMAfr. Armed Brothers B-16-3 (1).

[189] AGMAfr. Armed Brothers B-16-255-262. Correspondence with the Delegate of the Grandmaster of the Sovereign Order of Malta.

[190] AGMAfr. Armed Brothers B-16-1 (bis).

[191] AGMAfr. Armed Brothers B-16-4, B-16-9-10.

[192] AGMAfr. Armed Brothers B-16-82-96.

[193] AGMAfr. Armed Brothers B-16-180-262.

[194] AGMAfr. Armed Brothers B-16-3 (2).

[195] AGMAfr. Armed Brothers B-16-242-247; 255–262.

[196] AGMAfr. Armed Brothers B-16-97-156.

[197] AGMAfr. General Council Minutes 206, November 27th 1892.

[198] Ilboudo, 1993, *op. cit.*, p. 15.

4. God's Work in Africa

[1] *CT*, no. 147, (1908) [1907], p. 179.

[2] Hastings, Adrian, *The Church in Africa 1450–1950*, Oxford, Clarendon Press, 1994, p. 269

[3] *CT*, no. 100, (1903), p. 181.

[4] *CT*, no. 98, (1903), p. 205.

[5] Rooijackers, Marinus, *History of the White Fathers in Uganda*, Working Paper no. 15, n.d., pp. 2–5.

[6] *CT*, no. 134, (1907), p. 44; no. 139, (1907), p. 404.

[7] Nolan, Francis, Patrick, *Christianity in Unyamwezi 1878–1928*, Cambridge Ph.D. Dissertation, 1977, p. 121.

[8] Croegaert, Luc, *Les Pères Blancs au Rwanda—Jalons et Balises*, unpublished MS, no date, AGMAfr. Casier 341, p. 81; Alphonse Brard left the White Fathers to become a Carthusian in 1906. As Dom Pierre Claver, he died at the Charterhouse of Lucca in Italy in 1918.

[9] Garvey, Brian, *Bembaland Church—Religious and Social Change in South Central Africa 1891–1964*, Leiden, E.J. Brill, 1994, pp. 51–52.

[10] *CT*, no. 98, (1903), p. 223; no. 99, (1903), p. 62.

[11] *CT*, no. 77, (1898) [1897], p. 97.

[12] *CT*, no. 150, (1908) [1907], p. 453; no. 153, (1908), p. 720.

[13] Lavigerie, Charles, *Instructions aux Missionnaires*, Namur, Grands Lacs, 1950, pp. 73–75, 91–94.

[14] *Rapports Annuels*, no. 4, (1908–1909), pp. 348–349.

[15] Nolan, *op. cit.*, pp. 254–257.

[16] *CT*, no. 110, (1904), p. 98.

[17] *CT*, no. 122, (1905), p. 560; no. 144, (1907), p. 680.

[18] *CT*, no. 114, (1905), p. 123; no. 115, (1905), p. 208; no. 135, (1907), p. 78.

[19] *CT*, no. 135, (1907), p. 74.; no. 149, (1908), p. 350.

[20] *CT*, no. 133, (1906), p. 673; no. 141, (1907), p. 518.

[21] *CT*, no. 142, (1908), p. 593.

[22] *CT*, no. 135, (1907), p. 78.

[23] Statistics are taken from Casier, Jacques, *Développement de la Société*, 1961, MS in the General Secretariat of the Society of Missionaries of Africa, Rome.

[24] On January 1st 2006 brothers numbered 154, as compared to 1,498 priests, www.africamission-mafr.org.

[25] *CT*, no. 89, (1899), p. 467.

[26] *CT*, no. 162, (1909), p. 495.

[27] *CT*, no. 150, (1908), p. 432.

[28] *CT*, no. 141, (1907), p. 282; no. 159, (1909), p. 156.

[29] *CT*, no. 136, (1907), p. 93; no. 138, (1907), p. 281.

[30] *CT*, no. 145, (1908), p. 67.

[31] *CT*, no. 77, (1895), p. 119.

[32] *CT*, no. 81, (1899), p. 91.

[33] *CT*, no. 147, (1908), p. 234; no. 149, (1908), p. 385; no. 152, (1908), p. 633.

[34] *CT*, no. 162, (1909), p. 445.

[35] *CT*, no. 144, (1907), p. 694; *Rapports Annuels*, no. 5, (1909–1910), p. 118.

[36] *CT*, no. 80, (1898), p. 465.

[37] *CT*, no. 136, (1907), p. 105; no. 138, (1907), p. 314; AGMAfr. *Notices Nécrologiques*, vol. 3, pp. 66–68.

[38] AGMAfr. *Notices Nécrologiques*, vol. 8, pp. 319–327.

[39] *CT*, no. 113, (1905), pp. 105–106.

[40] *CT*, no. 115, (1905), p. 206.

[41] *CT*, no. 78, (1898), p. 227; no. 138, (1907), p. 261.

[42] *CT*, no. 155, (1908), p. 868; no. 124, (1906), p. 78; no. 161, (1909), p. 336.

[43] Lavigerie, *Instructions aux Missionnaires*, pp. 101–103.

[44] *CT*, no. 159, (1909), p. 159.

[45] Casier, *op. cit.*

[46] *MSOLA/CT*, no. 14, (1905), pp. 322–323.

[47] *CT*, no. 108, (1904), p. 401.

[48] *CT*, no. 77, (1898), p. 126.

[49] *CT*, no. 104, (1904), p. 160; no. 113, (1905), p. 115.

[50] *CT*, no. 138, (1907), pp. 253–259.

[51] Some informants ascribe his death to yellow fever, others to heat exhaustion.

[52] *CT*, no. 138, (1907), p. 255.

[53] *CT*, no. 103, (1904), p. 41; no. 122, (1905), p. 565; no. 130, (1906), p. 542.

[54] *CT*, no. 152, (1908), p. 636.

[55] AGMAfr. General Council Minutes, April 4th 1898, p. 469.

[56] AGMAfr. General Council Minutes, December 9th and 28th 1898, pp. 822, 824.

[57] *CT*, no. 74, (1897), p. 189.

[58] *CT*, no. 72, (1896), p. 377; no. 87, (1900), p. 369.

[59] It seems that this was due to *Propaganda Fide*'s growing commitments.

[60] *CT*, no. 124, (1906), 77–78; *Rapports Annuels*, no. 4, (1908–1909), p. 164.

[61] *Rapports Annuels*, no. 6, (1910–1911), p. 174.

[62] *CT*, no. 133, (1906), p. 653; *Rapports Annuels*, no. 2, (1906–1907), p. 164.

[63] *CT*, no. 146, (1907), p. 144.

[64] AGMAfr. General Council Minutes, June 24th 1907, p. 764.

[65] Duval, Armand, *Le père Siméon Lourdel, apôtre de l'Ouganda (1853–1890)*, Paris, De Guibert, 2004, pp. 34–35.

[66] Livinhac, *Lettres Circulaires*, Algiers, Maison Carée, vol. 1, 1891–1912; vol. 2, 1912–1922.

[67] Linden, Ian, with Linden, Jane, *Catholics, Peasants and Chewa Resistance in Nyasaland 1889–1939*, University of California Press, Berkeley and Los Angeles, 1974, p. 28.

[68] Society of Missionaries of Africa, White Fathers, *Constitutions*, Algiers, Maison Carée, 1908, p. 1.

[69] Society of Missionaries of Africa, White Fathers, *Directory of the Constitutions*, Algiers, Maison-Carée, 1914, pp. 9–15.

[70] Hastings, *op. cit.*, p. 263.

[71] *Directory of 1914*, p. 27.

[72] *Constitutions of 1908*, no. 78.

[73] *Ibid.*, no. 277.

[74] *Ibid.*, nos. 264 ff.

[75] *Directory of 1914*, p. 428.

[76] *Ibid.*, p. 429.

[77] Communication from Aimé Brunel (1904–1993), supplied by Dominique Arnauld M. Afr.

[78] *Ibid.*, pp. 500–502.

[79] Livinhac, *Lettres Circulaires*, no. 85, October 3rd 1909.

[80] *Directory of 1914*, pp. 16, 124, 126.

[81] *Constitutions of 1908*, no. 304.

[82] Livinhac, *Lettres Circulaires*, no. 85, October 3rd 1909.

[83] *CT*, no. 150, (1908), p. 442.

[84] *CT*, no. 159, (1909), p. 186.

[85] *Coutumier Général des Missionnaires d'Afrique*, Algiers, Maison Carée, 1895, pp. 16–22.

[86] *CT*, no. 85, (1900), p. 98.

[87] *CT*, no. 114, (1905), p. 178; no. 127, (1906), p. 317; no. 141, (1907), p. 499; no. 142, (1907), p. 599; no. 144, (1907), pp. 712–713.

[88] *CT*, no. 122, (1905), p. 561; no. 140, (1907), p. 455; no. 152, (1908), p. 644; no. 161, (1909), p. 328.

[89] Gray, Richard, "Christianity," in A.D. Roberts (ed.), *The Cambridge History of Africa*, Cambridge, Cambridge University Press, 1986, vol. 7, p. 169.

[90] This account follows closely that of Ahern, Patrick, *Maurice and Thérèse—The Story of a Love*, New York, Doubleday, 1998.

[91] Ahern, *op. cit.*, p. 281.

[92] *Ibid.*

[93] Dupont to Livinhac, Sept. 25th 1905, AGMAfr. Livinhac 106 141. Dupont writes "Louveau" as "Luneau."

[94] AGMAfr. General Council Minutes, January 2nd 1906, pp. 718, 720.

[95] Ahern, *op. cit.*, p. 282.

[96] Lavigerie, *Instructions aux Missionnaires*, p. 250.

[97] Comboni, Daniele, *Piano per la Regenerazione dell'Africa*, Turin, Comboni Missionaries, 1864.

[98] Storme, Marcel, *Rapports du Père Planque, de Mgr. Lavigerie et de Mgr. Comboni sur l'Association Internationale Africaine*, Brussels, Académie Royale des Sciences Coloniales, Mémoire, tome x1, fasc. 2, 1957, p. 116 and fn. 6.

[99] Waliggo, John Mary, "The Catholic Church in the Buddu Province of Buganda 1879–1925," Ph.D. Dissertation, Cambridge University, 1976, pp. 96–97.

[100] *CT*, no. 115, (1905), p. 199.

[101] *CT*, no. 125, (1906), pp. 165, 172.

[102] *CT*, no. 147, (1908), p. 206.

[103] *CT*, no. 87, (1900), p. 419; no. 108, (1904), p. 361.

[104] *CT*, no. 114, (1905), p. 127; no. 124, (1906), p. 100.

[105] *CT*, no. 156, (1908), p. 887.

[106] *CT*, no. 155, (1908), p. 820; *Rapports Annuels*, no. 7, (1911–1912), p. 155.

[107] cf. Hastings, *op. cit.*, p. 276.

[108] This account of the Malta Institute and its graduates is mainly based on Boom, Constant, "The Doctor-Catechists in Tanganyika—A Study in Evangelism," M.A. essay presented to the Centre of African Studies, (SOAS), London University, 1970, MS; Rooijackers, Marinus, *History of the White Fathers in Uganda*, Working Paper no. 14, *The Impact of Lavigerie's Project of Doctor-Catechists on the Mission of Uganda*, MS; Renault, François, *Cardinal Lavigerie, Churchman, Prophet and Missionary*, London, Athlone Press, 1994, pp. 274–276.

[109] Livinhac to Lavigerie, November 6th 1879 in *CT*, (1880), p. 276.

[110] The spelling of some of these names varies. I have tried to eliminate French spelling in some of them. Information about Nazara Yanaba was obtained in an interview with his daughter, Sister Agnes Yanaba, at Bamako on February 9th 2004.

[111] Kabeya, John, *Daktari Adriano Atiman*, Tabora, TMP Book Department and Arusha, Eastern Africa Publications, 1978; Fouquer, R., *Le Docteur Adrien Atiman*, Karema, Spes Publications, no date; Breedveld, Walter, *Atiman der Negerdokter bij het Tanganyikameer*, Gottmer, Nijmegen, The Netherlands, no date.

[112] *CT*, no. 141, (1907), p. 493; no. 150, (1908), p. 447.

[113] *CT*, no. 153, (1908), p. 693.

[114] *CT*, no. 150, (1908), p. 447.

[115] *Petit Echo*, vol. 1., no. 2, January 1913.

[116] Heremans, Roger, *L'Education dans les missions des Pères Blancs 1897–1914*, Brussels, Editions Nauwelaerts, 1983; Roelens, Victor (ed. Antoine, N.), *Notre Vieux Congo 1891–1917—Souvenirs du premier evêque du Congo Belge*, 2 vols., Namur, Grands Lacs, 1948; Kabeya, *op. cit.*

[117] *CT*, no. 57, (1893), p. 128.

[118] *CT*, no. 78, (1898), p. 236.

[119] *CT*, no. 117, (1905), p. 271.

[120] *CT*, no. 138, (1907), p. 305.

[121] *CT*, no. 159, (1909), p. 194.

[122] *CT*, no. 79, (1898), p. 313; no. 81, (1899), p. 155.

[123] *CT*, no. 99, (1903), p. 13.

[124] Hirth to Livinhac, April 15th 1891, AGMAfr. C13/509.

[125] Hirth to Livinhac, November 15th 1891, AGMAfr. C13/522; December 27th 1891, AGMAfr. C13/523.

[126] Interview with Sister Agnes Yanaba at Bamako, February 9th 2004.

[127] Ilboudo, Jean, "La Christianisation du Moogo (1899–1949), La contribution des Auxiliaires Indigènes," in Ilboudo, Jean (ed.), *Burkina 2000, Une Eglise en marche vers son centenaire*, Ouagadougou, Presses Africaines, 1993, pp. 106–107.

[128] Rooijackers, Marinus, "First Sub-Saharan Missionaries of Africa," *Petit Echo*, vol. 6, 2004, no. 952, pp. 333–339. Two other Ugandan Missionaries of Africa of this time, Léon Lwanga and Barnabé Walabieki, did not go to Malta.

[129] Cf. n. 132 below.

[130] Ogez, Louis, *Forget Me Not—Saved from Slavery He Became a Missionary to Zambia 1896–1910*, Ndola, Mission Press, 1992.

[131] Nolan, *op. cit.*, p. 221.

[132] *CT*, no. 86, (1900), p. 226. The signature "Jean Victor Mhoro" appears on a document of the Malta Institute of 1894–1895, together with those of Sambateshi (Mwijuma) and several other African Malta graduates whose names are known. Cf. Ogez, *op. cit.*, p. 38.

[133] AGMAfr. General Council Minutes, February 13th 1893, p. 230.

[134] Ceillier, Jean-Claude, *A Pilgrimage from Chapter to Chapter, The First General Chapters of the Society of Missionaries of Africa 1874–1900*, Rome, Missionaries of Africa History Series, no. 1, 2002, p. 66.

[135] *Rapports Annuels*, no. 8, (1912–1913), p. 560.

[136] Ilboudo, 2000, *op. cit.*, p. 175.

[137] This section on catechists owes a great deal to Nolan, *op. cit.*; also to Nolan, Francis, "History of the Catechist in Eastern Africa," in Shorter, Aylward and Kataza, Eugene (eds.), *Missionaries to Yourselves—African Catechists Today*, London, Geoffrey Chapman, 1972, pp. 1–28; also Nolan, Francis, *Mission to the Great Lakes, 1878–1978*, Tabora, TMP Book Department, 1978; and to Rooijackers, Marinus, *History of the White Fathers in Uganda*, Working Papers nos. 13, 15, 17 and 18, MS, which deal with different aspects of the work of catechists.

[138] *CT*, no. 100, (1903), p. 187.

[139] *CT*, no. 104, (1904), p. 124; no. 110, (1904), p. 105.

[140] Heremans, *op. cit.*, pp. 219–222; Stenger, pp. 111–137.

[141] *CT*, no. 125, (1906), pp. 165–166.

[142] *CT*, no. 110, (1904), p. 105.

[143] *CT*, no. 90, (1901), p. 83; no. 110, (1904), p. 178; no. 113, (1905), p. 93; no. 129, (1906), p. 419; *Rapports Annuels*, no. 8, (1912–1913), pp. 137–138, 604; Interview with Jules Keita at Kati, Mali, February 7th 2004.

[144] *CT*, no. 81, (1899), p. 75; no. 104, (1905), p. 107; no. 141, (1907), p. 498.

[145] Figures cited in Rooijackers, Working Paper no. 17, p. 2.

[146] *CT*, no. 138, (1907), p. 299; no. 150, (1908), p. 464.

[147] Nolan, *op. cit.*, pp. 242–244; *CT*, no. 152, (1908), pp. 613–614.

[148] *CT*, no. 132, (1906), p. 613; no. 135, 1907, p. 55.

[149] Croegaert, *op. cit.*, p. 121.

[150] *CT*, no. 114, (1905), p. 136; no. 140, (1907), p. 450.

[151] *CT*, no. 114, (1905), p. 139; no. 113, (1905), pp. 107–108; no. 124, (1906), p. 77; no. 136, (1907), p. 104; no. 149, (1908), p. 346.

[152] In Nyanza South, at Bukumbi and Kome in 1900, and at Kagondo in 1903; in Unyanyembe, at Ushirombo in 1900; in Upper Congo at Mpala in 1893, moved to Lusaka in 1905; in Tanganyika, at Utinta in 1895, Karema in 1899, and Zimba in 1912; in Nyasa, at Chilubula and Natakataka in 1909, the latter moving to Mua in 1911. In French Sudan, a catechetical school for children was opened at Kati in 1912. In Nyanza North, Streicher started a catechist training centre at Rubaga in 1902. This moved to Mitala Maria in the following year.

[153] *CT*, no. 103, (1904), p. 84; no. 114, (1905), p. 151; no. 124, (1906), p. 77.

[154] Sources for Munaku's story are Faupel, J.F., *African Holocaust, The Story of the Uganda Martyrs*, Nairobi, St. Paul's Publications Africa, fourth edition, 1984; Gray, Richard, "Christianity," in Roberts, A.D. (ed.), *Cambridge History of Africa*, vol. 7, Cambridge, Cambridge University Press, 1978, chapter 3, p. 165; Waliggo, John Mary, *A History of African Priests*, Nairobi, Matianum Press, 1988; Waliggo, 1976, *op. cit.*, p. 187.

[155] *CT*, no. 127, (1906), p. 292.

[156] Lavigerie, *Instructions aux Missionnaires*, pp. 17, 108–110; *Constitutions of 1908*, nos. 218–219; *Directory of 1914*, pp. 293–325.

[157] *Petit Catéchisme d'Alger traduit en Langue Kiswahili*, Paris, F. Levé, 1884; *Catéchisme en Langue Kiswahili*, Algiers, Maison Carée, 1885; *Catéchisme Kabyle*, Algiers, Maison Carée, 1904; *Katekismu Katolika*, Algiers, Maison Carée, 1911.

[158] Croegaert, *op. cit.*, p. 126.

[159] *CT*, no. 93, (1902), p. 116; no. 98, (1903), p. 248, van Waesberghe to Livinhac; no. 117, (1905), p. 261; no. 141, (1907), pp. 312, 484.

[160] *CT*, no. 98, (1903), p. 202; no. 114, (1905), p. 178; no. 158, (1909), p. 132.

[161] Streicher, Henri, *Extraits des Lettres Circulaires*, 1897–1909, Bukalasa, White Fathers, 1910.

[162] *CT*, no. 132, (1906), p. 620; no. 147, (1908), p. 179.

[163] Van Der Meersch, Jean, *Le Catéchuménat au Rwanda de 1900 à nos Jours*, Kigali, Pallotti Press, 1993, pp. 63–67, 71–73.

[164] *Rapports Annuels*, no. 7, (1911–1912), p. 197; Rooijackers, Marinus, *History of the White Fathers in Uganda*, Working Paper no. 4, MS, p. 10.

[165] *CT*, no. 153, (1908), p. 680; no. 154, (1908), p. 813; no. 155, (1908), p. 871.

[166] Van Der Meersch, *op. cit.*, p. 136.

[167] *CT*, no. 133, (1906), p. 683; no. 156, (1908), p. 938.

[168] Croegaert, *op. cit.*, p. 125.

[169] *Directory of 1914*, p. 296.

[170] Sundkler, Bengt, and Steed, Christopher, *A History of the Church in Africa*, Cambridge, Cambridge University Press, 2000, pp. 580–581.

[171] Hamilton, J. Taylor and Hamilton, Kenneth G., *A History of the Moravian Church: The Renewed Unitas Fratrum, 1722–1957*, Bethlehem, Penn., Moravian Church in America, 1967, p. 611.

[172] Cf. Missionaries of Africa, *Publications en Langues Africaines, Catalogue provisoire*, Algiers, Maison Carée, 1928. The Church Missionary Society produced a New Testament in Rutoro in 1902 and an Old Testament in 1906.

[173] Burlaton, Louis, *Monseigneur Léon Livinhac, Archevêque d'Oxyrhynque, Supérieur-Général de la Société des Missionnaires d'Afrique (Pères Blancs), Fondateur de la Mission de l'Ouganda*, typescript, Carthage, 1932, AGMAfr. B2 Livn. 1–4, p. 168.

[174] Van Der Meersch, *op. cit.*, pp. 60–62; Croegaert, *op. cit.*, p. 126.

[175] Rooijackers, Working Paper no. 4, MS.

[176] AGMAfr. 82134, Streicher to Livinhac, May 5th 1901.

[177] AGMAfr. General Council Minutes, February 17th 1908, p. 790; February 24th 1908, p. 791; April 21st 1909, p. 840.

[178] AGMAfr. Report of 1912 Chapter, p. 44.

[179] *CT*, no. 110, (1904), p. 97; no. 140, (1907), p. 140; no. 155, (1908), pp. 833, 859.

[180] *CT*, no. 113, (1905), p. 54; no. 90, (1901), p. 77.

[181] *CT*, no. 99, (1903), p. 56; no. 161, (1909), p. 402; no. 127, (1906), p. 308.

[182] Bourgade, F., *Les Soirées de Carthage*, Paris, 1847; *La Clef du Coran*, Paris, 1852; *Passage du Coran à l'Evangile*, Paris, 1855.

[183] Renault, *op. cit.*, p. 90, dismisses Bourgade as "narrowly apologetic." Arnulf Camps, "M. l'Abbé Bourgade (1806–1866) in Dialogue with Muslims at Carthage," in Cornille, Catherine and Neckebrouck, Valeer (eds.), *A Universal Faith*, Louvain Theological and Pastoral Monographs, no. 9, Louvain, Eerdmans, 1992, pp. 73–88, has the more positive assessment.

[184] Shorter, Aylward, *Christianity and the African Imagination*, Nairobi, Paulines Publications, 1996, pp. 49–50.

[185] Renault, *op. cit.*, p. 90; Goyau, Georges, *Un Grand Missionnaire Le Cardinal Lavigerie*, Paris, Plon, 1925, p. 256.

[186] Lavigerie, *Instructions aux Missionnaires*, p. 252.

[187] Cuoq, Joseph, *Lavigerie, Les Pères Blancs et les Musulmans Maghrebins*, Rome, Missionaries of Africa, 1986, pp. 40–41.

[188] Cuoq, *op. cit.*, pp. 14–21; Renault, *op. cit.*, pp. 93–98.

[189] Cuoq, *op. cit.*, p. 18; Ceillier, Jean Claude, "Les Missionnaires d'Afrique et le Dialogue Interreligieux: Quelques Jalons Historiques," Colloque de Paris, December 2002, unpublished typescript, p. 2.

[190] Cuoq, *op. cit.*, pp. 51–52; Ceillier, *op. cit.*, p. 3.

[191] Lavigerie, *Instructions aux Missionnaires*, pp. 99–100.

[192] Renault, *op. cit.*, pp. 178–184; Saadia, Ossilia, *Catholiques et Musulman Sunnites, Discours Croisés 1920–1950, Approche Historique de l'Alterité Religieuse*, doctoral thesis, University of Lyon, 2001, pp. 91–97 (AGMAfr. UE 1007).

[193] Cuoq, *op. cit.*, pp. 51–73; Ceillier, *op. cit.*, pp. 3–4.

[194] *CT*, no. 57, (1893), p. 19. The remark was made at the College of St. Charles at Tunis, but it reflects the attitude in Algeria.

[195] *CT*, no. 109, (1904), p. 35.

[196] Cuoq, *op. cit.*, pp. 85, 92.

[197] *CT*, no. 121, (1905), Annual Statistical Table for Algeria Province. Infant baptisms *in extremis* were 995.

[198] *CT*, no. 76, (1897), p. 459.

[199] Vanlande, René, *Chez les Pères Blancs—Tunisie, Kabylie, Sahara*, Paris, J. Peronnet, 1929, p. 69.

[200] *CT*, no. 57, (1893), p. 58.

[201] *Ibid.*; also *CT*, no. 101, (1903), p. 239; no. 148, (1908), p. 327.

[202] *CT*, no. 97, (1903), Supplement p. 27.

[203] Society of Missionaries of Africa (White Fathers), *Directoire des Constitutions*, Algiers, Maison Carée, 1914, pp. 244–245.

[204] Cuoq, *op. cit.*, pp. 39, 90; *CT*, no. 68, 1895, p. 2.

[205] *Rapports Annuels*, no. 9, (1913–1914), p. 73.

[206] *Rapports Annuels*, no. 6, (1910–1911), pp. 81–83.

[207] See discussion in Saadia, *op. cit.*, pp. 91–97.

[208] Lavigerie, *Instructions aux Missionnaires*, pp. 71–72; on the proposition, *extra ecclesia nulla conceditur gratia*, cf. Fransen, Piet, "How can Non-Christians find salvation in their own religions?," in Neuner, Josef (ed.), *Christian Revelation and World Religions*, London, Sheed and Ward, 1967, pp. 67–122.

[209] Cf. Renault, *op. cit.*, pp. 185–194, 257–262.

[210] Renault, *op. cit.*, p. 262; Grévoz, Daniel, *Sahara 1830–1881—Les mirages Français et la tragédie Flatters*, Paris, l'Harmattan, 1989, pp. 25–195.

[211] *CT*, no. 72, (1896), p. 449.

[212] *CT*, no. 93, (1902), p. 153; no. 100, (1903), pp. 156–157.

[213] *CT*, no. 100, (1903), p. 157.

[214] *CT*, no. 93, (1902), p. 158.

[215] AGMAfr. 071 348, Hacquard to Livinhac, Oct. 25th 1900.

[216] *CT*, no. 102, (1903), p. 11.

[217] Cf. AGMAfr. D:S d 268, Dupuis Dossier; Seabrook, William, *The White Monk of Timbuctoo*, London, Harrap, 1934.

[218] *Rapports Annuels*, no. 2, (1906–1907), p. 36.

[219] De Foucauld, Charles, *Lettres et Carnets*, ed. Jean-François Six, Paris, Editions du Seuil, 1966, p. 160.

[220] De Foucauld, *op. cit.*, p. 160; Saadia, *op. cit.*, pp. 290–295.

[221] Fleming, Fergus, *The Sword and the Cross*, London, Granta Books, 2003, pp. 278–279.

[222] Gaudeul, J.M., *Encounters and Clashes—Islam and Christianity in History—A Survey*, Rome, PISAI, 2000, p. 310.

[223] De Foucauld, Charles, *Correspondences Sahariennes*, ed. Thiriez, Philippe and Chatelard, Antoine, Paris, Editions du Cerf, 1998, pp. 941–952.

[224] Ceillier, *op. cit.*, p. 5.

[225] *Ibid.*, p. 6.

[226] *Petit Echo*, vol. 1, no. 8, pp. 81–82.

[227] Cuoq, *op. cit.*, pp. 76–77.

[228] Gaudeul, *op. cit.*, pp. 318–319.

[229] Ceillier, *op. cit.*, p. 7.

[230] *Ibid.*, pp. 9–10.

[231] This account is based on Cuoq, *op. cit.*, pp. 74–110; Ceillier, *op. cit.*, pp. 9–11; Gaudeul, *op. cit.*, pp. 314–320 and Saadia, *op. cit.*, pp. 299–236.

[232] Teissier, Henri, *Chrétiens en Algérie, un Partage d'Espérance*, Paris, Desclée de Brouwer, 2002, pp. 47–48; Duval, Armand, *C'était une longue fidélité à l'Algérie et au Rwanda*, Paris, Mediaspaul, 1998, quoting Bishop Pierre Claverie, p. 136.

5. Africa Re-invents the Church

[1] Wagner, Roy, *The Invention of Culture*, Chicago, University of Chicago Press, 1981.

[2] Mudimbe, V.Y., *The Invention of Africa*, London, James Currey, 1988; *The Idea of Africa*, London, James Currey, 1994.

[3] Stenger, Friedrich, *White Fathers in Colonial Central Africa*, Münster, Hamberg, London, Lit Verlag, 2001, pp. 208–210.

[4] Sanneh, Lamin, *Encountering the West—Christianity and the Global Cultural Process: The African Dimension*, London, Marshall Pickering, 1993, pp. 155–156.

[5] Hastings, Adrian, *The Church in Africa 1450–1950*, Oxford, Clarendon Press, 1994, p. 274.

[6] *Maximum Illud*, in Hickey, Raymond, *Modern Missionary Documents and Africa*, Dublin, Dominican Publications, 1982, p. 40.

[7] Shorter, Aylward, *Christianity and the African Imagination*, Nairobi, Paulines Publications Africa, 1996, pp. 37–40; de Montclos, Xavier, *Lavigerie, La Mission Universelle de l'Église*, Paris, Cerf, 1991, pp. 18–20, 78–82.

[8] Sanneh, *op. cit.*, pp. 139–151; Fabian, Johannes, *Language and Colonial Power—The Appropriation of Swahili in the Former Belgian Congo 1880–1938*, Cambridge, Cambridge University Press, 1986.

[9] Lavigerie, Charles, *Instructions aux Missionnaires*, Namurs, Grands Lacs, 1950, pp. 210, 270.

[10] *Ibid.*, p. 121.

[11] *CT*, no. 144, (1907), p. 710.

[12] *CT*, no. 82, (1899), p. 234.

[13] *CT*, no. 150, (1908), p. 444.

[14] *Rapports Annuels*, no. 8, (1912–1913), p. 206.

[15] *CT*, no. 159, (1909), p. 184.

[16] *CT*, no. 133, (1906), p. 664.

[17] *CT*, no. 90, (1901), p. 76.

[18] *CT*, no. 98, (1903), p. 268.

[19] *CT*, no. 87, (1900), p. 410.

[20] *CT*, no. 82, (1899), p. 236.

[21] *CT*, no. 135, (1907), p. 77; no. 141, (1907), p. 525; no. 143, (1907), p. 633.

[22] Celebrated hunters were: Pierre-Marie Thomas (1869–1958), Jean-Marie Chapdelaine (1876–1938) and Jean-Marie Stéphant (1876–1938).

[23] *CT*, no. 127, (1906), p. 308; no. 149, (1908), p. 376; no. 150, (1908), p. 495; no. 161, (1909), pp. 384, 386.

[24] *CT*, no. 138, (1907), p. 281.

[25] *CT*, no. 145, (1908), p. 60.

26 *CT*, no. 150, (1908), p. 440.

27 *CT*, no. 141, (1907), p. 487.

28 *CT*, no. 159, (1909), p. 213.

29 *Ibid.*, p. 184.

30 *CT*, no. 161, (1909), pp. 327–328.

31 *CT*, no. 87, (1900), pp. 422, 427; no. 162, (1909), pp. 461, 482.

32 *CT*, no. 152, (1908), pp. 628–629; no. 158, (1909), p. 98.

33 Heremans, Roger. *L'Education dans les Missions des Pères Blancs en Afrique Centrale 1879–1914*, Brussels, Editions Nauwelaerts, 1983, p. 201.

34 Stenger, *op. cit.*, pp. 62–103; Mudimbe, 1988, 1994, *op. cit.*, *passim*; Delathuy, A.M., *Missie en Staat in Oud Congo 1880-1914, Witte Paters, Scheutistenen, Jezïten*, Brussels, EPO, 1988, pp. 93–96.

35 Roelens,Victor (ed. N. Antoine) *Notre Vieux Congo 1891–1917—Souvenirs du premier evêque du Congo Belge*, Namur, Grands Lacs, 1948, vol. 1, pp. 199–214; vol. 2, p. 92; Roelens, Victor, *Instructions aux Missionnaires Pères Blancs du Haut Congo*, Baudouinville, 1920, pp. 61–65.

36 Roelens, *Instructions*, Part 6, p. 62.

37 Roelens, *A propos de "La Philosophie Bantoue" du R.P. Tempels*, AGMAfr. K3/9.

38 Lavigerie, *Instructions aux Missionnaires*, pp. 28, 70.

39 *Ibid.*, pp. 70–71.

40 Fabian, *op. cit.*, pp. 76–77.

41 Society of Missionaries of Africa (White Fathers), *Directory of the Constitutions*, Algiers, Maison Carée, 1914, nos. 345–347.

42 Bazin, Hippolyte, *Dictionnaire Bambara-Français*, Paris, Imprimerie Nationale, 1906; van der Burgt, Jean-Martin-Michel, *Un Grand Peuple de l'Afrique Equatoriale-Elements d'une monographie sur l'Urundi et les Warundi*, s'Hertogen-bosch, *Société d'Illustration Catholique*, 1903; van der Burgt, J.-M.-M., *Dictionnaire Français-Kirundi*, s'Hertogenbosch, 1904; van der Burgt, J.-M.-M., *Het Kruis geplant in een Onbekend Negerland van Midden-Afrika*, Boxtel, 1921.

43 *CT*, no. 143, (1907), p. 63.

44 *CT*, no. 117, (1905), p. 293; no. 146, (1907), p. 115.

45 *CT*, no. 113, (1905), p. 76.

46 1919 was the year of Brutel's departure from the Society. The Missionaries of Africa, however, reprinted his work at Algiers in 1914 and 1925.

47 Fabian, *op. cit.*, p. 83.

48 *CT*, no. 104, (1904), p. 109.

49 Fabian, *op. cit.*, p. 77.

50 *CT*, no. 141, (1907), pp. 502–503.

51 Meersch, van der, *Le Catéchuménat au Rwanda de 1900 à nos Jours*, Kigali, Pallotti Press, 1993, p. 57.

52 Dufays, Félix and de Moor, Vincent, *Au Kinyaga les enchaînés*, Paris, Librarie Missionnaire, 1939, p. 17.

53 *CT*, no. 104, (1904), p. 109; no. 153, (1908), p. 693.

54 It was the first piece of music ever broadcast by radio. Adolphe Adam lived from 1803 to 1856.

55 *CT*, no. 98, (1903), p. 267.

56 AGMAfr. 091/21, Letter of June 15th 1905, p. 2.

57 Fabian, *op. cit.*

58 Fabian, *op. cit.*, p. 81.

59 Fabian, *op. cit.*, pp. 155–161.

[60] De Benoist, Joseph-Roger, *Eglise et Pouvoir au Soudan Français*, Paris, Karthala, 1987, p. 47.

[61] *CT*, no. 130, (1906), p. 497.

[62] *CT*, no. 149, (1908), p. 351.

[63] Heremans, *op. cit.*, pp. 169–170.

[64] *CT*, no. 152, (1908), p. 640.

[65] *CT*, no. 120, (1905), p. 501.

[66] *CT*, no. 113, (1905), p. 67.

[67] *CT*, no. 140, (1907), p. 442.

[68] *CT*, no. 155, (1908), p. 822.

[69] *CT*, no. 109, (1904), p. 45.

[70] *CT*, no. 156, (1908), p. 910.

[71] *CT*, no. 149, (1908), p. 375.

[72] *CT*, no. 97, (1902), p. 66; no. 161, (1909), p. 349.

[73] *CT*, no. 150 (1908), p. 492.

[74] *CT*, no. 143, (1907), p. 638.

[75] *CT*, no. 150, (1908), p. 479.

[76] *CT*, no. 154, (1908), p. 765.

[77] *CT*, no. 152, (1908), p. 631; no. 156, (1908), p. 915; *Rapports Annuels*, no. 4, (1908–1909), p. 356.

[78] The author remembers that, on his first morning in Nairobi, June 28th 1951, at Langata Army Barracks, a servant was singing the *Missa de Angelis* outside his door.

[79] AGMAfr. General Council Minutes, p. 1056, February 9th 1914.

[80] *CT*, no. 114, (1905), p. 129.

[81] Aduonum, Oforiwaa, "Dance," in Zeleza, Paul Tiyambe (ed.), *Encyclopaedia of Twentieth Century African History*, London, Routledge, 2003, pp. 125–131; Slade, Ruth, *King Leopold's Congo, Aspects of the Development of Race Relations in the Congo Independent State*, London, Oxford University Press, 1962, p. 166; Hastings, *op. cit.*, p. 459.

[82] Information supplied by Didier Sawadogo M. Afr. and other informants in Bamako.

[83] *CT*, no. 158, (1909), p. 128.

[84] *CT*, no. 162, (1909), p. 482.

[85] Robert, Jean-Marie, *Coutûmes des Wafipa*, vol. 2, mimeographed folio in Swahili and French, pp. 12–18, AGMAfr. 104592.

[86] *CT*, no. 76, (1897), p. 497.

[87] Letter of Bishop Hirth to his brother, October 1st, 1902, quoted in Croegaert, Luc, *Les Pères Blancs au Rwanda—Jalons et Balises*, unpublished MS, no date, AGMAfr. Casier 341, p. 126.

[88] *CT*, no. 132, (1906), p. 628.

[89] *CT*, no. 126, (1906), p. 220.

[90] *CT*, no. 144, (1907), p. 695.

[91] *CT*, no. 117, (1905), pp. 264–265.

[92] Austen, Ralph, *Northwest Tanzania under German and British Rule: Colonial Policy and Tribal Politics, 1889–1939*, New Haven, Yale University Press, pp. 80–81.

[93] Nolan, Francis, Patrick, *Christianity in Unyamwezi 1878–1928*, Cambridge Ph.D. dissertation, 1977, p. 298; *CT*, no. 137, (1907), p. 225.

[94] *Rapports Annuels*, no. 2, (1906–1907), p. 38.

[95] *CT*, no. 156, (1908), p. 891.

[96] *CT*, no. 113, (1905), p. 69; no. 128, (1906), p. 220; no. 150, (1908), p. 430.

[97] *CT*, no. 161, (1909), p. 328.

[98] *Rapports Annuels*, no. 4, (1908–1909), p. 230; 8, (1912–1913), p. 478.

[99] *Rapports Annuels*, no. 8, (1912–1913), p. 607.

[100] *Rapports Annuels*, no. 6, (1910–1911), p. 427.

[101] Cf. Arens, William, *The Man-Eating Myth*, Oxford, Oxford University Press, 1979.

[102] *Rapports Annuels*, no. 4, (1908–1909), p. 351.

[103] *Rapports Annuels*, no. 8, (1912–1913), p. 554.

[104] *CT*, no. 57, (1892), p. 128.

[105] *CT*, no. 90, (1901), p. 149.

[106] *CT*, no. 117, (1905), p. 308. For a discussion of "the poison ideal," see *infra*, the section entitled "Negative Cultural Factors—Ritual Murder."

[107] Roelens (ed. Antoine), 1948, *op. cit.*, pp. 151–155.

[108] Cf. Shorter, *Chiefship in Western Tanzania*, (1972), pp. 107–111.

[109] *CT*, no. 107, (1904), p. 297.

[110] Cf. Shorter, *Chiefship in Western Tanzania*, (1972), pp. 140–147.

[111] *CT*, no. 84, (1899), p. 473; no. 161, (1909), p. 394.

[112] Cory, Hans, "The Buswezi," *American Anthropologist*, vol. 57, no. 5, 1955, pp. 923–952; *CT*, no. 147, (1908), p. 230.

[113] *CT*, no. 144, (1907), p. 683; no. 156, (1908), p. 885; *Rapports Annuels*, 4, (1908–1909); 6 (1910–1911), p. 131; 9 (1913), p. 287.

[114] *CT*, no. 133, (1906), p. 668.

[115] *CT*, no. 156, (1908), p. 885.

[116] Monteil, Charles, *Les Bambara du Ségou et du Kaarta*, Paris, Maisonneuve et Larose, 1977, pp. 234–280.

[117] *CT*, no. 130, (1906), p. 551; no. 155, (1908), p. 823.

[118] *CT*, no. 123, (1906), p. 26.

[119] *CT*, no. 130, (1906), p. 505.

[120] *CT*, no. 140, (1907), p. 432.

[121] *Ibid.*, pp. 437–438.

[122] *CT*, no. 155, (1908), p. 823.

[123] Communication from Joseph-Roger de Benoist, at Dakar, February 3rd 2004.

[124] *CT*, no. 135, (1907), pp. 70–72.

[125] My translation, with minor editing.

[126] The word used means "strangers." In the context, it refers to colonial officers and settlers.

[127] Iliffe, John, *Tanganyika Under German Rule 1905–1912*, Cambridge, Cambridge University Press, 1969, pp. 80–82; Austen, *op. cit.*, pp. 77–81.

[128] This account is based on Tiquet, Jean, *Une Expérience de petite colonisation en Algérie—Les colons arabes-chrétiens du Cardinal Lavigerie*, Algiers, Maison Carée, 1936.

[129] Cf. Dornier, François, *Pères Blancs, Soeurs Blanches, Thibar 1895–1975*, typescript, 1991, AGMAfr. 108187.

[130] Vanlande, René, *Chez les Pères Blancs—Tunisie, Kabylie, Sahara*, Paris, J. Peyronnet, 1929, p. 11.

[131] Tiquet, *op. cit.*, pp. 171–178.

[132] This section relies on: Vezeau, Roland, *The White Fathers' Contribution to the Civilizing of Central Africa through their Agricultural Activities and Improvement of Native Diet, 1878–1953*, Rome, F.A.O. and the Vatican, typescript, 1954, AGMAfr. K44; Byabazaire, Deogratias M., *The Contribution of the Christian Churches to the Development of Western Uganda, 1894–1974*, Frankfurt am Main, Peter Lang, 1979, European University Papers.

[133] *CT*, no. 87, (1900), p. 416; no. 131, (1906), p. 620; no. 162, (1909), p. 447.

[134] *CT*, no. 150, (1908), p. 480; no. 153, (1908), p. 714.

[135] *CT*, no. 161, (1909), pp. 350–351.

[136] *Ibid.*, p. 358.

[137] *CT*, no. 117, (1905), p. 301.

[138] *CT*, no. 119, (1905), p. 411.

[139] *Rapports Annuels*, no. 6, (1910–1911), p. 285.

[140] Byabazaire, *op. cit.*, p. 93.

[141] *CT*, no. 117, (1905), p. 300; no. 159, (1909), p. 198.

[142] *CT*, no. 138, (1907), p. 299; no. 141, (1907), p. 499.

[143] *CT*, no. 159, (1909), p. 224; no. 156, (1908), p. 926.

[144] Wright, Marcia, *Strategies of Slaves and Women—Life Stories from East/Central Africa*, London, James Currey, 1993, p. 69.

[145] *Ibid.*, p. 155.

[146] Cf. Oduyoye, M.A., *The Will to Arise: Women, Tradition and the Church in Africa*, New York, Orbis Books, 1992.

[147] *CT*, no. 85, (1900), p. 35.

[148] *CT*, no. 153, (1908), p. 697.

[149] Ilboudo, Jean, *Christianisation du Moogo—Pourquoi les Mossi se sont-ils convertis? Le point de vue de l'historien*, Ouagadougou, Centre Spirituel Paam Yoodo, 2000, p. 129.

[150] *CT*, no. 155, (1908), p. 874; no. 161, (1909), pp. 332–333.

[151] *CT*, no. 161, (1909), p. 388.

[152] *Rapports Annuels*, no. 8, (1812–1913), p. 354.

[153] *CT*, no. 108, (1904), p. 405; no. 112, (1905), p. 11.

[154] Marie-André du Sacré Coeur, *Histoire des origins de la congregation des Soeurs Missionnaires de Notre Dame d'Afrique*, 1869–1892, Algiers, MSOLA, 1946, pp. 779 ff.

[155] Information from Joseph-Roger de Benoist at Dakar, Senegal, February 3rd 2004.

[156] Ilboudo, 2000, *op. cit.*, p. 176.

[157] Seabrook, William, *The White Monk of Timbuctoo*, London, Harrap, 1934, p. 209.

[158] See the discussion of this in Waliggo, John Mary, *A History of African Priests—Katigondo Major Seminary 1911–1966*, Nairobi, Matianum Press, 1988, pp. 100–102.

[159] Waliggo, 1988, *op. cit.*, p. 102.

[160] This section is based on Hinfelaar, Hugo, *History of the Church in Zambia*, Lusaka, Bookworld Publishers, 2004, pp. 5–32; Stenger, *op. cit.*, pp. 111–137.

[161] Hinfelaar, 2004, *op. cit.*, p. 24.

[162] Stenger, *op. cit.*, p. 202.

[163] The full text in both Bemba and English is found in Hinfelaar, Hugo, *Bemba-Speaking Women of Zambia in a Century of Religious Change—1892–1992*, Leiden, E.J. Brill, 1994, p. 39; an incomplete version is found in Roberts, Andrew D., *A History of the Bemba—Political Growth and Change in North-Eastern Zambia before 1900*, London, Longman , 1973, p. 266. The original, recorded by Rev. T. van Diessen, is in the Missionaries of Africa Archives, Lusaka, Zambia.

[164] *CT*, no. 140, (1907), p. 456; no. 152, (1908), p. 657.

[165] *CT*, no. 134, (1907), p. 43; no. 143, (1907), p. 612; no. 150, (1908), pp. 445–446.

[166] McCoy, Remigius, *Great Things Happen*, Montreal, Missionaries of Africa, 1988, pp. 109–124.

[167]   *CT*, no. 109, (1904), p. 52.

[168]   *CT*, no. 141, (1907), p. 481.

[169]   *CT*, no. 153, (1908), p. 701.

[170]   Lavigerie, *Instructions aux Missionnaires*, pp. 66, 117, 311.

[171]   *Ibid.*, p. 75.

[172]   *Ibid.*, p. 114

[173]   *Ibid.*, p. 116.

[174]   *Diary of Makete Mission*, 1927–1956, 6 vols. in French and German, seen by the author at Kipalapala, December 28th 1964.

[175]   *Ibid.*, vol. 5, p. 143.

[176]   Leroy, Alexandre, "La religion des primitifs," and "Role scientifique des missionnaires," *Anthropos*, vol. 1, 1906.

[177]   Leroy, Alexandre, *La religion des primitifs*, Paris, Beauchesne, 1909, *Etudes sur l'histoire des religions*.

[178]   *CT*, no. 158, (1909), p. 147.

[179]   Achte, August, *Histoire des rois Baganda*, 1900, MS, longhand, AGMAfr. P157/1.

[180]   Dupuis, Auguste, *Monographie de Tomboctou*, MS, longhand, AGMAfr. N8 104233.

[181]   Van der Burgt, 1903, *op. cit.*

[182]   Van der Burgt, 1921, *op. cit.*

[183]   AGMAfr. General Council Minutes, p. 1046, December 9th 1913.

[184]   Lechaptois, Adolphe, *Aux Rives du Tanganyika, Etude couronnée pa la Société Géographique de Paris*, Algiers, Maison Carée, 1913.

[185]   Mangin, Eugène, *Essai sur les us et coûtumes du people Mossi au Soudan Occidental*, Vienna, Anthropos, 1916; also *pro manuscripto*, Algiers, Maison Carée, 1960.

[186]   Gorju, Julien, *Entre le Victoria, l'Albert et l'Edouard—Ethnographie de la partie anglaise du vicariate de l'Uganda—Origines, histoire, religions, coûtumes*, Rennes, Imprimerie Oberthür, 1920.

[187]   Gorju, Julien, *En zigzags à travers l'Urundi*, Namur, Missionaries of Africa, 1926.

[188]   Dufays, Félix, *Pages d'epopée Africaine—Jours troublés*, Ixelles (Belgium), René Weversbergh, 1928; Dufays and de Moor, *op. cit.*

[189]   The author had the privilege of meeting Fridolin Bösch at Tabora on December 18th 1964.

[190]   Cf. Nolan, *op. cit.*, p. 190. Bösch's most important work was *Les Banyamwezi, peuple de l'Afrique orientale*, Münster, Biblioteca Anthropos, 1930; Robert's major work was *Croyances et coûtumes magico-religieuses des Wafipa païens*, Tabora, Missionaries of Africa, 1949.

[191]   Schynse, Auguste Wilhelm, *Zwei Jahre am Congo—Erlebnisse und Schilderungen*, Köln, Karl Hespers, Bachem, 1889.

[192]   AGMAfr. *Bukumbi Mission Diary*, vol. 1, 1882–1890, p. 358.

[193]   *Ibid.*, vol. 2, 1890–1905, p. 387.

[194]   Schynse, Auguste Wilhelm, *A travers l'Afrique avec Stanley et Emin-Pacha*, Paris, Karl Hespers, 1889; *Mit Stanley und Emin Pascha durch Deutsch Ost-Afrika*, Köln, Bachem, 1890; *Con Stanley ed Emin Pasciá attraverso l'Africa orientale*, Milan, Antonio Vallardi, 1890.

[195]   Cf. McLynn, Frank, *Stanley, Sorcerer's Apprentice*, Oxford, Oxford University Press, 1992, pp. 305–307, 318.

[196]   Hacquard, Augustin, "La Mission Hourst," *Bulletin de la Société Géographique d'Alger*, 1897, vol. 2, pp. 110–112.

[197] *CT*, no. 64, (1894), p. 556; no. 68, (1895), p. 62.

[198] Hacquard, Augustin, "Promenade au Mossi," *Missions Catholiques*, vol. 32, 1901, pp. 94–96, 106–108, 117–120, 128–130, 142–144, 147–148, 174–178. A recent version of this article was edited by Ilboudo, Jean de la Théotokos, in *Le Christ au Burkina*, Ouagadougou, Presses Africaines, 1993.

[199] Dromaux, Théophile, "Nouvelle route à Karema sur le Tanganyika," *Geographical Journal*, vol. 13, no. 5, 1899, pp. 535–536; *Durchquerung von Deutsch-Ostafrika (Bagamojo-Kiwele-Karema)*, presented by Paul Langhans, *Petermann's Mitteilungen*, 1899, no.1, pp. 1–3, Map and Table 1.

[200] Freed, Joann, Centre d'Etudes et de Documentation Archéologique de la Conservation de Carthage (CEDAC), *CEDAC Bulletin* 20, March 2001.

[201] De Benoist, Joseph-Roger (ed.), *Voyage au Soudan 1896–1897 de Mgr. Anatole Toulotte*, AGMAfr. N 3 and LA 21/3.

[202] Mesnage, Joseph, *L'Afrique chrétienne, Evêchés et ruines antiques d'après les manuscripts de Mgr. Toulotte et les découvertes archéologiques les plus récentes*, Paris, Ministère de l'Instruction Publique, 1912; *Le Christianisme en Afrique, decline et extinction*, Paris, 1915.

[203] Vellard, André, *Carthage autrefois et aujourd'hui*, Lille, Victor Ducolombier, 1896.

[204] Vellard, André, *Aux Oasis Sahariennes*, MS, 1903, AGMAfr. L14 102033.

[205] *CT*, no. 93, (1902), p. 91; no. 109, (1904), p. 49; no. 136, (1907), p. 107; no. 141, (1907), p. 496; no. 142, (1907), p. 599; no. 147, (1908), p. 204; no. 149, (1908), pp. 398–399; no. 151, (1908), p. 578.

[206] *CT*, no. 77, (1898), p. 121.

[207] *CT*, no. 143, (1907), p. 629; no. 156, (1908), p. 931; no. 161, (1909), p. 361.

[208] *CT*, no. 78, (1898), p. 226; no. 86, (1900), p. 256.

[209] *CT*, no. 133, (1906), p. 672.

[210] *CT*, no. 162, (1909), p. 445.

[211] *CT*, no. 142, (1907), p. 545.

[212] *CT*, no. 124, (1906), p. 128; no. 129, (1906), p. 447.

[213] *CT*, no. 161, (1909), p. 343.

[214] *CT*, no. 72, (1896), p. 601; no. 132, (1906), p. 619; no. 136, (1907), p. 110; no. 139, (1907), p. 334.

[215] *CT*, no. 147, (1908), p. 224.

[216] *CT*, no. 143, (1907), p. 638.

[217] *CT*, no. 147, (1908), p. 237.

[218] The mountain is also called "Ninangongo."

[219] Dufays, Félix, *Le volcan du Nyirangongo*, Letter from Muler, June 15th 1905, AGMAfr. 103953.

[220] *CT*, no. 143, (1907), p. 648.

[221] This mountain is also called "Munanira."

[222] *CT*, no. 147, (1907), pp. 235, 241; no. 150, (1908), p. 497.

[223] *CT*, no. 150, (1908), p. 491.

[224] *Ibid.*, pp. 496–497.

[225] Cf. Ousby, Ian, *The Road to Verdun*, London, Pimlico, 2003, pp. 179–181.

[226] *CT*, no. 147, (1908), p. 184.

[227] *CT*, no. 150, (1908), p. 440.

[228] *CT*, no. 149, (1908), p. 407.

[229] Hastings, *op. cit.*, pp. 559–560.

[230] *CT*, no. 145, (1908), p. 11; no. 148, (1908), p. 291; no. 150, (1908), p. 444.

[231] Vandenberghe, An, "Rome and the Religious-Ethnological Activities of Father Wilhelm Schmidt SVD (1868–1954)," summary of a paper presented to the Belgian Academy, Rome, 2004.

[232] Nolan, *op. cit.*, pp. 190–192.

[233] Hebblethwaite, Peter, *John XXIII, Pope of the Council*, London, Geoffrey Chapman, 1984, p. 62.

6. Education and Denomination

[1] *CT*, no. 130, (1906), p. 532.

[2] *CT*, no. 115, (1905), p. 274.

[3] Yates, Timothy, *Christian Mission in the Twentieth Century*, Cambridge, Cambridge University Press, 1994, pp. 28–29.

[4] Pius XI, *Mortalium Animos*, January 6th 1928.

[5] Linden, Ian, with Linden, Jane, *Catholics, Peasants and Chewa Resistance in Nyasaland*, Berkeley and Los Angeles, University of California Press, 1974.

[6] This whole chapter relies heavily on Heremans, Roger, *L'Education dans les missions des Pères Blancs en Afrique Centrale 1879–1914*, Brussels, Nauwelaerts, 1983.

[7] *Benedicamus Domino*, "Let us bless the Lord," to which the reply was *Deo Gratias*, "Thanks be to God"; *Benedicite* means "Bless," the opening invocation of the monastic grace.

[8] *CT*, no. 84, (1899), p. 489.

[9] AGMAfr. Minutes of the Thirteenth Chapter: General Chapter of the Society, 1874–1947, pp. 215, 217, 227.

[10] *CT*, no. 113, (1905), p. 81.

[11] Heremans, *op. cit.*, p. 170.

[12] Nolan, Francis Patrick, *Christianity in Unyamwezi 1878–1928*, Cambridge Ph.D. dissertation, 1977, p. 223.

[13] *CT*, no. 87, (1900), p. 406.

[14] *Rapports Annuels*, no. 5, (1910–1911), p. 136; 7, (1911–1912), p. 533.

[15] *CT*, no. 108, (1904), pp. 375–376.

[16] *CT*, no. 141, (1907), p. 527.

[17] *CT*, no. 150, (1908) [1907], p. 602.

[18] Heremans, *op. cit.*, p. 162.

[19] *Rapports Annuels*, no. 8, (1912–1913), p. 514.

[20] *CT*, no. 162, (1909), p. 495.

[21] *CT*, no. 147, (1908), p. 180; *Rapports Annuels*, no. 7, p. 530.

[22] *CT*, no. 98, (1903), pp. 210, 215; no. 104, (1904), p. 117.

[23] Heremans, *op. cit.*, pp. 171–172.

[24] *Rapports Annuels*, no. 8, (1912–1913), p. 606.

[25] *CT*, no. 145, (1908), p. 66; Heremans, *op. cit.*,p. 192.

[26] Cf. Statistical Tables in *Rapports Annuels*, 8 (1912–1913); 9 (1913–1914).

[27] Heremans, *op. cit.*, p. 176.

[28] *CT*, no. 109, (1904), p. 50.

[29] *CT*, no. 152, (1908), p. 602.

[30] *CT*, no. 138, (1907), p. 262.

[31] *CT*, no. 144, (1907), p. 696.

[32] *CT*, no. 143, (1907), p. 616; *Rapports Annuels*, no. 5, (1909–1910), p. 117.

[33] *CT*, no. 98, (1903), p. 215.

[34] Heremans, *op. cit.*, p. 192.

[35] Ilboudo, Jean, *Christianisation du Moogo—Pourquoi les Mossi se sont-ils convertis ? Le point de vue de l'historien*, Ouagadougou, Centre Spirituel Paam Yoodo, 2000, pp. 183–184.

36 *CT*, no. 98, (1903), p. 244.

37 *CT*, no. 130, (1906), p. 538.

38 *CT*, no. 144, (1907), p. 66.

39 *CT*, no. 156, (1908), p. 925.

40 *CT*, no. 84, (1899), p. 461.

41 *CT*, no. 86, (1900), p. 210.

42 *Rapports Annuels*, no. 7, (1911–1912), p. 203.

43 Goodall, Norman, *A History of the London Missionary Society 1895–1945*, Oxford, Oxford University Press, 1954, pp. 271–278.

44 *CT*, no. 78, (1898), p. 244; no. 82, (1899), p. 246.

45 *CT*, no. 125, (1906), p. 204; no. 129, (1906), p. 426.

46 *CT*, no. 141, (1907), pp. 518–520.

47 *CT*, no. 150, (1908) [1907], p. 477; no. 156, (1908), p. 938; Hinfelaar, Hugo, *History of the Church in Zambia*, Lusaka, Zambia, Bookworld Publishers, 2004, p. 69.

48 *CT*, no. 150, (1908), p. 475; no. 156, (1908), p. 938; no. 162, (1909), p. 490.

49 Hinfelaar, 2004, *op. cit.*, pp. 52–71.

50 Goodall, *op. cit.*, p. 276.

51 *CT*, no. 97, (1903), pp. 94–95; no. 159, (1909), p. 224.

52 Hamilton, J. Taylor, and Hamilton, Kenneth G., *History of the Moravian Church—The Renewed Unitas Fratrum 1722–1967*, Bethlehem, Penn., Moravian Church in America, 1967.

53 A complete account of the Catholic-Moravian dispute is to be found in Shorter, Aylward, *Chiefship in Western Tanzania, A Political History of the Kimbu*, Oxford, Clarendon Press, 1972, pp. 346–350.

54 Hamilton and Hamilton, *op. cit.*, p. 610.

55 *CT*, no. 117, (1905), p. 297.

56 *CT*, no. 110, (1904), p. 120; no. 119, (1905), p. 444; no. 125, (1906), p. 200.

57 Information from Chief Karolo Ilonga II of Ubungu at Mwambani (Galula) August 28th 1966; Shorter, 1972, *op. cit.*, p. 348.

58 *CT*, no. 147, (1908), p. 199; no. 153, (1908), p. 698; no. 162, (1909), p. 466.

59 *Rapports Annuels*, no. 7, (1911–1912), p. 482.

60 Heremans, *op. cit.*, p. 203.

61 AGMAfr. General Council Minutes, p. 270, November 20th 1893.

62 Heremans, *op. cit.*, pp. 168–172; *CT*, no. 90, (1901), p. 82.

63 *CT*, no. 90, (1901), p. 108.

64 Oliver, Roland, *The Missionary Factor in East Africa*, London, Longmans, 1952, pp. 95–96, 167; *Rapports Annuels*, 4, (1908–1909), p. 231.

65 *CT*, no. 146, (1907), p. 158.

66 *Rapports Annuels*, no. 8, (1912–1913), p. 409.

67 *Rapports Annuels*, no. 2, (1906–1907), p. 213; 4, (1908–1909), p. 69; 7, (1911–1912), p. 97; *Petit Echo*, vol. 2, no. 19, (July 1914), pp. 109–110.

68 Ilboudo, 2000, *op. cit.*, pp. 138–145.

69 *Ibid.*; Information supplied by Joseph-Roger de Benoist at Dakar, February 3rd 2004.

70 *CT*, no. 114, (1905), p. 143.

71 Bell, C.R.V., *Education in Uganda before Independence*, Oxford Development Records Project, Report II, Rhodes House Library Oxford, 1985, p. 3; *CT*, no. 143, (1907), p. 617.

72 AGMAfr. General Council Minutes, p. 729, July 9th 1906.

73 AGMAfr. Minutes of the 1906 General Chapter, p. 217.

[74] *CT*, no. 124, (1906), p. 81.

[75] Heremans, *op. cit.*, pp. 303–310.

[76] AGMAfr. General Council Minutes, p. 1023, June 23rd 1913.

[77] AGMAfr. Livinhac 087 243, Prentice to Livinhac, November 23rd 1908.

[78] *Rapports Annuels*, no. 6, (1910–1911), p. 172.

[79] AGMAfr. General Council Minutes, p. 1023, June 23rd 1913; pp. 1051–1054, January 12th 1914.

[80] Oliver, *op. cit.*, pp. 212–213. Oliver, however, calls it "St. Joseph's," a confusion with St. Joseph's Technical School of later foundation, also at Kisubi.

[81] *CT*, no. 84, (1899), p. 416; no. 109, (1904), Supplement, p. 9.

[82] Renault, François, *Cardinal Lavigerie, Churchman, Prophet and Missionary*, London, Athlone Press, 1994, pp. 172–173; Finn, Peter, *The History of the Priory Bishop's Waltham*, Winchester, Hedera Books, 2002, p. 14.

[83] AGMAfr. General Council Minutes, p. 505, June 12th 1899.

[84] The following account of the foundation of St. Anne's is based on Page, Ivan and Trimbur, Dominique, *St. Anne's at Jerusalem—Historical Account of its Founding*, Missionaries of Africa History Series, no. 3, Rome, 2004, pp. 12–28.

[85] Page and Trimbur, *op. cit.*, p. 11.

[86] *Ibid.*, p. 28; Lavigerie, *Instructions aux missionnaires*, pp. 184–190.

[87] Dahbar, Nicolas, *Sainte-Anne de Jérusalem*, Yabroud, Lebanon, 1959; Gorra, Philippe, *Sainte Anne de Jérusalem, Séminaire Grec Melkite dirigé par les Pères Blancs 1882–1932*, Harissa, Lebanon, Imprimerie St. Paul, 1932.

[88] Gorra, *op. cit.*, p. 232.

[89] Gorra, *op. cit.*, p. 24.

[90] Gorra, *op. cit.*, p. 232.

[91] Hastings, Adrian, *The Church in Africa 1450–1950*, Oxford, Clarendon Press, 1994, p. 297.

[92] AGMAfr. Livinhac C 13–99, Livinhac to APF Lyon, May 21st 1888.

[93] This account follows Heremans, *op. cit.*; Waliggo, John Mary, *A History of African Priests—Katigondo Major Seminary 1911–1986*, Nairobi, Matianum Press, 1988; and Rooijackers, Marinus, "History of White Fathers in Uganda," Working Paper no. 14.

[94] Waliggo, *op. cit.*, 1988, p. 1.

[95] *CT*, no. 103, (1904), p. 47.

[96] *CT*, no. 124, (1906), pp. 105–106.

[97] Heremans, *op. cit.*, p. 369.

[98] Heremans, *op. cit.*, p. 306.

[99] Pirouet, M. Louise, *Black Evangelists—The Spread of Christianity in Uganda 1891–1914*, London, Rex Collings, 1978, p. 19.

[100] Pirouet, M. Louise, *Historical Dictionary of Uganda*, African Historical Dictionaries, no. 64, London and Metuchen, Scarecrow Press Inc., 1995, p. 335.

[101] The author was present on that occasion.

[102] Nolan, Francis Patrick, *Mission to the Great Lakes*, Tabora, TMP Book Department, 1978, p. 50.

[103] AGMAfr. Livinhac 098 214, Kuypers to Livinhac, April 11th 1910; Gahungu, Méthode, *Les methodes des Pères Blancs dans l'oeuvre des séminaries pour le clergé local en Afrique des Grands Lacs (1879–1936)*, Ph.D. thesis presented to Pontifical Salesian University, 1998.

[104] AGMAfr. 148 055, Hirth's Rule for Rubya, no date.

[105] *Rapports Annuels*, no. 8, (1912–1913), p. 476.

[106] *CT*, no. 117, (1905), p. 299.

[107] Heremans, *op. cit.*, pp. 385–389.

[108] *CT*, no. 141, (1907), p. 511.

[109] Heremans, *op. cit.*, p. 390, says four, but Kimpinde, Amando Dominique et al., *Stefano Kaoze, prêtre d'hier at d'aujourd'hui*, Kinshasa, Editions St. Paul Afrique, 1982, says three.

[110] Most of the details of the life of Stefano Kaoze are taken from Kimpinde, *op. cit.*

[111] Malishi, Lukas, *Kipalapala Seminary 1925–1975*, Tabora, TMP Printing Department, 1975, pp. 21–25.

[112] Cf. "Note Biographique, Prosper Kamara," *Petit Echo*, March 1962, no. 524, pp. 172–175.

[113] AGMAfr. Minutes of the 1912 General Chapter, pp. 285–286.

[114] Streicher, Henri, *Instructions Pastorales*, vol. 2, 1910–1932, Villa Maria, Uganda, 1932, p. 73.

[115] Waliggo, 1988, *op. cit.*, p. 55.

[116] Kimpinde et al., *op. cit.*, p. 216.

[117] Roelens to Livinhac, December 5th 1912, quoted by Delathuy, A.M., *Missie en Staat in Oud Congo 1880–1914, Witte Paters, Scheutistenen, Jeziten*, Brussels, EPO, 1988, p. 90; see also Heremans, *op. cit.*, pp. 391–394.

[118] Huys to Livinhac, January 12th 1914; Delathuy, *op. cit.*, p. 90.

[119] Delathuy, *op. cit.*, p. 90.

[120] Kimpinde et al., *op. cit.*, p. 158.

[121] Roelens, *Instructions aux missionnaires Pères Blancs du Haut Congo*, Baudouinville, 1910, AGMAfr. 011, Part 4, pp. 55–67.

[122] Kimpinde et al., *op. cit.*, p. 161.

[123] *Ibid.*, pp. 219–220.

[124] Heremans, *op. cit.*, p. 394.

[125] Cf. Kala parish in Upper Congo, and the dioceses of Masaka and Rutabo.

[126] This biography is based on: Faupel, J.F., *African Holocaust, The Story of the Uganda Martyrs*, Nairobi, St. Paul's Publications Africa, fourth edition, 1984; Gray, Richard, "Christianity," in Roberts, A.D. (ed.), *Cambridge History of Africa*, vol. 3, Cambridge, Cambridge University Press, 1978, chapter 3, p. 140 ff.; Rooijackers, Marinus, "History of the White Fathers in Uganda," Working Paper no. 13; Waliggo, John Mary, "The Catholic Church in the Buddu Province of Buganda 1879–1925," Ph.D. thesis, Cambridge University, 1976; and Waliggo, 1988, *op. cit.*

[127] Cf. Marie-André du Sacré Coeur, *Histoire des origines de la congregation des Soeurs Missionnaires de Notre Dame d'Afrique, 1869–1892*, Algiers, MSOLA, 1946, pp. 779 ff.

[128] This account is based on entries in *CT* 1908–1909; *Rapports Annuels*, no. 8, 1912–1913; notes supplied from the MSOLA archives by Sister Hildegunde Schmidt, June 25th 2004; and articles in *Missions d'Afrique*, 1908.

[129] Adolphe Lechaptois, in *Missions d'Afrique*, January–February, pp. 226–231; and March–April 1908, pp. 257–261.

[130] *CT*, no. 156, (1908), p. 911.

[131] *Rapports Annuels*, no. 8, (1912–1913), p. 515.

[132] *Ibid.*, p. 476.

[133] Sister Adolphina became blind and left the congregation in 1914. Communication from Sister Hildegunde Schmidt.

[134] *Rapports Annuels*, no. 8, (1912–1913), p. 553.

[135] Hastings, *op. cit.*, p. 431.

[136] Delathuy, *op. cit.*, p. 27.

137 Information from Gilles de Rasilly M. Afr., Ouagadougou, February 24th 2004.

138 Pirouet, 1978, *op. cit.*, p. 34.

139 *Petit Echo*, vol. 2, no. 13, (January 1914), p. 6.

140 Hastings, *op. cit.*, p. 263.

141 Oliver, *op. cit.*, p. 284.

142 *CT*, no. 98, (1903), p.200.

143 Hastings, *op. cit.*, p. 375.

144 Mercui, Joseph, *L'Ouganda—La mission Catholique et les agents de la compagnie Anglaise*, Paris, Procure des Missions d'Afrique, 1893, p. 74.

145 *CT*, no. 119, (1905), p. 444.

146 Missionnaires du Cardinal Lavigerie, *Le culte de la Sainte Vierge chez les noirs*, Malines, Grand Lacs, 1899, pp. 11–41.

147 *CT*, no. 75, (1897), p. 392; no. 86, (1900), p. 212; no. 82, (1899), p. 199.

148 *CT*, no. 124, (1906), p. 79.

149 *CT*, no. 113, (1905), p. 79.

150 *Rapports Annuels*, no. 3, (1907–1908), p. 73; 4, (1908–1909), p. 231.

151 *Rapports Annuels*, no. 8, (1912–1913), p. 202.

152 *CT*, no. 76, (1897), p. 489.

153 *CT*, no. 86, (1900), p. 210.

154 *CT*, no. 157, (1909), p. 59.

155 This biography of Pilkington is based on Sundkler, Bengt and Steed, Christopher, *A History of the Church in Africa*, Cambridge, Cambridge University Press, 2000, pp. 580–581; Tucker, Alfred R., *Eighteen Years in Uganda and East Africa*, London, Edward Arnold, 1911, *passim*; Baur, John, *2,000 Years of Christianity in Africa*, Nairobi, Paulines Publications Africa, 1994, p. 241; and on *CT* entries. Cf. also Battersby, Charles Forbes Harford, *Pilkington of Uganda*, London, Marshall Bros., 1898.

156 Tucker, *op. cit.*, pp. 141–143; Oliver, *op. cit.*, pp. 184–186.

157 *CT*, no. 64, (1894), p. 582.

158 *Ibid.*, p. 584.

159 Sundkler and Steed, *op. cit.*, pp. 580–581.

160 *CT*, no. 80, (1898), p. 455.

161 *CT*, no. 74, (1897), p. 252; Tucker, *op. cit.*, p. 198; Hastings, *op. cit.*, p. 422.

162 Quoted by Sundkler and Steed, *op. cit.*, p. 581.

163 *CT*, no. 74, (1897), pp. 455–456.

164 Pirouet, *op. cit.*, pp. 26, 193.

165 Hastings, *op. cit.*, p. 267.

166 Tucker, *op. cit.*, pp. 204–205.

167 Cf. Duval, Armand, *Le Père Siméon Lourdel, Apôtre de l'Ouganda (1853–1890)*, Paris, F-X de Guibert, 2004, p. 87, quoting the *CMS Intelligencer*, 1882, p. 95.

168 AGMAfr. Livinhac 083 200, Livinhac (to Le Veux?) May 22nd 1909. I am indebted to Ivan Page M. Afr. for this reference.

169 *CT*, no. 136, (1907), p. 110.

170 *CT*, no. 149, (1909), p. 405.

171 *CT*, no. 156, (1908), p. 940.

172 *CT*, no. 149, (1908), p. 404.

173 Hearne, Brian, *Ecumenical Initiatives in Eastern Africa*, Nairobi, AACC/AMECEA, 1982, pp. 5–7.

Epilogue

[1] Livinhac, Léon, *Lettres Circulaires*, Algiers, Maison Carée, 1912–1922, p. 108.

[2] *Petit Echo*, vol. 2, no. 20, (August 1914), p. 121.

[3] Lesourd, Paul, *Les Pères Blancs du Cardinal Lavigerie*, Orléans, Bernard Grasset, 1935, p. 280; Casier, Jacques, "Développement de la Société," MS, in AGMAfr. Secretariat Général, Rapports Statistiques, 1961.

[4] It resumed in June 1915.

[5] Lesourd, *op. cit.*, p. 280, gives a total of forty-eight; *Missionaries of Africa Necrological Calendar*, Rome, M.Afr. generalate, 2004, gives thirty-three priests, brothers, novices and scholastics who died in action. The list of 60 is my own compilation from archival and published sources and includes novices, scholastics and aspirants.

[6] Total membership was 899 in 1914, and 898 in 1918. Personnel in missionary work counted 549 in 1914, and 465 in 1918. Cf. Casier, *op. cit.*

[7] *Ibid.*

[8] The fifteen included Algeria, Tunisia, Mali, Burkina Faso, Ivory Coast, Ghana, Uganda, Tanzania, Rwanda, Burundi, Congo, Zambia, Malawi; the Vicariate Apostolic of French Sudan also covered parts of Niger and Chad, to which White Fathers later went. Missionary work started later on in countries not included in the original circumscriptions, such as Anglo-Egyptian Sudan, Kenya, Mozambique, Nigeria and South Africa. These are not counted in the fifteen.

[9] The phrase is from Hastings, Adrian, *The Church in Africa 1450–1950*, Oxford, Clarendon Press, 1994, p. 274.

[10] Oliver, Roland, *The Missionary Factor in East Africa*, London, Longmans, 1952, p. 288.

[11] Livinhac, *Lettres Circulaires*, p. 107.

GLOSSARY

Angelus [Latin]: The prayer recalling the Incarnation recited three times daily.

Askari [Swahili]: "Soldier."

Benedicamus Domino [Latin]: "Let us bless the Lord"; the wake-up call for religious.

Benedicite [Latin]: "Bless ye," the opening word of grace before meals.

Burnous: The white cloak of Missionaries of Africa.

Cappa magna [Latin]: The cloak and long train of a bishop.

Charitas, or *caritas* [Latin]: "Love," the motto of Cardinal Charles Lavigerie.

Chevalier [French]: "Knight."

Collectanea [Latin]: "Collection" of decrees.

Cujus regio ejus religio [Latin]: "The religion of the region is that of the region's owner."

Deo gratias [Latin]: "Thanks be to God."

Douillette [French]: A long, black clerical overcoat (in Italian, *Greco*).

Entente cordiale [French]: 1904 Anglo-French diplomatic and military understanding.

Force Publique [French]: Armed forces of the Congo Free State.

Gandourah: The white tunic of Missionaries of Africa.

Hongo [Swahili]: Toll fee for passage through a chiefdom.

In puris naturalibus [Latin]: "In a state of nature."

Jihad [Arabic]: Islamic holy war.

Joho [Swahili]: Black gown or robe.

Kabaka: "King" of Buganda.

Kanzu [Swahili]: A white cotton tunic.

Kingwana: Pidgin Swahili.

Liber usualis [Latin]: "Usual book"; the book of Gregorian chant for Mass and Vespers.

Maji-Maji: Rebellion which took place in German East Africa in 1905–1908.

Mangeur d'hommes [French]: "Eater of men," nickname of General Charles Mangin, brother of Eugène Mangin M.Afr.

Marabout [Arabic]: Muslim holy man.

Medersa [Arabic]: A school or faculty of learning.

Miserere [Latin]: Psalm 50 (51), "Have mercy on me, O God . . ."

Missa de Angelis [Latin]: "Mass of the angels," Gregorian Common no. VIII.

Monseigneur [French]: "My Lord," cf. *Monsignor*, Italian.

Moto-moto [Swahili]: "Firebrand."

Mwami: "King" in various languages, notably Rwanda.

Mwavi: Vegetable poison from *erythrophlaeum guineensis*.

Naba: Moore word for "chief" among the Mossi.

Palmes archéologiques: Archeological distinction of the French Legion of Honour.

Particular examen: Mid-day review or examination of conscience.

Pax Britannica [Latin]: "British peace/rule," cf. *Pax Romana*, "Roman peace/rule."

Personnage fêtiche [French]: "Ritual figure."

Pesa [Swahili]: "Coin, currency."

Placet [Latin]: Vote in favour.

Praeparatio evangelii [Latin]: "Preparation for the Gospel."

Prefect Apostolic: Priest in charge of a missionary diocese in formation.

Prefecture, prefecture apostolic: Roman Catholic missionary diocese in formation.

Prestations: Quota of rubber or other raw materials levied by the Congo Free State.

Prie-dieu [French]: Wooden kneeler.

Procure: A White Fathers appeal and/or supply centre.

Propaganda Fide, De [Latin]: "For the Propagation of the Faith," Vatican Mission Congregation.

Provicar Apostolic: Priest in charge of a provicariate.

Provicariate: Circumscription about to become a missionary diocese.

Province: White Fathers' constituency in Europe, cf. also "Vice-Province."

Rafiki Yetu [Swahili]: "Our Friend."

Region: White Fathers' administrative grouping of vicariates or countries.

Rituale [Latin]: Book of sacraments and sacramental blessing formulas.

Ruga-ruga: Professional soldiers, mercenaries.

Safari [Swahili]: "Journey."

Sakalani, Sakarani [Swahili]: Nickname for Tom von Prince (said to mean a warrior in a state of reckless exultation).

Scholasticate: Theological seminary.

Sixa: "Sister," girls' boarding school or residential catechumenate in West Africa.

Stagiaire(s) [French]: Trainee(s).

Tabula rasa [Latin]: "Clean slate."

Tembe [Swahili]: A square, flat-earth-roofed, fortified dwelling.

Union sacrée [French]: "Sacred union," political slogan of national integration in 1914.

Vade mecum [Latin]: "Handbook."

Vicar Apostolic: Bishop of a missionary diocese.

Vicariate, vicariate apostolic: Roman Catholic missionary diocese.

Wadi [Arabic]: Seasonal river course.

Wangwana [Swahili]: Afro-Arab free men from Zanzibar.

BIBLIOGRAPHY

Achte, Auguste, *Histoire des rois Baganda*, 1900, MS, longhand, AGMAfr. P157/1.

Ahern, Patrick, *Maurice and Thérèse: The Story of a Love*, New York, Doubleday, 1998.

Arens, William, *The Man-Eating Myth*, Oxford, Oxford University Press, 1979.

Arnauld, Dominique, *Les Débuts de l'évangélisation en Pays Mossi-Nakomse d'Après les Archives des Missionnaires d'Afrique (Pères Blancs)*, Mémoire pour la Licence, MS, Rome, 1979.

Ashe, Robert Pickering, *Chronicles of Uganda*, London, Hodder and Stoughton, 1894.

Austen, Ralph A., *Northwest Tanzania under German and British Rule: Colonial Policy and Tribal Politics 1889–1939*, New Haven, Yale University Press, 1968.

Baunard, Louis-Pierre-André, *Le Cardinal Lavigerie*, Paris, 1896, 2 vols.

Baur, John, *2,000 Years of Christianity in Africa*, Nairobi, Paulines Publications Africa, 1994.

Battersby, Charles Forbes Harford, *Pilkington of Uganda*, London, Marshall Bros., 1898.

Bazin, Hippolyte, *Dictionnaire Bambara-Français*, Paris, Imprimerie Nationale, 1906.

Bell, C.R.V., *Education in Uganda before Independence*, Oxford Development Records Project, Report II, Rhodes House Library Oxford, 1985.

Bell, Hesketh, *Glimpses of a Governor's Life*, London, Sampson Low, no date.

Boom, Constant, "The Doctor-Catechists in Tanganyika—A Study in Evangelism," M.A. Essay presented to the Centre of African Studies, School of Oriental and African Studies, London University, 1970, MS.

Bösch, Fridolin, *Les Banyamwezi, peuple de l'Afrique orientale*, Münster, Biblioteca Anthropos, 1930.

Bouniol, Joseph, *The White Fathers and Their Missions*, London, Sands, 1929.

Bourgade, F., *La Clef du Coran*, Paris, 1852.

Bourgade, F., *Les Soirées de Carthage*, Paris, 1847.

Bourgade, F., *Passage du Coran à l'Evangile*, Paris, 1855.

Breedveld, Walter, *Atiman der Negerdokter bij het Tanganyikameer*, Gottmer, Nijmegen, The Netherlands, no date.

Burgman, Hans, *The Way the Catholic Church Started in Western Kenya*, London, Mission Book Service, 1990.

Burlaton, Louis, *Monseigneur Léon Livinhac, Archevêque d'Oxyrhynque, Supérieur-Général de la Société des Missionnaires d'Afrique (Pères Blancs), Fondateur de la Mission de l'Ouganda*, typescript, Carthage, 1932, AGMAfr. B2 Livn. 1–4.

Byabazaire, Deogratias M., *The Contribution of the Christian Churches to the Development of Western Uganda, 1894–1974*, Frankfurt am Main, Peter Lang, 1979, European University Papers.

Camps, Arnulf, "M. l'Abbé Bourgade (1806–1866) in Dialogue with Muslims at Carthage," in Cornille, Catherine and Neckebrouck, Valeer (eds.), *A Universal Faith*, Louvain Theological and Pastoral Monographs, no. 9, Louvain, Eerdmans, 1992.

Ceillier, Jean-Claude, *Lettres d'un Supérieur Général à ses Confrères Missionnaires*, unpublished typescript, 2001.

Ceillier, Jean-Claude, "Les Missionnaires d'Afrique et le Dialogue Interreligieux: Quelques Jalons Historiques," Colloque de Paris, December 2002, unpublished typescript.

Ceillier, Jean-Claude, *A Pilgrimage from Chapter to Chapter, The First General Chapters of the Society of Missionaries of Africa 1874–1900*, Missionaries of Africa History Series no. 1, Rome, 2002.

Ceillier, Jean-Claude and Page, Ivan, *Les sources écrites internes à la société, Société des Missionnaires d'Afrique*, Missionaries of Africa History Series no. 4, Rome, 2004.

Comboni, Daniele, *Piano per la Regenerazione dell'Africa*, Turin, Comboni Missionaries, 1864.

Concise Dictionary of National Biography, Oxford, Oxford University Press, 1992.

Cory, Hans, "The Buswezi," *American Anthropologist*, vol. 57, no. 5, 1955, pp. 923–952.

Croegaert, Luc, *Les Pères Blancs au Rwanda—Jalons et Balises*, unpublished MS, no date, AGMAfr. Casier 341.

Cuoq, Joseph, *Lavigerie, Les Pères Blancs et les Musulmans Maghrebins*, Rome, Missionaries of Africa, 1986.

Cussac, J., *Evêque et pionnier, Monseigneur Streicher*, Paris, Éditions de la Savane, 1955.

Dahbar, Nicolas, *Sainte Anne de Jérusalem*, Yabroud, Lebanon, 1959.

De Benoist, Joseph-Roger, *Eglise et Pouvoir au Soudan Français*, Paris, Karthala, 1987.

De Foucauld, Charles, *Correspondences Sahariennes*, ed. Thiriez, Philippe and Chatelard, Antoine, Paris, Editions du Cerf, 1998.

De Foucauld, Charles, *Lettres et Carnets*, ed. Jean-François Six, Paris, Editions du Seuil, 1966.

De Montclos, Xavier, *Lavigerie, La Mission Universelle de l'Église*, Paris, Cerf, 1991.

Debrett's Peerage, London, Dean and Co., 1894.

Delathuy, A.M., *Missie en Staat in Oud Congo 1880–1914, Witte Paters, Scheutistenen, Jezïten*, Brussels, EPO, 1988.

Dornier, François, *Pères Blancs, Soeurs Blanches, Thibar 1895–1975*, typescript, 1991, AGMAfr. 108187.

Dromaux, Théophile, "Nouvelle route à Karema sur le Tanganyika," *Geographical Journal*, vol. 13, no. 5, 1899, pp. 535–536.

Dufays, Félix, *Pages d'epopée Africaine—Jours troublés*, Ixelles (Belgium), René Weversbergh, 1928.

Dufays, Félix and de Moor, Vincent, *Au Kinyaga les enchainés*, Paris, Librarie Missionnaire, 1939.

Dupuis, Auguste, *Monographie de Tomboctou*, MS, longhand, AGMAfr. N8 104233.

Duval, Armand, *C'était une longue fidélité à l'Algérie et au Rwanda*, Paris, Mediaspaul, 1998.

Duval, Armand, *Yohana Kitagana Catéchiste*, Condé-sur-Noireau, Corlet, 2002.

Duval, Armand, *Le Père Siméon Lourdel, Apôtre de l'Ouganda (1853–1890)*, Paris, F-X de Guibert, 2004.

Ewans, Martin, *European Atrocity, African Catastrophe—Leopold II, the Congo Free State and its Aftermath*, London, Routledge Curzon, 2002.

Fabian, Johannes, *Language and Colonial Power—The Appropriation of Swahili in the Former Belgian Congo 1880–1938*, Cambridge, Cambridge University Press, 1986.

Faupel, J.F., *African Holocaust, The Story of the Uganda Martyrs*, Nairobi, St. Paul's Publications Africa, fourth edition, 1984.

Finn, Peter, *The History of the Priory Bishop's Waltham*, Winchester, Hedera Books, 2002.

Fleming, Fergus, *The Sword and the Cross*, London, Granta Books, 2003.

Fouquer, R., *Le Docteur Adrien Atiman*, Karema, Spes Publications, no date.

Fransen, Piet, "How can Non-Christians find salvation in their own religions?", in Neuner, Josef (ed.), *Christian Revelation and World Religions*, London, Sheed and Ward, 1967.

Gahungu, Méthode, *Les methodes des Pères Blancs dans l'oeuvre des seminaries pour le clergé local en Afrique des Grands Lacs (1879–1936)*, Ph.D. thesis presented to Pontifical Salesian University, 1998.

Galton, Francis, *The Art of Travel or Shifts and Conveniences Available in Wild Countries*, London, John Murray, 1860.

Garvey, Brian, *Bembaland Church—Religious and Social Change in South Central Africa 1891–1964*, Leiden, E.J. Brill, 1994.

Gaudeul, J.M., *Encounters and Clashes—Islam and Christianity in History—A Survey*, Rome, PISAI, 2000.

Goodall, Norman, *A History of the London Missionary Society 1895–1945*, Oxford, Oxford University Press, 1954.

Gorju, Julien, *Entre le Victoria, l'Albert et l'Edouard—Ethnographie de la partie anglaise du vicariate de l'Uganda—Origines, histoire, religions, coûtumes*, Rennes, Imprimerie Oberthür, 1920.

Gorju, Julien, *En zigzags à travers l'Urundi*, Namur, Missionaries of Africa, 1926.

Gorra, Philippe, *Sainte-Anne de Jérusalem, Séminaire Grec Melkite dirigé par les Pères Blancs 1882–1932*, Harissa, Lebanon, Imprimerie de Saint Paul, 1932.

Gouraud, General, *Souvenirs d'un Africain au Soudan*, Paris, Pierre Tisné, 1939 (1899).

Goyau, Georges, *Un Grand Missionnaire Le Cardinal Lavigerie*, Paris, Plon, 1925.

Gray, Richard, "Christianity," in Roberts, A.D. (ed.), *The Cambridge History of Africa 1907–1940*, vol. 7, Cambridge, Cambridge University Press, 1970.

Gray, Richard, "The Catholic Church and National States in Western Europe During the Nineteenth and Twentieth Centuries, from a Perspective of Africa," *Kirchliche Zeitgeschichte*, no. 1, 2001, pp. 148–158.

Grévoz, Daniel, *Sahara 1830–1881—Les mirages Français et la tragédie Flatters*, Paris, l'Harmattan, 1989.

Hacquard, Augustin, "La Mission Hourst," *Bulletin de la Société Géographique d'Alger*, 1897, vol. 2, pp. 110–112.

Hamilton, J. Taylor and Hamilton, Kenneth G., *History of the Moravian Church: The Renewed Unitas Fratrum 1722–1967*, Bethlehem, Penn., Moravian Church in America, 1967.

Hansen, Holger Bernt, "The Colonial State's Policy towards Foreign Missions in Uganda," in Hansen, Holger Bernt and Twaddle, Michael (eds.), *Christian Missionaries and the State in the Third World*, Oxford, James Currey, 2002.

Hansen, Holger Bernt and Twaddle, Michael, (eds.), *Christian Missionaries and the State in the Third World*, Oxford, James Currey, 2002.

Hastings, Adrian, *The Church in Africa 1450–1950*, Oxford, Clarendon Press, 1994.

Hearne, Brian, *Ecumenical Initiatives in Eastern Africa*, Nairobi, AACC/AMECEA, 1982.

Hebblethwaite, Peter, *John XXIII, Pope of the Council*, London, Geoffrey Chapman, 1984.

Heremans, Roger, *L'Education dans les Missions des Pères Blancs en Afrique Centrale 1879–1914*, Brussels, Editions Nauwelaerts, 1983.

Hickey, Raymond, *Modern Missionary Documents and Africa*, Dublin, Dominican Publications, 1982.

Hinfelaar, Hugo, *Bemba-Speaking Women of Zambia in a Century of Religious Change—1892–1992*, Leiden, E.J. Brill, 1994.

Hinfelaar, Hugo, *History of the Church in Zambia*, Lusaka, Bookworld Publishers, 2004.

Hochschild, Adam, *King Leopold's Ghost*, London, Pan Books, 2002.

Houdebine, T.L. and Boumier, Marcel, *Capitaine Joubert*, Namur, Grands Lacs, no date.

Ilboudo, Jean, "La Christianisation du Moogo (1899–1949), la contribution des auxiliaries indigenes," in Ilboudo, Jean (ed.), *Burkina 2000, une église en marche vers son centenaire*, Ouagadougou, Presses Africaines, 1993.

Ilboudo, Jean, *Le Christ au Burkina: Les Actes des Premiers Chrétiens*, vol. 1, *Promenade au Mossi*, Ouagadougou, Presses Africaines, 1993.

Ilboudo, Jean, *Christianisation du Moogo—Pourquoi les Mossi se sont-ils convertis? Le point de vue de l'historien*, Ouagadougou, Centre Spirituel Paam Yoodo, 2000.

Iliffe, John, *Tanganyika under German Rule 1905–1912*, Cambridge, Cambridge University Press, 1969.

Iliffe, John, *A Modern History of Tanganyika*, Cambridge, Cambridge University Press, 1979.

Iliffe, John, *Africans, the History of a Continent*, Cambridge, Cambridge University Press, 1995.

Kabeya, John, *Daktari Adriano Atiman*, Tabora, TMP Book Department, and Arusha, Eastern Africa Publications, 1978.

Kelly's Handbook to the Titled, Landed and Official Classes, London, Kelly, 1931.

Kimpinde, Amando Dominique et al., *Stefano Kaoze, prêtre d'hier at d'aujourd'hui*, Kinshasa, Editions St. Paul Afrique, 1982.

Ki-Zerbo, Joseph, *Alfred Diban—Premier Chrétien de Haute-Volta*, Paris, Cerf, 1983.

Lavigerie, Charles, *Instructions aux Missionnaires*, Namur, Grands Lacs, 1950.

Lavigerie, Charles, *Cardinal Lavigerie—Selected Texts*, Rome, Missionaries of Africa, 1980.

Leblond, G., *Le Père Auguste Achte des Missionnaires d'Afrique (Pères Blancs)*, Algiers, Maison Carée, 1912.

Lechaptois, Adolphe, *Aux Rives du Tanganyika, Etude couronnée par la Société Géographique de Paris*, Algiers, Maison Carée, 1913.

Leloir, L., *Un Evêque Missionnaire—Roi des Brigands*, Brussels, Editions du Rendez-Vous, 1945.

Leroy, Alexandre, *La religion des primitifs*, Paris, Beauchesne, 1909, *Etudes sur l'histoire des religions*.

Lesourd, Paul, *Les Pères Blancs du Cardinal Lavigerie*, Orléans, Bernard Grasset, 1935.

Linden, Ian with Linden, Jane, *Catholic Peasants and Chewa Resistance in Nyasaland 1889–1939*, University of California Press, Berkeley and Los Angeles, 1974.

Linden, Ian and Linden, Jane, *Church and Revolution in Rwanda*, Manchester University Press, 1977.

Livingstone, David, *The Last Journals*, London, John Murray, 1874, 2 vols.

Livinhac, Léon, *Lettres Circulaires*, Algiers, Maison Carée, 1912.

Livinhac, Léon, *Lettres Circulaires; Instructions de Monseigneur Livinhac aux Missionnaires d'Afrique (Pères Blancs)*, Algiers, 1938.

Low, D.A., *Religion and Society in Buganda 1875–1900*, East African Studies, no. 8, EAISR, Kampala, no date.

Malishi, Lukas, *Kipalapala Seminary 1925–1975*, Tabora, TMP Printing Department, 1975.

Mangin, Eugène, *Essai sur les us et coûtumes du people Mossi au Soudan Occidental*, Vienna, *Anthropos*, 1916.

Mangin, Eugène, *Les Mossi—Essai sur les us et coutûmes du peuple Mossi au Soudan Occidental*, Algiers, Maison Carée, 1960.

Marie-André du Sacré Coeur, *Histoire des origins de la congregation des Soeurs Missionnaires de Notre Dame d'Afrique, 1869–1892*, Algiers, MSOLA, 1946.

Marin, Eugène, *Algérie, Sahara, Soudan, Vie Travaux, Voyages de Mgr. Hacquard des Pères Blancs (1860–1901)*, Paris, Berger-Levrault, 1905.

Matheson, Elizabeth Mary, *African Apostles*, New York, St. Paul's Publications, 1963.

Mazé, Joseph, *Origines des missions d'Afrique Belge*, Algiers, Maison Carrée, 1930.

McCoy, Remigius, *Great Things Happen*, Montreal, Missionaries of Africa, 1988.

McLynn, Frank, *Stanley—Sorcerer's Apprentice*, Oxford, Oxford University Press, 1992.

Mercui, Joseph, *L'Ouganda—La mission Catholique et les agents de la compagnie Anglaise*, Paris, Procure des Missions d'Afrique, 1893.

Mesnage, Joseph, *L'Afrique chrétienne, Evêchés et ruines antiques d'après les manuscripts de Mgr. Toulotte et les découvertes archéologiques les plus récentes*, Paris, Ministère de l'Instruction Publique, 1912.

Mesnage, Joseph, *Le Christianisme en Afrique, decline et extinction*, Paris, 1915.

Missionaries of Africa, *Quelques indications pouvant servir pour le Voyage des Missionnaires d'Europe en Ouganda*, Algiers, Maison Carée, 1894.

Missionaries of Africa, *Coutumier Général des Missionnaires d'Afrique*, Algiers, Maison Carée, Algiers, 1895.

Missionaries of Africa, *Publications en Langues Africaines, Catalogue provisoire*, Algiers, Maison Carée, 1928.

Missionnaires du Cardinal Lavigerie, *Le culte de la Sainte Vierge chez les noirs*, Malines, Grand Lacs, 1899.

Monteil, Charles, *Les Bambara du Ségou et du Kaarta*, Paris, Maisonneuve et Larose, 1977.

Mudimbe, V.Y., *The Invention of Africa*, London, James Currey, 1988.

Mudimbe, V.Y., *The Idea of Africa*, London, James Currey, 1994.

Nicq, A., *Le Père Siméon Lourdel et les premières années de la mission de l'Ouganda*, Algiers, Maison Carée, 1906, second edition.

Nolan, Francis, "History of the Catechist in Eastern Africa," in Shorter, Aylward and Kataza, Eugene (eds.), *Missionaries to Yourselves—African Catechists Today*, London, Geoffrey Chapman, 1972.

Nolan, Francis Patrick, *Christianity in Unyamwezi 1878–1928*, Cambridge Ph.D. dissertation, 1977.

Nolan, Francis Patrick, *Mission to the Great Lakes*, Tabora, TMP Book Department, 1978.

Nyakatura, J.W., *Anatomy of an African Kingdom: A History of Bunyoro-Kitara*, New York, NOK Publishers, 1973.

O'Neil, Robert, *Mission to the Upper Nile—The Story of St. Joseph's Missionary Society of Mill Hill in Uganda*, London, Mission Book Service, 1999.

Oduyoye, Mercy Amba, *The Will to Arise: Women, Tradition and the Church in Africa*, New York, Orbis Books, 1992.

Ogez, Louis, *Forget Me Not—Saved from Slavery He Became a Missionary to Zambia 1896–1910*, Ndola, Mission Press, 1992.

Oliver, Roland, *The Missionary Factor in East Africa*, London, Longmans, 1952.

Page, Ivan and Trimbur, Dominique, *St. Anne's at Jerusalem—Historical Account of its Founding*, Missionaries of Africa History Series no. 3, Rome, 2004.

Pakenham, Thomas, *The Scramble for Africa*, London, Weidenfeld and Nicolson, 1991.

Pelletier, Raynald, *Bishop John Forbes (1864–1926), Coadjutor Vicar Apostolic of Uganda, The First Canadian White Father*, Missionaries of Africa History Series, no. 2, Rome, 2003.

Perrier, Joseph, *Wind of Change, Cardinal Lavigerie 1825–1892*, Slough, St. Paul's, 1993.

Pichard, Gabriel, *Dii Alfred-Simon Diban—Témoin de Dieu . . . Fondateur d'Eglise*, Bobo-Dioulasso, Savane, 1997.

Pineau, Henry, *Evêque-Roi des Brigands—Monseigneur Dupont, Premier Vicaire Apostolique du Nyassa 1850–1930*, Paris, Pères Blancs, 1937.

Pirouet, M. Louise, *Black Evangelists—The Spread of Christianity in Uganda 1891–1914*, London, Rex Collings, 1978.

Pirouet, M. Louise, *Historical Dictionary of Uganda*, African Historical Dictionaries, no. 64, London and Metuchen, Scarecrow Press Inc., 1995.

Portal, Sir Gerald, *The Mission to Uganda of 1893*, London, Edward Arnold, 1894.

Renault, François, *Lavigerie, L'Esclavage Africain et l'Europe 1868–1892*, Paris, E. De Boccard, 1971, 2 vols.

Renault, François, *Tippo Tip—un Potentat Arabe en Afrique Centrale au XIXe siècle*, Paris, Société Française d'Histoire d'Outre-Mer, 1987.

Renault, François, *Cardinal Lavigerie, Churchman, Prophet and Missionary*, London, Athlone Press, 1994.

Robert, Jean-Marie, *Coutûmes des Wafipa*, 2 vols., mimeographed folio in Swahili and French, no date, AGMAfr. 104592.

Robert, Jean-Marie, *Croyances et coûtumes magico-religieuses des Wafipa païens*, Tabora, Missionaries of Africa, 1949.

Roberts, Andrew D., *A History of the Bemba—Political Growth and Change in North-Eastern Zambia before 1900*, London, Longman, 1973.

Roelens, Victor, *Lettre Ouverte à Messieurs les Membres de la Commission Chargée d'Examiner le Rapport sur l'Enquête au Congo—Protestation des Supérieurs des Missions Catholiques du Congo*, Brussels, J. Goemaere, 1905.

Roelens, *Instructions aux Missionnaires Pères Blancs du Haut Congo*, Baudouinville 1910, AGMAfr. 011.

Roelens, Victor, *Instructions aux Missionnaires Pères Blancs du Haut Congo*, Congo, Baudouinville, 1920.

Roelens, Victor (ed. Antoine, N.), *Notre Vieux Congo 1891–1917—Souvenirs du premier evêque du Congo Belge*, Namur, Grands Lacs, 1948, 2 vols.

Rooijackers, Marinus, "First Sub-Saharan Missionaries of Africa," *Petit Echo*, vol. 6, 2004, no. 952, pp. 333–339.

Rooijackers, Marinus, "History of the White Fathers in Uganda," Working Papers, *pro manuscripto*, no date.

Ross-of-Bladensburg, Lieutenant Colonel Sir John, *The Coldstream Guards 1914–1918*, Oxford, Oxford University Press, vol. 1.

Rowe, John, "Mutesa and the Missionaries: Church and State in Pre-colonial Buganda," Hansen, Holger Bernt and Twaddle, Michael (eds.), *Christian Missionaries and the State in the Third World*, Oxford, James Currey, 2002.

Saadia, Ossilia, *Catholiques et Musulman Sunnites, Discours Croisés 1920 –1950, Approche Historique de l'Alterité Religieuse*, doctoral thesis, University of Lyon, 2001 (AGMAfr. UE 1007).

Sanneh, Lamin, *Encountering the West—Christianity and the Global Cultural Process: The African Dimension*, London, Marshall Pickering, 1993.

Schynse, Auguste Wilhelm, *A travers l'Afrique avec Stanley et Emin-Pacha*, Paris, Karl Hespers, 1889.

Schynse, Auguste Wilhelm, *Zwei Jahre am Congo—Erlebnisse und Schilderungen*, Köln, Karl Hespers, Bachem, 1889.

Seabrook, William, *The White Monk of Timbuctoo*, London, Harrap, 1934.

Shorter, Aylward and Kataza, Eugene (eds.), *Missionaries to Yourselves—African Catechists Today*, London, Geoffrey Chapman, 1972.

Shorter, Aylward, *Chiefship in Western Tanzania—A Political History of the Kimbu*, Oxford, Clarendon Press, 1972.

Shorter, Aylward, *Christianity and the African Imagination*, Nairobi, Paulines Publications Africa, 1996.

Slade, Ruth, *King Leopold's Congo—Aspects of the Development of Race Relations in the Congo Independent State*, London, Oxford University Press, 1962.

Society of Missionaries of Africa (White Fathers), *Constitutions*, Algiers, Maison Carée, 1908.

Society of Missionaries of Africa (White Fathers), *Directory of Constitutions*, Algiers, Maison Carée, 1914.

Sondo, Rose-Marie, *Monseigneur Joanny Thévenoud, Père Fondateur des Soeurs de l'Immaculée Conception de Ouagadougou*, Ouagadougou, SOGIF, 1998.

Stanley, Henry M., *Through the Dark Continent*, London, Sampson Low, 1878; 1899 edition, London, George Newnes, 2 vols.

Stanley, Henry M., *How I Found Livingstone in Central Africa*, London, Sampson Low, 1895.

Stenger, Friedrich, *White Fathers in Colonial Central Africa*, Münster, Hamberg, London, Lit Verlag, 2001.

Storme, Marcel, *Rapports du Père Planque, de Mgr. Lavigerie et de Mgr. Comboni sur l'Association Internationale Africaine*, Brussels, Académie Royale des Sciences Coloniales, Mémoire, tome x1, facs. 2, 1957.

Strachan, Hew, *The First World War*, London, Simon and Schuster, 2003.

Streicher, Henri, *Extraits des Lettres Circulaires 1897–1909*, Bukalasa, White Fathers, 1910.

Streicher, Henri, *Instructions Pastorales*, vol. 2, 1910–1932, Villa Maria, Uganda, 1932.

Sundkler, Bengt and Steed, Christopher, *A History of the Church in Africa*, Cambridge, Cambridge University Press, 2000.

Teissier, Henri, *Chrétiens en Algérie, un Partage d'Espérance*, Paris, Desclée de Brouwer, 2002.

Thom, Alexander, *Thom's Irish Whose Who*, Dublin, 1923.

Thuillier, Guy, *La Bureaucratie en France aux XIXe et XXe Siècles*, Paris, Economica, 1987.

Tiama, Jean-Baptiste, *Les Missionnaires d'Afrique (Pères Blancs) et la lutte anti-esclavagiste au Mali 1895–1905*, licentiate dissertation, Rome, P.U.G., 1992.

Tiquet, Jean, *Une expérience de petite colonisation indigène en Algérie—les colons Arabes-Chrétiens du Cardinal Lavigerie*, Algiers, Maison Carée, 1936.

Toulotte, Anatole (Joseph-Roger de Benoist, ed.), *Voyage au Soudan 1 Oct 1896–14 Mai 1897*, no date, AGMAfr. N3 and LA 21/3.

Tourigny, Yves, *So Abundant a Harvest—The Catholic Church in Uganda 1879–1979*, London, Darton, Longman and Todd, 1979.

Tucker, Alfred R., *Eighteen Years in Uganda and East Africa*, London, Edward Arnold, 1911.

Van der Burgt, Jean-Martin-Michel, *Un Grand Peuple de l'Afrique Equatoriale—Elements d'une monographie sur l'Urundi et les Warundi*, s'Hertogenbosch, Société d'Illustration Catholique, 1903.

Van der Burgt, Jean-Martin-Michel, *Dictionnaire Français-Kirundi*, s'Hertogenbosch, 1904.

Van der Burgt, Jean-Martin-Michel, *Het Kruis geplant in een Onbekend Negerland van Midden-Afrika*, Boxtel, 1921.

Van der Meersch, Jean, *Le Catéchuménat au Rwanda de 1900 à nos Jours*, Kigali, Pallotti Press, 1993.

Vanlande, René, *Chez les Pères Blancs—Tunisie, Kabylie, Sahara*, Paris, J. Peyronnet, 1929.

Vellard, André, *Carthage autrefois et aujourd'hui*, Lille, Victor Ducolombier, 1896.

Vellard, André, *Aux Oasis Sahariennes*, MS, 1903, AGMAfr. L14 102033.

Vezeau, Roland, *The Apostolic Vicariate of Nyasa—Origins and First Developments 1889–1935*, Rome, Missionaries of Africa, 1989.

Vezeau, Roland, *The White Fathers' Contribution to the Civilizing of Central Africa through their Agricultural Activities and Improvement of Native Diet, 1878–1953*, Rome, F.A.O. and the Vatican, 1954, typescript. AGMAfr. K44.

Wagner, Roy, *The Invention of Culture*, Chicago, Chicago University Press, 1981.

Waliggo, John Mary, "The Catholic Church in the Buddu Province of Buganda 1879–1925," Cambridge Ph.D. dissertation, 1976.

Waliggo, John Mary, *A History of African Priests—Katigondo Major Seminary 1911–1986*, Nairobi, Matianum Press, 1988.

Walvin, James, *Black Ivory*, London, Fontana Press, 1993.

Wright, Marcia, *German Missions in Tanganyika 1891–1914*, Oxford, Oxford University Press, 1971.

Wright, Marcia, *Strategies of Slaves and Women—Life Stories from East/Central Africa*, London, James Currey, 1993.

Yates, Timothy, *Christian Mission in the Twentieth Century*, Cambridge, Cambridge University Press, 1994.

Zeleza, Paul Tiyambe (ed.), *Encyclopaedia of Twentieth Century African History*, London, Routledge, 2003.

INDEX

Numbers in italics indicate photographs.

285